Weberian sociological theory

Max Weber is undoubtedly one of the most important sociologists of all time, and his writings have been extensively commented upon. Yet, as Randall Collins convincingly argues in this book, much of Weber's work has been misunderstood, and many of his most striking and sophisticated theories have been neglected, or even overlooked. By analyzing these hitherto little-studied aspects of Weber's writings, Professor Collins is able both to offer a new interpretation of Weberian sociology and to show how the more fruitful lines of the Weberian approach can be projected to an analysis of current world issues.

Professor Collins begins with Weber's theory of the rise of capitalism, examining it in the light of Weber's later writings on the subject and extending the Weberian line of reasoning to suggest a "Weberian revolution" in both medieval Europe and China. He also offers a new interpretation of Weber's theory of politics, showing it to be a "world-system" model; and he expands this into a theory of geopolitics, using as a particular illustration the prediction of the future decline of Russian world power. Another "buried treasure" in Weber's corpus that he brings to light is Weber's conflict theory of the family as sex and property, which Professor Collins applies to the historical question of the conditions that led to the initial rise of the status of women. He also makes other applications of the Weberian approach – for example, to produce a comparative theory of technological innovation, and theories of the conditions for heresy disputes in both religious and secular form, and of alienation as a secular political ideology.

This broad view of the corpus of Weber's work shows that Weberian sociology remains intellectually alive and that many of his theories still represent the frontier of our knowledge about large-scale social processes. It will interest teachers and students of sociology, political science, history, philosophy, and economics, as well as appealing to any reader concerned with such current affairs as world politics, feminism, and the role of technology.

Weberian sociological theory

RANDALL COLLINS
University of California, Riverside

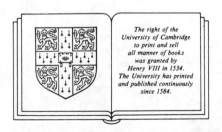

The right of the
University of Cambridge
to print and sell
all manner of books
was granted by
Henry VIII in 1534.
The University has printed
and published continuously
since 1584.

CAMBRIDGE UNIVERSITY PRESS

Cambridge
London   New York   New Rochelle
Melbourne   Sydney

Published by the Press Syndicate of the University of Cambridge
The Pitt Building, Trumpington Street, Cambridge CB2 1RP
32 East 57th Street, New York, NY 10022, USA
10 Stamford Road, Oakleigh, Melbourne 3166, Australia

First published 1986

Printed in the United States of America

Library of Congress Cataloging in Publication Data
Collins, Randall, 1941–
Weberian sociological theory.
Includes index.
1. Sociology – Germany.   2. Weber, Max, 1864–1920 –
Criticism and interpretation.   I. Title.
HM22.G3W4257   1986   301'.01   85-7879
ISBN 0 521 30698 1 hard covers
ISBN 0 521 31426 7 paperback

British Library Cataloging in Publication applied for

For Sam Kaplan

Contents

Contents

Contents

Preface

This book represents an effort to demonstrate that Weberian sociology is intellectually alive, in at least as full a sense as Marxian sociology is alive today. By this I mean not only that Max Weber's works are a landmark in the history of our discipline but also that in many respects his ideas still mark the frontier of our knowledge. This is particularly true in the areas of macrosociology: politics, economics, large-scale stratification patterns, and above all in the megasociology of long-term historical change. At the same time, I am no believer in the excessive adulation of past theorists, no matter how heroic. The best way to demonstrate the vitality of Weber's theories is to show they are capable of projection beyond themselves. That is what this book attempts to do.

Weber was an extraordinarily multisided figure, and I do not claim to develop more than a few sides of his approach. I have acquired some appreciation for what Weber's various sides have included, or at least engendered, from my teachers of some years past Talcott Parsons and Reinhard Bendix. Various parts of this book have benefited from comments or other assistance by Samuel W. Kaplan, Vatro Murvar, Stephen Kalberg, Guenther Roth, Walter Goldfrank, Norbert Wiley, Whitney Pope, Al Bergesen, Immanuel Wallerstein, Wolfram Eberhard, Jack Goldstone, Paul DiMaggio, Ken Donow, Craig Calhoun, Robert L. Hamblin, Michael Hout, Arthur L. Stinchcombe, Rae Lesser Blumberg, Richard Gordon, Melvin Seeman, Roy d'Andrade, and Victor Zaslavsky. Whether they approve of what has resulted here is, of course, another matter.

1

Introduction

Why another book about Max Weber? He is recognizably among the most important sociologists of all time and, except for Karl Marx, probably the most commented upon as well. Yet Weber's sociology is one of the least well understood. I say this even though everyone has heard of the Protestant ethic, charisma, and the iron cage of bureaucratization, and current Marxists write of legitimation crisis and make most of their revisions in a Weberian direction.

Very simply: because some of the most important parts of Weber's advanced work have been overlooked, underused, or drastically misunderstood. An instance is Weber's theory of capitalism. His early paper "The Protestant Ethic and the Spirit of Capitalism" (1904) has been the subject of an enormous literature. For many, it remains the "Weber thesis," despite the fact that others have pointed to his mid-period series on comparative world religions, which moves considerably beyond his early position (1916/1951, 1916–17/1958, 1917–19/1952; see Parsons, 1967). And, indeed, Weber's comparative analyses remained half finished, with pictures still to be drawn of ancient Mediterranean societies, Islam, and medieval Christendom; and Weber's last treatment of the subject, just after the end of World War I and in the aftermath of the German revolution, deals with Marxism much more extensively and moves his sociology of economics much farther from his early idealist interests.

In the case of Weber's theory of politics, I would argue that his explicitly stated position in his systematic work *Wirtschaft und Gesell-schaft* (1922) has never been fully set forth, let alone appreciated and developed. His views of politics have been the subject of much polemic (e.g., Mommsen, Adorno, Marcuse, Roth) and have been made the basis of some quite famous developments in subsequent social theory, of which the ideas of Mannheim (1935) and C. Wright Mills (1956) are only a few examples. Nevertheless, the views of Weber's politics have been constructed out of bits and pieces of his political sensibilities. One such is in his middle-of-the-road lecture to his radical students in 1919, "Science as a Vocation" ("Politics is a strong and

1

slow boring of hard boards. It takes both passion and perspective. Only he who in the face of all this can say 'In spite of all!' has the calling for politics." [Weber, 1946:128]), with its emphasis on the now rather maligned preference for academic value-freedom. Other scholars have concentrated on Weber's writings on legitimacy, pulling these in a strongly conventionalist, *Ordnung*-conscious direction (Parsons, 1947) or, alternatively, flourishing the possibility of charismatic revolution (Gerth and Mills, 1946). Still others have sought Weber's politics in his writings on bureaucracy (Mannheim, 1935; C. Wright Mills, 1956; Gerth, 1982). Whereas these writers have taken Weber's theme of rationalization in a pessimistic sense, others (Schluchter, 1981; Habermas, 1979) have put a progress-oriented and evolutionary construction on it.

But there is, in fact, a systematic exposition of the theory of politics by Weber himself. The last seven chapters of *Wirtshaft und Gesellschaft*, making up more than a third of his major book, are devoted to different aspects of politics (domination, legitimacy, bureaucracy, patrimonialism, feudalism, charisma, hierocracy, and so forth). Some (rather small) parts of this work are famous, but taken out of their context as segments of a general comparative treatment of the sociological dimensions of politics. One of the most often overlooked is the beginning part of chapter 9, "Political Communities," which introduces the entire analysis to follow. Segments of this have been reprinted in the famous Gerth and Mills reader (Weber, 1946), but without capturing the initial, key arguments and the logic that ties the whole scheme together. Weber's theory of politics turns out to be an unsentimental view of the conditions of domination and conflict. Legitimacy plays a central enough role in this, but in Weber's full model legitimacy is not the static typology that it has been in the hands of his commentators. Weber proposes a dynamic for legitimacy, one that is tied both to the status claims of the state in the international military arena and to the three-sided grid of contending interest groups within the society (the familiar "class, status, and party").

Weber's political sociology, I am going to argue, works essentially from the outside in. Societies cannot be understood alone, as independent functional units, cultures, or arenas delimited for the convenience of the analyst. Their politics is tied first and foremost to the shifting relationships of the external realm. Weber was oriented toward the "world system" long before Wallerstein popularized the term, but with a difference: Weber attempted to show (fairly successfully, I believe) that the key external dynamics of states is not economic but military – geopolitical in the largest sense. What this implies, I conclude, is that a great deal of political analysis has to be redone, and that the direction to follow is to consolidate and improve what is known of geopolitical theory – the causes and consequences of the military interrelationships of states – with an emphasis on extending it to link up with internal politics. Throughout the various interactions, in which internal politics reverberates back into the external arena, I think it is worthwhile keeping our attention on a central Weberian theme: that the guiding dynamic is a larger, international status system, not reducible to the economic (or bureaucratic or other) internal interests and resources of local political actors.

Perhaps enough has been said to make the point of there being much in Weber that has remained buried and that is well worth salvaging and using as the point of departure for ourselves. There are other areas, as well, in which Weber has hidden treasures, or in which the Weberian perspective can advance our theoretical understanding of some central issues. One such area is the treatment of sex. Weber has a powerful, and unsentimental, theory of the family; it has gone almost entirely unnoticed, but it offers a realistic conflict viewpoint on the issue of sexual stratification, and points to some of the crucial historical developments that have changed the status of women in the West. As in much of the rest of Weber, the analysis of the family is unique in showing how much of family structure hinges on politics.

I make no claim to have uncovered the "true" Weber. Perhaps such a thing exists, but we certainly do not know it. Surprisingly enough, we still lack a definitive full-scale intellectual biography of Weber. We know well neither his personal life, nor his social and intellectual milieu, nor the development and continuity of his ideas through the various phases of his life. What we have instead are the (somewhat censored) memories of his wife (Marianne Weber, 1925/1975), some psychohistorical speculations and sexual exposés (Mitzman, 1970; Green, 1974), and a series of very competent studies on selected themes (Parsons, 1937; Bendix, 1960) that nevertheless remain one-sided and selective. We have nothing like the fully rounded picture of Emile Durkheim and his milieu that emerges from Steven Lukes (1973) and Terry Clark (1973), although some useful building blocks exist (Bendix and Roth, 1971; Burger, 1976; Kalberg, 1980).

My aim is not to provide that intellectual biography, or even to offer a glimpse of what I think would be a well-rounded picture of Weber. My picture is one-sided, and quite consciously so. Weber was much more of a German idealist of the Dilthey type, and a historicist of the school of German historical economics, than I choose to emphasize here. There is no doubt that, especially in his early works, Weber is explicitly concerned to give the role of ideas in history their

3

Introduction

due, and to defend both ideas and history against the encroachments of positivist causal generalizations.[1] Personally I am much more sympathetic to that positivist effort to build an explanatory science, and I believe that the value of Weber's works is in just the leads he gives toward building a sophisticated and realistic conflict theory. Such are not the preferences of many theorists today, since we live in an era in which the spirit of Dilthey's *Geisteswissenschaft* is reechoed by trendy modes of Frankfurt Marxism and the various dialects of Paris structuralism, and further reinforced by the bias toward particularism and specialization characteristic of our crowded academic world. The existence of these trends is one of the reasons why Weber's treasures have remained buried so long, even after intense examination during the past half century.

Perhaps, then, I am going against Weber's posthumous wishes, putting emphasis where he would not have himself intended. Certainly my approach goes against much of his explicit methodological writings, which stress that theories can only take the form of ideal types with which to chart the particulars of the endless flow that makes up history. But ultimately it is of no importance to what degree I have drawn from a one-sided selection of Weber. My complaint

[1] This is particularly clear in his early articles in *Schmoller's Jahrbuch* on Roscher and Knies (1903, 1905, 1906/1975), written at just the time he was working up his approach to the Protestant ethic. These works are notably parallel to Durkheim's early work (in fact his Latin dissertation) on Montesquieu (1892). In each case, the writer was defining his own position vis-à-vis his principal intellectual ancestors, although the substantive content of the positions each took up was diametrically opposed. Durkheim praised Montesquieu as a predecessor in the scientific search for the basic structures of society, whereas Weber attacked precisely this type of belief in nomothetic laws, evolution, and the value premises implied in the image of the healthy or diseased social organism. Roscher, writing in the 1840s, marks the beginning of the distinctively German school of economics, repudiating classical economics in favor of the study of the historical development of economic institutions. Weber himself was, above all, just such a German historical/institutional economist, which should be borne in mind when considering his position on the *Methodenstreit* that makes up the background of his methodological essays. The *Methodenstreit* was, in fact, a debate within economics, set off by the Austrian Carl Menger's revival of neoclassical economics, which occasioned a furious attack by Gustav Schmoller, the leader of the historical/institutional school. Weber not only sides with Schmoller, bolstering his position with Rickert's neo-Kantianism, but purifies Roscher's style of economics of its vestigial Hegelianism of "spiritual" stages of development. Weber even uses Marxism to attack Roscher's concept of the *Volksgeist*: "From the point of view of the contemporary Marx-oriented conception, it is self-evident that the development of a Volk is to be understood as *determined* by these typical economic stages" (1903/1975:76). But Weber only wished to play off one-sided idealism against one-sided materialism; in his view, any systematic thought distorts the inexhaustible variety of reality. Weber directed this in particular against any deductive system of general principles; the most prominent examples he was combating were, of course, classical and neoclassical economics, although evolutionary sociology of the Spencer type also fell under its ban.

4

against previous selections from his treasure chest is not that they have been one-sided but only that they have chosen some of his lesser contributions and left some of the most important. Ideas are important merely for what understanding of the world we can get from them, and to the systematic extension of such knowledge I should be happy to subordinate all else.

Weber had certain strengths that make him still our greatest resource as a sociologist. One is that, of all the great sociologists, he was by far the most historically comparative. Marx certainly had very large intellectual ambitions, but in fact virtually all of his analysis was done of the economic history of northwestern Europe, and his scattered references to other societies are neither systematically thought through nor comprehensive. Durkheim, on the other hand, had a clear sense of the importance of comparative historical evidence for sociology. He stated that such comparisons constituted the main application of the method of concomitant variation characteristic of experimental science; for him, historical comparisons played for the sociologist a "role analogous to that of the microscope in the order of physical realities" (quoted in Lukes, 1973:404). But Durkheim himself knew far too little history to follow his own recommendation. For history he substituted static anthropological comparisons of tribal societies – a choice that has left its legacy by nearly monopolizing the more formal scientific part of comparative analysis; see, for example, Murdock (1967).[2] Durkheim was particularly deficient in comparative understanding of politics and economic institutions, especially since the rise of the large-scale state. This was, of course, where Weber shone. Despite their extreme methodological differences, Weber was

[2] Comparative sociology has suffered the consequence of a strong anthropological bias toward tribal societies and against the large-scale historical states that made up Weber's subject matter. This bias has been exacerbated by the methodological dogma that the search for general laws requires a solution to "Galton's problem," the possibility that similarities in the social structures of various societies were due not to structural causes but merely to the fact that the traits in question diffused from nearby societies. The answer generally accepted has been to choose samples of societies remote from each other in space; such societies are almost always tribal because large-scale historical empires are notably *non*isolated and "contaminated" by diffusion. One ironic result has been that comparative analysis gives the illusion that social structures leaped directly from tribal to "modern" forms – one of the main sources of simplistic fallacies about industrial society such as have been exposed by the recent family history. In fact, "Galton's problem" is an absurdity; *all* societies are affected by diffusion, and Murdock-style "world samples" simply pretend it doesn't exist by systematically excluding all possible data on how the diffusion might have occurred. The real problem is not to find mythically isolated societies for comparison, but to develop a theory of just how the larger "external" context of societies affects their internal traits. A moment's thought will indicate that this is hardly an automatic result; what diffuses and what does not is hardly indicated in any of the methodological beliefs popular among comparativists.

in the ideal position to carry out Durkheim's program of showing by comparative analysis the causal conditions underlying large-scale social structures.

Moreover, there is more than a hint that Weber himself got more from his comparative studies than would have been allowed inside the straitjacket of his philosophy of ideal types. For these ideal types are not merely a kind of Kantian universals through which we see the historical flux. Ideal types, like other complex concepts, themselves contain the embryo of scientific generalizations. Categories such as charismatic, traditional, and rational-legal legitimation do not exist merely for the sake of labeling and classifying history; they are embedded in a larger network of concepts and in an image of how they work. The three types of legitimation, for example, are related to another set of ideal types: Weber's concepts of organization (mainly political organization). Nor does bureaucracy stand by itself as an isolated ideal type; it is part of the set (1) bureaucracy, (2) patrimonial organization (with its relatives, patriarchism, sultanism, feudalism, etc.), and (3) the uninstitutionalized retinue of followers (one might say, "social movement") of a charismatic leader. Thus the routinization of charisma is not merely a psychological or cultural transformation from feelings of charisma into either traditional or rational-legal authority; it is part of a process of organizational transformation in which the original social movement, through the organizational impetus of its own success, acquires property and hence becomes transformed into either bureaucracy or patrimonialism (or mixtures and variants thereof).

One could go farther and show how Weber's famous dimensions of stratification – class, status, and power, with their less familiar subtypes (see Wiley, 1967) – are themselves meshed in a larger explanatory scheme. Since much of this comes out in the chapters to follow, I will limit myself to mentioning here that the "status" dimension is a crucial one in Weber's scheme. It is the area in which he made his most famous contributions: the importance of religion, both in economics and in politics; the diversifying of the Marxian class scheme with status groups, which gives the theoretical potential for treating ethnicity and sex, problems that have remained intractable from the Marxian viewpoint (as well as from most others). But status is closely linked with legitimacy, the dynamic element in Weber's political scheme; it is also linked with authority, the center of his sociology of organizations, and with monopolization of market opportunities, which is key to his treatments of economics and of social class. Weber's categories, in other words, do us relatively little service if we confine them to the doctrinal role of ideal types. Whatever Weber's own feelings about the matter turn out to have been at various stages of his life, it is apparent to me that his ideas are robust and burst the seams of the historicism and idealism he strove so mightily to defend.

Weber's historical comparisons, then, are among his great strengths, and a major reason why we continue to go back to him. They underlie his sheerly intellectual attraction, since Weber obviously lacks the kind of political appeal that draws people to Marx. Another of Weber's strengths is his capacity for breaking through normal modes of understanding. He is full of unexpected insights and subterranean connections, although many of them have proved too forbidding for most readers attempting to dig through the unaccustomed historical examples from which Weber induced (and constructed) his generalizations. Weber's Protestant ethic is, of course, a sufficiently well-known instance of digging through one institutional realm, the economic, to find a seemingly alien one beneath, religion. But this remains a superficial example. One might even lay out Weber's major insights as an extension of this overturning of the obvious.

Weber's threefold scheme – class, status, and party (or economics, culture, and politics) – echoes throughout his works. He is multidimensional in every respect. One might say that a vulgar version of Weber is to stress the status dimension (religion, culture, values) as underlying all else. Thus capitalism is but an offshoot of Christianity; stratification, of a status hierarchy; and politics, of legitimacy. A more complex version would be the route taken (to a certain extent) during his middle period by Talcott Parsons (1951; Parsons and Shils, 1951), in which certain analytic dimensions (in Parsons's case, four rather than three) are applied to every institution, so that each has its functional specialization, as well as containing within itself all of the other dimensions. (Thus religion has a political aspect and an economic aspect; politics, a religious aspect; etc.) I regard this as a mode of scholasticizing, and a diversion from constructing a genuinely explanatory and dynamic theory. But, for purposes of exposition, something like an "exposé" reinterpretation of Weber's three main dimensions might be facetiously used as a guidepost.

That is to say, one might "uncover" the underlying reality of these institutions as follows: (1) *Religion* is "really" *economics:* (2) *politics* is "really" *religion;* (3) *economics* is "really" *politics.*

Religion as economics

Weber is famous, of course, for arguing that religion provided the underpinnings of capitalism. And this is true, I shall argue, in a broader sense than that of the early Protestant-ethic thesis. But religion is economic in other respects as well. When Weber analyzes churches, he points above all to their economic organization: not in the sense that churches must rest upon this or that form of surrounding economy but, rather, that a church itself is an organization that has certain material requisites for its survival. The forms of religion change with its material resources. The principal ground for the routinization of religious charisma is the acquisition of property and sources of income (i.e., regular sources of support) for the religious specialists; how these properties are organized (here one may think of the economics of Buddhist temples, Islamic madrasahs, Christian bishops, or Protestant congregations) is a crucial determinant of the larger religion.[3]

Of course, religion is not merely, much less "really" or "ultimately," economics. But that unnatural slant gives us the proper position from which to see one of the crucial dynamics of world history, and a distinctively Weberian viewpoint. Within Weber's multidimensionality, religion occupies a privileged place for the analysis of capitalism in particular. The first step in professional sophistication is to show how complicated things really are; but this remains only the first step. Multidimensionality and complexity can end up merely muddying our picture of the world to unintelligibility. That is why the higher stage of scholarly insight is to point to a guiding thread through the labyrinth.

In the chapters of Part I of this book, grouped under the rubric "Economics," religion gives us that guiding thread. Chapter 2, "Weber's Last Theory of Capitalism," is a systematic outline of the full theory of the institutional characteristics and social prerequisites for the emergence of capitalism. The picture that emerges is predominantly institutional; apparently "free-floating" religious ethics, ideas of predestination, and the like fall into their proper places as part of a set of institutional patterns linking status communities, religious organizations, and the rational-legal state. The picture here is multidimensional, with a vengeance. Nevertheless, its skeleton consists of two long chains of historical conditions: one producing a particular kind of balance in the political sphere that can either regulate or plunder the productive economy; the other producing the social net-

---

[3] To give a modern application: One reason that the Catholic Church has maintained a continuing presence, despite the erosion of its community support in recent decades, is because its vast property holdings keep the institution going through "hard times." Given this viable organizational base, it seems only a matter of time before religious leaders emerge who make the "reforms" that regain its ideological appeal in some constituency. I owe this observation to Joseph R. Gusfield.

works and relationships that allow for a maximally dynamic capitalistic market. *Both causal chains are crucially dependent on religion.* It is the organizational side of religion that has made possible the rise of the bureaucratic state and, more remotely, the civic forms underlying a business-oriented legal system. And it is religion that reorganizes primal kin and ethnic communities so that they cease to be barriers to rationalized trade and labor, and instead become status systems rewarding rationalized economic success.

When we go on to make a concrete application of this model, we find ourselves even more obviously immersed in religion. "The Weberian Revolution of the High Middle Ages" is a phenomenon that I believe Weber would have discovered if he had lived long enough to complete his comparative studies of the world religions. For modern historiography now has abundantly documented what was scarcely visible in Weber's day: a full-fledged economic boom in the Europe of A.D. 1050–1300. My argument is that the institutional prerequisites of capitalism fell into place then. This theme is in keeping with the general line of revisionist economic history of recent decades, which finds many of the traits formerly thought to be associated with industrialism (e.g., family structures, property relationships) already present several centuries earlier. The boldest step along this line has been the claim of Macfarlane (1978) that modern individualism was already in existence in the 1200s (though perhaps only in England).

My argument differs by stressing the "Weberian" point that the transformations of the High Middle Ages are not basically cultural, but institutional; and that the capitalism of the Middle Ages was above all the *capitalism of the Church.* That is to say, the secular economy, which was apparent enough in merchant cities like Genoa, Florence, and Venice, remained essentially a premodern "merchants' capitalism" and as such had no very deep or lasting effects upon European institutions. Weber drew upon the scholarship of his time, concentrated primarily on this Mediterranean economy, whereas the new revisionist historiography has uncovered a different world in rural northern Europe. The key to this world, in my opinion, has not yet been recognized: it was the economy of the monastic "revolution" that in many ways marks the beginning and end points of the High Middle Ages. The rationalized capitalism that emerged was, above all, that of the dynamic monastic movements, and the appropriately regulatory bureaucratic state that went along with it was not the secular states but the Papacy in the period when it made a bid for theocratic power over all of Christendom.

The argument must wait for details later in this book. It can be

Introduction

pointed out, though, that the Weberian religious theme can be elaborated in several directions. The downfall of the medieval economy, I will suggest, was linked with religious politics, which is to say, with the failure of theocracy and the decline of the Papacy. The Reformation, which Weber (and so many others) took as the beginning point of modern capitalism, rather appears as the end point of one cycle in the larger world economy, and the beginning of another. Weber also bolstered his argument by comparisons of the other great world religions. China has been the closest competitor to Europe for an approach to rationalized capitalism; its technological developments, which led no farther in the Orient but which vitalized European growth, have often been remarked upon, although rarely explained. I attempt to show that Weber could have followed the logic of his own institutional analysis of capitalism farther, to uncover a crucial turning point in the social history of China: the crisis of Chinese Buddhism. For Buddhism, *as an institutional form*, had a monastic economy that played much the same role in medieval China (especially the northern dynasties, about A.D. 400–581, the Sui 581–618, and the T'ang, 618–900) as Christianity did in Europe. I suggest that the vicissitudes of religious politics in China, especially the increasingly successful Confucian counterattack during the late T'ang and Sung (960–1279), undermined the protocapitalist structure of China and eventually deflected it from a capitalist route.

The whole historiography of China, I would suggest, is overlaid with scarcely noticed religious bias. Weber himself, like most Chinese historians and the Westerners who draw upon them, tended to regard Confucianism as the archetypal religion of China, with a symbiotic Taoism providing a kind of private spiritual relief from its public formalism. What lends credence to this view is the fact that Confucianism, besides being very ancient, also dominated the bureaucratic examination system and the state ideology of the most recent dynasties (Ming, 1368–1644, and Ch'ing, 1644–1911). But in between the Han (202 B.C.–A.D. 220) and Sung (960–1279) one would have to say that medieval China was above all a Buddhist society. That is especially true of the innovative and state-building dynasties of the north (ca. 400–618), and the politics of the T'ang and early Sung tended to be a religious struggle – a kind of Confucian Counter-Reformation fought, by and large successfully, against Buddhism. The differing fates of East and West, I am going to suggest, can be placed upon the balance of their contrasting religious politics.

Thus far, we follow Weber's sociology in order to illuminate history, quite in keeping with his own preferences. But in the process certain more abstract points turn up. Weber's economic theory bears

10

upon the problem of technology, a topic that seems the antithesis of the theme I am imputing to him. Technology for us seems to have the quality of brute fact and sheer functional imperative. Perhaps this is because there is no real sociological explanation of technology, although it plays a central role as an independent variable in many treatments of comparative social structure and social change. Technology is the great *deus ex machina* of sociology, perhaps even a mysterious *machina ex deus*. All we seem to know is that technology suddenly appears, or evolves, or diffuses, sometimes with tremendous consequences like printing or gunpowder setting off the Gutenberg revolution, the military revolution, and so forth. Technology continues to play this overriding role in currently fashionable "post-industrial" pictures of the computerized electronic society today.

Nevertheless, it is possible to derive from Weber a theory of the social conditions for technology. One may take the hint from his remarks in *General Economic History* on the rationalization of production in eighteenth-century Europe. This analysis makes technology itself part of the realm of the spirit, so to speak. I bring in some tentative historical comparisons in sympathy with this idea, including both the medieval-European and Chinese cases mentioned above, along with a comparison with eras of very low technological change.

Finally, I round off Weber's economic sociology with a consideration of a central feature of the modern capitalism: the social organization of money. Norbert Wiley proposes in a brilliant essay (1983) that all great sociologies have an economics attached to them. Thus Parsonian functionalism is the sociological counterpart of neoclassical general equilibrium theory, whereas Marx's doctrine is, of course, a variant on Ricardian classical economics. For Weber, Wiley proposes, the equivalent economics is that of John Maynard Keynes, because of their underlying assumptions about uncertainty and cognition in the economic realm. I suggest another economist, one very close to Weber's own milieu: Joseph Schumpeter.

The connection is especially apt in that Schumpeter is probably the most sociologically oriented of economists. The comparison goes beyond Schumpeter's entrepreneur and Weber's Protestant ethic, as indeed it should if the Protestant ethic is only an early and partial aspect of Weber's model of capitalism. What we find, rather, is a convergence on the business organization as a locus for struggle over power and alliance. Weber and Schumpeter are in essential agreement on this. Weber adds a special emphasis on the importance of monopolization of opportunities in the labor market, which is surprisingly parallel to Schumpeter's defense of business monopolies as a necessary part of the profit-making system. What Schumpeter especially adds is a focus of an organizational realm that has received strikingly little attention: the financial world as "the headquarters of the capitalist system, from which orders go out to its individual divisions, and that which is debated and decided there is always in essence the settlement of plans for further development" (Schumpeter, 1911/1961:126).

We seem to be pursuing the essence of economics into the political mode, rather than into the religious one. But the connection is just around the corner. Money is another social phenomenon, like technology, about which there is virtually no sociological analysis. If we were to seek the beginnings of such a theory, a likely candidate would be the analysis of symbolic currencies. We find here the gift-exchange systems of Mauss and Lévi-Strauss (the latter of whom comes very close to what we are seeking, by his stress on how symbolic exchanges of women mesh with the hard economic exchanges of goods and services). Even closer to our target are analyses of the cultural capital whose circulation makes up the status networks of ordinary life, and the public currencies of ideology that are the dynamic vehicle for religious and political legitimacy (Bourdieu and Passeron, 1970/1977; Collins, 1981b). It is time, perhaps, that we stopped merely using money as a metaphor to explain other things and began to use it as a metaphor to explain the place of money itself. The central dynamics of capitalism, especially its cyclical character and its tendency to crisis, appear to lie in the realm of *cultural* circulation that constitutes a financial system.

The importance of money and that of markets are two essential points of contention between the Weberian and the Marxian world views. I would claim that Weber is right on these points and the Marxians are wrong – or, what comes to the same thing, the Weberian analysis is on a far more fruitful track, capable of moving ahead, whereas Marxism is at an impasse.

Politics as religion

On the face of it, the formula of politics as religion, however facetious, seems too great a distortion of Weber's position. I have already argued that the central feature of Weberian politics is the contest for military power in the world arena. The essence of politics thus seems to be force. Still, there is something to be gained from pursuing our "uncovering" transformation. For, as I show in Chapter 6, "Imperialism and Legitimacy: Weber's Theory of Politics," the geopolitical realm is the key to internal politics because of the connection between military force and domestic legitimacy. Weber stresses the point that there is an international arena of *status* competition, overriding and guiding economic considerations in "imperialism." This does not simply leave us with the brute irrationality of war, for there is a logic of status competition underlying the use of force.[4] The logic is the same, I would argue, as that underlying the major transformations of the world religions. A demonstration of this is attempted in Chapter 9, "Heresy, Religious and Secular," in which it is argued that the political vicissitudes of churches *as organizations* are essentially what is involved in heresy disputes.

My point is not the kind of reductionism that declares heresy is nothing but a reflection of politics. It is, rather, that religion, as an institution, has its own politics. As Weber stresses, during much of history, religion was so much better organized for politics than the secular realm (to the extent that we can speak of the latter) that secular power-seekers were necessarily drawn into the religious orbit. The point may also be put in a fashion to which Durkheim would have strongly assented: The symbols of religion always represent emotionally committed membership in a social organization. Hence any strong organization must be in essence "religious." The state is among the strongest of organizations precisely because its implied use of force generates the most emotionally committing of all situations. Politics in an important sense is ritual. If it is too much to say that politics is "really" religion, it is scarcely going too far to say that at the dynamic level they are virtually identical.

The set of "uncovering" formulas, if pushed very far, of course breaks down. If religion is economics and politics is religion, it follows that politics is economics. Indeed, everything in the circle is everything else. This is the Parsonian position of infinitely subrepeating analytical dimensions. It is true, in a sense, but also not necessarily fruitful to pursue this circle too far. It is only worthwhile to expose some significant points: the central role of religion (as *organization*, not merely ideas) in capitalism; the near identity of the status dynamics underlying violent politics with those underlying the ritual powers and contentions of religion; and finally, the way in which the "political" organization of everyday life is a crucial determinant of economic fate, as well as providing its ideological cover.

---

[4] One could go farther and show that actual military success in battle is to a considerable extent the result of a kind of psychological war. Violence is used above all as a ritual display, aimed at destroying the opposing army's *organization* while preserving one's own. Even pure force thus reduces, in an important sense, to the dimension of social ideas and emotions that may be indexed by the realm of "culture," "status," or "religion."

Introduction

Economics as politics

We have already noticed, in the proposed Weber-Schumpeter connection, that business is a realm of "political" manuever. Again, as in the case of religion, this does not mean so much that business people appeal to the state for favors and protection (although, of course, they do that too) as that the realm of business itself, the so-called market, is a sphere of organization with its own political relationships. Schumpeter describes the entrepreneur as an individual driven by the aim of setting up his own private sphere of control, the last vestige of independent baronial power after the rise of the bureaucratic state. But politics always involves alliances, and these are nowhere more apparent than in the financial relationships that are, according to Schumpeter, the essence of capitalism (which he defines as "enterprise carried out with borrowed money"). As in other realms, business alliances do not exclude calculated self-interest, and may even have it as their core.

Both Weber and Schumpeter emphasize that the key to stratification in a market economy is precisely the ability of certain organizations and classes to evade the vicissitudes of the market and find a protected place for themselves within it. Without this, Schumpeter argues, profit could not emerge. (As I shall show, this analytical point, which I call the "Adam Smith paradox," is taken by Marx as the crucial contradiction driving his economic scheme; I think, however, that Marx offers a mistaken resolution of the paradox.) On the level of labor markets, Weber stresses the importance of occupational groups that establish some degree of monopoly over market chances. This not only evades the "Adam Smith paradox" on the level of personal incomes, and hence generates income stratification; it also ties the phenomonen of status groups into the economic realm. Contrary to our usual interpretation, status groups are not the antithesis of economic class but precisely the way in which stratified classes are able to emerge and maintain themselves. It is through the organization of status groups that classes become distinctive entities in the market, instead of parts of the endless (and essentially profit-less) flux of labor with the tides of supply and demand. Thus, by a roundabout way, we come to the role of culture in economic stratification.

Another chapter, on alienation, provides a kind of double "uncovering" of a theme in modern culture. Cultural alienation, according to the Marxian critique, is reducible to the economic relations of capitalism. This analysis, however, is but another form of mystification. The Marxian view of the capitalist economy, with its focus on alienation of workers from the means of production, misses the central features of capitalist competition for profits, and the dynamics that produce both expansion and crisis. These dynamics, rather, are to be found in the realm of markets, including the intermeshing of financial and cultural markets I have suggested. Modern Marxism misses the very nature of the power struggles that go on in the economic realm. By the same token, it misses the political nature of the slogans of alienation itself. I shall attempt to show that feelings and ideas of alienation emerge precisely through the experience of political mobilization, in its characteristic ritual form. Economics, culture, politics constitute a series of "uncoverings." With this, hopefully, we can discard our makeshift formulas of Weberian alchemy, having emerged through them onto solid ground.

The organization of this book follows roughly the Weberian trichotomy of economics, politics, and culture. Each is transformed, more or less in the manner indicated. Some parts of these topics remain less transformed, of course. Weber's theory of politics not only gives the consequences of military force for legitimacy but also leads to the more immediate consideration of what would be an adequate theory of geopolitics. Two chapters attempt to develop this, including a discussion of whether geopolitical principles derived from the agrarian era, Weber's "home base," are applicable to the geopolitics of modern industrialized warfare. As might be expected from our discussion of the dependent role of technology, it turns out that the principles remain valid today. As an illustration of their utility, I shall give an application in the form of what they predict for the future of the Russian Empire in the world today.

I also add a fourth rubric: sex. It is, of course, more fashionable now to use the term "gender," but I hold to the traditional one here, for several reasons. Foremost among these is the fact that a Weberian approach to gender centrally emphasizes sexual – that is, erotic – relationships, along with economic ones. Here again the Weberian approach stresses something that currently popular modes of thought tend to ignore. I shall not attempt to "uncover" the analytical dimensions in the Weberian scheme that might be thought to underlie sexual relationships. But one more familiarly Weberian theme is apparent. As I show in an exegesis of Weber's neglected theory of the family, politics, is a centrally important determinant of those male-female relationships that make up the legitimate kinship system. My concluding chapter is an attempt at a rather far-flung comparison – of southern Indian, medieval Japan, and medieval Europe – to uncover the political dynamics responsible for the first major rise in the modern rights and status of women. The first feminist revolution, in a sense, can already be found deep in the courtly politics of certain

15

special types of agrarian states. An important implication, if the Weberian theory is right, is that the further success of the current feminist movement depends on its continuing to be explicitly political.

These, I venture to propose, are some central themes of a Weberian sociology. Whether this is authentically Weber is a less interesting question than whether it will prove fruitful. I have some hopes that it is in the spirit of Weber, and that if he were alive he would not be unhappy with the directions in which his thought has been taken.

Part I

Economics

2

Weber's last theory of capitalism

Max Weber had many intellectual interests, and there has been considerable debate over the question of what constitutes the central theme of his life work. Besides treating the origins of capitalism, Weber dealt extensively with the nature of modernity and of rationality (Tenbruck, 1975; Kalberg, 1979; 1980; Seidman, 1980), and with politics, methodology, and various substantive areas of sociology. Amid all the attention which has been paid to these concerns, one of Weber's most significant contributions has been largely ignored. This is his mature theory of the development of capitalism, found in his last work (1961), *General Economic History*.

This is ironic because Weber's (1930) first major work, *The Protestant Ethic and the Spirit of Capitalism*, has long been the most famous of all. The argument that the Calvinist doctrine of predestination gave the psychological impetus for rationalized, entrepreneurial capitalism is only a fragment of Weber's full theory. But many scholars have treated it as Weber's distinctive contribution, or Weber's distinctive fallacy, on the origins of capitalism (e.g., Tawney, 1938; McClelland, 1961; Samuelsson, 1961; Cohen, 1980). Debate about the validity of this part of Weber's theory has tended to obscure the more fundamental historical and institutional theory which he presented in his later works.

The so-called "Weber thesis," as thus isolated, has been taken to be essentially idealist. Weber (1930:90) defines his purpose in *The Protestant Ethic* as "a contribution to the manner in which ideas become effective forces in history." He (1930:183) polemically remarks against the Marxists that he does not intend to replace a one-sided materialism with its opposite, but his correcting of the balance sheet in this work concentrates largely on ideal factors. The germ of Weber's institutional theory of capitalism can also be found in *The Protestant*

Reprinted with modifications from *American Sociological Review*, 45 (1980), by permission of the American Sociological Association.

Ethic (1930:58, 76).[1] But it remained an undeveloped backdrop for his main focus on the role of religious ideas. The same may be said about his (1951; 1952; 1958b) comparative studies of the world religions. These broadened considerably the amount of material on social, economic, and political conditions, but the main theme still stressed that divergent ideas made an autonomous contribution to the emergence of world-transforming capitalism in the Christian West rather than elsewhere in the world.[2] Thus, Parsons (1963; 1967) treats these works as extending the early Weber thesis from Protestantism to Christianity in general, describing an evolution of religious ideas and their accompanying motivational propensities from ancient Judaism up through the secularized achievement culture of the modern United States.

From these works, and from (1968) Part II of *Economy and Society*, it is possible to pull out an extensive picture of institutional factors which Weber includes in his overall theory of capitalism. But *Economy and Society* is organized encyclopedically, by analytically defined topics, and does not pull together the theory as a whole. There is only one place in Weber's works where he brings together the full theory of capitalism as a historical dynamic. This is in the *General Economic History*, and, especially, in the 70-page section comprising Part IV of that work. These lectures, delivered in the winter and spring of 1919–20, before Weber's death that summer, are Weber's last word on the subject of capitalism. They are also the most neglected of his works; *General Economic History* is the only one of Weber's major works that remains out of print today, both in English and in German.

One important change in the *General Economic History* is that Weber pays a good deal more attention to Marxian themes than previously. This is a significant difference from the anti-Marxist comments scattered through *The Protestant Ethic* (e.g., pp. 55–56, 61, 90–91, 183). In the *General Economic History*, Weber reduces the ideal factor to a rela-

---

[1] The list of institutional characteristics given on pp. 21–25 of the English-language edition of *The Protestant Ethic* (1930), however, are not in the 1904–5 original, but are from an introduction written in 1920 (1930:ix–x).

[2] Cf. the closing words of *The Religion of China*: "To be sure the basic characteristics of the 'mentality,' in this case practical attitudes towards the world, were deeply co-determined by political and economic destinies. Yet, in view of their autonomous laws, one can hardly fail to ascribe to these attitudes effects strongly counteractive to capitalist development" (1951:249), and of *The Religion of India*: "However, for the plebeian strata no ethic of everyday life derived from its rationally formed missionary prophecy. The appearance of such in the Occident, however – above all, in the Near East – with the extensive consequences borne with it, was conditioned by highly particular historical constellations without which, despite differences of natural conditions, development there could easily have taken the course typical of Asia, particularly of India" (1958b:343).

tively small place in his overall scheme. During this same period, to be sure, Weber was preparing a new introduction and footnotes for the reissue of *The Protestant Ethic* among his collected religious writings, in which he defended his original thesis about Calvinism. But his claims for its importance in the overall scheme of things were not large, and the well-rounded model which he presents in *General Economic History* does not even mention the doctrine of predestination. Instead, what we find is a predominantly institutional theory, in which religious *organization* plays a key role in the rise of modern capitalism but especially in conjunction with particular forms of political organization.

In what follows, I will attempt to state systematically Weber's mature theory of capitalism, as it appears in the *General Economic History*, bolstered where appropriate by the building blocks presented in *Economy and Society*. This argument involves a series of causes, which we will trace backward, from the most recent to the most remote. This model, I would suggest, is the most comprehensive general theory of the origins of capitalism that is yet available. It continues to stand up well in comparison with recent theories, including Wallerstein's (1974) historical theory of the capitalist and world-system.

Weber himself was primarily concerned with the sensitizing concepts necessary for an interpretation of the unique pattern of history and, in his methodological writings, he disavowed statements in the form of general causal principles (cf. Burger, 1976). Nevertheless, Weber's typologies contain implicit generalizations about the effects of institutional arrangements upon each other, and statements of cause-and-effect abound in his substantive writings. There is nothing to prevent us from stating his historical picture of changing institutional forms in a more abstract and generalized manner than Weber did himself.

Weber's model continues to offer a more sophisticated basis for a theory of capitalism than any of the rival theories of today. I put forward this formalization of Weber's mature theory, not merely as an appreciation of one of the classic works of the past, but to make clear the high-water mark of sociological theory about capitalism. Weber's last theory is not the last word on the subject of the rise of capitalism, but if we are to surpass it, it is the high point from which we ought to build.

The components of rationalized capitalism

Capitalism, says Weber (1961:207–8, 260) is the provision of human needs by the method of enterprise, which is to say, by private busi-

21

nesses seeking profit. It is exchange carried out for positive gain, rather than forced contributions or traditionally fixed gifts or trades. Like all of Weber's categories, capitalism is an analytical concept: capitalism can be found as part of many historical economies, as far back as ancient Babylon. It became the indispensable form for the provision of everyday wants only in Western Europe around the middle of the nineteenth century. For this large-scale and economically predominant capitalism, the key is the "rational permanent enterprise" characterized by "rational capital accounting."

The concept of "rationality" which appears so often in Weber's works has been the subject of much debate. Marxist critics of capitalism, as well as critics of bureaucracy, have attacked Weber's alleged glorification of these social forms (e.g., Hirst, 1976). On the other hand, Parsons (1947), in his long introduction to the definitional section of *Economy and Society*, gives "rationalization" both an idealist and an evolutionary bent, as the master trend of world history, involving an inevitable upgrading of human cognitive and organizational capacities. Tenbruck (1975) claims the key to Weber's works is an inner logic of rational development found within the realm of religious solutions to the problem of suffering.

It is clear that Weber himself used the term "rationalism" in a number of different senses.[3] But for his *institutional* theory of capitalist development, there is only one sense that need concern us. The "rational capitalistic establishment," says Weber (1961:207), "is one with capital accounting, that is, an establishment which determines its income yielding power by calculation according to the methods of modern bookkeeping and the striking of a balance." The key term is *calculability*; it occurs over and over again in those pages. What is distinctive about modern, large-scale, "rational" capitalism – in contrast to earlier, partial forms – is that it is methodical and predictable, reducing all areas of production and distribution as much as possible

---

[3] In Part I of *Economy and Society* (written 1918–20), Weber distinguishes formal and substantive rationality of economic action (1968:85–6). In "The Social Psychology of the World Religions" (written 1913), Weber (1946:293–4) defines three different types of rationalism: (1) a systematic world view based on precise, abstract concepts; (2) practical means-ends calculations; (3) a systematic method, including that of magic or prayer. In *The Protestant Ethic* (1904–5), Weber (1930:76–78) attacks the notion that the spirit of capitalism is "part of the development of rationalism as a whole," and says he is interested in "the origin of precisely the irrational element which lies in this, as in every conception of a calling." Kalberg (1980) points out that under one or another of Weber's types of rationality, *every* action, even the most superstitious, might be called "rational." Kalberg argues that only one type of rationality is relevant for the methodical conduct of affairs.

to a routine. This is also Weber's criterion for calling bureaucracy the most "rational" form of organization.[4]

For a capitalist economy to have a high degree of predictability, it must have certain characteristics. The logic of Weber's argument is first to describe these characteristics; then to show the obstacles to them that were prevalent in virtually all societies of world history until recent centuries in the West; and, finally, by the method of comparative analysis, to show the social conditions responsible for their emergence.

According to his argument, the components of "rationalized" capitalism are as follows:

There must be *private appropriation of all the means of production*, and their concentration under the control of entrepreneurs. Land, buildings, machinery, and materials must all be assembled under a common management, so that decisions about their acquisition and use can be calculated with maximal efficiency. All these factors must be subject to sale as private goods on an open market. This development reaches its maximal scope when all such property rights are represented by commercial instruments, especially shares in ownership which are themselves negotiable in a stock market.

Within this enterprise, capital accounting is optimized by a *technology which is "reduced to calculation to the largest possible degree"* (1961:208). It is in this sense that mechanization is most significant for the organization of large-scale capitalism.

Labor must be free to move about to any work in response to conditions of demand. Weber notes that this is a formal and legal freedom, and that it goes along with the economic compulsion of workers to sell their labor on the market. Capitalism is impossible without a propertyless stratum selling its services "under the compulsion of the whip of hunger" (1961:209), for only this completes a mass market system for the factors of production which makes it possible to clearly calculate the costs of products in advance.

---

[4] It is plain that Weber (1968:85–6) is referring to what in *Economy and Society* he calls "formal" rationality, efficiency based on quantitative calculation of means, rather than "substantive" rationality, the adequacy of actions for meeting ultimate values. Such values could be criteria of economic welfare, whether maximal production, quality of life, or a socialist economic distribution, or they could be ethical or religious values. Weber makes it clear that formal and substantive rationality can diverge widely, especially in his late political writings about the dangers of bureaucracy (1946:77–128; 1968:1393–1415). Weber himself tended to defend the formal rationality of modern capitalism as coinciding to a fair degree with substantive rationality in meeting the value of maximizing the economic welfare of the population at large (1968:108–9). It goes without saying that this is an empirical, not an analytical judgment.

Economics

Trading in the market must not be limited by irrational restrictions. That is to say, noneconomic restrictions on the movement of goods or of any of the factors of production must be minimized. Such restrictions include class monopolies upon particular items of consumption (such as sumptuary laws regulating dress), or upon ownership or work (such as prohibitions on townspeople owning land, or on knights or peasants carrying on trade; more extensively, caste systems in general). Other obstacles under this heading include transportation difficulties, warfare, and robbery – which make long-distance trading hazardous and unreliable.

Finally, there must be *calculable law, both in adjudication and in public administration.* Laws must be couched in general terms applicable to all persons, and administered in such a way as to make the enforcement of economic contracts and rights highly predictable. Such a legal system is implicated in most of the above characteristics of rational capitalism: the extension of private property rights over the factors of production; the subdivision and easy transferability of such rights through financial instruments and banking operations; formal freedom for laborers; and legally protected markets.

The picture that Weber gives us, then, is of the institutional foundations of the market as viewed by neoclassical economics. He sees the market as providing the maximal amount of calculability for the individual entrepreneur. Goods, labor, and capital flow continuously to the areas of maximal return; at the same time, competition in all markets reduces costs to their minimum. Thus, prices serve to summarize all the necessary information about the optimal allocation of resources for maximizing profit; on this basis, entrepreneurs can most reliably make calculations for long-term production of large amounts of goods. "To sum up," says Weber (1961:209), "it must be possible to conduct the provision for needs exclusively on the basis of market opportunities and the calculation of net income."

It is, of course, the model of the laissez-faire capitalist economy that Weber wishes to ground. At the extreme, this is an unrealistic view of any economy that has ever existed. Weber treats it as an ideal type and, hence, in a fuller exposition would doubtless have been prepared to see it as only partially realized even in the great capitalist takeoff period of the nineteenth century. But it is worth noting that a critique of Weber along these lines could certainly not be a classical Marxian one. The central dynamic of capitalism in Marx's theory, in fact, depends even more immediately than Weber's on the unrestricted competitiveness of the open market for all factors of production (cf. Sweezy, 1942). And Weber and Marx agree in claiming that

24

the initial breakthrough to an industrial society had to occur in the form of capitalism. Thus, although Weber may have a personal bias toward the neoclassical market economy, both as analytical model and as political preference, this would give no grounds for a critique of the adequacy of his explanation of this phase of world history. Even for a later period, Weber is hardly dogmatic. As we shall see, he recognizes the possibility of socialism emerging, once capitalism has matured – although he does not admire the prospect – and he even gives some indications of the forces that might produce it. Like German and Austrian non-Marxist economists of his generation, Weber includes socialism within his analytical scheme.

Weber's model of the modern economy is particularly striking with regard to the concept of the "industrial revolution." For it is not mechanization per se that is the key to the economic transformation, despite the far-reaching consequences of shifts from agrarian to inanimate-energy-based technologies (cf. Lenski, 1966). In Weber's scheme, technology is essentially a dependent variable. The key *economic* characteristic of mechanization is that it is feasible only with mass production (Weber, 1961:129, 247). The costs of even simpler machines such as steam-powered looms would make them worthless without a large-scale consumers' market for cloth, as well as a large-scale producers' market in wool or cotton. Similar considerations apply a fortiori to machinery on the scale of a steel rolling mill. But large-scale production is impossible without a high degree of predictability that markets will exist for the products, and that all the factors of production will be forthcoming at a reasonable cost. Thus, mechanization depends on the prior emergence of all the institutional factors described above.

Weber does not elaborate a systematic theory of technological innovation, but it would be possible to construct one along these lines. He does note that all the crucial inventions of the period of industrial takeoff were the result of deliberate efforts to cheapen the costs of production (1961:225–6, 231). These efforts took place because previous conditions had intensified the capitalist pursuit of profits. The same argument could be made, although Weber did not make it, in regard to the search for methods to improve agricultural production that took place in the seventeenth and eighteenth centuries. The "green revolution" which preceded (and made possible) the industrial revolution was not a process of mechanization (agricultural mechanization took place only in the late nineteenth century) but was, more simply, the application of capitalist methods of cost accounting to hitherto traditional agriculture. Thus, it is the shift to the calculating practices of the capitalist market economy which makes technological innovation itself predictable, rather than, as previously, an accidental factor in economic life (1961:231).[5]

The causal chain

What are the social preconditions for the emergence of capitalism as thus described?

Note, first of all, that economic life, even in the most prosperous of agrarian societies, generally lacked most of these traits. Property systems frequently tied land ownership to aristocratic status, while commercial occupations were often prohibited to certain groups and monopolized by others. The labor force was generally unfree – being either slaves or tied to the land as serfs. Technologies of mass production hardly existed. The market was generally limited either to local areas or to long-distance trade in luxuries, due to numerous near-confiscatory tax barriers, unreliable and varying coinage, warfare, robbery, and poor transportation. And legal systems, even in literate states, tended to be characterized by patrimonial or magical-religious procedures, by differential application to different social groups and by different localities, and by the practices of officials seeking private gain. Reliable financial transactions, including the operation of a banking system relatively free from political interference and plundering, were particularly handicapped by these conditions.

The social preconditions for large-scale capitalism, then, involved the destruction of the obstacles to the free movement or economic transfer of labor, land, and goods. Other preconditions were the creation of the institutional supports for large-scale markets, especially the appropriate systems of property, law, and finance.

These are not the only preconditions of capitalism, but, specifically, Weber is seeking the organizational forms that made capitalism a world-transforming force in the West but not elsewhere. By a series of comparisons, Weber shows that a number of other factors that have been advanced to account for the Western takeoff cannot have been crucial. Against Sombart, he points out that standardized mass production for war cannot have been decisive, for although a good deal

---

5 Weber does mention "rational science and in connection with it a rational technology" (1961:232) as one of the features of the West important for modern capitalism. On the other hand he says: "It is true that most of the inventions of the 18th century were not made in a scientific manner. . . . The connection of industry with modern science, especially the systematic work of the laboratories, beginning with Justus von Liebig [i.e., *Circa* 1830], enabled industry to become what it is today and so brought capitalism to its full development." On the balance, I think science comes out as a secondary factor in the model.

of this existed in Europe in the seventeenth century, and thereafter, it also existed in the Mogul Empire and in China without giving an impetus to capitalism (1961:229). Similarly, the enormous expenditures for court luxury found in both Orient and Occident were incapable of generating a mass market (1961:229–30). Against the simpler arguments of Adam Smith, which attribute the industrial division of labor to the extension of trade, Weber points out that trade can be found everywhere, even in the Stone Age. In ancient Babylon, for example, trade was such as to disintegrate "primitive economic fixity" to a considerable degree (1961:232). On the other hand, politically determined agrarian economies show how "specialization takes place without exchange" (1961:103). Nor is the pursuit of profit per se the crucial motive for mass capitalism: the "ruthlessness" and "unscrupulousness" of the traditional foreign trader was incapable of transforming the economy at large (1961:232). Nor can population growth have been the cause of Western capitalism, for the same trend occurred in China without the same result (1961:258–9). Neither, finally, can the price revolution of the sixteenth century, due to the influx of precious metals from the Americas, have been decisive (see the later discussion on Wallerstein).[6]

The features that Weber finds unique to the West constitute a causal chain.[7] I have represented this schematically in Figure 2.1. The characteristics of rational capitalism itself are the entrepreneurial organization of capital, rational technology, free labor, unrestricted markets, and calculable law. These make up a complex: the markets for goods, labor, and capital all mesh around entrepreneurial property using mass production technology; the operation of all of these factors together creates further pressures to both rationalize technology and expand each factor market – while yet distributing wealth in such a way as to further the demand. The legal system is both an ongoing prop for all of these features and a causal link backward to their social preconditions. At this intermediate causal level there is a second crucial factor which, like the law, is essentially cultural, al-

---

6 Weber (1961:260) also mentions geographical conditions as more favorable to capitalism in Europe than in China or India, due to transportation advantages in the former via the Mediterranean sea and the interconnecting rivers. But he goes on (p. 261) to discount this, in that no capitalism arose in Mediterranean antiquity, when civilization was predominantly coastal, whereas early modern capitalism in Europe was born in the cities of the interior.
7 Weber does not clearly describe a chain, and sometimes he lumps characteristics of rational capitalism with its preconditions. Although some of these preconditions continue into the operation of modern capitalism, a logical chain of explanation, I believe, requires something like the separation I have given. It should be understood that Weber gives a highly condensed summary in these lectures.

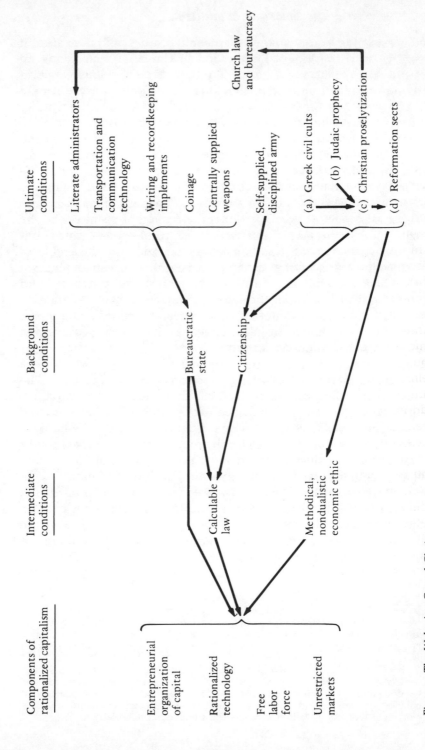

Fig. 2.1. The Weberian Causal Chain

though not in the sense of disembodied ideas, but, rather, in the sense of beliefs expressed in institutionalized behavior. This is the "lifting of the barrier . . . between internal and external ethics" (1961:232).

In virtually all premodern societies there are two sharply divergent sets of ethical beliefs and practices. Within a social group, economic transactions are strictly controlled by rules of fairness, status, and tradition: in tribal societies, by ritualized exchanges with prescribed kin; in India, by rules of caste; in medieval Europe, by required contributions on the manor or to the great church properties. The prohibition on usury reflected this internal ethic, requiring an ethic of charity and the avoidance of calculation of gain from loans within the community (cf. Nelson, 1949).[8] In regard to outsiders, however, economic ethics were at the opposite extreme: cheating, price gouging, and loans at exorbitant interest were the rule. Both forms of ethic were obstacles to rational, large-scale capitalism: the internal ethic because it prevented the commercialization of economic life, the external ethic because it made trading relations too episodic and distrustful. The lifting of this barrier and the overcoming of this ethical dualism were crucial for the development of any extensive capitalism. Only this could make loans available regularly and promote the buying and selling of all services and commodities for moderate gain. Through innumerable daily repetitions, such small (but regular) profits could add up to much more massive economic transactions than could either the custom-bound or the predatory economic ethics of traditional societies.

What, then, produced the calculable legal system of saleable private property and free labor and the universal ethic of the pursuit of moderate economic profit? The next links in the causal chain are political and religious. The bureaucratic state is a crucial background determinant for all legal and institutional underpinnings of capitalism. Moreover, its legal system must be based on a concept of universal citizenship, which requires yet further political preconditions. The religious factor operates both as a direct influence on the creation of an economic ethic and as a final level of causality implicated in the rise of the rational-legal state and of legal citizenship.

The state is the factor most often overlooked in Weber's theory of capitalism. Yet it is the factor to which he gave the most attention; in *Economy and Society,* he devoted eight chapters of 680 pages to it, as

---

[8] Hence the role of "guest peoples" such as the Jews and the Caursines in Christian Europe, or the Christians in Islamic societies, or the Parsees in India, as groups of tolerated outsiders who were available for making loans, which otherwise would not be forthcoming within the controlled internal economy (1961:267).

29

opposed to one chapter of 235 pages to religion, with yet another chapter–the neglected but very important chap. XV of Part II–to the relations between politics and religion. In the *General Economic History*, he gives the state the two penultimate chapters, religion the final chapter. For Weber, this political material was not an extraneous interest but, instead, the key to all of the *institutional* structures of rational capitalism. Only the West developed the highly bureaucratized state, based on specialized professional administrators and on a law made and applied by full-time professional jurists for a populace characterized by rights of citizenship. It is this bureaucratic-legal state that broke down feudalism and patrimonialism, freeing land and labor for the capitalist market. It is this state that pacified large territories, eliminated internal market barriers, standardized taxation and currencies. It is this state that provided the basis for a reliable system of banking, investment, property, and contracts, through a rationally calculable and universally applied system of law courts. One may even argue that the bureaucratic state was the proximate cause of the impulse to rationalization, generally – above all, via the late seventeenth- and eighteenth-century spirit of enlightened absolutism, which set the stage for the industrial revolution.

There are three causal questions about the rational/legal state. Why did it rise to predominance? Where did its structural characteristics come from? How did its legal system take the special form of conceiving of its subjects as holding the rights of citizenship?

The first question is easily answered. The bureaucratic state rose to predominance because it is the most efficient means of pacifying a large territory. It is effective externally in that it can supply a larger military, with better weapons, than can nonbureaucratic states; and it is effective, internally, as it tends to be relatively safe against disintegration by civil war or political *coup*.[9]

The sources of the bureaucratic state are, to a degree, quite familiar. In the widely reprinted section on bureaucracy from *Economy and Society* (1968:956–1005), Weber outlines the prerequisites: literate administrators, a technology of long-distance transportation and communication, writing and record-keeping materials, monetary coinage. The extent to which these could be put into effect, however, depended on a number of other factors. Geographical conditions such as easy transportation in river valleys, or favorable situations for state-controlled irrigation (1961:237), fostered bureaucratic centralization, as did intense military competition among adjacent heartlands.

---

[9] The main exception is that revolutions can occur after the military breakdown of the state itself due to foreign wars.

Types of weapons which are centrally (rather than individually) supplied also favor bureaucratization. If such conditions make central control easy, however, bureaucratization need not proceed very deeply, and the society may be ruled by a thin stratum of officials above a local structure which remains patrimonial. In China, for example, this superficial bureaucratization constituted a long-term obstacle to capitalism, as it froze the economy under the patrimonial control of local clans.

The most thorough bureaucratization, as well as that uniquely favorable to capitalism, is that which incorporates a formalistic legal code based on citizenship. Citizenship meant, first of all, membership in a city; by extension, membership in a state and hence holding political rights within it. This was an alien concept throughout most of history. In the patrimonial state, political office was a form of private property or personal delegation, and even in most premodern quasi-bureaucratic states the populace at large was only subject to the state, not holders of rights within it. The latter condition arose only in the West. In both Mediterranean antiquity and the European Middle Ages, cities came under the control of brotherhoods of warriors banded together for mutual protection. Such cities had their own laws and courts, administered by the citizens themselves, all of whom stood under it in relation of formal equality. Such citizenship rights remained historically significant after the original civic forms changed or disappeared. The formal rights and legal procedures originally applied only to a local elite, but when cities were incorporated into large-scale bureaucratic states, they provided the basis for a much more widely inclusive system of adjudication. This was the case when Rome, originally one of these military-fraternity cities, became an empire and, again, in the Middle Ages, when cities in alliance with kings lost their independence but contributed their legal structures to the larger states.[10]

Nearing the end of our chain of causality, we ask: What factors enabled this distinctive type of city to arise in the West? Weber gives two conditions: one military, the other religious.

The military condition is that in the West the city consisted of "an organization of those economically competent to bear arms, to equip and train themselves" (1961:237). This was the case in the formative period of the ancient Greek and Italian cities and, again, in the medieval cities with their disciplined infantries fielded by the guilds. In

---

[10] Contractual forms of feudalism also contributed somewhat to legal citizenship. Weber neglected this in the *General Economic History*, but considered it in *Economy and Society* (1968:1101). The earlier preconditions (military and religious) for contractual feudalism and for independent cities, however, are essentially the same.

both cases, the money power of the cities bolstered their military power and, hence, democratization and concomitant legal citizenship. In the Orient and in ancient Egypt, on the contrary, the military princes with their armies were older than the cities and, hence, legally independent cities did not arise; Weber attributed this pattern to the impetus to early centralization given by irrigation.

The second condition is that in the East, magical taboos prevented the organization of military alliances among strangers and, hence, did not allow formation of independent cities. In India, for example, the ritual exclusion of castes had this effect. More generally, in Asia and the Middle East, the traditional priests held monopolies over communion with the gods, whereas in Western antiquity it was the officials of the city who themselves performed the rites (1961:238). In the one case, the boundaries of religious communion reinforced preexisting group divisions; in the other, religious boundaries were an explicit political tool by which civic alliances could be established and enlarged. It is at this point that the two main lines of Weber's chain of causality converge.

We have been tracing the causal links behind the emergence of the rational/legal state, which is one of the two great intermediate conditions of the emergence of an open market economy. The other great intermediate condition (noted earlier) is an economic ethic which breaks the barrier between internal and external economies. Now we see that the religious factors that produced the citizenship revolution and those that produced the economic ethic are essentially the same.

Our last question, then, is: What brought about this religious transformation? Weber gives a series of reasons, each intensifying the effects of the last (1961:238). Ethical prophecy within ancient Judaism was important, even though it did not break down ritual barriers between Jews and Gentiles, because it established a tradition of hostility to magic, the main ethos within which barriers flourished. The transformation of Christianity from a Jewish sect into a proselytizing universal religion gave this tradition widespread currency, while the pentacostal spirit of Christian proselytization set aside the ritual barriers among clans and tribes, which still characterized the ancient Hellenistic cities to some degree. The Judeo-Christian innovations are not the whole story, however; the earlier development of Greek religion into the civic cults had already done much to make universalistic legal membership possible.

The religious factors, as we have seen, entwine with political ones, and their influence in the direction of legal citizenship and upon an economic ethic have fluctuated historically. There is no steady nor inevitable trend toward increasing rationalization of these spheres, but Western history does contain a series of episodes which happen to have built up these effects at particular points in time so that, eventually, a whole new economic dynamic was unleashed. On the political side, the Christian cities of the Middle Ages, drawing upon the institutional legacies of the ancient world, were able to establish religiously sworn confraternities which reestablished a legal system based on citizenship. A second political factor was fostered by religion: the Christian church provided the literate administrators, the educational system, and the example of its own bureaucratic organization as bases upon which the bureaucratic states of the West could emerge. And, on the strictly motivational side, the development of European Christianity gave a decisive ethical push toward rationalized capitalism.

Here, at last, we seem to touch base with Weber's original Protestant Ethic thesis. But in the mature Weber, the thesis is greatly transformed. Protestantism is only the last intensification of one of the chains of factors leading to rational capitalism. Moreover, its effect now is conceived to be largely negative, in the sense that it removes one of the last institutional obstacles diverting the motivational impetus of Christianity away from economic rationalization. For, in medieval Christianity, the methodical, disciplined organization of life was epitomized by the monastic communities.[11] Although the monasteries contributed to economic development by rationalizing agriculture and promoting their own industries, Weber generally saw them as obstacles to the full capitalist development of the secular economy. As long as the strongest religious motivation was siphoned off for essentially otherworldly ends, capitalism in general could not take off (1961:267–9). Hence, the Reformation was most significant because it abolished the monasteries. The most advanced section of the economy would, henceforth, be secular. Moreover, the highest ethics of a religious life could no longer be confined to monks but had to apply to ordinary citizens living in the world. Calvinism and the other voluntary sects were the most intense version of this motivation, not because of the idea of predestination (which no longer receives any mention in Weber's last text) but only because they required a specific religious calling for admission into their ranks, rather than automatic and compulsory membership in the politically

---

11 Weber did not live to write his planned volume on medieval Christianity. If he had, I believe he would have found that the High Middle Ages were the most significant institutional turning point of all on the road to the capitalist takeoff. His commitment to the vestiges of his Protestantism argument may have kept him from recognizing this earlier. I will deal with this point in Chapter 3.

more conservative churches. Weber's (1961:269–70) last word on the subject of Protestantism was simply this:

The development of the concept of the calling quickly gave to the modern entrepreneur a fabulously clear conscience – and also industrious workers; he gave to his employees as the wages of their ascetic devotion to the calling and of co-operation in his ruthless exploitation of them through capitalism the prospect of eternal salvation, which in an age when ecclesiastical discipline took control of the whole life to an extent inconceivable to us now, represented a reality quite different from any it has today. The Catholic and Lutheran churches also recognized and practiced ecclesiastical discipline. But in the Protestant ascetic communities admission to the Lord's Supper was conditioned on ethical fitness, which again was identified with business honor, while into the content of one's faith no one inquired. Such a powerful, unconsciously refined organization for the production of capitalistic individuals has never existed in any other church or religion.

Weber's general theory of history

Is there an overall pattern in Weber's argument? It is not a picture of a linear trend toward ever-increasing rationality. Nor is it an evolutionary model of natural selection, in the sense of random selection of the more advanced forms, accumulating through a series of stages. For Weber's constant theme is that the *pattern of relations among the various factors* is crucial in determining their effect upon economic rationalization. Any one factor occurring by itself tends to have opposite effects, overall, to those which it has in combination with the other factors.

For example, self-supplied military coalitions produce civic organizations and legal systems which are favorable to capitalism. But if the self-armed civic groups are too strong, the result is a series of guild monopolies which stifle capitalism by overcontrolling markets. Cities, on the other hand, have to be balanced by the bureaucratic state. But when the state is too strong by itself, it, too, tends to stifle capitalism. This can happen by bolstering the immobility of labor (as in the case of "the second serfdom" produced in Russia and eastern Europe as absolutist states developed in the seventeenth and eighteenth centuries); or by directly controlling the division of labor by forced contributions instead of allowing a market to develop. In the areas of the world where bureaucratization was relatively easy, as in ancient Egypt or China, or the Byzantine Empire, the unrestrained power of the state stereotyped economic life and did not allow the dynamics of capitalism to unfold.

The same is true of the religious variables. The creation of the great world religions, with their universalism and their specialized priesthoods, was crucial for the possibility of breaking the ritual barriers among localized groups, with all the consequences this might have for subsequent developments. But, in the absence of other factors, this could actually bolster the obstacles to capitalism. This happened in India, where the development of Hinduism fostered the caste system: the universalistic religion set an external seal upon the lineup of particularistic groups that happened to exist at the time. Even in Christianity, where moral prophecy had a much more barrier-breaking and world-transforming effect, the Church (in the period when it was predominant) created another obstacle against its capitalist implications. This was the period of the High Middle Ages in Europe, when monasticism proliferated and, thus, channeled all the energy of religious motivation into a specialized role and away from the economic concerns of ordinary life.[12]

Weber saw the rise of large-scale capitalism, then, as the result of a series of combinations of conditions which had to occur together. This makes world history look like the result of configurations of events so rare as to appear accidental. Weber's position might well be characterized as historicist, in the sense of seeing history as a concatenation of unique events and unrepeatable complexities. Once a crucial conjuncture occurs, its results transform everything else – and not just locally but also in the larger world of competing states. This was true of the great charismatic revelations of the world religions, which shut off China, India, or the West from alternative lines of development as well as determined the ways that states upon these territories would interact with the rest of the world. Similarly, the full-scale capitalist breakthrough itself was a once-only event, radiating outward to transform all other institutions and societies. Hence, the original conditions necessary for the emergence of capitalism were not necessary for its continuation. The original religious ethic could fade, once the calculability of massive economic transactions had become a matter of routine. Hence, late-industrializing states need not follow the route of classic capitalism. In the advanced societies, the skeleton of the economic structure might even be taken over by socialism.

Weber's account of the rise of capitalism, then, is in a sense not a theory at all, in that it is not a set of universal generalizations about economic change. Nevertheless, on a more abstract level, Weber is at least implicitly proposing such a theory. On one level, he may be read as a collection of separate hypotheses about specific processes and their effects.[13] The foregoing caveat about the necessary balance

---

[12] This was also the time when the church took the offensive against incipient capitalism, in the form of pronouncements against usury (Weber, 1968:584–6).
[13] One clearly formulated proposition, for example, is that armies based on coalitions

among factors may be incorporated by specifying that the causal variables must operate at a given strength – that is, by turning them into quantitative generalizations specified to a given range of variation.

On a second level, one may say that the fundamental generalizations in Weber's theory of capitalism concern the crucial role of balances and tensions between opposing elements. "All in all," says Weber in a little-known passage (1968:1192–3), "the specific roots of Occidental culture must be sought in the tension and peculiar balance, on the one hand, between office charisma and monasticism, and on the other between the contractual character of the feudal state and the autonomous bureaucratic hierocracy."[14] No one element must predominate if rationalization is to increase. More concretely, since each "element" is composed of real people struggling for precedence, the creation of a calculable, open-market economy depends upon a continuous balance of power among differently organized groups. The formal egalitarianism of the law depends upon balances among competing citizens and among competing jurisdictions. The nondualistic economic ethic of moderated avarice depends upon a compromise between the claims of in-group charity and the vicious circle of out-group rapaciousness.

The capitalist economy depends on this balance. The open-market system is a situation of institutionalized strife. Its essence is struggle, in an expanded version of the Marxian sense, but with the qualification that this could go on continuously, and indeed must, if the system is to survive.[15] Hence, if there is any generalization implicit in Weber's theory applicable to economic history after the initial rise of capitalism, it is this: The possibility for the follower-societies of the non-Western world to acquire the dynamism of industrial capitalism depends on there being a balance among class forces, and among

of self-supplied individuals produce citizenship rights. (For a series of such propositions, see Collins, 1975:356–64.)

[14] In other words, the main features of the West depend on a tension between the routinization of religious charisma in the church and the participatory communities of monks, and on a tension between the democratizing tendencies of self-supplied armies and the centralized bureaucratic state. These give us Weber's two great intermediate factors, a nondualistic religious ethic and calculable law, respectively.

[15] "The formal rationality of money calculation is dependent on certain quite specific substantive conditions. Those which are of a particular sociological importance for present purposes are the following: (1) Market struggle of economic units which are at least relatively autonomous. Money prices are the product of conflicts of interest and of compromises: they thus result from power constellations. Money is not a mere 'voucher for unspecified utilities,' which could be altered at will without any fundamental effect on the character of the price system as a struggle of man against man. 'Money' is, rather, primarily a weapon in this struggle, and prices are expressions of the struggle: they are instruments of calculation only as estimated quantifications of relative chances in this struggle of interests" (Weber, 1968:107–8).

competing political forces and cultural forces as well. In the highly industrialized societies also, the continuation of capitalism depends on continuation of the same conflicts. The victory of any one side would spell the doom of the system. In this respect, as in others, Weber's theory is a conflict theory indeed.

An assessment: Weber's confrontation with Marxism

How valid is Weber's theory? To fully answer this question would require extensive comparative analyses and a good deal of explication of principles on different levels of abstraction. These tasks are beyond the scope of what is intended here. What I can present is a confrontation between Weber's theory and the one rival theory of capitalism which claims a comparable degree of historical and theoretical comprehensiveness, Marxism. This is especially appropriate because Weber himself devoted a great deal of attention in the *General Economic History* to the points at which his analysis impinges on Marxist theories.

The book begins and ends on Marxian themes. The first chapter deals with the question of primitive agrarian communism. Characteristically, Weber finds it to be only one variant of primitive agriculture; where it does exist, it is usually the result of fiscal organization imposed from above (1961:21–36). The closing words of the book speak of the threat of working class revolution which appears once capitalism matures and work discipline loses its religious legitimation (1961:270). In between, there are numerous references to Marxism, far more than in any other of Weber's works. His attitude is critically respectful, as in his comment on the Engels-Bebel theory of the origins of the family: "although it is untenable in detail it forms, taken as a whole, a valuable contribution to the solution of the problem. Here again is the old truth exemplified that an ingenious error is more fruitful for science than stupid accuracy." (1961:40)[16]

Weber's intellectual maturity coincides with a period of high-level debate in Germany and Austria between Marxian and non-Marxian economists. In the years between 1885 and 1920 appeared Engels's editions of the later volumes of *Capital*, as well as the principal works

---

[16] Weber goes on to say, "A criticism of the theory leads to consideration first of the evolution of prostitution, in which connection, it goes without saying, no ethical evaluation is involved." There follows (1961:40–53) a brilliant outline of a theory of the organization of the family as one set of variants on sexual property relations, in which material transactions and appropriations are fundamentally involved. Later versions of this line of theory are found in Lévi-Strauss (1949/1969) and in Collins (1975:228–59). See also Chapters 11 and 12 of this book.

of Kautsky, Hilferding, and Luxemburg. On the other side, Sombart, Bortkiewitz, and Tugan-Baranowski provided what they considered to be revisions in the spirit of Marxian economics, while Böhm-Bawerk (1898) and Schumpeter (1911) launched explicit efforts to shore up the weaknesses of neoclassical economics vis-à-vis Marxism, and attacked the technical weaknesses of Marxian theory.[17] This period was in many ways the high-water mark in political economy, for an atmosphere of balanced debate is beneficial for intellectual advance. Weber in particular was concerned to meet the Marxian challenge on its own grounds, leaving out nothing that must be conceded, but also turning up whatever factors the Marxists left out. Moreover, the German Marxists had suddenly become stronger with the end of the World War and the downfall of the German monarchy. Weber delivered his lectures in Munich just after the short-lived Communist commune of 1919, and his lecture room contained many radical students. It is not surprising that Weber was so much more explicitly concerned with Marxism in his last work than in the religious studies he published while the war was going on.

Weber had one great advantage over the Marxists. The discipline of historical scholarship reached its maturity around the end of the nineteenth century. Not only had political and military history reached a high degree of comprehensiveness and accuracy, but so had the history of law, religion, and economic institutions not only for Europe and the ancient Mediterranean but for the Orient as well. The historical researches of the twentieth century have not brought to light any great body of facts about the past that has radically changed our view of world history since Weber's day. Weber was perhaps the first great master of the major institutional facts of world history. By contrast, Marx, pursuing his assiduous researches in the 1840s and 50s, had much narrower materials at his disposal (Hobsbawm 1964:20–7). The histories of India, China, Japan, or Islam had scarcely begun to be available; the permeation of the ancient Greco-Roman world by religious institutions was only beginning to be analyzed; and the complex civilization of the European High Middle Ages was hidden beneath what Marx considered the "feudal rubbish" of the *Ancien Regime* of the eighteenth century. Marx wrote before the great coming-of-age of historical scholarship; Weber, just as it reached its

---

17 Böhm-Bawerk also made an analysis of socialist economies. He regarded these as possible *politically* (as did Schumpeter and Weber), but denied that production would be organized differently than in capitalism. Socialism could affect only the distribution of capitalist profits among the populace. For the economic thought of this period, see Schumpeter (1954:800–20, 843–55, 877–85) and Sweezy (1942:190–213).

peak. Weber thus represents for us the first and in many ways still the only effort to make a truly informed comparative analysis of major historical developments.

It should be borne in mind that Marx and most of his followers have devoted their attention primarily to showing the dynamics of capitalism, not to the preconditions for its emergence. Weber's concerns were almost entirely the reverse. Hence, it is possible that the two analyses could be complementary, Marx's taking up where Weber's leaves off. Only in the 1970s have there been efforts comparable to Weber's from within the Marxian tradition, notably that of Wallerstein (1974). Interestingly enough, Weber anticipated Wallerstein's major points in the *General Economic History*. On the other side, Wallerstein's revision of Marxism is in many ways a movement toward a more Weberian mode of analysis, stressing the importance of external relations among states.

The classical Marxian model of the preconditions for capitalism covers only a few points (Marx, 1967:1, 336–70, 713–64;II, 323–37, 593–613; 1973:459–514). Some of these are a subset of Weber's model, while two of them are distinctive to Marx. Weber and Marx both stressed that capitalism requires a pool of formally free but economically propertyless labor; the sale of all factors of production on the market; and the concentration of all factors in the hands of capitalist entrepreneurs. Marx did not see the importance of the *calculable* aspect of technology; at times, he seemed to make the sheer productive power of technology the central moving force in economic changes, while at others, he downplayed this as part of a larger economic system – much in the way Weber did. Unlike Weber, Marx gave no causal importance at all to calculable law, nor did he see the earlier links in Weber's causal chain: economic ethics, citizenship, bureaucratization, and their antecedents.[18]

The uniqueness of Marx's discussion is in two factors: primitive accumulation and revolution. About the latter, Marx had surprisingly little to say beyond the dramatic imagery of revolution breaking the

---

[18] Marx (1973:459–514) gave a very general outline of early forms of property as based on family and tribal membership, and he recognized that the ancient cities were military coalitions. He missed the central organizing role of religion in these developments, and failed to see the crucial effect of the revolutions within the ancient cities upon the uniquely Western legal tradition. For Marx, the rise of cities simply meant the growing separation of town and country, an instance of dialectical antithesis, and of the progress of the division of labor (1967:1, 352). For the period immediately preceding the capitalist takeoff, Marx noted that the state had hastened the transition from feudalism to capitalism by creating public finance and conquering foreign markets. These effects Marx subsumed under his concept of "primitive accumulation."

bonds imposed by the property system upon the growing engines of production (Marx, 1959:43–4). Primitive accumulation takes up nearly the whole of his historical discussion. It means the accumulation of enough raw materials, tools, and food for laborers to live on before subsequent production was completed; hence, it is the quantitative prerequisite for any takeoff into expanded economic production. Such accumulation took place historically in two ways. One was by the expropriation of peasants from their land, which simultaneously concentrated wealth in the hands of the capitalists who received the lands and required the expropriated masses to sell their labor on the market. The other means of primitive accumulation was by usury and merchants' capital. Marx downplayed the importance of monetary factors by themselves, as they operated only in the realm of circulation and did nothing to productive relations: but he did assert that the growth of money capital furthered the dissolution of the feudal economy once it was already under way (1967:III, 596–7).

Of these two factors, Weber says almost nothing explicitly about primitive accumulation. However, the entire earlier sections of the *General Economic History* (1961:21–203) deal with the various forms of appropriation of material and financial means, which have made up, among other things, the capitalism that has been omnipresent throughout history, although not in a rationalized form. The idea that there must be a specific accumulation of surplus for the purpose of a capitalist takeoff, I suspect, is one that Weber would reject. The assumption ought to be subjected to proof. After all, agrarian societies already have the most extreme concentration of wealth at the top of the social hierarchy of any type of society in world history (Lenski, 1966); the industrial takeoff need only have been fueled by a shift in the use of this wealth, not by a further extraction process. As Weber understood, and as subsequent research has shown, capitalists do not have to rise "from below," having amassed their own wealth; it has been far more typical for the aristocracy themselves to go into capitalist production (Stone, 1967; Moore, 1966).[19]

Weber is somewhat more sympathetic to the importance of revolutions. Perhaps the final conditions for the capitalist takeoff in England were the revolutions of 1640 and 1688. These put the state under the control of political groups favorable to capitalism, thus fulfilling the condition of keeping markets and finances free of "irrational" and predatory state policies. Of more fundamental institutional conse-

---

[19] Weber also anticipated Barrington Moore's (1966) theory of the political consequences of different property modes in the commercialization of agriculture (1961:81–94).

quence were the revolutions within the cities of ancient Greece and of medieval Italy. The latter Weber lists among "the five great revolutions that decided the destiny of the occident" (1951:62).[20] For it was the uprising of the plebeians which replaced the charismatic law of the older patrician class with the universalistic and "rationally instituted" law upon which so much of the institutional development of capitalism was to depend (Weber, 1968:1312–3, 1325). In effect, this was a revolution in a system of property, but not in the gross sense of a replacement of one form of appropriation with another. For Weber, a system of property is a complex of daily actions – above all, the making of transfers and contracts and the adjudication of disputes. Hence, political revolutions are most crucial where they set the pattern for ongoing legal actions in a highly calculable form, with all the consequences noted above.

Wallerstein's (1974) theory, as developed in volume I, emphasizes two conditions in the origins of capitalism. One is the influx of bullion from the European colonies, which caused the price inflation of the 16th century. During this period, wages remained approximately constant. The gap between prices and wages constituted a vast extraction of surplus which could be invested in expanding capitalist enterprises (Wallerstein, 1974:77–84).[21] This is Wallerstein's version of the primitive accumulation factor.

Wallerstein's (1974:348) second condition also emerges from the international situation. "[C]apitalism as an economic system is based on the fact that economic factors operate within an arena larger than that which any political entity can totally control. This gives capitalists a freedom of maneuver that is structurally based." He (1974:355) goes on to say that the different states must be of different strengths, so that not all states "would be in the position of blocking the effective operation of transnational economic entities whose locus were in another state." Capitalists in effect must have opportunities to shift their grounds among varied political climates to wherever the situation is most favorable.

Weber (1961:259) was generally aware of both conditions. Regarding the effects of gold and silver influx, however, he was largely unfavorable.

---

[20] The others were "the Netherland revolution of the sixteenth century, the English revolution of the seventeenth century, and the American and French revolutions of the eighteenth century."

[21] To this, Wallerstein adds the argument that surplus is further extracted by coerced labor on the periphery, to be consumed in the core, where however (somewhat contrary to the point about the price revolution) labor is well enough paid to constitute a potential consumers' market for capitalist production.

41

It is certainly true that in a given situation an increase in the supply of precious metals may give rise to price revolutions, such as that which took place after 1530 in Europe, and when other favorable conditions are present, as when a certain form of labor organization is in the process of development, the progress may be stimulated by the fact that large stocks of cash come into the hands of certain groups. But the case of India proves that such an importation of metal will not alone bring about capitalism. In India in the period of the Roman power, an enormous mass of precious metal – some twenty-five million sestertii annually – came in exchange for domestic goods, but this inflow gave rise to commercial capitalism only to a slight extent. The greater part of this precious metal disappeared into the hoards of the rajahs instead of being converted into cash and applied in the establishment of enterprises of a rational capitalistic character. This fact proves that it depends entirely upon the nature of the labor system what tendency will result from an inflow of precious metal.

In another passage, Weber (1961:231) does say that the price revolution of the sixteenth and seventeenth centuries "provided a powerful lever for the specifically capitalistic tendencies of seeking profit through cheapening production and lowering the price." This came about for industrial (but not agricultural) products, because the quickened economic tempo put on pressures toward further rationalizing economic relations and inventing cheaper technologies of production. Weber thus gives the influx of precious metals a place as a contributory factor, though apparently not an indispensable one, *within* the framework of economic institutions which had already appeared in Europe at the time.[22]

Weber (1961:249) largely agrees, however, with Wallerstein's argument about the international character of capitalism. Modern cities, he points out,

came under the power of competing national states in a condition of perpetual struggle for power in peace or war. This competitive struggle created the largest opportunities for modern Western capitalism. The separate states had to compete for mobile capital, which dictated to them the conditions under which it would assist them to power. Out of this alliance of the state

[22] Weber's (1961:223) comment on the economic benefits of the colonies is even more negative: "This accumulation of wealth brought about through colonial trade has been of little significance for the development of modern capitalism – a fact which must be emphasized in opposition to Werner Sombart. It is true that the colonial trade made possible the accumulation of wealth to an enormous extent, but this did not further the specifically occidental form of the organization of labor, since colonial trade itself rested on the principle of exploitation and not that of securing an income through market operations. Furthermore, we know that in Bengal for example, the English garrison cost five times as much as the money value of all goods carried thither. It follows that the markets for domestic industry furnished by the colonies under the conditions of the time were relatively unimportant, and that the main profit was derived from the transport business."

with capital, dictated by necessity, arose the national citizen class, the bourgeoisie in the modern sense of the word. Hence it is the closed national state which afforded to capitalism its chance for development – and as long as the national state does not give place to a world empire capitalism will also endure.

Here the coincidence with Wallerstein is remarkable. Weber does not emphasize the contours of Wallerstein's world system, with its tiers of core, semiperiphery, and periphery, but Weber does show the central importance of mobile capital among military competing states, and he gives a more specific analysis than Wallerstein of the mechanism by which this is transformed into an advantage for capitalism.

In general, there is considerable convergence, as well as complementarity, between Weber's last theory of the origins of capitalism, and the mature Marxian theory which is only now emerging. Weber largely rejects Marxian theories of primitive accumulation, or at least relegates them to minor factors. On the other side, Wallerstein, as well as modern Marxism in general, has moved the state into the center of the analysis. Weber had already gone much further in that direction, so that the main Weberian criticism of the Marxian tradition, even in its present form, is that it does not yet recognize the set of institutional forms, especially as grounded in the legal system, upon which capitalism has rested.

For Weber, the state and the legal system are by no means a superstructure of ideas determining the material organization of society. Rather, his theory of the development of the state is to a considerable extent an analogy to the Marxian theory of the economy. The key factor is the form of appropriation of the material conditions of domination. We have seen the significance of the organization of weapons for Weber's chain of causes of capitalism. In this connection, Weber (1961:237) remarks:

Whether the military organization is based on the principle of self-equipment or on that of military equipment by an overlord who furnishes horses, arms and provisions, is a distinction quite as fundamental for social history as the question whether the means of economic production are the property of the worker or of a capitalistic entrepreneur . . . [T]he army equipped by the war lord, and the separation of the soldier from the paraphernalia of war, [is] in a way analogous to the separation of the worker from the means of production. . . .

Similarly, state bureaucracy depends upon a set of material conditions, and upon the separation of the administrator from treating the office and its incomes as private property (1968:980–3). Weber diverges from the Marxian analogy by being a more thoroughgoing conflict theorist. As we have seen, and as the quotation given above on the international basis of capitalism bears out, for Weber the conditions of rationalized organization, in political and economic spheres alike, depend upon a continuous open struggle.[23]

The main disagreements between Marx and Weber have less to do with the origins of capitalism than with its future. Weber thought that capitalism could endure indefinitely as an economic system, although political factors could bring it down. As we have seen, he thought that the disappearance of religious legitimation in mature capitalism opened the way for workers to express their discontents in the form of a political movement for socialism. Ironically, it is the rationalized world view promoted by the underlying conditions of capitalism that gave birth to rational socialism, a doctrine that proclaims that the social order itself, rather than the gods, is to blame for economic distress; and that having been deliberately instituted, that order is capable of being consciously changed (1961:217–8). For Weber, however, economic crises may be endemic to modern capitalism, but they are not caused by a fundamental contradiction in it, nor is there any necessary tendency for them to worsen toward an ultimate breakdown. He attributes crises to overspeculation and the resulting overproduction of producers' (but not consumers') goods (1961:217). To decide who is right on these points requires further consideration than can be given here.

Conclusion

Weber's last theory is still today the only comprehensive theory of the origins of capitalism. It is virtually alone in accounting for the emergence of the full range of institutional and motivational conditions for large-scale, world-transforming capitalism. Even so, it is incomplete. It needs to be supplemented by a theory of the operation of mature capitalism, and of its possible demise. And even on the home territory of Weber's theory, there remain to be carried out the comprehensive tests that would provide adequate proof. But sociological science, like any other, advances by successive approximations. The theory expressed in Weber's *General Economic History* constitutes a base line from which subsequent investigations should depart.

[23] It is true that Weber continues to leave more room for religious conditions than any of the Marxians. Yet even here, military conditions play a key role in the ultimate determinants of religions. The earliest Greek civic cults were war coalitions; and the this-worldly, antimagical character of Judaism derives from the cult of Yahwe, the war god of the coalition of Jewish tribes.

3

The Weberian revolution of the High Middle Ages

The European High Middle Ages, the period between approximately A.D. 1050 and 1450, occupies an anomalous position in most treatments of social change. This is true in the theories of Immanuel Wallerstein and Max Weber, as well as those of Marx and many others. Medieval Europe is taken as representing a structural obstacle to the development of capitalism and modernity, or at least no more than a prelude to it. I intend to argue, on the contrary, that the Middle Ages experienced the key institutional revolution, that the basis of capitalism was laid then rather than later, and that at its heart was the organization of the Catholic Church itself.

Wallerstein (1974:15–38) is interested in the Middle Ages only as a backdrop to the capitalist world economy that followed. He notes that the medieval economy grew from 1150 to 1300, then contracted from about 1300 to 1460, whereupon came the crucial world expansion. His analysis focuses on the contraction and subsequent takeoff, not on the original growth of medieval society itself. To explain the contraction, he gives various reasons: a period of unfavorable climate; a long-term secular trend in which a thousand years of feudal appropriation reached the stage of diminishing returns; a shorter-term economic cycle in which intolerable burdens were placed on the peasantry, leading to revolts and further declines in productivity. None of these in itself seems quite satisfactory, but Wallerstein decides that their conjunction created a crisis of such magnitude that only a major transformation, including overseas expansion, could solve it. This seems to be Toynbee's challenge-and-response model again, and I think that its implicit teleology makes it implausible. The Middle Ages are left as a continuing question-mark in the logic of Wallerstein's theory. And all the more so because it seems to have a cyclical character. As Nicole Bousquet (1979) points out, if the nature of capitalism is held to be peculiarly cyclical, the existence of long cycles in precapitalist periods is something of a theoretical embarrassment. Bousquet proposes that such precapitalist cycles ought to be regarded as something like dinosaurs, prehistoric beasts that have nothing to do with the cycles we see today. But the logical possibility remains open that we have misclassified and that "modern capitalism" is a subtype of something much larger.

Weber is famous, of course, for emphasizing the role of the Protestant Reformation in bringing about modern capitalism. But although there is a tone in *The Protestant Ethic and the Spirit of Capitalism* that Catholicism was an obstacle to capitalist development, it is clear from Weber's later comparative studies of the world religions that Christianity in general rather than Protestantism in particular is the fundamental basis from which rationalized capitalism grew. Moreover, as we have seen, Weber ended up with a model for the preconditions of capitalism involving a long chain of historical conditions. These conditions are primarily institutional rather than motivational, and the famous argument about the psychological effects of the Calvinist belief in predestination is greatly diminished in importance in the overall scheme. Most interpreters of Weber, though, have continued to stress the importance of the Reformation for the capitalist takeoff (Parsons, 1971; Schluchter, 1981). This is consonant with Weber's last words on the subject, at the end of *General Economic History*, where he describes the abolition of the monasteries in the Reformation as releasing the power of religious asceticism in a worldly direction and thus creating the work ethic of capitalism (1923/1961:267–8).

Weber and Wallerstein agree on the timing of the rise of capitalism, if not on its mechanism. Nevertheless, I would propose that the logic of Weber's later arguments can be pursued much further, and that they lead us to a drastic reevaluation of the crucial turning point in the rise of capitalism. Weber's comparative work on the world religions, which was to establish a kind of experimental proof for his thesis on the Western origins of capitalism, was left unfinished at his death. In addition to his existing treatments of the religions of China and India, and of ancient Judaism, there were to be further studies of Islam and ancient and medieval Christianity. My contention is that if the latter were to be carried out, it would result in the Weberian theory shifting its emphasis to the "revolutionary" development of medieval European society.

The Weberian model

Weber's institutional model characterizes capitalism by a complex of traits: rationalized technology; free labor; unrestricted markets for mass-produced products; and the entrepreneurial organization of capital. Behind these are a series of institutional developments, including a combination of the bureaucratic state with political citizenship, resulting in a calculable legal system; as well as a methodical, nondualistic economic ethic. In general, the interplay of religious and political organizational forms has been responsible for creating these institutional preconditions. If we examine Weber's causal chain as a whole, it can be seen that the *institutional preconditions* for capitalism fell into place for the first time in the High Middle Ages. And not only the *institutional preconditions* but a version of the *developed characteristics of capitalism* itself can also be found then.

We all know now that the Middle Ages experienced a revival of trade, the growth of towns, and a rise in population. Medieval Europe was an expanding economy, clearing forests, draining swamps, and occupying more land with a denser population than had existed in Roman times. But what kind of economy was it? We are accustomed to calling it a feudal economy, with its serfdom and its vassalage, and hence to see it as incompatible with capitalism. The growth of trade and the rise in population are attributed to shifts in military fortunes vis-à-vis Arab, Magyar, and Viking raiders, and thus dismissed in ad hoc fashion as outside the notice of an economic theory. The existence of craft guilds in the towns, and of class conflict in them as well, is merely an ancillary phenomenon in a society characterized as profoundly uncapitalist.

Nevertheless, there are a number of features of medieval Europe that set it off from the economies of other agrarian and feudal societies. First, there was the growth of rationalized technology in this period. Lynn White (1962) draws attention to the fact that the European Middle Ages is one of the major periods of technological innovation in the history of the world. Ancient Mediterranean society was stagnant by comparison. Medieval agricultural productivity was drastically increased by innovations in plowing, crop rotation, the harness and iron horseshoes, and new crops. Land transportation was made cheaper, faster, and more wide-ranging by new methods of harnessing and riding the horse, and by improvements in wagons and carts. Sea transportation, too, experienced what Frederic Lane (1973:119–34) calls the "nautical revolution of the Middle Ages" in the years after 1250, with the development of the sternpost rudder, new ship and sail designs, the mariner's compass and maritime charts allowing dead reckoning in the open seas. The bronze metalworking of the ancient world was displaced, for the first time, by an economy based *primarily* on iron (Gimpel, 1976:63–4). Mining became a major activity, and not merely in precious metals, while stone quarrying surpassed the total output of several millennia of ancient Egypt, and timber cutting reduced the primeval forests of France to a lower acreage in 1300 than in the mid-1900s (Gimpel, 1976:59, 76).

Above all, medieval Europe experienced a revolution in the use of machinery, so much so that Jean Gimpel entitled his book on the period *La Revolution industrielle du Moyen Age*. Ancient, inefficient models of water mills and windmills were transformed by gears and other devices into highly productive engines for grinding corn, fulling cloth, tanning leather, and making paper. Water-powered triphammers were used for crushing ore and forging iron, and mechnical bellows were operating blast furnaces by the 1300s. The spread of these innovations goes back to the 900s and even earlier, but the real boom period for their spread was the 1100s and 1200s, the acknowledged height of the medieval economy. Even in its mentality medieval Europe was fascinated by the machine, and in the 1300s the first really intricate machines, mechanical clocks, enjoyed an almost faddish popularity.

Rationalized technology of this sort, however, is not a precondition for capitalism, but tends to go along with the economic boom itself. Weber pointed out that industrial technology is of little value if it cannot be used for mass production, and that requires the regularized provision on a large scale of the factors of production, as well as markets on which mass products can be regularly disposed of. The medieval boom in technology thus implies a larger institutional transformation. This seems especially likely in the period of the 1200s, when a veritable "mill-building craze" took place, financed by shareholders who traded freely like a modern stock exchange, and subject to numerous lawsuits (Gimpel, 1976:12–27).

And in fact the other institutional features of capitalism were being put into place. The crucial *preconditions* include the bureaucratized state, a rationalized legal system, and citizenship rights. The significance of the Middle Ages for the last is in little dispute. Modern autonomies and corporate privileges of self-government under enacted law derive from the chartered cities of medieval Europe. This is particularly noticeable in merchant-dominated republics such as Venice or many of the cities of the Hanseatic League. At the same time, these citizenship elements were scattered on the medieval scene; together with some of the contractual elements of feudalism, they provided the seedbed for later developments of universal citizenship, but only after massive political revolutions of later centuries widened their application. The point I would like to stress, though, is that the institutional preconditions for capitalism were developed in medieval Europe, not so much in the wider society as in one specialized part of it, the Church.

The Weberian revolution: High Middle Ages

The bureaucratic Church

The first bureaucratic state in modern times was not a secular state at all but the Papacy. Beginning around A.D. 1050, the Papacy developed a centralized administrative organization to regulate affairs and settle disputes within the far-flung monasteries and churches of Christendom. Because it was the only centralized, literate organization in Europe, and because its properties amounted to approximately one-third of the territory of Europe, the Papacy soon established political preeminence, and made a claim for theocratic rule. Its efforts to enforce peace within Europe among rival feudal lords, and to direct their energies outward on the Church's behalf in crusades, were part of its attempt at theocracy. This attempt did not in the end prove successful, although it dominated European politics during the High Middle Ages. But what is most important from our viewpoint is the fact that *Europe had a bureaucratized government that nevertheless had just the right degree of organizational decentralization within it to foster Weber's institutional preconditions for capitalism.*

The crucial characteristics of bureaucracy, as Weber emphasized, are a continuous administration on the basis of formal rules, record-keeping files, the separation of the person from the office, specialized jurisdictions, fixed salaries, autonomous institutional finances, and "expert" rather than particularized recruitment. The reformed Papacy was uniquely qualified to promote these. Indeed, if we except some tendencies in the late Roman Empire, it was the first true bureaucracy to exist in the West. Clerical celibacy was a central concern of the reforming Popes precisely because it counteracted the tendency to hereditary appropriation of office, and hence the melding of personal with institutional rights and properties that was so prominent in the patrimonial-feudal organization of most agrarian societies. The Church was able to create a successful bureaucratic rule within its own ranks by stressing its character as an organization of freely recruited individuals, educated into "expert" literate qualifications on the basis of its own texts and laws, and subject to the administrative control of a chief whose legitimation was given within the formal laws of the organization itself. Quite likely there was no other way that a pure bureaucracy could be initially established, except on the basis of a religion of celibate priests following a sacred book.

In accordance with Weber's model, the bureaucratic Papacy provided the regularization of public law and order that was necessary for any extensive economic activities. To be sure, the Church was not completely successful in this. But it is no coincidence that the height of economic boom within Europe was in the very centuries (1100–

49

1300) when the Papacy was at the height of its power, and that the European economy declined during the 1300s and 1400s, when the Papacy became split and secular princes grew increasingly autonomous and at war among themselves.

I have already commented that the seedbed of modern citizenship may be found in the cities of medieval Europe, as well as in such feudal institutions as the *Standestaat* (including the parliament-style assemblies). But these played a comparatively small role in the overall feudal system of the secular society. If we concentrate on the Church, however, as the "real" government of medieval Europe, the citizenship elements are much wider. For the organization of the Church itself was permeated by the rights and duties of legal citizenship *in that body itself*. To be sure, these citizenship rights were not uniform throughout its ranks. But almost everywhere there was some degree of participatory rule under law. The Pope himself was chosen by election, initially by the people and clergy of Rome, later by a restricted body of cardinals. Similarly, each monastic order elected its own general, or head, and many instituted safeguards in the form of a council of overseers who watched against abuse and had the power to turn him out of office (Davis, 1961:62–6). At a lower level, cathedral chapters elected their own bishops and monasteries their abbots. There was also a strong conciliar tradition within the body of the Church as a whole, which may have been manipulated by strong autocratic Popes but, nevertheless, represented the tradition of collective responsibility for legislation. Powers of election and appointment shifted over time, with lay people becoming excluded and the powers of the Pope increasing (Bloch, 1961:348–51; Southern, 1970:151–68).

The Church had numerous hierarchical and even autocratic elements. At the same time, even its autocracy was embodied in a rule of laws and was balanced by collective powers and responsibilities at various levels. There is the further fact that the members of the clergy and the religious orders entered the Church voluntarily; they entered into a contractual relationship that not only involved oaths of obedience and self-abnegation but also gave them certain legal privileges.

It is these elements that are important from the point of view of Weber's institutional preconditions for capitalism. Citizenship is important because it balances the authoritarian tendencies of bureaucracy and gives some autonomy of action to the individual, as well as fostering the rule of a calculable law that provides rights from below as well as from above. The spread of citizenship rights within the Catholic Church for its own professional members allowed the lower branches of the Church their own dynamism. It was also the key to the development of the Canon law.

The Weberian revolution: High Middle Ages

From our usual secular viewpoint we are used to considering the effect of legal systems on the development of capitalism only in terms of the secular law systems, especially in the contrast between the Common Law and the Civil Law of the Roman codes. Weber (1922/1968:890) remarks, in fact, that neither form was of exclusive significance for fostering capitalism. The more important point was that *some* form of regularized and objective law should exist, in a political situation of balancing powers that gave businesspeople proper access to it. What I would argue is that *the Canon Law had exactly this place within the economic activities of the Church itself.*

For the rise of the Papal Curia was connected with adjudicating economic disputes within the Church. In the early Middle Ages, when Christian missionaries were converting the pagan tribes of the north, the Church had little central direction or control. Locally successful missionaries acquired considerable grants of land and other property from local lords, and monasteries were active in settling thinly populated areas. These largely self-governing church properties often found themselves in disputes: between neighboring monasteries, or among seceding factions dividing a common property, or over rival claims in local church elections. It was to settle these property disputes without appealing to secular authorities that in the 1000s and 1100s monks and priests from all over Christendom made increasingly frequent appeals to Rome. It was this development that gave rise to the bureaucratic Curia, and simultaneously to the extension of Papal power throughout Europe, as well as to the formulation of Canon law (Southern, 1970:105–24). The first universities were founded during this time, primarily to train lawyers and administrators; their most flourishing period was during the height of Papal power. The outpouring of litigation within the church courts was largely over property matters, and it accompanied an economic boom within the Church.

If we wish to concentrate on the significance of church law for later developments in secular capitalism, the connection is not hard to find. Modern corporate law, which has been of such central importance for the development of so-called monopoly capitalism since the late nineteenth century, is its direct descendant. In the English Common Law tradition, the modern conception of the corporation was already clearly formulated in the writings of Coke and Blackstone, well before the Industrial Revolution. It is true the most general conceptions of corporations may be traced to ancient Roman law. But Roman corporations had no economic significance, consisting rather of ritual-performing and mutual burial-insurance societies; they were considered neither as associations of individuals nor as fictive legal

51

personalities, and they did not own property as such (Davis, 1961:233–6; MacMullen, 1974:78–82). The key legal change occurred within the Canon law of the 1200s. There, in cases relating to monasteries and cathedral chapters as corporate entities, the legal principle was established that these were legal individuals. Pope Innocent IV has thus been described as "the father of the modern learning of corporations" (Davis, 1961:236–8, 242–3).

Monasteries as economic entrepreneurs

In the medieval economy, the ecclesiastical forms were not merely harbingers of the institutions that would later dominate secular capitalism. The dynamism of the medieval economy was primarily that of the Church itself. And within that economic structure the key role was played by the monks.

The High Middle Ages were above all a period of expansion in Christian monasticism. Since ancient times there had been only one order, the Benedictine. Around A.D. 1100 there was an outpouring of rival orders: the Cistercians, the Augustinians, the various Crusading orders. A century later came a second wave, the mendicant friars of the rival Franciscan and Dominican orders. Still later there were further waves, especially of devotional lay orders such as the Beguines.

The most important of these monastic orders were those of the first reforming wave, whose expansion between the years 1100 and 1300 coincides with the boom period of the medieval economy. Their contrast with the previous Benedictine monasteries was sharp. The Benedictines had thrived on large-scale donations of property by local barons, in return for which the monks accepted their children as members and kept up a continuous round of ritual penances for the souls of their benefactors (Southern, 1953:156–63; 1970:223–30). Benedictine monasteries tended to be wealthy adjuncts of the upper class, where their children lived in comparative luxury, often surrounded by magnificent buildings and carrying on a rich ceremonial routine. The number and wealth of such monasteries grew considerably from the late 900s through about 1100, and their increasingly dispersed property was one of the sources of the litigation to Rome that gave the Papacy its start as a centralizing bureaucracy (Southern, 1970:232–5). Such monasteries represented quite literally a sedentary and parasitical upper class, supported by their relatives as part of a ritual status competition among the nobility.

The new orders that revolted from this model were intensely activist. The most familiar of them are the Crusading orders: the Templars and the Knights Hospitalers of St. John, who took part in the recapture of the Holy Lands of Palestine and the adjacent coast. These orders of military monks, most of whom adopted the Cistercian rule, became politically powerful but also wealthy, not only from plunder but from trade and banking. They had an important role in expanding European trade with the Middle East. Even more significant for the shape of the European economy were the Crusading orders that conquered and converted the pagan Baltic, the Brethren of the Sword and the Teutonic Knights. These were part of a massive German migration into Slavic lands in the 1200s, resulting in the trading network of the Hanseatic cities, which dealt not in luxury goods but in bulk commodities (Scammell, 1981:38–85).

Most central of all was the order of Cistercians. It was founded in 1098 and underwent spectacular growth during the next two centuries. It was most prominent in France but was also notable in opening up Europe's frontiers: Iberia, Austria, Hungary, Poland, Scandinavia, and the borders of England. Unlike the earlier Benedictines, the Cistercians accepted no rents or labor services from feudal donors but would take only full possession of land to do with it as they wished. These estates they worked themselves in a highly rationalized manner (Southern, 1970:250–72). Much of the land they took consisted of uncleared or marginal areas within France itself, upon which they carried out an internal colonization by bringing the land into productive cultivation. Their prime concern was these economic activities. The ritualism of the Benedictines was abjured. Cistercians refused to perform confessions, burials, or perpetual masses for the surrounding populace. They prohibited adornment in dress or buildings, but plowed back all income into buying up land to consolidate their estates. By the end of the 1100s, the Cistercians' asceticism had brought them not only tremendous economic success but also a reputation for covetousness and greed, especially among neighboring landowners.

The Cistercians were innovative in numerous respects. They were the first highly centralized organization, following a deliberate plan of expansion throughout Europe. They also established a new form of hierarchy within their organization, a division between the fully ordained monks and a second class of monastic laborers. The latter took oaths of celibacy, poverty, and obedience, but remained illiterate and were ineligible for advance to full monastic rank. The Cistercians were thus divided into a managerial class and a class of manual laborers, both working under religious incentives and subject to a strong asceticism.

These monasteries were the most economically effective units that had ever existed in Europe, and perhaps in the world, before that time (Gimpel, 1976:3–9, 46–7). The community of monks typically operated a factory. There would be a complex of mills, usually hydraulically powered, for grinding corn as well as for other purposes. In iron-producing regions, they operated forges with water-powered trip-hammers; after 1250 the Cistercians dominated iron production in central France (Gimpel, 1976:67–8). Iron was produced for their own use but also for sale. In England, the entire monastic economy was geared toward producing wool for the export market. The Cistercians were the cutting edge of medieval economic growth. They pioneered in machinery because of their continuing concern to find laborsaving devices (Gimpel, 1976:230). Their mills were not only used by the surrounding populace (at a fee) for grinding corn but were widely imitated. The spread of Cistercian monasteries around Europe was probably the catalyst for much other economic development, including imitation of its cutthroat investment practices.

We find here, then, not only the complex of institutional preconditions for capitalism but the main features of capitalism itself. To be sure, this capitalism was not primarily in the cities, which as yet hardly existed in Europe. But we have been led astray by the old image of capitalism as an urban phenomenon, and have searched for a "rising bourgeoisie" where it was not the significant thing to be seen. (One might equally note that in the economic takeoff of England in the 1500s and 1600s, the major role was again played not by the cities but by a business-oriented segment of the landed aristocracy, which established rural ironworks and other capitalist ventures in the countryside [Stone, 1967:163–82]).

Was medieval Europe capitalist?

Weber characterizes capitalism in terms of rational technology, entrepreneurial organization of capital, free labor, and mass commodity markets. The rational technology we have seen, especially in the Cistercian "factories." The Cistercians also represent the entrepreneurial organization of capital, indeed in a more massively centralized and effective form than most private capitalists were to achieve before the late nineteenth century. They followed a form of rational cost accounting, and plowed back their profits into the business. One could say that they represented Weber's "inner-worldly asceticism" in the most literal form. They had the Protestant ethic without Protestantism. Moreover, because they had a centrally controlled organization, they could move capital around internally from one enterprise to another, building up prospering ones and cutting their losses in unsuccessful areas (Southern, 1970:264). Although we know relatively little about the financing of church enterprises, it

54

appears that this kind of "religious capitalism" was equivalent to evading usury laws on investments. The religious orders generally, and to some extent also other parts of the Church, took in donations and incomes from widely scattered sources and invested them internally in church enterprises. Other religious orders, less commercially oriented than the Cistercians, nevertheless followed their example. The Augustinian canons, who grew up contemporary with the Cistercians but specialized in collecting small endowments within the towns, were taking money on deposit by the 1200s and investing it in property. Many Augustinian houses became prosperous small bankers (Southern, 1970:246). The immobility of capital that operated as a hindrance to economic development in the secular economy was thus circumvented to a considerable degree in the centralized features of the Church.

Feudalism, of course, is notoriously lacking in a freely moving labor market responding to the pressure of wages. But, to a degree, the Church provided a way of circumventing this as well. The Church and the new monastic orders were the only international organizations in Europe. Moreover, they recruited freely and from all social ranks, and thus provided a channel for movement outside the rankings that were being made hereditary in secular society in the 1100s and 1200s (Bloch, 1961:320–1). To be sure, vertical movement within the Church was not common either, but of greater economic significance is the horizontal, geographical movement of the labor force to areas of greatest opportunity. This is precisely what was provided by the Crusading orders (especially those that colonized the Baltic), by the Cistercian enterprises, and by the later mendicant orders. In contrast to the old Benedictines, whose vows included staying perpetually in one place, the new-style orders moved their labor force around, and some even took the vow *not* to have a permanent domicile. Given that the Church held one-third of the land in Europe, and constituted its most dynamic sector economically, one might well propose that the equivalent of a labor market had been established within its own ranks, even if much of the surrounding society was legally (if not de facto) immobile. The Church also had its effect on secular society in this respect. One of the largest economic enterprises of the High Middle Ages was the building of the great cathedrals during this period. These required large numbers of skilled as well as unskilled laborers, who moved from place to place in response to demand, also taking part in secular building such as castles. Stonemasons operated on a wage labor market, at levels of real wages that were considerably higher in the early 1300s than they were four and five centuries later (Gimpel, 1976:106–13).

Economics

The one feature of capitalism that would seem not to be well represented was a mass market. It is true that the movement of goods was restricted by multiple political authorities and unsafe conditions of travel. Nevertheless, as we have noted, the entire Cistercian economy in England could be oriented to the wool-export trade, and there was considerable movement of stone, textiles, timber, metals, and other bulk commodities throughout Europe. The Baltic trade of the Hanseatic cities was almost entirely in bulk goods, and by the late 1200s entire countries such as Norway had becom wholly dependent on imported grain (Scammell, 1981:67). Clearly there was a mass market in some areas. Moreover, the Church was active in attempting to shore up one of the crucial institutional underpinnings of a mass market: security from robbers and military predators. The Church held the doctrine that it was a sin to kill a fellow Christian in secular battle, and attempted to confine military action to Crusades against foreign enemies and domestic heretics. This ban was not very effective, and sins of violence were usually commuted upon payment of penances. But in the 1000s and 1100s, just as the medieval economy was beginning to develop, there was a widespread movement to establish peace (Bloch, 1961:412–21). Certain days of the week and times of the year were declared "God's Truce" in the wars among the nobility. More significantly, bishops took the initiative in organizing "peace associations," whose members swore to abjure private violence and also acted to put down robber barons and brigands. Monks and especially wandering friars took the initiative in ending local vendettas. These efforts were only partially successful, and there is no doubt that the volume of trade was kept down by the unsafe conditions that prevailed. But the peace associations and the friars did pave the way in settling the atmosphere of violence, and their gains were consolidated for a while in the 1200s by the strengthening of major secular states.

The Church thus brought about at least an approximation to a capitalist economy within the larger feudal economy of the High Middle Ages. To be sure, there was also some capitalism outside the Church. There was a flourishing textile business in Florence and in Flanders, and prosperous trading cities such as Venice, Genoa, and Pisa. Venice was notably free of church influence, and it promoted successful investment banking that ignored the restrictions of usury laws (Scammell, 1981:114). It also had the largest and most modern factory in Europe, the state-owned Arsenal, which built ships in a mass-production, assembly-line fashion through the employment of several thousand wage-paid workers (Scammell, 1981:131–2). Nevertheless, I would argue that Venice had little institutional potential (and Genoa even less) for transforming Europe into a capitalist economy on its own. It was a typical merchants' capitalism, dealing in luxury goods and involving little manufacturing for the market. The output of the Arsenal, which might seem an exception, was in fact confined to state-owned vessels that were leased to private merchants. Moreover, the rise of the Italian maritime cities was to a considerable degree dependent on the Crusaders, who provided them with shipping profits as well as political leverage in the Levant. One may see the expansion of the Italian maritime states, along with that of the Hanse into the Baltic, as part of a typical pattern: a drive into the periphery that takes place whenever a core area becomes consolidated within a world system (Wallerstein, 1974). But the hegemonic center of that core was the Church, and most of the drive toward the periphery was carried out by religious orders of military monks.

Among the institutional preconditions for capitalism in Weber's model is *a nondualistic economic ethic*. Typically, this is taken to mean that the energies devoted to achieving the highest human status must be directed toward secular tasks in the world, rather than siphoned off into the mystical or ascetic activities of religious virtuosi. The same religious ethic of salvation must apply to everyone; there must be no division between world-escaping monks and a religious lower class of lay people. The nondualistic ethic also must apply universally to all people rather than reserving religious membership, and hence duties of ethical behavior, within a particular ethnic group of tribal or kin community. Christianity certainly had the universalistic aspect of such an ethic. But it has usually been held, including by Weber himself, that medieval Christianity had a very acute case of religious dualism, in which the monks absorbed the energies that could otherwise go into an economic transformation of the world. The facts, though, show us a paradoxical situation in which the monks themselves harnessed their energies and created the first dynamic, world-transforming capitalism, albeit in religious form.

Yet is this so paradoxical? We are used to conceiving of capitalism as individualistic, secular, and bourgeois. But the twentieth century shows us a capitalism that is corporate and that sometimes even appears, it is said, under the guise of socialism. We may be led astray here by a historical accident that makes us mistake the capitalism of nineteenth-century England for the general form. Weber (1922/1968:1181–91) consistently saw medieval hierocracy as an impediment to capitalism, and its ascetic workers as no more than unfair competitors to secular craftsmen. He points to the ban on usury, which was explicitly aimed against investments in international trade by the Italian cities, and which was counterattacked by civic guilds that prohibited their members from suing in ecclesiastical courts. But surely here one should be alive to the political context: the battle between Papacy and the Holy Roman Empire that was fought at precisely this period for control of Italy. The northern Italian cities whose commercial practices were attacked by the usury laws were by and large allies of the Empire against the Papacy. I would suggest that insofar as the Church attacked private capitalism, it did so not simply because its religious ethics disagreed with the uncharitable profit-making of capitalism, but because there was a political battle between two economies: church capitalism and secular capitalism. And there is little doubt that between the two, church capitalism was both more successful in its own day and more forward-looking for the future.

Weber's characterization of monastic religiosity as siphoning off energies and assets from the secular economy is accurate for many historical periods, including the pre-Reformation. It is certainly true for the Benedictine monasteries before the period of the Cistercian movement, and it becomes true again after the end of the 1200s. But this is only to say that institutional economies may go through a long-term cycle, in which the dynamic forms of the earlier period become its impediments later on.

Rival developments: religious capitalism in Buddhist China

There are, in fact, many instances throughout history in which we see an economically productive effect of monasticism. The earliest orga-nized Christian monasteries in Egypt, in the 200s and 300s A.D., were strikingly like the Cistercians' in many respects. They had a two-class system of illiterate workers, plus an elite of ascetics whom they sup-ported, both under a unified discipline. These monasteries supported themselves economically by producing mats and other goods for sale in nearby cities, constituting factories that prospered by plowing back their profits (Borkenau 1981:332–7). The Irish monks of the Dark Ages carried a similar spirit of "asceticism within the world" (Borkenau 1981:308–9), which had an important effect on reestablishing civiliza-tion in Europe. In China, the economic role of the Buddhist monas-teries was particularly important.

If Weber missed the way in which his own logic should have led to an appreciation of the "Weberian revolution" of the European Middle Ages and the place of the monastic orders within it, he was even less able to see a corresponding development in medieval China. The historical treatment of China is one of Weber's main weak spots. Weber's picture of Chinese institutions derives largely from the classical texts of Confucius, Lao-tzu, Mencius, and the other philosophers predating the Han unification (ca. 200 B.C.), and descriptions of the years following the establishment of the Ming dynasty (1368). Weber's analysis of the social organization of China is particularly dependent on the late dynasties, especially the Ch'ing (Manchu) dynasty (1644–1911). Weber drew heavily on accounts by nineteenth-century travelers and missionaries and other authorities on *contemporary* China, with a resulting picture of administrative corruption, familistic control, popular superstition and magic, which he then projected backward into the intervening centuries. This picture of an unchanging agrarian/bureaucratic society was reinforced by a kind of optical illusion. Since modern China was officially Confucian with an undercurrent of Taoism, and ancient China shows these same traditions in their "classic" phase, it is a natural assumption that China has been dominated by the same cultural system for two thousand years.

But this assumption is in error. Medieval China, from the fall of the Han (ca. A.D. 200) virtually until the rise of the Ming (1368), was technologically and economically dynamic, and underwent the greatest economic development yet seen in world history. Moreover, it was far more a Buddhist society than a Confucian or Taoist one, although Confucianism made its comeback at the end. For this reason, the Chinese historiographical tradition itself introduces a serious bias that has affected most sinological scholarship. It was the great Confucian scholars, particularly of the 1600s and 1700s, who laid the systematic foundation for the treatment of their own past, and they were prone to minimize or disparage the role of the Buddhists in it. Weber falls into the same attitude. His treatment of the Chinese "world religions" is confined to Confucianism and Taoism, with only the most offhand treatment of Buddhism. In fact, the pages (Weber, (1966/1951:213–9) in *The Religion of China* that touch on Buddhism deal only with the Chinese attitude toward heresy. Chinese Buddhism receives attention in its own right only in a few pages (Weber, 1916–17/1958a:264–9) of *The Religion of India*, where Weber dismisses the economic influence of the monasteries as "seats in part of irrational asceticism, in part of irrational meditation" (p. 269).[1]

To assess the economic impact of Buddhism, a sketch of Chinese economic history is in order (Eberhard, 1977; Elvin, 1973). In the period of Warring States that preceded the rise of the Han, indepen-

---

[1] Weber rather contemptuously asserted: "Gambling, drinking, opium, and women presumably played a considerable role in some monasteries. Any beginnings of a systematic ethical rationalization of conduct of the laity was out of the question" (1916–17/1958a:268).

Table 3.1. *Population and urbanization in China and Europe*

China			Europe	
Population of greater China[a] (in millions)	Percent urbanized (cities over 40,000)	Year	Population (in millions)	Percent urbanized
12	3.3	600 B.C.	10	0.5
28	2.3	400	20	3.5
45	1.6	200	26	—
60	1.8	A.D. 100	33	3.6
53	1.3	400	31	4.1
50	2.8	600	26	2.5
50	3.6	800	29	2.1
66	2.4	1000	36	3.5
115	1.6	1200	58	2.0
86	3.0	1300	79	2.5
81	3.5	1400	60	3.2
110	2.7	1500	81	3.6
160	2.0	1600	100	4.6
160	2.3	1700	120	4.4
330	1.9	1800	180	4.9

[a]Includes not only the political boundaries of the Chinese state at each date, but the entire east Asian territory including Manchuria, Mongolia, Chinese Turkestan, and Tibet.
Sources: McEvedy and Jones, 1978; Chandler and Fox, 1974.

dent clans and fiefs gave way to centrally controlled states that levied massive peasant infantries, as well as worker corvées to build roads, canals, and border walls, and to clear land. Metal coinage figured in an expansion of trade and the systematic collection of taxes. As we can see in Table 3.1, population quadrupled during these four hundred years and went through an additional but more moderate rise during the early Han dynasty.

The Han Empire officially comprised a kind of bureaucratic state socialism in which all land belonged to the state, all persons were subject to corvée labor on state projects, and welfare needs were to be met from state granaries. In practice, this was considerably mitigated by the survival of a class of nobility who held (or were awarded) their own fiefs, and who jostled for power with the office gentry through an endless series of mutual denunciations, confiscations, and purges. Political centralization broke down increasingly during the second century A.D., followed by four hundred years of division: at first into three states, with a brief period of reunification (280–307); then came the Hun conquest of north China (309–16) with considerable devastation and population loss. Many Chinese fled to the south, which became densely settled for the first time (and changed Chinese agriculture from wheat and millet to rice); the southern state underwent considerable economic development, but under a weak government subject to many uprisings, civil wars, and changes of dynasty. In the north, there was a flux of tribal states of the Huns, Turks, Mongols, and Tibetans, with the only period of considerable unification lasting from 440 to 530 under the Toba (Turkish) Empire. The money economy largely disappeared during this time, and was not reinstituted until late in the T'ang; coins were in very short supply, and salaries were paid in silk or grain, while trade was carried out largely through barter. Nevertheless, this was a time of considerable economic dynamism. Despite the devastation produced by continuous warfare, population held fairly steady, and the urbanization level increased considerably over the Han level. As we shall see, this was a period during which Chinese technology acquired a large lead over Europe and the rest of the world.

When reunification was achieved by the Sui dynasty (589–618) and, after brief civil wars, the T'ang (618–900), a high level of economic productivity prevailed. It is customary to date the decline of the T'ang from its midpoint about 755, when a combination of military defeats on distant central Asian battlefields, military revolts, and governmental budget crisis greatly diminished the power of the state. Nevertheless, it is precisely in this period of political weakness, which continues into another "interdynastic" period of rival states during 900–60, that the Chinese economy makes a particularly strong take-off. The inability of the state to collect taxes went along with the withdrawal of land into large-scale capitalist agriculture, often in connection with the tax-exempt privileges of the Buddhist monasteries. It is *after 780* that the predominantly monetary economy makes its reappearance. Taxes thereafter were always collected in money; coinage expanded, followed by the appearance of paper money *in the warring states period 900–60*. New large-scale trade appeared, especially from tea plantations of the south, but also in the emerging porcelain industry. Despite the fighting and its toll on the population, another boom set in. This one (Table 3.1) took the population to 115 million by the 1100s, by far the largest and densest of any historical state up to that time.

The period from the 700s through the 1100s comprised what Elvin called the "medieval economic revolution." Agricultural productivity expanded and rationalized, especially due to migration into new rice- and tea-growing areas of the south. Whole districts came to specialize in textile production. There was a corresponding revolution in water transportation, the perfection of a national network of canals and rivers, with a great expansion of commercial traffic. Local market towns sprang up to go along with the growth of large cities (which nevertheless did not keep up with the overall boom in population: Table 3.1). Large parts of the countryside were "industrialized" (Elvin, 1973:179, 204), and the world's first mechanized industries emerged during 900–1200, including some factories with up to five hundred workers. With the increasingly specialized division of labor came a financial revolution (Elvin, 1973:146). Increasing interdependence and volume of transactions accompanied a higher velocity of circulation of monetary means, and implied an increasing wealth per capita. Pressure on the coinage led, as we have seen, to the expansion of paper money and thence to financial speculation. There was considerable investment in commercial agriculture, especially near the heavily urbanized belt in central China, the large markets. The government, too, became financially calculating.

Much is often made of the financial distress and signs of growing poverty during the Sung. But these features should not be distorted by our biased hindsight, which looks for the crucial weakness as to "why China did not succeed in industrializing first." The fact is that China in the 1000s was far ahead of Europe; its iron production, for example, was equal to the entire output of Europe in 1700, and indeed somewhat higher on a per capita basis (Jones, 1981:202; cf. Hartwell, 1966, 1967). Sung China's problems were to a considerable extent those of a capitalist economy: a system, as we know, prone to cycles and crises that are market-based and hence exceedingly difficult to control. Thus the inflation and governmental crisis of tax revenues during 1020–60 is a sign of modernity, hardly characteristic of earlier command economies; so is the famous outbreak of factional "party politics" at the end of the century, with the in-again-out-again fortunes of Wang An-shih's reforms. Eberhard (1977:269–73) even traces the reform and traditionalist factions to economic interest groups: Wang An-shih's deflationary reforms were supported by the smaller, commercial landowners of the economically dynamic south, whereas the large landowners of Szechuan and Kiangsi were the core of the traditionalist Confucian opposition. These blocs were to remain active in Chinese politics for centuries thereafter. Similarly, the highly visible division that was appearing in Sung times between rich and poor, and the increasing numbers of beggars and wanderers, is a sign of the displacement of the rural population similar to that which took place in Tudor England with its own takeoff of capitalist agriculture. Is it not, in fact, the free propertyless labor force moving in response to economic forces? Sung China, in short, is already well into capitalism and its problems.

In hindsight, the fall of this system appears to have begun with a series of barbarian conquests: first of north China by the Jurchen Tartars in 1127, and then, in the next century, the long and bloody fifty years of war with the Mongols, who eventually took all of China. In the process, the north was largely depopulated, hence the kink in the population curve at this time (Table 3.1: with another smaller decline during the expulsion of the Mongols in the civil wars of the 1300s). Nevertheless, the large cities prospered, and, indeed, one result was to shift the center of the Chinese economy even more firmly to the more dynamic South. It is true that Mongol economic policies were rather destructive; forced labor led to a decline of taxes and a general impoverishment of China; north China had been turned largely to pasturage; world commerce was fostered but left in the hands of foreigners, and metal money flowed abroad. Nevertheless, technological growth and industrialization continued up to about 1400, and in some sectors there was a large expansion: printing, which had its springtime during the 1000s, was so widespread in the 1600s that Jesuit visitors noted that it was much more common than in Europe (Needham, 1965:1).

With the restoration of Ming Chinese rule (1368–1644), and the highly sinicized Manchu (Ch'ing) dynasty that followed (1644–1911), the Chinese economy entered a paradoxical situation. We are accustomed to regarding this period as typical Chinese economic stagnation. But this is true in only one sense. Technological development did stop, and governmental policy became notably anti-innovative (and, as is well known, antagonistic to continuing China's lead in world naval exploration). But, in fact, as Elvin (1973:204) concludes, post-Mongol China was undergoing vigorous economic growth. Serfdom disappeared, markets towns expanded, the industralization of large parts of the countryside went on. Population recovered its wartime losses and went on to an impressive growth *that can only be considered a sign of economic prosperity*. For we are dealing here not with a nineteenth- or twentieth-century–style "demographic transition" of declining death rates due to public health gains, but with the traditional agrarian population process in which the birthrate was closely attuned to economic feasibility (cf. Laslett, 1971:84–112). The enormous population of China, which we have come to take for granted as a sign of "backwardness," in fact had nothing to do with European colonial penetration, but antedates it by many centuries. It is primarily a result of the rationalization of agriculture that had taken place in preceding centuries (Eberhard, 1977:255–6, 283). Economic growth on a per capita basis apparently continued until about 1750, when the continuing population boom got out of hand. In Elvin's (1973) judgment, Chinese economic growth did not fail in the takeoff; instead, it became caught in the high-level equilibrium trap.

Chinese technology

The history of Chinese technology underscores the general point. Already in the ancient Han dynasty or in the preceding Warring States, Chinese technology was moving ahead of contemporary Greco-Roman society (which may be one reason why it got a jump in population size at this time). Chinese mastery of iron-casting and other metalwork was ahead of Europeans', and complex gears were already in use (Needham, 1965:1). Efficient breast-harness for horses was already universal in the Han, whereas the West was continuing to use (down through the 700s) the old throat-and-girth harness, modeled after the ox yoke, which partly strangled the horse as it pulled and greatly reduced its power. Thus, Roman chariots were always small, carrying two passengers at most and often pulled by four horses, whereas Chinese chariots and carts were much larger and used fewer horses (Needham, 1965:247, 312–17). Considering the emphasis that White and Gimpel have given to the improved harness and the "horsepower revolution" in medieval Europe, it is notable that China had already reached this plateau of energy production a millennium earlier.[2]

China was similarly ahead in the development of machinery. The first use of waterpower is for metallurgical bellows, much later used for hammers, sawmills, air-conditioning fans, and textile machinery. There are records from the 400s A.D. of water-powered mills used for blowers at the government Iron Authority, and similar instances can be probably be found, according to Needham (1965:362–404), in most other centuries. Around 500, Chinese officials used trip-hammers, and a combination of eccentric, connecting-rod, and piston rod

---

[2] The availability of cheap labor in China, contrary to a popular interpretation, was no bar to laborsaving devices. China early developed efficient trace-harness for horses (400s B.C. and after), the still better collar harness in the 400s A.D., the wheelbarrow in the 200s A.D. (a thousand years before Europe). China never used slave-manned oared warships like the omnipresent Mediterranean galleys, despite its extensive use of inland waterways. When the water mill appeared in the 100s A.D. for blowing metallurgical bellows, it was recorded as more humane and cheaper than human or animal power. About 1280, waterpower was widely applied to textile machinery. Nor was there rejection of technologies because of fear of unemployment, unlike in Roman, Venetian, Elizabethan, and other instances. Needham comments (1965:29), "If China was so often in fact first in the field with labour-saving devices, had Confucian benevolence and Buddhist compassion nothing to do with it?"

(equivalent to the inverse pattern of the reciprocating steam engine), a thousand years before Europe. Germany, Denmark, and France had their first mechanized forge-hammers about 1100, with the application of waterpower to bellows in the early 1200s. Another important commercial application of machinery, the silk-reeling machine (a system of complicated gears) was standard in the 1000s, although it changes little over the next seven hundred years. But the silk industry is much older, and the water-powered blower may have been developed in T'ang and Sung. A similar gear system was found in Europe only occasionally in the 1400s. In China, hydraulically powered triphammers for forges were widespread from the 1300s onward. But late Han already had them along canals from mountain streams, and they were considered to be relatively new in the 200s and 300s A.D. Water mills were used for palace air-conditioning fans about 747. By 1313, water mills for textile machinery were very common in textile districts.

China also had the lead in the development of more refined machinery. Printing has already been mentioned; escapements, the mechanical key to clocks, developed about 725. Late Han (A.D. 100 and following) and every century thereafter had astronomical globes or spheres rotated mechanically by water power. The Chinese Middle Ages had large, cumbersome mechanical clocks, equivalent to those that became something of a mania in Europe in the 1300s, although the Chinese versions were probably not widespread (Needham, 1965:436, 481). And in military technology and naval warfare, the Chinese had a substantial priority (see Chapter 4). Needham (1965:600) summed up: "The balance shows a clear technological superiority on the Chinese side down to about +1400." Europeans' view of China as late as the 1700s was generally that they were in contact with a *superior* civilization (cf. the Chinoiserie of the Enlightenment period), and Needham points out that one reason the British introduced the opium trade into China in the early 1800s was because there were yet no European manufactures that the Chinese wanted in return for their own.

The contribution of Buddhist monastic capitalism

It is during this medieval period that Buddhism entered and became the dominant religion of China (Ch'en, 1964; Wright, 1959). The early missionaries were patronized especially by the alien dynasties that held northern China after the fall of the Han, but Buddhism also had fervent royal patrons from time to time in the Chinese south. Buddhism at this time bore a strong resemblance to early medieval Christianity when it was converting the pagan northern Europe; in

China, though, there was the added complication of rivalry from other literate religions, Confucianism and Taoism (both of which had been transformed by now from their individualistic form into ritualistic churches). Buddhist monks were revered as magicians and rainmakers, and artifacts such as the alleged bones of the Buddha were centers of cult worship and public festivals.[3] Monasteries, particularly in the vicinity of the capitals, were lavishly endowed with great buildings, gold and jeweled works of art, huge monuments, and grants of land.

Like early European monasticism, Buddhism at first was largely a ritual-producing enclave attached to the status structure of the aristocracy, having lost most of its original philosophy and meditative detachment. But in the two centuries after A.D. 530, Buddhism underwent a kind of "reform" comparable to that which took place in the Europe of 1050–1250. The earlier magical/ritual monasticism was criticized and supplemented (if not entirely supplanted) by a revival of traditional Buddhist meditation, monastic discipline, and philosophy. At the same time, proselytizers of a simplified Buddhism worshipping the deities Maitreya and Amitabha spread an often millennial fervor among the people, and succeeded in giving Buddhism a popular basis in small local temples throughout the countryside. This made Buddhism by far the strongest religion among the common people, as Confucianism was a self-consciously elitist cult of the gentry, and Taoism was similarly an upper-class luxury (although in emulation of Buddhism it, too, developed a more popular structure, which largely amalgamated with Buddhism in the popular mind in later centuries). Buddhism thus developed another leg to stand on, besides the patronage of ruling houses, whose support was subject to the volatile shifts and purges of factional politics at the capital. The founder of the unifying Sui dynasty (581–618) was a strong supporter of Buddhism, although its revolutionary overthrow and replacement by the T'ang brought a temporary crisis when Confucianism was reestablished in 624 as the basis of a government examination system for selecting officials.[4]

---

[3] This "bone worship" of sacred relics was also central in early medieval Christianity, before the reforms of the 1000s (Southern, 1970:30–1).

[4] The examination system had existed in rudimentary form for some positions in the Han dynasty, but became the major, regularized bureaucratic route to office only in the Sung and had its greatest development in the Ming and Ch'ing dynasties (Galt, 1951; Franke, 1960). The later dominance of the long-studying Confucian scholar should not be read back unreservedly into the T'ang. At first the T'ang examination topics were not exclusively Confucian; candidates were recommended by provincial officials rather than presenting themselves at their own initiative; and the aristocracy maintained the privilege of nominating their sons for office without examina-

But Buddhism remained too strongly entrenched to be eliminated and, in fact, during the next century remained one of the rotating "ins" and "outs" in government religious politics – for instance, receiving support from two reigning empresses for a Buddhist "theocracy" during the years 680–701 and 705–12. Eventually, by the 800s, Buddhism lost most of its leverage in *court* politics, but the Amidaist and Ch'an (Zen) sects kept it flourishing throughout the country: the former as the main form of popular Chinese religiosity, the latter as a pure meditative Buddhism. Organizationally, Ch'an Buddhism owed its success to its policy of establishing monasteries far from the capital, especially on remote mountains; and of *economic self-sufficiency*, replacing reliance on alms (such as a royal patronage) by the requirement that lower-level monks, before achieving meditative "enlightenment," engage in agricultural labor. The Ch'an monasteries, in fact, became centers of tea production, and their missionaries were also the traders who introduced tea into Japan.

The economic impact of Buddhism, however, was not primarily in these later popularized or "rationalized" forms, but in the earlier monasteries of the northern, Sui, and early T'ang dynasties. In the period of depopulation and lapse from the monetary economy after the fall of the Han, the Buddhist monasteries became the economic basis upon which the great unifying dynasty could eventually arise. The early monasteries acted as entrepreneurs (Gernet, 1956). At first they were donated land in infertile highlands and other lands that were undeveloped or had been lost to cultivation. Their patrons also gave them the labor to cultivate them in the form of slaves, especially Chinese families subdued by the alien conquerors and given into the care of the church as a gesture of religious charity. Freed convicts were also donated to temples as laborers, eventually forming villages of hereditary serfs under monastic control (Ch'en, 1964:154–8). Later, these holdings expanded into the lowlands, and in the T'ang (at least according to hostile reports) the Buddhist temples became the largest landed possessions in China (Ch'en, 1964:269): again, comparable to the position of the Christian Church in Europe.

The monasteries were in several respects the most dynamic and rationalized economic force in China during this period (Ch'en, 1964:261–75). Monastic celibacy meant that unlike all other Chinese

tion. During the alien dynasties (Tartars and Mongols), examinations were limited to Chinese competing for minor appointments, whereas important positions were reserved for non-Chinese. Only in the Ming did a rigidly Confucian orthodoxy take command, and the lengthy series of local, provincial, and metropolitan examinations was established.

institutions, the monasteries escaped from the patriarchal/patrimonial family basis of organization. The vow of personal poverty automatically converted all wealth into organizational possessions, to be plowed back into communal property. To be sure, much of this took the form of ostentatious buildings and works of art; but these, as in the cathedral-building phase in Europe, had the important effect of supporting artisans and encouraging the movement of materials. It is true that the store of gold and jewels in the form of religious artifacts removed currency from circulation, but it also acted as a type of bank. If the government made numerous "irrational" gifts to the monasteries, they also repaid themselves on occasion by purges that confiscated monastic wealth to finance wars and other government enterprises. Moreover, these treasuries expanded into genuine banks. Goods were accepted for safekeeping, or were rented or loaned for interest. Temples served as pawnbrokerages, auctions, and sponsors of commercial fairs. They also became hostels for travelers – initially for pilgrims and monks but eventually serving traveling merchants, government-examination candidates, and others, thus becoming commercial hotels aiding the development of long-distance travel.

These economic activities were rationally directed in a spirit of calculating management of assets. Systematic financial reports were made by monastic officials who were specifically charged with accounting for temple incomes and expenditures. The internal structure of the larger monasteries became bureaucratized, regulated by rules and supervised by specialized officials. Grain crops and other temple wealth, beyond what was needed for local consumption, were usually put in the hands of a monastic agent, who was expected to invest them and return a profit. These gains were in turn reinvested in the acquisition of further land and goods.

Because of their position outside the secular and familistic structure of Chinese society, the monasteries were a focal point for other profit-oriented interests. In the absence of a money economy or (in the period before the Sui unification) state machinery strong enough to collect taxes reliably, the monasteries, with their stores of wealth and their system of trading, were the banks and much of the long-distance commercial structure of China. As the state regained strength, the monasteries continued to expand, this time in symbiosis with a private or "hidden" capitalism of the gentry landowners. Because the temples had tax-exempt status, noble landlords, especially in the T'ang, would give land to a temple but retain a private agreement to keep most of its proceeds; alternatively, a family would establish its own Buddhist "merit cloister" on its burial grounds, thereby acquiring tax exemption for the entire property. The latter form flourished particularly during the Sung (Ch'en, 1964:272). Although the practice was sharply criticized by Confucian enemies of Buddhism, and by the official party generally, for diminishing state revenues, from an economic point of view it was a major device by which resources were withdrawn from a strictly command system and put into the burgeoning market economy. With this accelerating accumulation of wealth, the Buddhist property-holders were able to buy further land and consolidate their holdings into rationally operable estates. During the T'ang, Eberhard concludes (1977:185), the monasteries were the leading edge of capitalism in China, serving as centers for foreign trade and dominating the money market through their accumulation of precious metals.

Buddhism, manufacturing, and technology

Medieval Buddhism also was a center of manufacturing, and of the use of production machinery. Again, we have a parallel with the Cistercians in Europe and their rationalizing methods. This is not to say that the Chinese monasteries were as much centers of technological innovation. One major difference was that the Chinese government itself had a tradition of supporting and even leading in the development of technology. It is not true, as we so often assume, that a centralized command system is inevitably technologically stagnant. There were Imperial Workshops and Arsenals in most dynasties, and the trades with the most advanced techniques were usually "nationalized," such as Salt and Iron Authorities in the Former Han (Needham, 1965:10, 17, 20). Technicians usually gathered as personal followers around prominent officials. Of course, most handicraft production was carried out by common people, but larger or new and complex machines (e.g., early water mills) were usually made by imperial workshops or under provincial officials. Many Han inventions, such as the invention of paper in A.D. 105, were announced by the Director of the Imperial Workshops.

Such innovations, particularly in industrial machinery, were especially prominent in the Middle Ages. The traditional pattern of development and control by government agents continued, but with a tendency for ownership (or at least profits) to spill over into private hands (Needham, 1965:400–3). For instance, celebrated water mills were built by an official engineer in 488. About 600, a chief technologist of the Sui dynasty owned or controlled thousands of them. Mills were used as "fiefs" to be given away to nobles, ex-emperors, and others. Buddhist monasteries were often recipients of such machinery, either as government patronage or as donations from faithful laymen. Because of their economic dynamism, the monasteries became major entrepreneurs in their use, and owned large numbers of water-powered rolling mills for processing flour, as well as oil presses and other sources of manufacture. Some mills had multiple water-wheels, capable of grinding large amounts of wheat. The machinery was often leased to private businesses, although temples also operated their own trade caravans for sale of their products. Monks brought the water-mill technology to Korea, Japan, and Tibet in the 600s.[5]

These manufacturing enterprises were also sheltered behind the monasteries' exemption from taxation. For this reason, among others, they became objects of contention. Already in 612 there were quarrels with monks about water mill revenues, and about 800 an official fought with them over their claim to tax-immunity. Mill dues were one of richest sources of income for great abbeys during the Chinese Middle Ages. Emboldened by their example, merchants also built mills, especially in cities lacking governmental control (hence the continued economic boom during and after the breakdown of the T'ang). There was also conflict between waterpower users and irrigation controllers. Sometimes mills were sealed or destroyed, as in 721 and 764, when aggressive officials attacked water mills belonging to wealthy families or to Buddhist abbeys. The biggest destruction took place in 778, including some mills belonging not only to abbeys but also to an important general. Mills were generally property of imperial concubines, powerful eunuchs, Buddhist abbeys, or rich merchants, and hence Confucian bureaucrats were often antagonistic. But by the early Sung, presumably after uncontrolled growth during an intra-dynastic period, the government decided to recognize officially the private mills (970) by establishing a Commissioner for Water Mills.

The balance sheet of Buddhist capitalism
The greatest economic effect of Buddhism was in the early Chinese Middle Ages, continuing through the early T'ang. By the late T'ang, when governmental controls disintegrated, a private agrarian/capitalist economy was already on its feet, and expanded beyond its Buddhist beginnings. Hence the Buddhist economy, although still substantial, no longer had the same visibility in the larger secular economy of the Sung. The various confiscations of Buddhist property, especially the great purge that took place in 845, all had the effect

---

5 Religious capitalism was not confined to Buddhism. Taoist hermits (especially in the T'ang and Sung dynasties) were known for their remote mountain mills, using trip-hammers for crushing materials for drugs. This appears to have been a Taoist cottage industry: in fact, the economic basis of the independent, nongentry Taoism that appeared by this time may well have been this pharmaceutical industry.

of transferring Buddhist economic power into private hands, and probably fostering even further capitalist development there.

If we compare Buddhist "monastic capitalism" with its Christian equivalent in Europe, we see at least a partial filling of the checklist of institutional factors of the "Weberian revolution." Most importantly, the Buddhist monasteries, like the Cistercians and some other Christian orders, acted as corporate entrepreneurs. They provided the leverage to escape from the familistic organization of the economy, and a methodical economic ethic that rationally calculated and plowed back profits into further investments. Buddhism also opened up a market in land, the most important factor of production in an agrarian economy, and pioneered in the application of mass-production technology. The temples organized the first financial markets. Again, as in Europe, the mass labor market based on free labor moving in response to economic demand is absent; but one might well conclude that this is a late factor, which falls into place once the other institutional conditions are present and economic growth begins to build up steam. (Indeed, this is what did happen in later centuries, with the disappearance of serfdom in China at the time of the Ming [Elvin, 1973].)

One feature that Christianity provided in Europe is notably lacking in China: the bureaucratization and the legal system of the Church. There is nothing equivalent to the Papacy and its chancery courts, which became the model for secular bureaucracy and for the system of property law on which Western capitalism developed. The lack of this type of governmental and legal infrastructure indeed severely cramped the later development of Chinese capitalism. But certainly its lack did not prevent the early religious phase of capitalism from emerging in China or from spilling over into a private economy by the time of the Sung. And the seeds were there within the Buddhist temples themselves; the internal organization of the great enterprises comprised specialized officials with fixed duties and terms of office, operating by rules and keeping records. The Buddhist *Sangha*, or body of monks, also was in principle a self-governing group with its internal "citizenship" equivalent to that in the Christian Church, and governed by the *Vinaya*, or code of monastic laws. It was not the internal deficiencies of Buddhism that made it less fateful than Christianity for the surrounding economy; it was the higher political organization of Buddhism that kept it from maintaining the same centralized structure vis-à-vis secular government as the Papacy and its courts did in Europe.

This brings us to the question of the downfall of medieval Chinese capitalism. I have already argued that it is mistaken to ask, "Why didn't China produce the Industrial Revolution?" As far as technological and institutional structure was concerned, one might as well say the Chinese *did* produce the revolution – if it makes any sense to use a word like "revolution" for a process that took many centuries. Industrialism in Europe did not suddenly appear in 1770 but was merely a culminating form of a series of institutional developments going back at least eight hundred years. Similarly, China had its own development of eight hundred or a thousand years, starting earlier than Europe and maintaining a notable lead over Europe until what Elvin calls a "high-level equilibrium trap" set in after 1400 (or even later). The question that now must be asked, rather, is: Given that Chinese Buddhism was the driving edge of medieval Chinese capitalism, can it be that the revival of Confucian hegemony and the near destruction of Chinese Buddhism was the crucial factor that eventually led to Chinese economic stagnation?

The formulation has much to recommend it. In its favor is the fact that Japan, a far more Buddhist country than China in its later centuries, was able to make a spectacular economic takeoff, even despite its enclosed command structure. Bellah (1957) attributed to Japanese Buddhism a cultural ethic equivalent to Protestantism, although differing in content. But we have seen that it is a matter not of any particular religious ethic but of the organizational structure of monastic religion itself that is economically crucial. Did the political attacks that eventually wrecked the vitality of Chinese Buddhism then undermine the source of Chinese economic dynamism? I have mentioned that in 845, under the pressure of military catastrophe and the instigation of Taoist opponents, virtually all Buddhist wealth was confiscated and hundreds of thousands of monks and nuns returned to secular life. This was the culmination of a series of earlier attacks. Thirty thousand monks had been defrocked in 712, after the overthrow of an empress who had ruled with strong Buddhist support; in 573, in the maneuvers just before the military coalition fell into place that established the Sui dynasty, one of the northern states confiscated both Taoist and Buddhist properties in an effort to fill the governmental treasury; and a similar confiscation occurred as early as 446 in another northern state. Yet Buddhism was able to come back in strength and prosperity after the earlier persecutions, and, indeed, by 1221 there were 460,000 monks and nuns, compared to the previous high of 260,000 at the time of the great persecution of 845.

More deadly to Buddhism was the creeping spread of government regulation, which eventually made monastic positions themselves part of the system of government patronage and sinecures. Administrative supervision began in the 620s, as a compromise move after

Confucians and Taoists failed to institute an official purge of Buddhism. Later, after the overthrow of the Empress Wu's effort at Buddhist theocracy (690–701, perhaps a crucial turning point in the history of China), the church became subject to increasing government regulation. In 747, people wishing to become monks were required to obtain an ordination certificate from the Bureau of National Sacrifices. During a military crisis in 755, certificates began to be sold to raise revenue. As government authority disintegrated over the next two centuries, local officials began surreptitiously to sell certificates on their own. The practice was officially revived in 1067 during the Sung dynasty, giving rise to a speculative market in which certificates were bought not for personal use but for resale, speculating on their rise in price. The Sung government also raised revenue by selling the higher monastic ranks, and in the 1100s added a series of monastic titles to spur purchases (Ch'en, 1964:241–4, 391–3).

This inflationary market for certificates and offices was perhaps not entirely negative in its overall economic effects. Given the shortage of hard currency, the certificates served as officially redeemable paper, which was pressed into use as financial instruments. No doubt their shifting value had less to do with the actual utility of a monastic ordination than with their purely mediating role within the financial world itself. Thus once again the Buddhist "economy" seems to have played a useful role in facilitating growth of the secular economy. But Buddhism itself was choked and could no longer play the role of corporate entrepreneur and leader of dynamic, rational capitalism. It is a thought worth following that the political vicissitudes of Chinese Buddhism may be the key to the rise, and high-level stagnation, of economic development in China.

The downfall of religious capitalism in Europe

Let us ask a similar question about the West. If in fact medieval Europe had a system of religious capitalism, how do we explain its downfall? Elsewhere (Collins, 1981f) I have proposed a model of cyclical growth and decline in culture-producing sectors generally. One of the cases included is the rise and fall of the medieval university system, which was closely attached to the rise and fall of the Papacy. I would propose that this model may be extended to provide a plausible explanation of the fate of medieval capitalism. In its original form, I argued for a three-sector model. (1) The expansion of *cultural production*, through investment in monasteries, schools, and churches, increases social mobilization and organization-building capacity. (2) This leads to an increasing scale of *political organization:* in the medieval case this comprised above all the Papal bureaucracy but also spilled over into building up secular states. (3) The framework of political organization in turn provided the institutional infrastructure (law, regularized markets, etc.) for *economic growth.* This in its turn fed back into the generation of material resources that could be invested in further culture-producing institutions and political organization.

I would now modify part of this model to include the monasteries as major units of economic production in their own right. The circle of growth among the three sectors, at least initially, was to a great extent the mutually stimulated growth of three different parts of the Church: monastic capitalism, religious culture-production, and religious political organization. In every respect, the Church was the modernizing sector within a surrounding feudal society. But also the circle of growth among the three religious sectors spilled over into corresponding growth in secular society, fostering both the secular economy and a secular status-culture, and encouraging the growth of secular states.

The mutually supporting circle of growth in these three sectors generates a crisis in the following way: Extremely high levels of cultural production, such as exist when there is a widespread status-competition for religious or educational credentials, tend to accelerate political mobilization. Whereas earlier phases of mobilization support the centralizing power of one or at most a few political organizations, later phases produce massive mobilization that spills over the bounds of centralized power. Competing organizations are consolidated, and the level of political conflict rises. This puts disproportionate weight on the economic sector to support the political and culture-producing sectors. A top-heavy credentialized society takes hold, characterized by destructive political conflict that eats up or destroys more economic resources than it helps create (cf. Collins, 1979). Eventually the economy goes into decline, the political system breaks down, and the culture becomes delegitimated. A downward phase of the cycle takes over; like the upward phase before it, this may last several hundred years.

This, roughly speaking, is what happened to medieval Christendom. The early phases of cultural status-competition took the form of nobles contributing to the ritual-performing sector, the traditional Benedictine monasteries, to enhance their own religious status. The increased power and wealth of the monasteries fostered a political growth within the Church itself, the Papal bureaucracy. It also gave rise to religious movements that escalated the competition for religious status to a new level of intensity: the reform movements within monasticism that arose in the 1100s, of which the Cistercians were the most dynamic and the most economically productive. The mutually supporting circle of growth went on for two centuries. Church capitalism emerged, providing resources that could be used to increase both cultural production and new political organization. Culture-producing institutions went into mushrooming growth. The escalating competition of different localities to found universities was one aspect of this; another aspect was the second round of reform movements within monasticism, the outburst of wandering friars in the 1200s.

But these movements were now more oriented toward status conflict and church politics than to economic production. Whereas the Cistercians had worked and invested, the Dominicans and Franciscans begged, theologized, persecuted heretics, and fought the battles of church politics. The Papacy had consolidated its control, but the same organizational and economic resources upon which it had grown were also being diverted into building strong state apparatuses for secular princes. The height of medieval Christian society, in the years around 1300, degenerated into chronic political battles both within the Church and between it and the increasingly potent princes. The 1300s and 1400s are the down side of the cycle, with their widespread internal warfare and their political anarchy. Together with this came economic decline, and the fading legitimation of the religious and educational credentials that had characterized the earlier period of medieval growth (Collins, 1981f). The end point of this delegitimation was to be the Reformation, which overthrew the cultural standards of the preceding period.

Historically, the bourgeois capitalism that we take as its "pure" form emerged upon the ruins of medieval religious capitalism. In its degenerate form, after the down phase of the medieval cycle, the remnants of the church economy did indeed appear as obstacles that needed to be swept away so that a vigorous capitalism could again appear. But I think this tells us less about the real nature of the religious economy at its height than about the long-term cycles that seem to be involved in capitalism generally. The first such cycle – in the West – was that of medieval Europe; the period of the Protestant Reformation began the second cycle; and apparently there have been others since then (Research Working Group, 1979). I stress that the medieval European cycle was the first *in the West*, because monastic capitalism in Buddhist China gives a strong suggestion of having set off a prior example of market dynamics on the world scale.

Conclusion

I would urge two main conclusions. One is that the rise of medieval Christendom was the main Weberian revolution, creating the institutional forms within which capitalism could emerge. The Protestant Reformation is just a particular crisis at the end of a long-term cycle; it gave rise to a *second* takeoff, which we mistakenly see as the first. If this is correct, incidentally, it means that the role of the Protestant doctrine of predestination was by no means a central or necessary one. The Cistercian rationale for their ascetically driven economics served the same ends. And there are earlier examples (both in early Christian monasticism and in Chinese Buddhism) where we see the same kind of "Protestant ethic" connection between religiously motivated asceticism and economic productivity, but under quite different theological outlooks.

The other conclusion is to warn us that capitalism has a much broader nature than the "classic" nineteenth-century bourgeois individualism enshrined in most sociological and economic theories. Against the backdrop of religious capitalism, the corporate capitalism of the twentieth century – which has gone under the silly misnomer of "postindustrialism" – does not look so incongruous. Neither does the state capitalism of the contemporary socialist world. This is not to say that all of history consists of capitalism, or that within the historical epochs fitting that rubric there are not significant variants to be explained. But it is to claim that there are certain long-term dynamics that no genuinely explanatory theory can afford to overlook.

4

A theory of technology

Technology is one of the unexplored dark spots in the social sciences. It is true that there is a branch of economics that models the profitability and costs of technology in the abstract, in relation to growth, interindustry productivity, and rates of diffusion. The evolution of particular technologies and the behavior of particular firms have also been studied. But this research lacks explanatory leverage, since it assumes the prior existence of the entire social and economic complex that makes up an ongoing market economy. We lack, in short, the kind of historical comparisons that can do for technology what Weber provides for the other institutional features of modern capitalism. Technology plays a crucial role throughout history, but we cannot be sure that its dynamics are similar in different historical epochs. Only a comparative historical analysis can provide this.

Weber provides some useful leads, although he does not pay a great deal of systematic attention to technology. The very omission is indicative of his attitude. Regarding the organization of the modern factory, for example, Weber (1923/1961) comments that its major prerequisite is a mass demand for its products – else mass-production machinery is of little use – and moreover a relatively constant demand. It requires a "certain organization of the market" (1923/1961:129). A further prerequisite is *relatively inexpensive techniques of production*. Entrepreneurs with fixed capital must be able to keep their establishments going even in bad times; that means that the factory type of organization must be able to produce more cheaply than the traditional household form or its offshoot, the putting-out system.

Weber goes on to argue (1923/1961:136) that the modern factory is *not* created by machines. He defines the factory as "labor discipline within the shop . . . combined with technical specialization and coordination and the application of non-human sources of power." (1923/1961:133). The factory, in other words, is a form of social and economic organization that maximizes the control of all factors of production in the hands of the entrepreneur and thus makes their rational calculation possible. Nonhuman sources of energy are important not because they enhance productivity per se but because they are more amenable to entrepreneurial control. If there was a deliberate search for machinery as capitalism took off, it was because machines favored labor discipline and specialization of work in the factory.

"Economically, the significance of the machines lay in the introduction of systematic calculation" (Weber, 1923/1961:136). Machines not only made possible a calculating enterprise; they also were the products of this spirit of calculation. Systematic experimentation was behind the inventions that overcame bottlenecks in production in the 1700s: the spindle (1769 and after), which overcame the shortage of yarn for the new machine looms; or the Cartwright power loom (1785), which overcame the resulting bottleneck now that there was an overabundance of yarn (Weber, 1923/1961:225). Similarly, Weber (1923/1961:226–7) mentions that the capitalist revolution would have been brought to a halt by deforestation, using up the wood that provided heat for smelting iron, if coking coal had not been developed in 1735 and used in the blast furnace in 1740. Another self-created threat to the mining industry occurred when the deeper mine shafts reached levels with serious water inundation; this was overcome by a series of devices for lifting water developed over the period 1670–1770, culminating in the steam engine.

Weber does not systematically theorize these examples, and they give the superficial impression of crucial "accidents." But they fit into Weber's general themes. It is *prior* capitalist development in each case that creates the threat or bottleneck; and it is the systematic efforts at innovation over a time period (which may be up to one hundred years) that brings about the mechanical solutions. Mechnical inventions are part of the spirit of capitalism. The catalyst, Weber asserts (1923/1961:230–1), was the price revolution following upon the influx of gold and silver in the 1500s and 1600s. This brought a tendency for capitalistic profit-seeking through cheapening production and lower prices, which in turn created the tendency to rationalize technology and economic relations in order to reduce price in relation to costs. Whereas in the "precapitalist" era, inventors such as Leonardo da Vinci were motivated not by cheapening production but by sheer artistic interest, by the 1600s capitalism had brought about a "feverish pursuit of invention."

Many of the specifics of Weber's argument have been widely supported. His point that factory machinery was a vehicle for tightening labor discipline is echoed by present-day Marxists (although for a later historical period; see Braverman, 1974; Gartman, 1979; Jeremy,

A theory of technology

1981); it is also supported by mainstream historians of early industrialization (Landes, 1969:60, 81, 115; cf. Jones, 1981). Similarly, Weber is correct that economic expansion preceded these technological innovations (Landes, 1969:57–8). Landes (1969:42) also concurs with the larger point that "steeply rising costs per unit of one or more factors of production under conditions of growing demand would imply an opportunity for and incentive to technological improvement."[1]

But this leaves us nevertheless in the realm of historical particulars and does not develop the fundamental Weberian point that makes technological innovation part of a general rise of an attitude of rational calculation. We need Weber-style historical comparisons to lay bare the proper social context. Weber was not interested enough in technology to provide these. In what follows, I will attempt to sketch some of the relevant materials, with special stress on comparing Europe and China. The technological innovations during long periods of Chinese history remain a major mystery for Western social science. They are invoked in an ad hoc way, since their diffusion into Europe plays an important role in all accounts of Europe's modernization. But so far they simply play the role of a historical accident, and the

---

[1] The concern with "bottlenecks" in production, which Weber shares with many subsequent economic historians, has however been increasingly critiqued in recent research. Richard Gordon, in an unpublished manuscript, points out that the "challenge-and-response" of particular technological problems at a given time generally *could* have been met in quite different ways, and these did not necessarily lead toward the centralization of production in the factory. Spinning jenneys and mules could have been made more compact and been diffused into the putting-out system, with little difference in productivity; the choice to do otherwise was a "political" question, not a technological imperative. The factory form was a control mechanism, and the first textile factories were organized not around machines but around hand technologies. This is of course Weber's general point too; the factory concentrates the factors of production in the control, and in the *sphere of calculation*, of the entrepreneur; and in fact this is precisely what makes it distinctively "modern," "rationalized" capitalism. Not that technological innovation is calculable in the sense that innovations become strictly foreseeable and plannable; but they are the result of systematic searches, and moreover they are searches for procedures *whose results in the work process are calculable.*

In common with many other authors, including Immanuel Wallerstein, Weber overestimated the importance of the influx of Spanish gold and silver in producing the price revolution of 1500–1650. Goldstone (1984) shows that most of the precious metal was either reexported to Asia or withdrawn from circulation in the form of ornaments and domestic plate. The price revolution was due, rather, to the heightened velocity of monetary circulation in the increasingly interlinked networks of occupational specialization that emerged with the commercialization of agriculture and the urbanization of this time. Goldstone's theory has the effect of further "dehistoricizing" an "accidental" factor – the influx of New World metals – and placing the European technological revolution in the context of an ongoing commercial transformation. The causes of *that*, in turn, are social and undoubtedly of the institutional nature outlined in Chapters 1 and 2.

79

conditions for their own development in China – and for the technological stagnation that set in there after A.D. 1400 – remain undertheorized.

I shall pursue, then, a general historical comparison, with an aim to isolate the social conditions underlying technological innovation. It is not to be assumed, however, that these conditions are limited to those Weber laid out for modern capitalist innovations. There may be other types of social mechanisms underlying innovation in various historical epochs.

What is an invention?

Apart from studies of industrial technology since the 1700s, historians' concern with technology has traditionally been limited to the question of whether any particular case is a diffusion from elsewhere, an indication of migration, or an independent invention, and if the last, who is to be assigned priority. All this assumes that it is quite clear what is an invention. Usually some example is given, whether of an idea (Leonardo's flying machines), a model (Hero of Alexandria's toy steam engine), or a full-scale working device (Watt's steam engine). These are, of course, heterogeneous types; the one thing they have in common is that somehow they acquired fame. Dates based on this kind of comparison are arbitrary and misleading.

The dichotomy between "invention" and "diffusion" is sociologically naive at both ends. Initial ideas, models, or even working examples are generally worthless without development; cataloguers of "independent inventions" ignore the essential "D" component in "R and D." Socially and economically, an innovation cannot be really said to exist until it can be used. But inventions almost always change during the process of becoming socially adopted (Sahal, 1981); a major part of the innovation is thus an aspect of the widespread adoption itself. Moreover, inventions do not appear suddenly at some point in time, despite our preference for a historical shorthand that assigns to each a convenient date. There is a long series of small improvements, which finally culminate in a technology that becomes economically dominant. This pattern is found, for example, in European textile machinery, from the 1500s on through the 1800s; in metallurgy throughout the coal and iron revolution of the same period; and in chemicals (Landes, 1969:81, 87, 90–92, 218). Landes (1969:92) comments that "small anonymous gains were probably more important in the long run than the major inventions that have been remembered in the history books." Moreover, "an invention" is in fact often a whole series of different types of technologies; this was the case, for example, in the development of locomotives and railroads, farm trac-

A theory of technology

tors, electrical power, and early versions of television (Sahal, 1981; Udelson, 1982). It is a complex of parallel and successive developments that constitutes the "innovation."

Different kinds of technological innovations feed off each other. The application of steam power to textile machinery was a typical combination of inventions with different histories. The steam engine came from water-draining problems in the mines, whereas the textile machinery (initially made of wood, incidentally) had been variously powered by hand, water mills, or animals. Both areas had long periods of independent development, fueled by economic demands. Similarly, the cost-cutting search for uses of chemical by-products led to a long series of new compounds, as each reaction yielded other compounds (Landes, 1969:109). Nor are innovations merely linked positively by the opportunities they provide for each other. As Weber and others have noted, technological innovations cause bottlenecks in the production process, or come up against limits of exhaustion of natural resources, which motivates a further search for technologies to overcome these challenges. Surprisingly often, the challenge is met, although it may take a century or more to do so – as in the difficulties of refining wrought iron, the object of continuous efforts since the 1730s but not overcome before about 1870 (Landes, 1969:91, 218–19).

To compare where various inventions are made really means comparing whole complexes of social activity. Isolated "independent inventions" taken out of context are in fact rarely the same thing.[2] Socially real technologies – those that have actually been put into normal use – are linked to a larger pattern of technical and social activity that had to be sustained over a relatively long time and large area (cf. Hughes, 1969, on the concept of a "technological system"). The importance of this social context is shown by the long lags that may occur between the isolated occurrence of some technique and its coming into general social use. Thus it is not incorrect, as is usually done, to date the "discovery" of agriculture to around 6000 B.C. in Mesopotamia, with another "discovery" in Mexico around 3000–2000 B.C., even though in each case the technique of cultivating seeds was known for some two thousand to three thousand years before (Edwards, Gadd, and Hammond, 1970:248–51) or even longer.[3] Agri-

---

[2] The same point has been demonstrated in the realm of allegedly "multiple discoveries" of scientific ideas or facts (Patinkin, 1983). Most such alleged discoveries were marginal to the central message of their "discoverers," and hence were buried by their own context. The significant "discovery" is one that is made socially central.

[3] More recent archeology keeps turning up earlier instances of agricultural cultivation: 12,000 B.C. in Egypt, 16,000 B.C. in Africa, metallurgy in southeast Asia in

81

culture was not socially real until after the later date. The reasons for the delay, incidentally, are of considerable interest for a theory of technology; it appears that the social costs of shifting from a relatively easy and pleasant economy of hunting and gathering to an arduous (and socially stratifying) agriculture were such that people were not willing to pay, until perhaps forced by population pressure (Cohen, 1977).

To be first in the development of a technique is often of no importance. Ironworking first occurred in Anatolia around 1500 B.C., but was expensive and little developed, and did not set off the "Iron Age" innovations until the two centuries after restrictions on its trade were broken with the downfall of the Hittite Empire around 1200 B.C. (Edwards et al., 1973:513–14; 1975:518.) The first European paper mills were operating in Spain in the 1100s, but there was no regular paper industry until the 1300s in Italy, where waterwheels were used to operate mechanical beaters (Braudel, 1967/1973:295). In the same vein, it is of no real imporatnce if Phoenicians sailed around Africa two thousand years before the Portuguese, or that the Vikings were the first Europeans to reach Greenland or even America. None of these counted as a socially real "discovery," because none occurred in a social context that could sustain its importance. Particular events recede in importance in this scheme. The fact the Chinese fleets under Admiral Cheng Ho reached Africa in the 1420s, and could even have circumnavigated Africa and opened up the route to Europe if they had not been called back, does not present us with a "crucial turning point." The decision of the Chinese Emperor to pull back from sea expeditions does not loom so large when we realize that later governments had plenty of opportunities to rescind the decision; "technological" developments (like all "discoveries") take a long time to develop, and the delay of a few decades means nothing in this time scale. We can be assured it was the larger social context that was missing, that could have sustained this kind of development of the technology of world navigation from the Chinese side.

There are innumerable further examples. A French doctor described the use of natural gas in 1618, two centuries before gas-lighting came into use; the electric telegraph was proposed on the basis of magnetic needles in 1635, two hundred years before Oersted's experiments (Braudel, 1967/1973:323). Newcomen's steam engine was built in 1711, but thirty years later only one existed in England. It was invented, Braudel says (1967/1973:245), "a long time before it

---

12,000 B.C. (Struver, 1971). These isolated, nonreproducing instances merely strengthen the general point.

launched the industrial revolution – or should we say before being launched by it?"

We are further struck by the importance of the social context when confronted by the long delays and periods of stagnation in technologies. European ships, after a series of major improvements in the High Middle Ages, reached a plateau that lasted from the 1400s to the 1800s (Braudel, 1967/1973:316–17); Chinese ships similarly experienced a long period of stagnation, after reaching a size and level of handling that far excelled, and long preceded, the Europeans' (Needham, 1971:509, 695–9). After the printing "revolution" in Europe in the 1400s and the development of the bar press around 1550, the technique remained unchanged until the late 1700s; Braudel (1967/1973:297) remarks that Gutenberg would have felt at home, except for a few minor details, in a print shop three hundred years after his death. Even more extreme than these instances of delay and stagnation are cases where inventions actually go out of use for long periods of time: coined money, for example, which disappeared in China for some six hundred years after the fall of the Han dynasty (ca. A.D. 200). And even in the modern era, when the socioeconomic system puts on continuous pressure for interlocking innovations, there are long periods when particular techniques remain fixed. The automobile is a familiar example; beneath the style changes, the basic engine remains mechanically the same today as it was in the 1920s (when speed records for conventional automobiles were set that have not greatly altered since). Only the automatic transmission has been added (about 1950), and that is not universally adopted or regarded as an improvement. Sahal (1981:110) sums up: "Innovative activity involves as many instances of deadlock as of progress."

To try to pin down exactly when and where an invention occurs is equivalent to asking who ought to make the profit from an invention today. Our sympathies are with the "inventor" because that is the figure around which the individualistic mythology of invention centers. But, in fact, the person who organizes production and makes it economically feasible is more likely to reap the profits than the one who supplied the "original" idea; given that the invention only becomes socially real through this process of development, the economic payoff may actually be more closely tied to social reality than our historical images are. If and when a particular individual is named as inventor depends on specific economic and legal conditions; to speak of the inventor of agriculture, for instance, is absurdly anachronistic. Our history is biased by the fact that our best-known examples of inventions are from a period when these social conditions did elevate individuals into the spotlight: such are the technological heroes like Alexander Graham Bell, or Thomas Alva Edison, who made money on some of his inventions (when he developed and marketed them himself), but not on others (when outmaneuvered by his financiers). With shifts in the scale of industry today, organizational politics has made this kind of individual credit again somewhat historically dated.

If the idea of a discrete invention, then, is a mirage, its traditional opposite, "diffusion," is equally unsatisfactory. All socially successful innovations involve diffusion, at least within some particular society. It is precisely this spread and adoption that makes it a true (i.e., socially real) invention. At the same time, as we have seen, the process of adoption (local diffusion) involves many adjustments and developments that form an intrinsic part of the "innovation" itself (see Sahal, 1981). From a different viewpoint, *this rapid local diffusion is exactly what we mean by a business boom.* We see the process all around us in the recent spread of transistors and silicon chips and subsequently of computers through their application to new economic and technical niches.

Diffusion, then, looks more and more like just another aspect of the social context that produces innovations. Existing theory about diffusion is modeled too narrowly on the idea of discrete and static inventions traveling calculable distances to static units of potential adopters. This does not capture the sociological differences between the diffusion that occurs within the modern capitalist context described above, and the long-range historical pattern that covers hundreds of years and dozens of generations. Diffusion can be fast or slow, depending on the state of the *total* social universe involved. If diffusion is very fast, such as the spread of the horse stirrup in Asia, Europe, and the Middle East after A.D. 500, it becomes impossible to tell where it was first introduced (McNeill, 1982:20). The conventional historical and anthropological notion of diffusion, then, depends on societies' being quite isolated from each other physically but nevertheless establishing some regular means of contact.

What is it, then, that we should conceive of as diffusing? An idea, such as the hearsay that a method of writing existed in Egypt, which allegedly inspired the different writing-systems of the Indus and of ancient China? Or does it require a physical instance itself, as we might imagine horses galloping across the Eurasian continent with stirrups for copy? Both versions are suspect from a sociological viewpoint. Given the embeddedness of technology in a social context, and the fact that technical development and diffusion are always linked in some geographical area, what we need instead is a model of different forms of social organization, including some that include very long-

A theory of technology

distance components. From this viewpoint, the famous (but rather distorted) instances of historical diffusion (e.g., gunpowder, printing) are to be explained not as ad hoc but as results of a particular state of social organization of the "world system" (Wallerstein, Braudel), the "ecumene" (McNeill), or the geopolitical network or world market. Social organization, both local and long-distance, becomes the key to all phenomena of technological change.

The case of military technology

The long-term development of military technology is a convenient example with which to study these themes. Much has been made of the effects of military technology on social organization (including by Weber, 1923/1961:237; see also Collins, 1975:355–64). The expensive bronze weapons and chariots of the Bronze Age fostered a small military aristocracy; the introduction of cheaper iron weapons expanded the size of armies and changed social structure accordingly. The shift to democracy in Athens was partly a result of changes in naval technology that made propertyless citizen rowers militarily indispensable. The development of heavily armored knights was correlated with decentralized feudal landholdings to equip them. Much later, artillery destroyed the nobles' castles and helped replace feudalism with centralized governments. These effects of technology are much better known than its causes.

In many ways military technology is like other forms of technology. It shows the pattern in which a complex of technological innovations feed off each other, both inside and outside the military realm. Usually there is a long, slow development, taking several hundred years or more: some hundred and fifty years in the case of cannon after their introduction in Europe in the 1320s; three hundred years in the case of handguns (McNeill, 1982:80–98, 141–2). During these periods a variety of competing forms of technology existed, along with other ones not yet displaced. Catapults remained superior to European cannon until 1425 (McNeill, 1982:83); and armor plating developed far beyond the earlier chain mail precisely during the period of the gunpowder revolution, feeding off of the growth of metallurgy it had fostered. And all these innovations were preceded by a revolutionary development of the crossbow during 1000–1300. Originally Chinese, it was improved by the introduction of steel and a windlass mechanism to wind it back: in short, typical applications of the medieval machine revolution. In defense against it, armor had already begun to improve (McNeill, 1982:66). Similarly, the field cannon was perfected in the wars between France and Burgundy of 1465–77; it was made smaller and more mobile by casting stronger barrels, and it fired iron cannonballs instead of stones. The result was a cheaper and more reliable weapon that could demolish any stone fortification in a matter of hours (McNeill, 1982:87–91). But although this cannon made the castle obsolete, it was quickly matched by a new type of fortification: the loosely packed sloping earthwork developed by northern Italian cities in the 1520s. This proved impregnable (although very expensive), and brought the art of siege warfare to a standstill for several centuries.

The rhythm of offensive and defensive counterweapons is thus similar to the challenges that industrial technology produced for itself in the form of bottlenecks and other problems. Moreover, military technology also depended on developments in nonmilitary fields. This rise of the armored knight, for example, took some six hundred years (500 B.C.–A.D. 100) of slow breeding in Iran of a large horse capable of supporting an armored warrior. This in turn required a shift in agricultural techniques, feeding horses with planted alfalfa rather than, as before, merely allowing them to graze (McNeill, 1982:18–19).

Military technology, like every other, is part of a larger economic and social complex. Economic conditions precede particular technical innovations (although, of course, these economies need not have the particular form of market capitalism out of which Weber took his examples). This dependence explains both the long lags found in the adoption of inventions and anticipations, and the periods of stagnation, as well as outright resistance to military inventions.

The heavily armored horse-knight was not adopted in China, for instance, despite its appearance there around 100 B.C. (McNeill, 1982:20). Its value was not great, given the countervailing development of powerful crossbows, which could easily penetrate existing armor; moreover, agricultural conditions in China did not favor horses (or animals in general), and hence they were expensive and hard to acquire. They remained luxury items, matters of status and curiosity but not of military importance. Nor did the Romans adopt armored cavalry to any extent. Their military system was organized around centrally administered legions, and perhaps there was explicit recognition that the heavy investment in supporting armored knights, especially according to the Iranian manner of assigning land to each, was antithetical to centralized control. This interpretation is bolstered by the fact that the small cavalry units the Romans did raise were paid in cash out of a central treasury.[4]

---

[4] The geopolitical situation was relevant here. Although the Roman and Iranian em-

A theory of technology

Military inventions were often resisted because they threatened the stratification of existing military classes. Weapons differ in their relative expense and in the collective or individual nature of their use (see Collins, 1975:357–9). The crossbow, like the handgun after it, was reviled by the European aristocracy, and efforts were made to ban both of them from warfare according to rules of honor. Even the Pope intervened, declaring in 1139 the use of the crossbow against Christians to be cruel and inhumane (McNeill, 1982:68). The argument from inhumanity was specious, given the brutality of knightly warfare (see Keegan, 1977:79–116). The real issue was one of stratification. At the very time an aristocracy was crystallizing on the basis of monopolizing the practice of arms, it was being challenged by plebeian warriors who could kill their social betters, and from a distance, without risking themselves in hand-to-hand combat. Nevertheless, in these instances the social resistance was gradually overcome by the superior power of those who adopted the new weapons. Crossbows proliferated in naval warfare, especially in the fleets of Genoa, a commercial city-state with no cavalry-aristocracy to impede it. (In China, by comparison, the challenge perhaps never existed; armies were centrally supplied after the showdown wars, after 350 B.C., of the pre-Han Warring States, and the crossbow was their principal weapon.) The spread of crossbows into land warfare was slowed primarily by their expense; it took considerable consolidation of state finances to arm and support troops of this sort, despite their superiority on the field of battle whenever they could be mustered.

The development of handguns went through the same series of obstacles. In addition, their adoption had to wait until improvements finally made them superior to crossbows, the earlier machine-weapon. The demonstrated military superiority of the Spanish infantry, which became armed with muskets around 1500, finally led to the musket's general adoption, although the cavalry clung to its social superiority in France and Germany for several centuries thereafter (McNeill, 1982:94). The experience of Japan tells us something of the conditions under which the social reaction can be successful in turning back the technological tide. Guns were introduced into the civil warfare of the 1500s, despite opposition from the samurai to plebeian warriors and the methods of regimentation that went along with them (Perrin, 1979). The armies of Nobunaga, Hideyoshi, and Tokugawa, which eventually unified the island, were successful

pires fought along their common frontier for some six hundred years, it constituted a relatively stable border, at the limits of the practical logistics of both empires. Thus, military competition did not give rise to technical imitation, unlike in other instances.

87

above all because they were able to make the technological transition. The introduction of the guns came from Portuguese and Dutch sailors, but with the usual process of further improvements during their diffusion (Perrin, 1979:17). Then, after the consolidation of Tokugawa power in the early 1600s, the samurai ethos reestablished itself. The wearing of swords (two of them) was carefully upheld in sumptuary regulations, whereas guns were degraded as plebeian and eventually all but forgotten. Special social conditions were involved in this triumph of conservatism. Although the status ideal that was exalted was that of the personally armed samurai, it was enforced by a centralized state that had successfully destroyed the feudal system.

We have here a case of something like the "second feudalism" in Europe, with an absolutist state enforcing and elaborating older status distinctions as part of a system of courtly controls. (The Tokugawa regime had numerous such controls, including its extensive use of ritual, enforced educational attendance for the nobility, and the like.) Thus although there was both a centralized bureaucratic government, of the type that in Europe brought in the gunpowder-equipped standing army, and an extensive commercial development in Japan at this time, neither favored the new military technology. The explanation must be found in the overriding importance of geopolitical circumstances. Once unification was achieved and the immediate attempts to conquer Korea proved unsuccessful, Japan embarked on a policy of isolation. This was made possible by its geographical position: not only its natural defenses as an island but its proximity to societies that also were without a booming military technology. As we shall see in other cases, this kind of military stagnation can be feasible for many centuries, in the absence of challenges in the local geopolitical environment.

The history of guns offers many opportunities to compare the conditions for innovation, as well as for lags and periods of stagnation. We have already noted that guns, like all weapons, are part of a social and economic complex. In isolation, they are worth relatively little. This was especially true in the early period, when gunpowder was used as little more than an adjunct to the bombs and flames used in sieges, both offensively and defensively. In the Mongol conquest of south China (1258–77), catapults and other traditional "artillery" were far more significant (Grousset, 1953:231–3), even though the Mongols were instrumental in spreading the use of gunpowder from the Chinese (who had discovered it around A.D. 900), and soon after introduced it to the West. For the Mongols, the economic infrastructure of metallurgy and all that it took to support it did not exist. This does not imply that they were technologically backward; in the technical organization of troops, they were at the forefront, establishing clear and centralized chains of command, capable of coordinating extremely large armies (by the standards of the time) over long distances. This was done on the basis of light horses, leather armor, and bows and arrows (not the more expensive crossbows); but the effect of organization was that their massed volleys of arrows were as devastating as the guns of much later days. The Mongols' organizational capacity was also shown in their extensive use of catapult-like machinery (operated by foreign technicians). But all this could be done on the basis of existing economic arrangements, which, proving satisfactory for their purposes, obviated the need to press further with guns. In any case, the Mongols could not wait the several hundred years of development necessary to make these weapons effective; by the time that length of time had elapsed, the Mongol empire had already disintegrated for conventional geopolitical reasons.

The question remains why the Chinese did not develop gunpowder weapons earlier. The basic chemical technology was already present; the necessary economic infrastructure was in existence in the 1000s and 1100s, indeed to a greater degree in China than anywhere else in the world at the time. Chinese metallurgy in particular involved large-scale ironworks, operating under government orders and with abundant sources of raw materials (McNeill, 1982:26–33). Again, the social and geopolitical factors took control. For the Sung dynasty (960–1279), with all its prosperity, was strongly pacifist in sentiment. Although there were threats from nomads to the north and northeast, these were successfully dealt with for more than a century by the method of buying alliances among the tribes to counter other tribes. Eventually the policy failed, as barbarian coalitions formed, adopted Chinese-style military and civil organization, and took first north China (the Jurchen regime, 1127), and then all of China in the Mongol conquests of the following century. But these enemies did not pose a threat by technological innovation and, indeed, for a long period did not appear to pose any substantial threat at all. As is often true in the geopolitical sphere, power shifted in sudden tipping-points as coalitions were formed, not by a steady increment of threat. The Sung state, the largest and richest in the world, had little reason to engage in an arms race, and the social interests of the Confucian gentry were best served, in their own lifetimes, at least, by their maintaining strict superiority over the military. China's relative geopolitical isolation thus made possible a stratification system oriented to civilian and commercial but not military development.

Guns were in fact developed in China, but at a slow pace – even slower than the long period in which European guns were made effective. The difference is thus one of degree. The first record of a gun in China is from 1322, six years after the first known in Europe. This was during the Mongol dynasty, and there was some small development thereafter. One might say the Chinese world lost its lead by delaying so long during the previous four centuries. But there were also comparable periods of stagnation in the West, after guns had reached a certain plateau. Here again, social and economic causes were responsible. The siege gun perfected during 1465–77 underwent only marginal improvements until the 1840s. Similarly, muskets remained largely the same from the late 1600s until 1840 – except for the substitution of more reliable flintlocks for matchlocks around 1710 (McNeill, 1982:87, 98, 141–2). European naval warfare also hit a plateau; after a revolution in sailing design and techniques from 1250 to 1350 and the introduction of cannon on board in the late 1400s, there was no further development until the steamship and the metal hull in the mid-1800s (McNeill, 1982:99–104).

These weapons required and fitted into a particular form of social and economic organization. The operation of a fleet required the amassing of substantial provisions; it thus was an even bigger investment than an army, which under the logistics of the time tended to live off the land it was marching through. The capacity to expand a navy, and to develop it technologically, had to wait for a larger period of economic boom, and for a privileged position within the world geopolitical lineup that made military investment profitable. The Spanish infantry, with its heavy investment of new muskets in the 1500s, represented what could be done by the wealthiest state of its time; stagnation set in when states, having raised the costs of armies to a new level by the general diffusion of the new technology, could not afford to push it farther. On a smaller scale, the standardization of arms, which had taken place in the 1600s with the introduction of coordinated drill procedures, provided an obstacle to easy and frequent experimentation with new weapons. Different firing mechanisms necessitated wholesale revision of battlefield routine. Flintlocks were available, for instance, about 1615, but the clumsier matchlock held sway for another hundred years: partly because a whole new form of drill would have to be instituted, and partly because of its greater expense (McNeill, 1982:141).

The superiority of European armies over Oriental ones became clear only after the late 1700s. Portuguese cannon destroyed a far larger Moslem fleet off India in 1509 with long-range fire (at two hundred yards), and some important victories were won over the

A theory of technology

Ottomans during 1593–1606 by the use of disciplined infantry gunpower (McNeill, 1982:101). But in fact guns had diffused to the Middle East and to India at about the same time they appeared in Europe. The Moslems had cannon in the 1300s and 1400s and destroyed the walls of Constantinople in 1453 by forging the largest siege-cannon yet seen (Braudel, 1967/1973:286). Relatively up-to-date cannon were found among the Mughals in India after 1525, and in Iran in the 1590s (McNeill, 1982:95). The difference was that the Europeans alone went through the larger social and economic transformation that made the new military technology effective.

Partly this was a matter of sheer economic resources, the wealth to support a large and well-equipped army and navy with the necessary metals and chemicals. This factor was to be a drag upon European armies as well, until the industrial revolution massively changed the scale of such resources. Even before then, though, European armies manifested a superiority that had more to do with their organization than the weapons they used. As indicated, the development of infantry armed with muskets went along with the introduction of systematic drill (McNeill, 1982:125–35). Given the general unreliability of aim and of firing mechanisms, guns were effective only if fired in unison. Since they took considerable time to reload, armies were organized into ranks firing in staggered order. Dutch armies in the 1590s introduced systematic firing-and-reloading drills, along with marching in step, which made for much better discipline in battle. Troops could now be maneuvered according to officers' strategy, instead of merely unleashed into melees, as were Swiss pikemen who were uncontrollable once a battle had begun. The "organizational technology" of military drill spread by diffusion and emulation, just as the hardware itself did.

Within Europe, the relatively rapid diffusion of techniques among nearby states negated any permanent advantage of one over another. Overseas, where the greater distances and different traditions of adaptation to local military conditions prevailed, European arms were able to rack up impressive conquests. The Spanish conquests of Mexico and of Peru were carried out with tiny armies of a few hundred men. But their superiority was not merely in their guns – which at these dates, the early 1500s, were not overwhelmingly effective. The Spaniards played on dissensions among the Indians, and made alliances in the traditional manner, tipping the balance with the weight of their superior organization and the psychological effect of their weapons and especially of the epidemic diseases that accompanied their incursions. Their enemies, moreover, were much poorer and

91

more primitive societies, with total populations and resources far below the level of a European state, hence not comparable to the sustained efforts the Spaniards could make.

In India, the situation was different. Here Europeans confronted civilizations of approximately their own level. Indian armies were equipped with cannon and often with muskets; the French and British troops that began the conquest of India in the late 1700s were generally little superior in firepower, if at all. Moreover, the numbers of European troops were frequently minuscule, hence they always operated in alliance with native troops. The major advantage was sheerly organizational. What European officers introduced was their methods of drill and hence of concerted battlefield discipline. It was this that enabled them to defeat far larger and well-armed Indian forces. Moreover, the Indian soldiers had a reputation for ferocity and a well-developed military tradition; it is mythical to assume that a pacifist India was caught napping. But the military tradition of India was its weakness, precisely because it honored individual exploits of arms in a grand melee of forces. The huge armies, complete with elephants, that the Indians were able to muster were liabilities in the field, incapable of maneuvering and prone to disorganized panic in the face of much smaller numbers of European-trained troops. Frequently the British or French merely supplied the officers, who reorganized native troops. These units had such great organizational superiority over the traditional Indian troops that they soon acquired a reputation for invincibility, which in turn became a psychological weapon ensuring their success (Mason, 1979:39–60). Their victory, in short, was that of one social system over another, not a superiority of technologies.[5]

---

[5] After new industrial technologies were applied to weaponry after 1840, the superiority of European weapons on colonial battlefields tended to grow as well. But this is a matter of degree. The British army introduced a series of new rifles throughout the late 1800s and early 1900s, each more powerful, longer-ranged, and more accurate than the last. Native enemies, now confined largely to the Himalayan frontier, nevertheless acquired "modern" weapons, if only about a generation behind, through the apparently universal process of military diffusion that more advanced countries are never able to prevent. But the major weakness of the Afghan and other hill tribes was essentially organizational and economic. They remained undisciplined mobs with chaotic supply systems, drawing on relatively small populations and weak economic resources. The importance of these is shown by the experience of the Europeans' arms when they confronted the larger, more bureaucratic, and wealthier societies of China and Japan. Despite momentary technical superiority, their advantages in troop discipline or in supplies were rarely so great; thus although inroads were made in China, neither it nor Japan was ever conquered by the West, until World War II, when the defeat of Japan was that of one industrialized nation by others. The modern Japanese conquest of China was a matter of geopolitical more than technological weakness, showing the vulnerability

A theory of technology

Who innovates?

What, then, can be said about the places where inventions originate, and about the relative weight of long-distance diffusion as against locally circumscribed processes of development?

From the military cases, we see that inventions can occur at centers of civilization as well as on the periphery. Ironworking began in eastern Anatolia about 1500 B.C., and horseback riding emerged in central Asia (after fragmentary instances elsewhere) around 800 B.C.: in both cases, in areas of little economic development or military importance. What these areas did have was simply the right geographical location for the necessary natural resources: ease of access to iron deposits, or plentiful grazing land and abundance of animals. In general, such factors always enter into the development of any technique. *But the crucial aspect of the development, its being made "socially real" by becoming part of a form of organization, generally seems to happen in areas of greater geopolitical importance.* Thus, horseback riding became a military technique when combined with mounted bowmen (bows, of course, had existed since the Mesolithic period, ca. 8000 B.C.). This step was taken by the Assyrian army in the 700s B.C., the largest and most aggressive army in the world, which just then was creating the first multiheartland empire in the Middle East (McNeill, 1982:14–15). The technique apparently diffused quickly to the steppes, where it was perfected and then used against the Assyrians and other civilizations – which is to say, the nomads who had first learned to ride horses did not make a military innovation out of the technique but only acquired it on the rebound.

In general, then, although elements of innovations may occur because of the geographical particularities of where certain natural resources are most easily available, it appears that the geopolitical centers are where they become organized into effective military technologies. The same is true in the case of guns.[6]

We can see now that "diffusion" patterns are structured by geopolitical organization. Sometimes the "diffusion" is of the local sort that goes more properly under the name of "competitive emulation" – or, as we might say, an arms race. Thus there was a period of consider-

of a divided land of warlords and political factions against a unified marchland enemy.

6 Geographical resources can also limit technical developments. As noted, heavily armored knights did not develop in China, partly because the agricultural economy was not suited to feeding large horses. Similarly, chariot warfare was of little use in the hilly terrain of Greece (Snodgrass, 1980:73–4; McNeill, 1982:10). Its diffusion there was thus limited, although the prestige associated with it motivated the local chief to own a chariot he could use to ride in ceremoniously, although he would have to dismount in order to fight.

able technical innovation in ships in the eastern Mediterranean beginning during the Persian/Greek wars and reaching its height during
the wars among the Hellenistic successor states to Alexander's empire (Foley and Soedel, 1981). Galleys expanded from open ships with
single rows of oars, to triremes (three banks of rowers, with oars one
above another or multiply manned), and then to quadriremes and
quinqueremes. At the height of the arms race, 320–250 B.C., there was
an escalation to seven, thirteen, or even sixteen banks, culminating in
gigantic (and clumsy) ships of twenty, thirty, or even forty banks.
Each expansion increased the speed of the galleys and hence their
military effectiveness in ramming, as well as the numbers of troops
for boarding. These increases demanded corresponding improvements in the hull design and other engineering developments. The
escalation of naval-warfare technology led to the development of new
artillery of the torsion catapult type, which could be mounted on
ships, and thus led to a kind of long-range artillery duel fending off
the earlier tactics of ramming and boarding. At the same time, engines for siege warfare and defense were also perfected (Adcock,
1957:58–61).

All this is remarkable because Greco-Roman civilization generally
had a rather low level of technological innovation in the civilian economy (Finley, 1973:146–7). The example shows that innovation can be
sector-specific, and need not involve a societywide boom. There is
innovation in command economies, too; the pressure of the market is
not a necessary factor. But there is something analogous to the market in the military sphere: that is, an active period of military competition among rivals that are relatively well matched and hence not
capable of overwhelming competition at a single stroke. This allows
the time period for the successive technological improvements of an
arms race. Balance-of-power situations may be crucial in all such
innovations.[7]

Geopolitical competition may also take a capitalist form, however.
This was the situation in Italy during the arms race of the late Middle
Ages and the Renaissance; not only was there a development in
crossbows, ships, and subsequently in artillery, guns, and fortifica-

---

[7] Jack Goldstone (1983) has argued that geopolitical competition alone is not a sufficient condition for technological innovation, however. The states of India during
many periods, Spain after 1600, the Austro-Hungarian Empire, all faced long-standing geopolitical rivalries and shifting borders but were nevertheless conservative,
even in military technologies. Goldstone argues that sheerly external geopolitical
pressures may have innovative effects, but *internal* geopolitical problems of maintaining control within a "centrifugally explosive state" (i.e., an ethnically divided
one) fosters the drive to maintain control by a conservative domination of ideology
and economy, which stifles innovation.

tions, but warfare was carried out as a kind of business enterprise by professional mercenaries (McNeill, 1982:73–8). *Condottieri* (the word means "contractor") contracted to raise troops for specific tasks and short time-periods, offering their services among a market of city-states and princes. Here the geopolitical situation actually was organized as a military market. Military innovations were thus doubly emphasized, by two superimposed forms of competition.

The obverse side of this formula is that technological stagnation – whether in the form of long delays in using "anticipations," or of a static plateau once a technique is developed – occurs whenever this kind of geopolitical competition is absent. Thus the stagnation of military technology of China after 1300, as well as of India and the Moslem world after the introduction of cannon in the 1400s, is probably due to the extent to which they were insulated from military rivals with more advanced technologies. There was no arms race in China during the Ming dynasty (1368–1644) because there was no serious military threat. Even though there was an eventual conquest by the Manchus at a time of domestic breakdown, this was in the form of a threat from familiar northern "barbarians," themselves lacking in technology other than what they could imitate from China. Geopolitical isolation was responsible for stagnation of military technology.

The long-term perspective

The question of technology needs to be put in long-term and world-wide perspective. We have already noticed some lengthy sequences of development: some 700–800 years from the discovery of gunpowder in China in the 800s until the plateau of European gunnery reached in the 1500s and 1600s; or the growth of Chinese nautical technology from the late Han to the massive 1,500-ton vessels of the 1400s (Needham, 1971:509). Within these centuries, of course, there may have been crucial takeoff periods, such as occurred about 1300–1500 for the cannon. But the long sequence cannot be overlooked. This is equally striking in the agricultural revolution of medieval Europe, a long period from around A.D. 500 to 1000, which saw the introduction of the wheeled moldboard plow, horse teams with harness, the horseshoe, new crops (legumes), and crop rotation (Whyte, 1962). There were also long sequences of improvements in tools and metallurgy in China (Needham, 1964), which, with the additional time for their diffusion and adaptation in Europe, could cover more than a thousand years. Still earlier, the series of developments that made up the neolithic revolution culminating around 6000 B.C. may well have spread over several thousand years.

Economics

Fernand Braudel, certainly a proponent of the *longue durée* (although perhaps not quite of these proportions), argues for a picture of technological history as gradually accelerating in speed and scale (Braudel, 1967/1973). He points out that developments moved very slowly until the late 1700s, or even half a century later, when capitalism finally achieved a critical mass to sustain rapid and pervasive innovations.[8] We have a problem, then, analogous to that of when we shall say capitalism began. Was it the 1770s, as advocated apparently by Braudel, by Schumpeter, who makes capitalism hinge on entrepreneurs operating in a developed credit market, and by Rostow, who calls this the "takeoff into sustained growth"? Or shall we say the 1500s, a period agreed on by Marx, Weber, and Wallerstein? But a case can also be made for a development stretching to the 1100s, the revolution of the High Middle Ages, as discussed in Chapter 3 (see also Macfarlane, 1978). The problem is compounded because each technological "revolution" draws upon the one that went before. The industrial technology of the late 1700s goes back in an unbroken chain to innovations of the previous hundred years at least, and these in turn were fostered, as Weber points out, by capitalist market pressures and resource problems of previous expansion. This takes us back to the 1500s, a period with such convenient "revolutionary" emblems as the Reformation and the ocean voyages establishing the modern world economy. But the preceding two centuries were precisely the period of the military revolution, with its tremendous impetus to metallurgy, and those overlap with the nautical revolution that began around 1250, and without which later expansion would have been impossible. This also pushes us back into the middle of the medieval machine revolution and its surrounding economy (which, I have argued, especially resides in the monastic economy), the starting point of which brings us into the latter part of the medieval agrarian improvements, which stretch back to A.D. 500. Add to this the influx of Chinese techniques, some of which have a history beginning in the Han dynasty, and we arrive at a conception of Eurasia in continuous technological change for the last 2,000 years, or for 1,400 (or, to put it conservatively, 1,000) years in the West.

Almost any slice of this is a very long time-period, which raises a serious problem with the mechanism of change. When this many generations take part in technological development – even holding to

[8] Braudel may overstate this acceleration, however. His study comes to an end in 1800; but if one examines the following century, one still finds typical periods of fifty to a hundred years to develop a product such as the automobile, the steel furnace, or even the computer – which has a history stretching back to the calculating machines of the mid-1800s.

the narrowest view of the industrial revolution as a phenomenon of the 1700s (which gives us at least three generations) – we are forced to ask, What forces acting on real human beings in their own lifetimes can produce phenomena that sustain themselves far beyond what they can foresee? We cannot invoke the kinds of mechanisms that sustain traditions over long time-periods, because the problem here is exactly the opposite. It is a mechanism of tradition-breaking, but extending over equivalent time-scales. The very existence of such patterns should warn us to abandon the idea of tradition as a force to be taken for granted, even in agrarian societies. Rather, one might say, if things stay the same it is because they are enforced by specific social interests, just as innovations are. It is the balance between these different interests that counts, not the necessity of very special circumstances to break up the otherwise normal "cake of custom."

We have already seen that it does not take capitalism (in the modern sense) to bring about innovation, even in rapid-fire periods (such as the Hellenistic arms race). An even earlier period had what Renfrew (1976:230) calls a "prehistorical arms race" as bronze daggers spread throughout the ancient Aegean. There may well be different social mechanisms of technological innovation in different historical periods. I will explore this briefly in what follows, separating out the innovations of tribal societies, command societies, and modern capitalism. At some higher level of abstraction, to be sure, we may find some more basic principles. One of these must certainly be a structure that makes it possible for innovations produced under one social system to provide a basis for innovations in systems of a different historical type.

Tribal societies

We are used to regarding tribal societies as the savage periphery, stagnant and immobile until inundated by an exploitative contact with more advanced societies. Even if we admit that they too have a continuing history, we generally do not see this in terms of technological innovation. Yet this cannot always have been true.[9] At one time tribal societies were the only locus of technological develop-

---

[9] In fact, we have grossly overstated the stasis of tribal societies even for the period in which they have been known by Western anthropologists. Such societies have been changing continuously throughout the last few hundred years; it is only that we have made a deliberate effort to discount this, because we ourselves have been the causes of much of this change. The process of subtracting out modern change leaves us with an artificial conception of a pristine society that never existed, and blinds us to the importance that intersocietal contact in general – what I call (later in this chapter and in Chapter 11, "Weber's Theory of the Family") the "geopolitics of tribal societies" – has always had on innovation.

ment. They produced a series of revolutions in many different parts of the globe. We may notice the following:

First, the *primitive revolution,* although it is straining the term to speak of revolution for a process that may well have taken half a million years or more. It included the discovery of the most basic tools (stonecutting implements), energy sources (fire), wild food sources, use of wood and animal materials, and communication by symbolic language, all of which was in place by 500,000 B.C. Better to skip over this with only the reminder that very long time-spans could well be involved (though our ignorance may hide shorter bursts). If, in fact, this was the slowest and most drawn-out "revolution" of all, it suggests a possible principle: *The smaller and more spread out the populations, the longer it takes for innovations.* The reason is that diffusion and competition would be least intense under these circumstances, and these are, by hypothesis, the prime mechanisms of innovation. Each tribe is a little self-contained and unthreatened Ming dynasty in itself.

The *neolithic revolution* is best known for its first widespread instance, in Mesopotamia around 6000 B.C. Its "discoveries" included the systematic gathering and cultivation of food: barley, wheat, and corn horticulture with digging sticks; herding goats, sheep, pigs, cattle; new "manufactured" materials of cotton and wool fibers, as well as clay fired into ceramics; the working of copper, the first metal; and the first machines (the potter's wheel and the loom).

The social effects of the neolithic revolution are well known; they include the increase in population, the shift to sedentary conditions, increased complexity of kinship networks, and many other social features that go along with the existence of a surplus and the possibility of stratification (see Lenski, 1966). On the causal side, there is a tendency to ad hoc explanations. The neolithic revolution is considered to have been brought about by climatic changes; with the receding of the Ice Age and the drying of the climate, uplands turned into deserts and forced people down into the river valleys. This also led to the gradual extermination of the large game animals and hence a pressure of starvation forcing technological change. Similar scenarios have been proposed for Mesopotamia and for Mexico.

As already noted, this cannot be the whole story, because the knowledge of plant cultivation was already available many centuries before it became the basis of the economy (Cohen, 1977). We may have, in fact, a typical pattern in which diffusion itself is the source of innovation. Scattered knowledge of cultivation would have been applied as populations became more concentrated (through the climatic changes or otherwise) and, in the process of spreading from one group to another, would have been changed and developed.

The climate explanation cannot be a full one, because, among other reasons, the neolithic breakthrough was made in many different places and in different ways (Edwards et al., 1970:90–6; McNeill, 1963:26–34).[10] The melting of the polar ice cap in the last ice age (Pleistocene) affected the climate of Europe and the Middle East during 10,000–8300 B.C., and somewhat later that of North America (7000–5000 B.C.). But this could not have affected the apparently independent development of rice culture in southeast Asia (ca. 4500 B.C.), or of other local varieties of horticulture in the Andes region (2000s B.C.) or in Melanesia (3000s B.C.). These many independent developments should not surprise us. As Cohen (1977) points out, it is hardly possible that hunters-and-gatherers should not have observed the varieties of edible wild plants and their patterns of propagation; and in fact seeds were stored by paleolithic peoples, presumably as food, but could easily have been available for planting.

The different neolithic breakthroughs were in fact different technological innovations, since each related to the special problems and opportunities of local environments (Flannery, 1973). Wheat in Mesopotamia had to be cultivated by a different method than corn in Mexico (which itself had many varieties, based on hybridization in different locales). Quite different again was the cultivation of root crops (potatoes) in the cooler Andes region, of rice in east Asia, and of tree fruits (breadfruit, bananas, coconuts) and yams in Melanesia. Different kinds of animals were domesticated (llamas in South America, turkeys in Mexico, chickens and pigs in Melanesia, cattle in the Middle East), each requiring their own special techniques, according to wild breeds locally available and the food that could be used to domesticate them.

It is also clear that paleolithic cultures were neither stagnant nor impervious to environmental influences. Stone implements show quite different styles, including important developments in many parts of the world from crude manufactures to finely chipped and flaked ones (such as the successive advances in Europe labeled Aurignacian, 40,000 B.C., Solutrian, 20,000 B.C., or Magdalenian, 13,000 B.C.; or the well-shaped spear points that appear in Mexico about 12,000 B.C.), and eventually to advanced grinding techniques (Semenov, 1964). What possible impetus there may have been behind these innovations has not received as much attention as the more

[10] See footnote 3 to this chapter.

spectacular neolithic inventions, but they show us that a theory must encompass more than just one factor of glacial retreat and climatic desiccation. Why, indeed, should there be a special importance in the most recent retreat of the glaciers, rather than earlier interglacial periods (which have occurred at least half a dozen times during the existence of paleolithic peoples, at intervals of forty thousand years)? The same kind of question arises in the case of the mesolithic innovations – the development of bows, fishing, and boats, which took place in various areas around the ninth millennium B.C. Again, each different environment had its own potential (and perhaps impetus) for innovation. Thus the paleolithic people of late Pleistocene northern Europe were specially adapted to hunting reindeer, and hence were not positioned to move toward horticulture when plant cover reappeared after the receding of the glaciers.

Paleolithic peoples, far from being seen as stagnant, should be regarded as a race of pioneers. Their long history involved innumerable migrations that eventually led them over almost the entire globe. Nor should migrations be regarded, in the conventional fashion, as merely bringing techniques from elsewhere; more importantly, the movement itself would have been responsible for many innovations. Boats, for instance, had to be devised for the colonization of Australia around 40,000 B.C. – a time far preceding the rise of more familiar mesolithic fishing cultures – just as much later the neolithic peoples who colonized Oceania had to develop an advanced nautical technology.

We notice throughout the long tribal period the familiar features of technological innovation in more recent times. Small, anonymous gains there surely were, along with long lags and anticipations. Different technologies must have fed off each other. Pottery must have developed along with the potter's wheel, which no doubt influenced other wheels including such machines as pulleys; and copper could hardly have been smelted without some advances in receptacles, such as those provided by the new pottery, and in firing techniques common to both. The simultaneous cultivation of crops and animals probably implies the use of feeding as a new control device, which could have then been extended to keeping animals merely by grazing. The canoe and fishing could easily have gone together, and the innovation of chipped stone spear-points, together with bone hooks, could have been an impetus behind both; primitive nets would have been made possible by the new fibers, and woodworking (for making boats) would have improved with metal implements.

The overall impression one gets from the neolithic revolution is that innovation does not seem to depend critically on new ideas. "Seed" ideas may well be widely available in every society, much like germ pools, which usually survive unnoticed and only break out into diseases when health defenses break down. And the existence of prior technologies always provides a starting place for subsequent spin-offs and transfers. Movement into new environments, as well as climatic changes (which, of course, had gone on long before the end of the Pleistocene), and population buildups (Renfrew, 1976) all would have provided frequent impetus to innovation. A significant question, then, may be what causes innovations to cease, as much as what makes them happen. Social interests must have brought about the triumph of conservatism, just as other interests at various times would have pushed for innovation. We catch a glimpse of this in the long resistance to (or neglect of) full-scale agriculture in both Mexico and Mesopotamia, perhaps because of resistance to its increased work load, greater regimentation and stratification.

I am suggesting, then, that there is a politics of technology, stretching back to its earliest history. There is no simplistic evolution of technical advances, each one eagerly received and building upon the last. There is, in fact, no universal set of stages. Some cultures, like the Chinese, skipped directly from stone to bronze; others, like the Americans, had no wheeled implements, few domesticated animals, and little metal but evolved extremely advanced techniques of construction in stone. Such patterns are readily understood as the result of combinations of local environmental conditions, selective diffusion, and particular patterns of innovation and specialization. We should envision a *geopolitics of tribes*, spread out across very specific landscapes. They lacked, to be sure, the capacity to build conquest empires over one another, but their external contacts influenced their technological patterns in more than a simpleminded process of diffusion. For although they could not conquer one another, they could fight or compete over available resources, and thereby both outbreed one another (given differences among their technologies) or find themselves forced to migrate elsewhere.[11] A third alternative is that

---

[11] Rae Lesser Blumberg (1984a) points out that the neolithic revolutions might not have been so much the spread of innovations as the spread of innovating persons because of the demographic revolution set off by the introduction of horticulture. Formerly nomadic hunters-and-gatherers would have acquired a higher birthrate as women became more sedentary, put on more body fat, and thus reduced the times between births. This, in turn, would have brought about increasing population density and the beginnings of migration and fighting over scarce land. The surrounding hunters-and-gatherers would have been forced, by the military pressure of their horticultural neighbors, to adopt cultivation (if without enthusiasm) in self-defense; and this in turn would set off yet another round of demographic/geopolitical "diffusion" of the technology. This is consonant with archeological evidence (such as the

these geopolitical contacts, under particular conditions not yet well understood, could lead to amalgamation of cultures – in itself a problem of politics that we have only begun to imagine. All of these geopolitical patterns must have had particular consequences for technological innovation; they would have set in motion the mechanisms already noted: innovation through the process of diffusion itself, crossovers and spin-offs bringing together different technologies, as well as mobilizing both conservative and innovating factions in the politics of the time.

Command economies

Our image of agrarian state societies is that they are antithetical to innovation. They are authoritarian, lacking the freedom and the incentives of the market, and legitimated by a traditionalism hostile to novelties. Weber (1916–17/1958:329–43) himself states this theme, arguing that religion and magic stereotype economic activities and inhibit economic rationality. Nevertheless, several considerations make it appear that Weber overstated this point for the sake of contrast to the rationalistic "capitalistic spirit."

For one thing, the agrarian state societies owe their origins themselves to a great technological revolution. This is the so-called urban revolution, first occurring around 4000–3000 B.C. in Mesopotamia and Egypt. It included the development of irrigation, with its considerable increase in the agricultural surplus; the first complex metalworking, in bronze; large buildings and monuments; tools including wedges, levers, pulleys, and oars; and revolutionary developments in transportation including the wheeled cart, the sailing ship, and later the oared galley; and the first writing systems (ideographs written on clay, stone, or shells) and number systems. Moreover, there was a long and continuous development of several such techniques; mathematics, for instance, evolved the use of fractions by about 2000 B.C., capping a thousand years of technological change *within* agrarian societies.

The same centers of civilization produced yet another major revolu-

---

building of fortifications) of the outbreak of widespread warfare, for the first time in human history, in the midneolithic period (around 6000 B.C. in the Middle East). One might argue that somewhat earlier in this process, by around 15,000 B.C., the hunting-and-gathering population had spread fairly evenly over the usable land of the world, in such a way that any further movements would encroach on someone else's subsistence. This puts a "geopolitical" factor at the very beginning of the neolithic revolution. Once again, as we shall see in Chapter 6 on the theory of politics and Chapter 11 on the theory of the family, the importance of geopolitical factors lurks everywhere.

tion, some millennium and a half after the first one, in the form of the iron and animal power revolution around 1500–800 B.C.[12] It included not only the development of iron implements and weapons but an unprecedented combination with animal power. Perhaps the two-wheeled war chariot was instrumental in getting this sequence going. The chariot appeared about 1500 B.C., drawn by horses, the first instance of animal power.[13] It spread rapidly around the Middle East and nearby Europe and central Asia, bringing about major political upheavals on the periphery by its military effectiveness. Around 1200 B.C. we find the camel domesticated for use in North Africa, and the elephant in India: likely cases of innovation by diffusion, as the example of horsepower was applied in different environments. Finally, around 1000 B.C., there is the epochal development of yoked oxen in Mesopotamia, which together with the iron plow greatly transformed the territorial scope of agriculture as well as its productivity. It was

[12] Iron was known a long time before (as early as 300,000 B.C.) but chiefly in the forms of raw ore used for pigments in art and cosmetics and of meteorites (the "thunder-bolts" of mythology), to which were attributed magical and religious significance (Eliade, 1962:21–5; Wertime and Muhly, 1980). Iron was scarcer than gold, exchanging for twice the price of silver and sixty times that of copper in the Middle East around 1400 B.C., and was monopolized as a gift for kings (Edwards et al., 1973:513–14). There is a peculiar *geopolitics* in its rise to widespread use for tools and weapons after 1200 B.C. Knowledge of the smelting and forging of iron (a process very different from the casting of bronze) became common in the mountains of Armenia and eastern Anatolia around 1400 B.C. but was kept secret and local (Forbes, 1950). The Hittite overlords of the area, an imitative Mesopotamian-style kingdom that had arisen in central Anatolia at about the time of the spread of chariot warfare in the 1700s B.C., kept strict control over its trade, which they confined to the traditional pattern of royal treasure. The Hittites in general seem to have been a conservative aristocracy, with no urban settlements beyond military citadels. In the 1300s B.C., they continued to hire chariot specialists from the steppes, even though iron was to prove revolutionary in other hands in creating cheaply armed mass infantry armies (McNeill, 1963:108–9, 135, 138). It was only after the breakup of the Hittite empire in barbarian invasions around 1200 B.C. that the subject ironsmiths began to migrate, whereupon iron spread rapidly throughout the Middle East and Europe. An additional factor in its spread may have been that the same migrations (including the Dorians in Greece) disrupted the Mycenaean sea commerce in copper and tin, creating an incentive to substitute iron for bronze (Wertime and Muhly, 1980). There remain some puzzles, such as why, although cheap iron weapons were rather quickly introduced in Assyria to build up a massive army, the conservative style of cavalry warfare remained dominant in Greece until about 600 B.C. (McNeill, 1963:217–8). We seem to have again a politics (and geopolitics) of technology: The expensive and therefore aristocratic horse warfare may have had explicit conservative support in Greece that was broken down only after considerable maneuvering, with the victory of the iron-armed phalanx and its attendant tendency to democracy.

[13] North Asian pastoralists had horses as early as 2500 B.C., but widespread horseback riding did not appear until well over a thousand years later. Early horse domestication was probably a development of paleolithic hunting of horses for food (Edwards et al., 1970:53, 140; Eberhard, 1977:5).

after this, as we have seen, that the Assyrians extended the sequence to horse-mounted archers, rounding off this series of mutually stimulating innovations. Simultaneous with this sequence came improvements in communications techniques: the invention of papyrus (the first lightweight writing material) in Egypt about 1300 B.C.; the displacing of ideographs by a consonantal alphabet in Syria around 1500 B.C., with vowels added about 800 B.C. in Greece making for maximum flexibility and abstraction.

Thus it can hardly be said that agrarian societies are necessarily technologically stagnant, although, of course, there is no lack of instances where this is so. The long history of agrarian societies in India, for instance, produced little in the way of technological innovations; and there is little in the Middle East and Mediterranean – with the exception of the military inventions of the Hellenistic arms race just discussed – from about 800 B.C. to A.D. 500. Since this is our "classical" period of ancient history, its relative stagnation may perhaps have loomed overlarge in our image of agrarian technology. With the fall of the Roman Empire in the West, however, Europe began yet another period of innovation, already mentioned in Chapter 3: the "agricultural revolution" of A.D. 500–900, which resulted in the improved crops and use of horsepower and hence a great expansion of agricultural productivity, along with a proliferation of rural windmills and water mills with new gear systems that greatly increased their effectiveness over ancient prototypes.

The secret of Easter Island

To find a key explaining agrarian technologi al innovativeness, let us return to the early urban revolution. Certainly the most visible part of this achievement came in the realm of construction. Whereas previous tribal societies had lived in small thatched huts and pit dwellings, we suddenly now find enormous walled cities, palaces, temples, and monuments.[14] The newfound power for large-scale construction also transformed agriculture, by the development of canals

---

[14] A few of the earliest neolithic settlements were sizable towns, such as Catal Huyuk in Anatolia (ca. 6700–5700 B.C.), which covered one-twentieth of a square mile and may have housed ten thousand people; and the walled hamlet Jericho in Palestine (at about the same time), which was about one-third the size (Edwards et al., 1970:309, 499–508). The extent of this early "urbanization" shows that trade and perhaps military factors already could produce concentration in some places. But these constructions are trivial compared to what we find with the command economies. One of the earliest cities of Shang China, for instance (ca. 1500 B.C.), had earthen walls averaging 10 meters in height and 20 in width, enclosing a circumference of some four miles; it is estimated that its construction would have required 10,000 workers for eighteen years (Eberhard, 1977:13–14).

for irrigation; and it greatly facilitated expansion of the scale of societies, with the construction of paved roadways and bridges. Society had suddenly become not only large but, for the first time, visibly imposing.

How does this sequence begin? I suggest that the very dates of the most monumental constructions give us a key. For, in fact, the large scale of construction is very early. The largest pyramids date from the earliest dynasties in Egypt, as does the huge stone Sphinx. Similarly, the most incredible construction project in Chinese history, the Great Wall, was largely built during the late Warring States period, before the rise of the first great centralized dynasty. The massing of huge numbers of workers seems to be the key "invention" underlying all of these.[15] It is a discovery, moreover, that all societies seem to make at the point when the early state is created. We notice similar pyramids in Mexico, built successively by the Olmecs, the Mayans, and their successors; and as emulation of Mexican state prestige spread into the Mississippi valley, cruder earth mounds built by the more powerful tribal chiefdoms. The Mississippi and Ohio valley mounds are smaller, built merely by sheer piling up of earth; the Mexican and Andean civilizations transformed these by adding stone facings. But the building techniques grew up by easy accretions; however marvelous subsequent observers have found the ability of early civilizations to move huge blocks weighing many tons, it was originally a matter of heaping up a solid mound, which only much later was hollowed out inside to any degree. Similarly, in India, the characteristic "beehive" temple shape derived from such solid mounds, which only later acquired rather narrow interior chambers. Egypt, China, and India alike built tombs, temples, and religious monuments by burrowing caves into stone hillsides, again following the path of least resistance. One can see that the initial step was simply to use large numbers of workers to heap up or hollow out natural materials; stonecutting, beams, measurements, and other technical advances would follow naturally as emulation strove to make these constructions still more impressive.

Here, incidentally, I believe we have an answer to puzzles of the type of the "secret of Easter Island." It has often been wondered how

[15] The first step pyramid, about 2700 B.C., was 200 feet high with a base of 413 by 344 feet; it was soon followed by the Great Pyramid of Khufu (Cheops), 450 feet tall and constructed of 2 million stone blocks of some 2.5 tons each. Later dynasties built smaller tombs, and eventually abandoned pyramid building entirely at the end of the Middle Kingdom. The Great Wall of China, the major portion of which was built 350–100 B.C., eventually exceeded 2,000 miles in length (with loops bringing the total to 3,900 miles); the old parts are 25 feet wide and 20 to 30 feet high, with 40-foot towers every 100–200 yards (Needham, 1971:46–55).

primitive tribesmen could have built the huge stone statues on an isolated island two thousand miles off the coast of Chile, and fanciful explanations have been conjectured, usually with a theme of extraterrestrial intervention. In the same vein we have the megalithic monuments spread out across precivilized Europe (ca. 2500–1500 B.C. or even earlier), of which Stonehenge is the most famous example (McNeill, 1963:113–17; Renfrew, 1976:133–82). The mystery is dissipated when we realize that the size of such monuments (the Easter Island statues reach heights of thirty feet) is well within a gradient leading up to the much grander scale of even the smallest pyramids or earth mounds. The tribal societies that reached Easter Island about A.D. 400 were far from primitive, having gone through successive waves of migration across the Pacific, perfecting their nautical technology for large-scale expeditions (Bellwood, 1981). They also achieved the highest degree of political centralization in the Pacific in the kingdoms found throughout Polynesia and in Hawaii. Their ability to carry and set in place these stone monuments seems to be in keeping with the political trend that enabled them to coordinate large numbers of men. And indeed, monuments comparable to those of Easter Island are found throughout Polynesia, including huge pyramid-like temple platforms of earth and stone.

And here may be the important lesson. The earliest constructions seem to be less for practical purposes than simply for their sheer impressiveness. A solid mound is useless as a dwelling, or even as a fortress; it is in the lineage of the great stone faces of Easter Island or the megaliths. They all represent, rather, what can be done by the sheer labor of massed bodies and are probably the first instances in which such large numbers of people had been coordinated. One might even conjecture that the rise of the state itself is simply an extension of this "discovery" – a social technique for coordinating people as a sheer mass, outside of the necessarily smaller and more particularistic linkages of tribal kinship. There is every reason to believe that this was done under religious auspices. The nature of the monuments themselves tends to confirm it. It is also in keeping with this interpretation that the earliest social organization we find in Egypt and Mesopotamia is not yet the conquest state but the temple organizing agricultural production collectively out of its central storehouse.

The whole social and technological revolution that goes under the name of the "urban revolution" or "the rise of the state," then, is best seen as a shorthand for a longer process that begins with religious politics. It is an innovation in religion but not so much an abstract idea as a set of material and social techniques, the development of improved "means of emotional impressiveness." It is this that makes the god of the society its effective externalizing symbol. In this sense, Durkheim's thesis, that religion is the society worshiping itself, should be translated into a series of developments in the *material* emblems used as "religious technology." From drums and masks and carved totems, there is an escalation to monumental stone faces, themselves both more impressive to behold, and impressive for the sheer amount of labor it took to raise them. These developments need not and would not have occurred all at once. Rather, we have a process feeding upon itself, as is typical with technological innovations. Improvements in the technology of religious impressiveness bring more worshipers into the fold, which in turn makes possible still grander projects. Along with the increase in social organization, of course, goes the capacity to use these coordinated hands for economic projects – for collective agriculture, irrigation, and the like; and for political power and eventually, at the end of the sequence, military coercion. Apparently the latter is a development that follows the former, although once military power takes off, it sets in motion a process of expansion and counteremulation that eventually becomes all-determining.[16]

The fundamental technique of agrarian technological innovation, then, may well be the discovery of the use of massed human energy. Once set in motion, the constructions to which it gave rise could result in a long series of changes. Not only the size of constructions but their techniques could develop through the typical emulation of impressiveness in command societies. The spin-offs of this process could then result in technological changes far afield from the original constructions. Massive coordination would have given rise to some form of record-keeping and hence to writing systems; construction tools, to oars; and so forth.

The authoritarianism of a command economy thus is compatible with technological innovation; it does not require the freedom and market competitiveness associated with independent merchants and craftsmen. Our image of technological innovation is perhaps too closely modeled on what we think happened in industrial societies. Thus it is often claimed (e.g., Farrington, 1953) that the slave econo-

---

[16] Thus the rise of the state is not merely a transformation of the "big-man" style of redistributive system found in some horticultural tribes. The fact that the temples of Egypt and early Mesopotamia did take in the harvests and store them to be doled out to the people as needed constitutes some parallel; but I am suggesting that the mechanism that brought about this kind of collective organization – and, incidentally, the monumental buildings that made large-scale stores possible – was different, in the realm of a competitive escalation of the technology of impressiveness.

my of classical Greece and Rome was what inhibited its technological development. My argument, instead, is that conditions of religious and political competitive emulation were central. In this type of society, the importance of the market recedes considerably.

We can see this by examining just how trade took place in command societies. There was the interregional exchange of goods, to be sure. Numerous essential (as well as luxury) products had to be brought from considerable distances: timber from Lebanon for construction in Egypt, for example, or tin from Armenia or even Cornwall to make bronze, as well as silver, gold, ivory, and many other products. But trade was carried out as part of the command system itself (Edwards et al., 1973:190–6). Traders were generally agents of the state, sent out on expeditions to procure particular goods. Sometimes these expeditions simply commandeered their objects, hence differing little from military plunder. Others entered into peaceful exchanges. But this differed from a market in that exchanges were carried out at traditional and fixed rates, rather than by a price interactively set by competition among different buyers and sellers. Typically there is only one buyer and one seller, perhaps both of them political authorities. The grain trade, which was essential for the survival of the Greek city-states, was nevertheless carried out in just this fashion (Polanyi, 1977). Under these conditions, the exchange system (which we cannot strictly speaking call a "market") does not lead to a calculating rationality, nor to the search for cheapening methods of production that Weber described as essential to capitalist innovation. And this was the case even though exchanges were often carried out in money (i.e., in weights of precious metal) as early as the third millennium B.C. (Edwards et al., 1973:389–90; McNeill, 1963:146); money itself does not carry any special significance for economic rationality in the absence of the larger market complex.

It is true that at times something closer to a true "market" did appear. We have records of Babylonian and Assyrian merchants about 1800 B.C., dealing on their own and calculating profits and costs in a modern manner (Edwards et al., 1973:190–6; cf. 381–90, 506–9). And during the Hellenistic period (ca. 325–100 B.C.), there seems to have been a true international market in grain, in which information about prices was gathered at Alexandria and Rhodes and used to direct ships to the ports where the highest prices could be gained (Polanyi, 1977:238–51). But neither of these instances seems to have provoked any wave of technological innovation such as we associate with capitalism;[17] perhaps they were too superficial or short-lived.

17 One possible exception to this statement may be the development of alphabetic

That genuinely independent merchants could appear was because there was, after all, some pluralism of economic units. In addition to the powerful state, temples usually maintained their own properties and hence bought and sold on their own account. And in the patrimonial-bureaucratic form of political organization, the state itself crumbled at its base as its officials managed to appropriate some of its lands or revenue sources for their own uses. Thus, numbers of independent estates might constitute some degree of competitive economy among themselves. The temples were particularly important in generating some economic leverage, since they tended to have a more impersonal organization, freed to some degree from family ties. They also served as primitive banks, places where treasure was kept and offerings made, which could on occasion be lent out. The situation does not yet approximate Schumpeter's definition of capitalism – enterprise carried out with borrowed money – since the money lent out was not itself part of a money market; it did not carry interest, nor could it be lent out many times over in the form of pure credit. But nevertheless the economics of temples (and, later, monasteries), and of the other private estates, provided an element inside command economies that could provide a potential opening toward out-and-out market capitalism.

How, then, did the structure of command economies give way to yet another form of technical innovation? We can collect a number of contributing factors.

1. There is a long, slow process of technological innovation at the center of command economies themselves. This tends above all to manifest itself in military innovations, given the appropriate geopolitical situation; but it also emphasizes works of construction. Some of these are especially important in creating the infrastructure for any extensive market economy: the spread of roads, canals, and bridges that is so characteristic, for instance, of China, especially during the great centralized dynasties (Needham, 1971:1–378).[18] The develop-

---

writing in Syria around 1500 B.C. (Edwards et al., 1973:516–9). This was a considerable improvement over the long series of ideographs used in Egypt, or the cumbersome Mesopotamian cuneiform with its hundreds of characters. The conservatism of the scribes in the command centers was part of their social interest in monopolizing the technique of writing; for them, a system of writing that was difficult to learn only bolstered their social position. The intersticial merchants of Syria, however, had only a purely business interest in writing technique and thus were motivated to provide "laborsaving" and "cheapening" technology in this sphere.

[18] Though it is also carried out in decentralized periods; often monasteries or particular priests are responsible, since building roads or bridging rivers and gorges were suitable tasks for acquiring religious merit (e.g., Needham, 1971:154, 160, 173, 197, 202). The biographies of the famous Tibetan Buddhist monks are full of examples.

ment of such a transportation system has more potential than merely as an infrastructure; for the first phase of the industrial revolution in Europe (and in North America) was itself to a considerable extent a boom in transportation. We see this in the appearance of the stage-coach (regarded by many contemporaries as dangerous and demoniacal [Braudel, 1967/1973:319]) in England in the 1670s, the mail service at about the same time, investments in private turnpikes and canals throughout the 1700s, and, of course, the railways in the 1800s. Wherever a transport construction boom occurred, one would have to conclude, at least one component for a potential capitalist expansion was present.

2. The command economy itself is subject to competitive emulation in the form of military and political struggles, and this has resulted in occasional periods of innovation, even, as already noted, of revolutionary proportions.

3. Religious institutions provide private leverage for market enterprise within the command structure, as does the patrimonial appropriation of state property by officials as private estates. A good example of this is the breakdown of the T'ang "state socialism" into a booming monetary economy in China after A.D. 780 (see Chapter 3).

4. Diffusion of technologies from civilizations to peripheral tribes creates an area in which innovations are likely, by the very fact of diffusion resulting in new applications. This may be part of the reason for the "agricultural revolution" of northern Europe after A.D. 500. Religious organization may be implicated in this as well, since the greatest agent of civilized "diffusion" was precisely the missionary colonization of the north. A different instance is the innovation in military technique that the Mongol coalition achieved around A.D. 1200 outside the borders of China.

5. Diffusion also occurs from one agrarian civilization to another, when geopolitical links among them are established, such as the Mongol "corridor" of the High Middle Ages. Again, the formula applies that *diffusion produces innovation.*

To be sure, there are strong social forces favoring conservatism in a command system. Highly labor-intensive methods may be firmly ensconced, so that they are actually cheaper than the introduction of machinery, especially before the latter was perfected. Thus the technology of inanimate energy sources (or even of animal power) was neglected in China in favor of sheer human muscle power, which was relatively cheap (Braudel, 1967/1973:246–9), and indeed became progressively cheaper with the population explosion after 1650. Economic rationalities of this sort, as well as status interests, probably play a larger role than the "magical stereotyping" Weber mentions.[19]

Capitalist innovation

We have already seen the major social determinants of innovation under modern capitalism. The crucial point is not any particular technological breakthrough, or the oft-cited application of inanimate energy sources or the use of machinery. The "industrial revolution" is a gloss for a set of innovations across a wide front, including chemicals and agriculture as well as machinery (initially run by traditional power sources), and stretching back for at least a hundred years before the perfection of the steam engine and the power loom. The crucial characteristic, as Weber stressed, was an attitude of systematic calculation applied to all economic factors. We can see this very strikingly in the movement to rationalize agriculture, which goes back to the 1600s and achieved its greatest gains before 1750 (Landes, 1969:76). The process involved neither mechanization nor new energy sources but consisted of systematic breeding of livestock and crops, carefully planned rotation, improvement of drainage and fertilizer, elimination of fallow and more intensive cultivation. The motivation behind it was purely economic and followed directly from the enclosures that gave capitalist farmers control over large holdings. This is strictly analogous to the way in which factory machinery gave the manufacturing entrepreneur calculable control over the factors of production.

The driving force thus was the spirit of calculation, brought on by the intensification of the competitive capitalist market. In this perspective, the use of inanimate energy and the development of machinery are just so many applications of this spirit. Their continuous improvements were due to systematic experimentation carried out with an emphasis on precision and measurement. It is when this precision achieved a sufficiently high level – in the development of machine tools with interchangeable parts – that the full power of mass production could be unleashed (Landes, 1969:105–7).

It remains to clear up the relation between modern technology and

---

[19] Though this is consonant with Weber's point (1923/1961:129) that mechanization is favored when there is a pressure for inexpensive techniques of production. Where the older techniques are cheaper, it follows that they would be preserved.

modern science. Weber (1923/1961:232), to be sure, does speak of one of the distinguishing characteristics (among others) of Western capitalism as "rational science and in connection with it a rational technology." Weber does not stress the point, which does not loom large in his scheme, commenting only that "union with science" emancipated production from the bonds of tradition (Weber, 1923/1961:227). But he does admit that most inventions of the 1700s were not made in the scientific manner, mentioning Cartwright's 1785 power loom as one of the first instances of applying scientific theory to technology (Weber, 1923/1961:225–6). The linkage of industry with systematic laboratory science, he says, begins only with Liebig in the 1830s, which "brought capitalism to its full development."

We should beware of making too much of this, or of falling into the facile modern ideology that declares we have evolved a knowledge-based economy. This frequently made assertion, offered without too careful a look at the evidence, operates to justify the massive modern educational system and the expenditures on academic science that accompany it – perhaps laudable enough institutions in their own right, but in fact with relatively little impact on industrial productivity (see evidence in Collins, 1979). The coincidence in time of modern science with technology may well be misinterpreted.

As Landes remarks (1969:61), "If anything, the growth of scientific knowledge owed much to the concerns and achievements of technology; there was far less flow of ideas or methods the other way; and this was to continue to be the case well into the nineteenth century." Even the steam engine, commonly cited as an instance of the application of science, owed relatively little to scientific theory, and none at all after Watt established the principle of the separate condenser in 1769 (Landes, 1969:104). It is true that a number of the inventors of this period were educated men, and Watt had worked as a maker of scientific instruments at Glasgow University. But this connection has not been correctly understood. As Landes points out (1969:62), the entrepreneurs of the period tended to be men of the professional or gentry classes, who deliberately sought apprenticeship to such technicians as weavers or joiners; Watt's father (a prosperous merchant, and son of a mathematics teacher) had been apprenticed to a carpenter-shipwright. This was not downward mobility, although it clearly broke with the status traditions of an aristocratic age; it meant, rather, a deliberate search for technical skills by persons who wished to make successful entrepreneurial developments. Thus came about the observed mixtures of two cultures, in which some scientific theory came along as part of the upper-class education. But this does not show that the theory itself was the crucial addition; Watt's experience with scientific *apparatus* – for example, with the technology that happened to be found in scientific laboratories – was doubtless more important than the rather inchoate science he found there.

There is a crucial Weberian point here: The movement of high-status persons into the sphere of technology marks a shift in social motivations. For low-status artisans have never been at the cutting edge of technological innovation. As we have seen, development into a socially successful technique is what makes an innovation successful, and it has always taken persons with power or economic resources to carry this out. If Schumpeter is right that private empire-building through the deliberate search for technological innovation is the essence of capitalist dynamics, then this shift in the status system of business was a key development.

In general, there is considerable evidence that science and technology are not closely linked, even in the mid-1900s. Studies of citation-chain patterns (Price, 1969) show that technical patents and scientific papers run separate and parallel courses, with only occasional cross-linkages. Each has its own genealogy, so that new technologies derive by increments from earlier technologies, just as new science derives from previous science.[20] The importance of the independent traditions in technology – which precede the scientific ones by many centuries – has generally not received the recognition it deserves.

The so-called scientific industries, such as modern chemicals, pharmaceuticals, and now electronics, may actually be best viewed as organizations practicing large-scale systematic trial and error, in a fashion not qualitatively different from that of earlier, "prescientific" eras. We find metallurgy or brewing, for instance, practicing systematic variation in processes over a period of centuries, resulting in incremental improvements and the gradual evolution of new combinations. Ought we not to entertain the possibility that, beneath the facade of scientifically trained professionalism, modern pharmaceutical labs, for instance, follow the traditional method of systematic experimentation around earlier successes, together with occasional lucky new combinations (such as penicillin) that start off further sequences? And further: The activities even of academic laboratories – which themselves resemble little factories, repeating experi-

---

[20] Thus it is not surprising that historians of technology should turn out to be different persons than historians of science, or that they should have separate and independent scholarly societies.

ments endlessly, with careful measurement of systematic variations – may well owe more to organizational technique than to theory per se. In fact, they are laboratory *factories*.

In this light, it should not surprise us (although it is certainly unconventional to say it) that technology may have always had more influence over science than the other way around. Modern physics would not be possible without a series of improvements in experimental apparatus. The branch of scientific thermodynamics was itself an effort to understand theoretically the processes occurring in the new steam engines; although the science developed elegantly in the French Ecole Polytechnique of the 1820s, it was in England rather than France that the technical innovations themselves continued to be made. Similarly, modern physics feeds off the development of autonomous improvements in electrical apparatus, from the electric generator coils that made possible Clerk Maxwell's mathematical theories to the massive engineering achievements underlying the discoveries in nuclear physics of the 1900s.

The scientific revolution of the 1600s is itself in many ways the result of the prior technological revolution. Let us recall some dates: how a revolution in machinery, gears, and many other areas goes back to the 1200s in Europe; how the first complex machines, mechanical clocks, were produced in a virtual mania during the 1300s; how Leonardo da Vinci's fanciful geared contraptions of the 1490s preceded by some thirty years the first real intellectual achievements of modern science, Copernicus's astronomy and Cardan and Tartaglia's solution to the cubic equation in the 1530s. And these intellectual events remain something like predecessors; the main "takeoff" of the scientific revolution is after 1600, in the mathematical mechanics based on Galileo's experiments, the physics of Torricelli and Huygens, the theoretical treatise of Gilbert synthesizing observations on the magnet and the compass that had been known – and technically applied – for centuries before. But, in fact, Galilean science was largely the application by intellectuals of the technologies that had begun to achieve a new level of precision in this period. The 1600s saw a boom in the business of lens making (eyeglasses had been known since the 1200s, and were in general use in the 1400s), which resulted in the development of the telescope and microscope. Other new instruments became available: the thermometer, the barometer, the air pump, precise weights and measures. It is little exaggeration to say that the scientific revolution was simply the exploration of the theoretical significance of these new instruments. Notice, moreover, that these are the first real precision instruments; they represent an application of the spirit of calculation and systematic measurement that Weber sees as the essence of the new economy.

The history of science has never been written in this fashion, but in principle it should be possible to do so. ("Hard science" is science that uses hardware.) Even in our own day, one might say, the development of new technologies for instrumentation, measurement, and experimental apparatus is a major driving force behind the development of science. Even the content of scientific ideas may be correspondingly shaped. The sociologists of science David Edge and Michael Mulkay (1976) have shown, in a pioneering case study, that differing technical organization of equipment by rival groups in the new field of radio astronomy was a prime determinant of the way in which discoveries were made and of the theoretical interpretation placed on them. Modern sociology of science is only just beginning to appreciate the material organizational basis for the production of scientific ideas.[21]

Conclusion

A remarkable fact seems to be emerging from this overview of the determinants of technological innovation. It appears that innovation is relatively easy, as far as the production of new ideas is concerned. The initial idea itself is rarely the crucial part of any invention, and, indeed, possible ideas seem to be far more widely available than their utilization. It is the social conditions for their sustained development that is more central. This should not be too surprising, given that technological innovations occur largely by incremental extension of previous inventions and by responses to crossovers and problems generated in the process of expansion and diffusion itself. It appears that wherever the social organization is such that enterprisers – whether private entrepreneurs or state or military officials – have the aim of improvement clearly in view, and the motivation and the resources to pursue it over a period of time, then technical innovations will result.

We are used to thinking of technological inventions as a kind of miraculous breakthrough, almost gifts of the gods of chance. This is

[21] This technological influence is not always what one would judge to be good for the intellectual advance of the discipline. For example, the widespread use of computers in sociology and economics has shaped the kind of data that is preferred – in sociology, easily obtainable responses to attitude surveys – and thus tended to limit the theoretical significance of what can be obtained, instead of letting theoretical considerations determine the optimal type of data needed.

almost the opposite of the truth. It follows that whenever there is the social pressure to innovate, solutions will always be found. The possibility of future inventions, at any point in history, always extends to infinity.[22]

[22] An analogous principle applies to intellectual history. Whenever the social conditions exist in which intellectuals are motivated to aim for new discoveries, the discoveries will be made. We can be sure that increasing the numbers of intellectuals – of scholars who need to publish to obtain tenure – or intensifying any other type of motivational system, will bring about a corresponding increase in the amount of discovery. The sheer numbers in the intellectual community, of course, create political problems of recognition and stratification within the field, and this further shapes the kinds of ideas that will be "discovered" (see Collins, 1975:506–23). Although "discovery" by its very nature means finding things that were unknown before, the shape of the unknown is, in fact, to a certain degree predictable.

5

Weber and Schumpeter: toward a general sociology of capitalism

Weber's economic sociology is essentially historical and institutional. It attempts to establish the conditions within which the market economy of modern capitalism can exist, but it does not deal with the principles by which such an economy actually operates. The latter is, of course, the task of economics in the conventional sense: to show the determinants of prices, the quantities of goods produced and services offered, as well as their dynamics and distributions. In this respect Weber represents the split between the German historical economics of his day and the classical and neoclassical economics found outside Germany.

Even today, conventional economics needs the aid of a sociological approach. For current economics, despite its relevance to practical matters and the technical sophistication of its apparatus, is nevertheless far from being able to provide satisfactory answers to its own problems (Leontieff, 1982). It is particularly weak on the dynamic issues of modern capitalism: on the causes of economic growth and downturn, on the fundamental reasons for the business cycle, and especially on the issues of economic inequality that are at the focus of much policy discussion. The failure of conventional economics is one reason for the renewed popularity of Marxist economics, even though Marxism itself has a less than impressive track record of real-world prediction. The parallel is not surprising, in that Marxist and conventional neoclassical economics are intellectual cousins. Both are offspring of classical British economics, with Marxism retaining the Ricardian fundamentals while neoclassical economics has followed the marginalist revolution associated with Jevons, Menger, and Walras.

Weber's economic sociology provides an alternative. A key conceptual difference concerns the nature of markets. The market is, of course, the central conception of both classical and neoclassical economics; it is via supply and demand operating in the market that all economic processes are explained, while the general equilibrium model itself is nothing more than a grand abstraction of the interconnection of all economic factors in the market. The mathematics of modern economics have been designed to model the market. Hence, any move away from the fundamental market paradigm would be a very hard one to establish, both on ideological and intellectual grounds and because of vested interests in existing technique. It is widely recognized that the idealized conditions for perfect competition in a market are rarely realized, and large branches of economic analysis have developed concerning the conditions of limited information, restricted competition, and the like, which result in these imperfections. Nevertheless, these are elaborations on a model that remains analytically centered around the market itself.

It is true that Weber, on one level, seems to have accepted the neoclassical conception of the market as the end point toward which his institutional analysis tends. As we have seen in Chapter 2, Weber focuses on the structures that make possible a calculating pursuit of profit, in which an open market for all the factors of production is taken as the ideal type of modern capitalism. Nevertheless, the historical comparisons in Chapters 3 and 4, intended as extension of Weber's leads, imply that "rational capitalism" is not an all-or-nothing phenomenon. The economic growth of medieval Europe or of Buddhist China must be characterized as at least quasi-capitalist, even though the full development of the market is the weakest aspect of the Weberian checklist in these instances. In fact, there is an implication that other features, especially the rationalized entrepreneurial organization of capital such as we have seen in the monasteries of both places, is more central, and that the market is to a certain extent *created* as the result of such entrepreneurship. It is true that competition seems to be important, especially in technological innovation and its spread. But we have seen that geopolitical conditions provide an alternative source to market competition, especially in military innovations, but also in the development of early agricultural technologies. From a historical comparative view, the market begins to resemble just one kind of competitive structure within a larger nexus of social structures.

What the sociological tradition can offer is a conception of the capitalist economy that is much more political in its emphasis. This means not simply that it takes cognizance of the state as an agent in the economic process, but that the economy itself should be regarded as a political process. Not supply and demand, but political maneuvering and power within the business community itself become the central concepts. Closely connected with this is the emphasis found in Weber on the process of monopolization: Economic politics is aimed precisely at ways of controlling opportunities on the market, and the variations in this process, we may surmise, are at the heart of the dynamics governing productive and distributive processes, inequalities, and economic change. Our interest is no longer confined to instances of industrial monopoly or oligopoly, but extends to the much more pervasive *process* of monopolization as it occurs in labor markets and through the financial world as well as in industry.

For an analytical overview of this process, it is useful to sketch the economics of Joseph A. Schumpeter. Schumpeter is an even more appropriate starting place than Weber, because he himself represents the mixture of conventional economics with economic sociology that we are looking for. The degree of resemblance to Weber is not accidental: Schumpeter came out of the same intellectual milieu as Weber, and in fact they were contemporaries and even associates. Despite the important differences between the two thinkers, there is a fundamenal compatibility in their conceptions that makes them the ideal opening wedge into a sociological politics of the economy. I will argue, following Schumpeter, that this politics centers increasingly on the social organization of money, as rationalized capitalism becomes successively more advanced.

Weber and Schumpeter

Schumpeter is perhaps the most sociologically oriented of the great economists (although, of course, Marx in his own way incorporated a sociological dimension), and it may seem needless to reintroduce him to sociologists. Nevertheless, like a number of other important thinkers, Schumpeter is known to sociologists primarily for peripheral work rather than his most central conceptions. Schumpeter's *Capitalism, Socialism, and Democracy* (1942) deals explicitly with the social issues of the modern economy, and hence has come to stand for Schumpeter's position in the minds of most sociologists. But his major contribution to economic (and, I would claim, to sociological) theory was made much earlier in his life: his *Theory of Economic Development*. Originally published in 1911, it contains the basic model that Schumpeter was to maintain throughout his life – part of which model he attempted to bolster later by his massive empirical study *Business Cycles* (1939).

Although Weber (1864–1920) was about twenty years older than Schumpeter (1883–1950), their first major works appeared at almost the same time. Weber, a late starter, did not publish *The Protestant Ethic and the Spirit of Capitalism* until 1904–5 (in the *Archiv für Sozial-*

wissenschaft und Sozialpolitik, which he had just taken over as editor); Schumpeter, an early starter, published his major book in 1911 at the age of twenty-eight. Although each knew of some of the other's work, there was little mutual influence. Weber's mature institutional-historical analyses of world economic systems had not yet been written, and Schumpeter knew him mostly as a forceful personality in academic politics and as the formulator of the methods of ideal types and *Verstehen,* which Weber published in the *Archiv* in 1904 and 1906 (Schumpeter, 1954:817–19). At the 1909 meeting of the Verein für Sozialpolitik, to which both men belonged, Weber led an attack on the partisan attitude of prevailing standards of research, which precipitated a furious debate. Schumpeter strongly agreed with Weber on the value-freedom issue, which in this context meant upholding an interest in "scientific" economics against merely topical and practical concerns. Schumpeter (1954:803) later reminisced that German economics, under the influence of the Verein, had little intellectual standing, quoting a contemporary joke: "Economics, what is that? Oh, yes, I know . . . you are an economist if you measure workmen's dwellings and say that they are too small."

Weber, for his part, invited Schumpeter to write a history of economic doctrines for the economic encyclopedia Weber was editing, the *Grundriss der Sozialoekonomik.* Schumpeter did so, and it was published in the first volume of the series (Schumpeter, 1914). It was this same series, of course, for which Weber wrote his massive *Wirtschaft und Gesellschaft,* but which appeared only after his death (1922). Schumpeter also published (1918) in Weber's *Archiv.* This does not, however, indicate Weber's assent to Schumpeter's point of view; Weber nowhere refers to Schumpeter in his own published works, and he had invited Schumpeter's contribution to the *Grundriss* expressly as a representative of an opposing camp of economics.

The dominant school in German economics since the 1870s had been the "Historical School," under the leadership of Gustav Schmoller. This was a position to which Weber strongly attached himself, indeed he was regarded as a leader of it (along with Werner Sombart) in his generation. The Historical School was unique in the world of economics in its sharp rejection of abstract theoretical models and its insistence on specific historical accounts of each type of economy as it actually existed. The earlier generation had rejected the "Smithian" doctrines of English economics, and in the 1880s, Schmoller had launched the *Methodenstreit* by attacking the new marginalist theory propounded in Austria by Karl Menger. The bad feelings between the two camps, "historical" and "theoretical," had died down somewhat by the time of Weber and Schumpeter, but the two men remained on opposite sides of the divide, even though both moved in their own way to mend it.

Weber's doctrine of ideal types, which is usually viewed in the context of purely sociological problems, was originally more concerned with overcoming the effects of the *Methodenstreit* and giving a qualified place to general economic principles within the flux of real-life history. Weber claimed, however, that the purpose of ideal types was merely to facilitate concrete historical understanding. Schumpeter, although impressed with Weber's efforts, nevertheless had a very strong commitment to building economics as a generalizing science, and respectfully rejected Weber's doctrine (Schumpeter, 1954:818–19; he remarks, "Indeed, he [Weber] was not really an economist at all . . . it would be the obvious thing to label him a sociologist"). On his side, Schumpeter shows much more concern for historical processes than any other theoretical economist; his lifework is an effort to capture the dynamic processes that he held were the very essence of capitalism. Schumpeter's respect for Marx, with whom he otherwise disagreed, was because Marx alone had grasped this crucial point. Schumpeter agreed with the historicists in criticizing the static bias of conventional economic theory, especially in the general equilibrium system then emerging; his solution, however, was not a retreat to pure history but the effort to develop a dynamic theory.

Schumpeter and Weber shared yet another important influence. Both were very much aware of the challenge of Marxism in contemporary intellectual life. Germany is where Marxist doctrines first emerged from the underground and came to the notice of academic intellectuals. The way was prepared by the growing influence of the Socialist Party as a parliamentary bloc, and by the readiness of the conservative German parties to adopt social welfare programs – in part, to forestall the Socialists. In Weber and Schumpeter's academic profession of economics, the so-called *Kathedersozialisten* ("socialists of the chair") were a major influence, along with the Historical School, and dominated the policy studies of the Verein für Sozialpolitik. Thus, although Social Democrats, as members of an alleged revolutionary party, could not hold academic positions, Marxian economics was promulgated and debated at a high intellectual level: partly through the party press of the Socialists, which published such writers as Hilferding, and partly by academic defenders such as Ferdinand Toennies. Considerable technical discussion followed upon the posthumous publication of volumes II (in 1885) and III (in 1894) of Marx's *Das Kapital*, and no less an official economist than Eugen von Böhm-Bawerk, the most famous of the Austrian marginalists, delivered a polite but far-reaching critique of the Marxian system (1896/1949).[1]

Weber and Schumpeter were highly aware of the debates. Weber published in his own *Archiv* an article by Bortkiewicz (1907) favoring Marxian economics. Again, Weber was demonstrating his usual punctilious fairness. His own attitude was much closer to the laissez-faire economics of the capitalist center. Both Weber and Schumpeter merit the label a "bourgeois Marx," in that each did for capitalism what Marx had done against it: produce a scholarly system explaining capitalism and showing why it was both rational and linked to Böhm-Bawerk: Schumpeter was his student and developer of his theoretical ideas, while Weber, too, generally accepted Böhm-Bawerk's technical theory, as the content of the capitalism to be explained historically within the social framework whose origins Weber analyzed (see Weber, 1922/1968:69). The challenge of Marxian economics was significant both ideologically and intellectually, and both Weber and Schumpeter learned from it as they rose to meet it.

Where do profits come from?

Schumpeter (1911) accepts the basic analytical construction of conventional economic theory: an all-encompassing market in which the supply and demand for all the factors of production influence each other's prices. Schumpeter describes this as a "circular flow." In its simplest, static form (rather like the general equilibrium model of Walras) there is a continuous transformation of (1) land and labor (the basic factors of production) into (2) produced means of production, which in turn produce (3) commodities for consumption, which return in payment to (1) land and labor. Schumpeter stresses that in this theoretical model the stocks from each phase always balance each other out in time. There must be an accumulation of consumers' goods from a previous cycle to support people while they are producing the next round of producers' and consumers' goods, while this is renewed in the next round. Despite these necessary overlaps in time, on the whole everything is consumed and nothing is left over. The existence of money and credit merely facilitates and reflects these

---

[1] Böhm-Bawerk's (1896–1949:118) conclusion to his critique of Marx is worth quoting for its tone: "Marx, however, will maintain a permanent place in the history of the social sciences for the same reasons and with the same mixture of positive and negative merits as his prototype Hegel. Both of them were philosophical geniuses. . . . The specific theoretical work of each was a most ingeniously conceived structure, built up by a fabulous power of combination, of innumerable storeys of thought, held together by a marvelous mental grasp, but – a house of cards."

exchanges but does nothing to change them. In this, Schumpeter merely follows the conventional practice of treating money as a veil.

What Schumpeter wishes to show from this analytical model – the essence of conventional economic theory – is a crucial way in which it deviates from reality. For in the circular flow, there is no profit. According to the workings of supply and demand, all of the receipts for each phase of production are exchanged in the next phase. Ultimately, all payment for goods flows back to the land and labor that was put into their production. There is, in short, no room for the capitalist, except in the role of either landlord or laborer.

This means there is something fundamentally wrong with the economists' conception of capitalism. Yet the profitless equilibrium is logically part of their systems, even if they did not explicitly recognize it. Schumpeter remarks (1911/1961:31–2) that the Ricardian labor theory of value strongly suggests this conclusion, and that "very plain suggestions are to be found in Smith." If the existence of profit was not an explicit problem in economic theory before it was raised by Böhm-Bawerk, it was because the classical economists "were not very rigorous in recognising the consequences of their own principles." But the problem follows, in fact, quite closely from Adam Smith's market principles, in which elevated prices anywhere automatically bring more producers into that sector, until the price falls to just the level of the cost of producing the goods. This is true for the production of producers' goods as well as for that of consumers' goods, so that machinery ultimately does not contribute to any profit, because competition drives down its returns to exactly the point where it merely repays the cost of the machinery itself.

The radicalism of Adam Smith

At this point there emerges a decidedly radical strain in Smith's doctrine. The market, if left to itself and operating without impediments on the action of supply and demand, brings about not only the maximal returns on land and labor but also complete economic justice. No one receives more than he or she has put in, since competition drives all returns down to the level of costs. Taken to its consistent extreme, Smith's system is an economic utopia, in which there is no inequality among laborers, and capitalists do not exist.

It was exactly this logic that was picked up by Marx. If the capitalist system logically tends toward this perfect equality, yet empirically shows just the opposite, there must be a contradiction within the system. Marx located this in the exploitation of labor – the derivation of surplus value by working laborers longer hours than it takes to reproduce the cost of their labor – and in the tendency to a falling rate of profit as laborsaving machinery cuts into the employment of labor. Invoking Smithian principles, Marx deduces that the returns on laborsaving devices are washed out as competition brings them down to the bare level of their original costs. One might say that Marx is a radical Smithian, who takes the utopian consequences of Smith's system to an appropriately radical conclusion.[2]

Böhm-Bawerk and Schumpeter, scrutinizing the technical details of Marx's system, were impressed by his grasp of the problem but proposed an entirely different solution. Böhm-Bawerk found this in the element of time, which had previously played no significant part in the economic theory of value. By locating the idealizations of economics in the rhythms of the real world, he attempted to show that profit is due to differences in valuation that take place between future and present goods. Schumpeter was not satisfied with this solution (1911/1961:32–9), and argued that Böhm-Bawerk's psychological premises were not consistent with an economic determination of values by the interacting parts of the market system itself. (Similarly, Schumpeter disposed of the other candidate source of profit, friction in movement of competitors to areas of greatest return, by pointing out that friction can be a source of loss as well as of profit, so that in the aggregate there is no reason to expect a structure of profit in the economic system on this basis.)

Where, then, does profit come from? Schumpeter argues that it cannot be found in a static model of the economy at all. Böhm-Bawerk was on the right track in pointing to time as the crucial factor, but he erred by concentrating on psychological time (as befitted a major proponent of the "psychological" marginalist conception of value) instead of on the historical time of the self-transforming capitalist system itself.

The entrepreneur as originator of new combinations

Schumpeter's technical solution to the problem of profits centers on the role of the entrepreneur. Existing economic theory, he complains, is static; his own role is to introduce into its fundamental apparatus the processes of change in technology and in productive organization that have been the most notable characteristics of modern capitalism throughout its history. For the entrepreneur is the person who finds new ways to organize existing factors of produc-

[2] It is, of course, heretical to say this, since the fundamental contradictions of capitalism in Marxian economics are alleged to flow from relationships to the means of production. But, as I point out in Chapter 10, this is merely the Hegelian dogmatics of the system, which shadows but does not really figure in the technical model of the dynamics of capitalism.

tion, taking portions of land, labor, and producers' goods and recombining them in ways that yield new economic products. It is this that may be called economic "development," as apart from the circular flow of economic routine. And where the circular flow is essentially profitless, development is the source of profit. The entrepreneur finds new combinations that yield goods that previously did not exist; hence the return on this is pure profit. It is not a lasting state of affairs, however. Once the innovation is established, other businesses enter that area, and the process of competition drives down prices to the normal level of the circular flow. Entrepreneurship is always temporary and self-liquidating; renewed profit depends on renewed innovation. (If the innovation remains monopolized because of barriers to the entry of competitors, then the gains, in Schumpeter's argument, are not profits but monopoly price, a distinct phenomenon.)

In a certain sense, the entrepreneur has a monopolistic position merely by the fact of being the first. Here, as elsewhere, Schumpeter parts company with economic orthodoxy by declaring himself in sympathy with a certain amount of monopoly. Without the protection of some degree of monopoly, he argues (1942), businesses could not afford to innovate at all. Monopolies thus are part of the dynamism of the economy. The other side of the same coin is the principle that monopolies are temporary over the long haul. Ultimately, a business that is not moving ahead is falling behind. It cannot merely remain in place, because it will lose out in the competition with other organizations, even those in quite different sectors of the economy, because of the pervasive competition for capital (credit) that ties together all economic sectors.[3] More will be said about this, under the heading of financial politics.

Monopolization as a key economic process

On this point, Schumpeter's themes lead into those of Weber. Various types of monopolization are very common historically; before the rise of modern Western capitalism with its fixed capital, free labor,

[3] This is not merely a matter of Schumpeter's faith in the self-correcting powers of capitalism. He is also pointing to a recognizable phenomenon, illustrated by the way in which even large oligopolistic corporations – one might think of Ford or Lockheed in recent years – can become threatened. Similarly, the wave of corporate take-overs of prospering businesses through purely financial manipulations indicates the vulnerability of any business entity to the strains of the financial market and the power of financial politics. The crucial point is the up-and-down process of making and unmaking monopolies of varying degrees, which is the continual dynamic of capitalism.

125

and rational calculation, capitalist enterprise typically took the form Weber termed "politically oriented capitalism." This consisted of financing or supplying lords, politicians, or the state; or carrying out production and trade backed up by force in colonial plantations, compulsory deliveries, and monopoly trade; or the farming of taxes and offices (Weber 1922/1968:164–5). All of these have important elements of monopoly. But Weber describes monopolization as a fundamental process in modern capitalism as well, especially as defining the characteristics of fixed occupations.

This points to the crux of the difference between Weberian and Marxian models of stratification. Marx stresses the relationship to the means of production, hence the major dividing line between capitalists and propertyless workers. This analytical model has been strongly defended by the Marxists, even though it has resulted in considerable scholastic juggling in dealing with the major contemporary classes of managerial and clercial workers. The Weberian approach has been criticized because it defines classes according to their relationship to the market rather than to the means of production. Thus Weber (1922/1968:927–30) defines class as a set of individuals who have similar life chances on the market, and points out there are three different kinds of class conflict possible on three different markets: employers and employees on the labor market; lenders and creditors on the financial market; and consumers and producers on the commodity market. Marxians allege that this analysis is superficial (and have made the same criticism of Wallerstein's world-system analysis, alleging that it is merely "neo-Smithian Marxism" or even "Weberian" [see Bergesen 1984]).

The Marxian point is not merely a querulous clinging to its traditional definitions. The relationship to the means of production is analytically crucial in the overall Marxian scheme because it links social classes to the mainspring of economic history, via the production of surplus value and its subsequent vicissitudes governed by the law of the falling rate of profit. Nevertheless, the overall system has not performed so well empirically as to leave us no alternative but to be attached to it. The Weberian model is more fruitful, and not only analytically but historically as well. It enables us to see, for example, that different types of class conflict have dominated in different historical eras: Revolts of debtor classes characterized ancient Mediterranean city-states, whereas struggles in the commodity market dominated medieval Europe, shifting to price wars in the labor market in recent centuries (Weber, 1922/1968:930–1). But the categories are not exclusive; all three types of class conflict remain operative today, and conflicts outside of the labor market have been especially prominent in the United States (Wiley, 1967).

Class conflict, in short, is more complex than the Marxian scheme allows for. Weber uses his scheme of market position to overcome a weakness in the analysis proceeding from economic self-interest. For according to economic logic, capitalists are not merely struggling with workers but even more immediately are competing against each other. Similarly, workers have an interest in competing against one another for wages and jobs. The combination of workers is not automatic; though it no doubt rises to their consciousness at some time that labor organization would be useful, the extent of the organized group can vary tremendously. It is rational for workers in a particular branch of industry to defend their self-interest against workers in other branches, or for union members to defend their interests against nonunion workers. The history of the union movement shows exactly these types of particularisms; although political doctrine may declare the alleged advantage in an overarching union of all workers, in fact political union involves sacrifices and compromises that specialized groups of workers may not find to their liking. Workers in a particular industry may have stronger economic interests in common with their own bosses than with workers in rival industries, as witnessed by such modern phenomena as the politics of government defense contracting or national protectionism, or ethnic exclusiveness (including immigration restriction policies) on the part of labor unions.

For Weber, these are not accidental or anomalous features of capitalism, although they do not fit conventional market theory with its treatment of labor as a single generalized factor of production. Marxian theory here is closer to the conventional economic heritage. For Weber, monopolization is a fundamental process in the economy. It is a dynamic, not a given state of affairs; certain tendencies move toward the formation of closed economic groups, whereas certain other tendencies act to break down their exclusiveness. Thus:

When the number of competitors increases in relation to the profit span, the participants become interested in curbing competition. Usually one group of competitors takes some externally identifiable characteristic of another group of (actual or potential) competitors – race, language, religion, local or social origin, descent, residence, etc. – as a pretext for attempting their exclusion. It does not matter which characteristic is chosen in the individual case: whatever suggests itself most easily is seized upon. . . . In spite of their continued competition against one another, the jointly acting competitors now form an "interest group" toward outsiders; there is a growing tendency to set up some kind of association with rational regulations; if the monopolistic interests persist, the time comes when the competitors, or another group whom they can influence (for example, a political community), establish a legal order that limits competition through formal monopolies; from then on, certain persons are available as "organs" to protect the monopolistic practices, if need be, with force. In such a case, the interest group has developed into a *"legally privileged group"*. . . . . Such closure, as we want to call it, is an ever-recurring process; it is the source of property in land as well as of all guild and other group monopolies. [Weber, 1922/1968:341–2]

Weber's description thus encompasses the formation of ethnically exclusionary groups, as well as the establishment of the modern licensed professions; but it also extends deep into the history of landed property and guild organization. By extension, it is applicable to the "technically" ultramodern organization of the labor force by educational credentials (which Weber refers to as "occupational patents" [1968:342]), as well as traditional privileges of master-craftsmen and apprentices. The degree and kind of occupational monopolization among different group structures is determined by a complex of political forces, and hence varies even among technically modern societies, as I have shown in the case of the medical, engineering, and legal professions (Collins, 1979:131–81).

Weber tends at times to speak of classes and status groups as antithetical phenomena. For example, he speaks of status group–based monopolies as characteristic of traditional societies, where they act as irrational restraints on the market (Weber, 1968:638–9). Thus in many feudal and patrimonial societies, the hereditary appropriation or exclusion of groups from military, landowning, mercantile, or other occupations is a phenomenon antithetical to rationalized capitalism. In general, Weber comments that stratification by status is favored when bases for economic acquisition are stable, but gives way to the naked class situation in times of technical and economic change (1922/1968:938). But on a deeper analysis, status-group formation and class formation are part of the same process of monopolization.

This process itself is dynamic, carried along by struggle. Moreover, it is undermined by its very success. For, as Weber points out, the further extension of group monopolization of economic opportunities is to appropriate those opportunities as the exclusive property of individuals, whereupon they become available for sale on a market. Thus a typical process of status-group monopolization restricted officeholding in parts of Europe to an aristocracy of birth, but its members in turn pressed their rights to the point at which they could sell their offices to the highest bidder (Weber, 1922/1968:343, 638). A similar process in the appropriation of land led to a market open even to outsiders, provided they had sufficient money. There are processes both creating monopolies and, by the further extension of property rights, dissolving them again in a financial marketplace. Weber's picture seems congruent with Schumpeter's emphasis on both sides of the monopolization process: both its ubiquity (at Schumpeter's innovation stage) and its transitoriness (as the competition for money and its pressure upon prices throughout the economy forces monopolists who are no longer growing to sell their holdings).

Status groups should be conceived of not as noneconomic phenomena but as an example of the type of process that is central to the economy. The strongly organized professions of today – for example, those that have monopolistic licensing requirements guaranteeing high incomes, occupational power, and hence prestige – are, as I have pointed out elsewhere (Collins, 1979:171–81), the equivalent of strongly closed status groups such as ethnic groups. Cultural groups based on educational credentials might be regarded as pseudo-ethnicity: Not only do they usually originate in the culture of a particular ethnic group and class, but even if widened from that base, they continue to operate to form subjective communities that favor one another in economic dealings and appropriating occupational positions. The theory of ethnic groups has not been systematically developed; nor has the larger topic of the theory of status groups (though see Chapter 6, "Weber's Theory of Politics"). But both are parts of the general theory of group formation and group dissolution, which is an intimate part of the organization of any economy.

The existence of status groups does not eliminate class conflict. Rather, it provides the specific form in which it takes place. It is not usually possible for all the members of a Marxian class – essentially reifications of the abstract factors of production in economic theory – to act together as a unified group. Status-group organization (which we may widen here to include consciousness of a particular life-style as an occupational group, especially an exclusionary profession) is the natural form in which economic interests can act socially. This model of stratification, then, cannot be determined by mere relationship to the means of production; the actual form of that relationship is itself the result of specific social processes. Weber lists a large number of forms of property in agriculture and industry found throughout world history (1922/1968:144–50). He argues that modern capitalism develops through a *series of monopolizations:* first, of money capital by entrepreneurs who make advances to labor; then, of market information and hence of sales opportunities; subsequently, of all material means of production, thereby expropriating workers from their tools as well as excluding seigneurial and other outsiders' control over the place of work. Finally, there is the expropriation of the manager and even the owner, who becomes in effect "a trustee of the suppliers of credit, the banks" (1922/1968:148). Weber thus subsumes Marx's concern with the expropriation of workers, into a larger process of monopolization that is directed against feudal lords as well as against workers, and that ultimately expropriates the owners themselves. Only in Weber's "dialectic" it is not socialism that triumphs but the credit market.

Various stages of the up-and-down process of monopolization may go on simultaneously in different areas. Thus the monopolistic medieval guilds and the hereditary landholding estates were circumvented as their individual members succeeded in appropriating their own shares for sale on the market, at the same time that new occupational and trade monopolies were being created. The transformation of capitalistic enterprises, having monopolized the means of production in particular branches, into entities to be sold and recombined according to the vicissitudes of stock markets and banks, goes along with the growth of new monopolies, both by Schumpeterian innovation and by cartelization and other forms of monopolistic business politics.

Moreover, the process of monopolization can operate within business organizations themselves. A similar up-and-down process occurs as occupational groups form: not only the various licensed professions, as well as ethnic and other culturally based exclusions of particular job categories, but also any use of group culture to define particular occupational positions and career channels. The culture may include technical culture, which gives a veneer of "technocracy" to the modern occupational structure, although the actual form of occupational monopolization by particular credentials is a political process dependent on the relative organizational resources of different groups. Capitalist organizations (and of course governmental and other public organizations as well) thus are sites for struggles over the creation of fixed positions of various sorts that can be monopolized, at least temporarily, by individuals who are thereby removed from the pressures of the labor market. Mature capitalist organizations do not lose power merely upward to the holders of financial credit, but also downward and inward. They are vulnerable to the growth of predatory interests in their own administrative sector, to occupational monopolies that are impossible to control because they are the very locus of organizational politics. I have referred to this organizational locale as the "sinecure sector" – though it should be borne in mind that a good deal of time and effort may be expended in such jobs on "political labor" (Collins, 1979:49–72). The workings of the labor market are not limited merely by "internal labor markets" within organizations

(Williamson, 1975). The size and shape of these organizational labor pools are due to occupational politics – which is to say, to the Weberian process of monopolization.

It should be stressed that our term "monopoly" or even "monopolization" carries rather misleading connotations from its traditional usage. Even disregarding the practice of Marxian commentators to speak of "monopoly capitalism" or the "monopoly sector" (in "dual labor market" theory) when what is actually referred to is "oligopoly," the term "monopoly" implies less dynamism and tension than is actually the case.[4] More accurately, we are speaking of a process of appropriation of market opportunities, although the instruments of appropriation themselves can thus become available for transactions on a superordinate market. Thus the sale of monastic ordination certificates in medieval China (Chapter 3) – or the comparable sale of governmental offices in early modern Europe – is a "corruption" of the usual channels of open occupational recruitment, but at the same time it opens up a market in which purely financial speculation and investment can take place. A modern analogy would be the growth of the highly credentialized occupational world, which fragments occupational markets and appropriates ("monopolizes") opportunities for groups of specialized degree-holders; at the same time, it creates market-like phenomena in the realm of the credentials themselves, such as the "credential inflation" that has diluted their value in recent decades.[5]

The market economy exists even in this situation, but its laws do not consist of the familiar processes of adjustment of supply and

---

[4] Thus, Hirsch (1983) points out that the "dual labor market" theory of the early 1970s, which distinguished a protected, price-setting "monopolistic" sector from a competitive, "secondary" economy, now seems static and historically dated. Crises within supposed "monopolistic" sectors such as automobiles, or the more recent wave of take-overs and shake-outs in the even more lucrative oil business, imply a fundamental deficiency in the model.

[5] The organization of occupations is not determined by their techniques, but varies according to the political circumstances that enable groups to achieve varying degrees of closure along particular membership lines. For example, the practice of law may be split among solicitors and barristers (as in England), or organized as part of government bureaucracy (as in continental legal systems), or left as a decentralized but internally unified profession of lawyers (as in the United States). These occupational forms arose under particular political circumstances; countermonopolizing periods are also possible, such as during the time of political democratization in the United States after 1800, which broke down monopolistic licensing requirements in the bar for almost a century (Collins, 1979:147–51). Similarly, particular political histories have been important both for creating unified ethnic groups and, under other circumstances, for dissolving their boundaries.

demand to produce equilibrium prices. Rather, the key dynamic may be the up-and-down fluctuation of monopolization in various sectors. Weber gives the outline of this process as it applies to labor of all degrees of skill and power, including managerial and "professional" labor (the latter being only a modern phrase for a successful type of licensed monopoly legitimated by a technocratic ideology). Schumpeter concentrates on monopolies of productive organization, which emerge and dissolve regularly within the economy. Together they add up to a general process of appropriation covering all aspects of the economy.

Recent sociological theory, from a different direction, proposes a scheme that makes monopolization even more central in the sphere of production. Harrison White (1981) proposes that each branch of production tends to have a small number of producers, each of which attempts to create a distinctive niche, so that it is not competing with anyone. Organizations do this, not by orienting toward the autonomous workings of supply and demand, but by *monitoring each other*. Each productive sector thus is organized as a clique or network, in which each gauges from others' quality, price, and sales volume some *different* combination of such factors it can use to find its own successful product niche. White's model shows that the widespread existence of "oligopoly" is not an anomaly, as in conventional market economics. In reality, producers in a given area are not anonymous and hostile competitors but readily join together socially in trade associations and other contacts, precisely because they depend on one another for information. (This has the effect of making their personnel a single labor pool, with automatically exclusionary effects in the Weberian sense.) Even in sectors that have numerous competitors (e.g., small retailers of goods or services), the same kind of relationships prevail, because these markets are usually organized locally among a small group of competitors, who attempt to differentiate their products or their localities to achieve unique niches – again, an aim for which mutual monitoring is important.

Similarly to Schumpeter, White argues that production does not occur in response to demand, but in fact producers create demand by these maneuvers. Schumpeter proposes that this happens as entrepreneurs make new combinations of the factors of production, offering goods that did not exist before and that, therefore, do not meet an existing demand. White generalizes this process to the everyday workings of production in every branch of the economy. To gather market information, in other words, producers cannot directly monitor demand (which is unorganized, potential rather than actual, and spread out), but must instead monitor competitors, with an eye not to competing directly but to finding a noncompetitive niche amid existing product lines.

Again, the demand site of the market does not disappear from the picture, but it is a secondary or "reactive" factor more than a primary shaper of organizational patterns. Population ecology models that stress natural selection of organizations by their success in finding niches in response to demand (e.g., Hannan and Freeman, 1977; Aldrich, 1979) assume too much the automatic working of the openly competitive market, and miss the "prestructured" pattern that develops as mutually monitoring organizations attempt to avoid this competition in advance. To be sure, organizations are not always successful at this, and some do go head to head in efforts to take a share of another's market, with the predictable results of long-term attrition among competitors. And it is not a foregone conclusion that even where organizations try to avoid competition, they will be able to calculate successfully how to do so. Nevertheless, White's model, which is congruent with Schumpeter's and Weber's, seems to capture correctly one essential side of the process of *appropriation of opportunities* that makes up the market.

White's model suggests that economic dynamics come from interorganizational politics among cliques of producers. This leads naturally to a network approach, and some empirical studies already available show the fruitfulness of the lead. Burt (1982), for example, shows that the kinds of interlocks among boards of directors predicts the profitability of different industrial sectors, with high profits going to industries that are little constrained by links to their suppliers, while strongly constraining those who must buy from them. This only begins to scratch the surface, since mutual monitoring among organizations is a network process with many manifestations, not confined to overt interlocking directorships. Such interlocks as exist (Pfeffer and Salancik, 1978) are often interpreted as devices of stable "monopolistic" power, especially industries and financial institutions, but the direction of control may in fact go either way (Hirsch, 1983). More realistically, we can say that interlocks indicate a network structure that involves White's mutual monitoring, and that this is part of the two-sided Weberian appropriation of opportunities. Competition of certain sorts is restricted, to the advantage of the organizations involved. At the same time, a superordinate system, or "market," is established, specifically in the form of financial markets, which can have an overriding influence on the politics of the business community. The way this occurs may be seen from Schumpeter.

Economics

The organizational politics of money

Schumpeter's picture of the economy is heavily imbued with politics, even in his analysis of the entrepreneur.[6] But structurally, Schumpeter's analysis focuses largely on the politics of the financial world. The sphere of organization-building, in which the entrepreneur's power motive is most immediately manifested, is not given much space, although Schumpeter's hints are congruent with Weber's picture of organizations as sites for domination and struggle over control (a picture amply documented in organizational research; see Collins, 1975:286–347). But the entrepreneur's first success must be in assembling the resources for a new organization, and that means action in the external environment. Here, the crucial role is played by the financial system.

[6] The entrepreneur bears a strong resemblance to Weber's puritan businessman driven by the Protestant ethic. Schumpeter (1911/1961:91–2) describes the entrepreneur as "irrational" in the sense that his motive is not hedonistic enjoyment of life but the opposite – his sheer interest in overcoming obstacles. At the same time, the entrepreneur can be described as "the most rational and the most egotistical of all" (1911/1961:91) because of the high level of conscious rationality involved in carrying out new plans, as opposed to the routine of running an established business. Schumpeter comments that the entrepreneur breaks up traditions – economic, moral, cultural, and social. "It is no mere coincidence that the period of the rise of the entrepreneur type also gave birth to Utilitarianism" (1911/1961:92). This sounds like the same personality type that Weber attributed to the Calvinistic Reformation. Schumpeter casts it in another light, however. Its theme is not religion but politics:

"First of all, there is the dream and the will to found a private kingdom, usually, though not necessarily, also a dynasty. The modern world really does not know any such positions, but what may be attained by industrial or commercial success is still the nearest approach to medieval lordship possible to modern man. The fascination is specially strong for people who have no other chance of achieving social distinction. The sensation of power and independence loses nothing by the fact that both are largely illusions" (Schumpeter 1911/1961:93).

The passage could almost have been written by Weber himself, especially the worldly disillusionment expressed in the last line. Schumpeter is expressly making the entrepreneur a political figure, motivated by a drive for power. It is for this reason that the search for profits is endless, just as in the case of Weber's Protestant ethic the profits are not ends in themselves but merely emblems or by-products of another type of success. Schumpeter connects this not with a religious motivation but with the political change that ushered in modern times: the rise of the bureaucratic state. The resulting centralization and depersonalization of political power eliminated political empire-building as an arena for this kind of ambition. The business organization comes on the scene as a private kingdom substituting for a political one; the robber baron of industry emerges precisely because the military robber baron is no longer possible. Since religion is a veiled political sphere in its own right, there may be even closer affinities between Weber and Schumpeter on this point. The Protestant Reformation was part of the same movement that saw the rise of the modern nation-state, eliminating the cross-cutting claims of the Papacy and sealing the doom of the feudal system. Schumpeter sees a displaced political motivation migrating into the economic sphere, whereas Weber sees a newly individualized religious motivation descending on secular society. Both, in fact, may be different readings of the same emotional energy released by this historical transformation.

For new combinations to be carried out, resources must be diverted from the circular flow. Advances are needed until these resources repay themselves. Innovation thus requires credit. Whereas the routine workings of the economy do not essentially depend on money – here, money is only a veil, facilitating exchanges but in no way changing them – in economic development credit is essential. In fact, Schumpeter (1939) goes so far as to define capitalism as "enterprise carried out with borrowed money," a definition that stresses the dynamism of capitalism as its most important characteristic.[7]

Development credit is not limited by the current amount of resources in existence. Banks are able to take money that would otherwise lie idle in deposits and lend it out in the interim. With appropriate juggling of time periods for repayment, and with use of paper credit, several times the amount of money on deposit may be lent out at any given time. (Similar processes may occur wherever funds are accumulated – in insurance, pensions, and so forth.) Thus the monetary system is a massive institutional example of Böhm-Bawerk's time lags, which were put forward as a solution to the problem of profits. For Schumpeter, it is the interaction of entrepreneurs and financiers that answers the question.

Schumpeter extols the entrepreneur, while viewing bankers more in shades of necessary evil. Bankers' interest on loans, in his analysis, is not profit but a kind of tax on entrepreneurial profit. From the viewpoint of the overall system, different development plans are competing for available credit. Interest payments dissuade entrepreneurs from the least remunerative schemes, and thus constitute a "necessary brake" that keeps development within bounds (Schumpeter, 1911/1961:210). One might put it in somewhat less sanguinely functionalist tones: interest is the tribute money-politicians (bankers) can exact from organization-building politicians (entrepreneurs).

Given the power of bankers to decide among different business plans, the financial world emerges as the command center of the economy, "the headquarters of the capitalist system" (Schumpeter 1911/1961:126). Having set up his model with these political overtones, Schumpeter does not linger on the sociological details of how

---

[7] Weber's definition of "capitalism" is less succinct, because he wishes to distinguish among varieties of economically acquisitive activities according to their degree of rationally calculative orientation. He does, however, come close to Schumpeter in defining "capital" as the "money value of the means of profit-making available to the enterprise at the balancing of the books," "defined strictly with reference to the individual private enterprise" (Weber, 1922/1968:91, 94). He also points out (p. 95) that the origins of the term was *capitale*, the principal sum of a loan. Weber, however, broadens the focus from Schumpeter's "borrowed money" to the accounting aspect of "rational profit-making activity."

its politics might work. As he retreats into the abstractions of economic theory, however, we should note that in the world he describes, banks do not simply give funds through a kind of anonymous competition to the best-qualified bidder, in order to optimize the allocation of economic resources. This would return us to the old neutral "veil" theory of money, which Schumpeter discards. In fact, as we learn from recent empirical studies, the financial world operates according to the politics of personal networks, and thus constitutes a formidable source of social and economic inequalities in its own right.

Is this congruent with Weber's view of money? Weber actually touched on the topic relatively little. What he does say largely consists of historical comparisons establishing the uniqueness of modern Western capitalism. Traditional forms of capitalism, almost all of them "politically oriented," arose wherever money-based exchange and money financing existed, including financing of wars, revolutions, and party leaders; tax farming; sale of offices; and trade monopolies (Weber, 1922/1968:164–6). The existence of money is thus crucial for any form of capitalism. Modern capitalism is unique in that it is oriented to profit from the *continuous* production of goods or from the *continuous* financial operations of political bodies, and from speculation in securities and promotional financing of new enterprises. "Apart from the rational capitalistic enterprise, the modern economic order is unique in its monetary system and in the commercialization of ownership shares in enterprises through the various forms of securities" (Weber, 1922/1968:166). Weber's ensuing discussion is a typology of kinds of money, with little concern for its dynamic aspects except in an excursus on a topical question of monetary policy and inflation (pp. 166–93). It is apparent that finance is central to the Weberian economic picture, though we are left on our own to fill in its organizational politics.

It is surprising how little the financial realm, given its importance, has been studied in social science. Economists tend to keep it in a separate compartment. Marxists follow a long-standing polemic by Marx against monetarists and refuse to grant the financial realm any independent singificance. Nevertheless, some sociological pictures are available (Mayer, 1976; Beveridge). Primarily these are concerned with banks, although by extension the same kind of processes are likely to be found throughout the modern financial community: the insurance companies, the mortgage and loan companies, the stock market, pension and trust funds, as well as the governmental treasuries, tax, and licensing agencies. Together they constitute the empirical core of capital as an organized social phenomenon.

Weber and Schumpeter

What theoretical consequences can we draw from a view of the modern organization of finance? Even with limited data, certain things stand out. Money is part of a network of interorganizational communication, but at the same time it is embedded in relations of a strikingly personal sort. Status communities leap to the sociological eye on almost every page of empirical reportage (see Mayer, 1976). New banks become successful or not, depending on the loans their officers can generate; in interviews, "knowing the community" is the slogan under which their success is ascribed. Modest loans to little-known walk-in customers are scrutinized at length; huge loans to well-known corporation executives are okayed with a minimum of investigation. Bankers proudly peer into the lives of small borrowers ("I expect him to undress completely. It's like a doctor" [Mayer, 1976:254]) while kowtowing to the big ones ("Banks will send lending officers around to big borrowers to chat about this and that, have a drink with friends, and make sure the number still looks right" [Mayer, 1976:272]).

We have, in short, a system of power relations in which deference is exacted according to one's relative standing in the community. There is a mutually reinforcing connection between two orders of stratification – personal status groups and economic domination. Banks do not merely assess entrepreneurial schemes against a total competitive allocation of resources; they assess them primarily on the degree of personal trust they have in the individuals involved. Given Harrison White's model of businesses as cliques of mutually monitoring organizations, this emphasis on personal connections perhaps represents economic rationality. But whatever its rationality in a situation of risk and uncertainty, it nevertheless means that those who share a common culture and outlook will do most of the financial transacting. The status group, in short, dominates the business system. And because the financial system is the key to business power, the politics of status groups rules the economic realm.

Inside organizations, line authority is essentially the power to dispense or withhold money. If it is problematic in the real life of organizations, it is only because the people who constitute the authority network are engaged in a game of social communications to keep the network together and themselves in favorable positions within it, and that means drawing on their status culture – the "conversational capital," as I have called it elsewhere (Collins, 1981a). Even talk about financial prospects and "realities" nevertheless operates as cultural exchange, and hence as a currency that can be exchanged, if the *social* rate of exchange is right, for the financial power of hard cash (or easy credit). Thus, inside organizations the politics of organized interpersonal communities and of line authority are tightly linked (cf. Kanter, 1977:164–205; Collins, 1979:22–72).

If money is power within organizations, it also is the key link that makes interorganizational relations into a power hierarchy. Business enterprises are linked to particular sources of capital. The large corporations are tied to the big banks, whereas small businesses get their funds from smaller "country" banks. Regionally powerful lead banks organize consortiums to finance large-scale loans – not only to business but also to municipalities at home, and entire states abroad – a circumstance that has led some Marxist analysts to the conclusion that a "fiscal crisis of the state" is built into the structure of governmental financing (O'Conner, 1973). The important element in this argument is that governments are themselves economic units (employing a sizable segment of the work force, and dispensing as much as half of the total GNP) and as such are subject to the same financial politics that ties together the rest of the business realm.

The connection between the capitalist class and the state, in this perspective, is hardly hidden or mysterious. Debates about "structuralist" and "instrumentalist" interpretations of the state are beside the point; empirically, capitalism does not have to depend on the machinations or the insight of politicians, nor does it rest on any teleological rationality of the system to make welfare concessions to protect itself. What exists in fact is a network held together by the financial system. The business world is tied together hierarchically through the size of the financial institutions upon which each enterprise can draw. The financial world, in turn, is hierarchically structured from the thousands of small and medium banks, organized around lead banks that act as regional clearinghouses, up through the dozen giant banks at the top (in the United States; other structures exist elsewhere) that stand in close relation with the financial agencies of the federal government. It is through these huge banks that the government exercises financial policy and releases its own funds. The government is committed to never allowing these banks to fail, precisely because they are the center for the entire economy. The structure of capitalism is shored up by the government itself, because the government needs a viable financial system for its own ends (as well as to prevent political unrest). Left-wing revolution is particularly difficult because any political moves that disturb the financial system bring about economic chaos, which in turn undermines the political support for a left government.[8]

---

[8] See Polanyi (1944) for examples of downfalls of revolutionary regimes by this process in the 1920s; many further examples could be multiplied from Latin America and

The overall structure of any economy may be seen as a hierarchy of social networks. Throughout, there are the dual aspects of appropriation of opportunities by restricted networks that exercise mutual monitoring and sometimes coercive power, but also the competitive pressures and price adjustments that exist on one level or another. Superordinate markets emerge, for money, credit, and cultural capital, which exert their own dynamics on appropriated opportunities. The financial system is one such superordinate market. Although it is itself structured as a network system par excellence, permeated by the favoritism of status groups and acting as the "headquarters of capitalism," nevertheless it is subject to a competitive market structure. In terms of Harrison White's model, product differentiation itself hardly exists in finance, since all banks and other financial institutions provide a homogeneous commodity, money. Thus, banking itself can be a highly competitive sector (as it is today), even though financial institutions monitor one another and attempt to find separate niches in particular locales, as well as hierarchically inside the internal transactions of the monetary system itself. Similarly, the government is a superordinate system of great potential influence because it can both structure and destroy all lower-level organizations and can affect the monetary system through its own spending and taxation. Nevertheless, governments are entrapped in the competitive-market aspects of any large-scale network of transactions, and hence are subject to political shocks from financial crises, inflations, or other economic phenomena they are attempting to control.

Conclusion: the nature of capitalist development

The conception of the economy implied in Weber and Schumpeter, and extended by modern network analysis, is broader than capitalism in any narrow definition. Schumpeter defines capitalism as "enterprise carried out with borrowed money" and restricts its historical appearance to the business cycles that have emerged in Western Europe since the late 1700s. Any such emphasis on a financial "headquarters" for capitalism would, of course, rule out the capitalist

elsewhere in recent decades. The monetary phenomenon of inflation seems to be crucially implicated in a theory of revolutions and especially counterrevolutions. A full-scale comparative study of inflation in different historical periods, and its political consequences, would be instructive. Given the frequent connection of inflation with wars, and of wars (and military overextension) with political downfall of regimes (see Chapter 6), the causal dynamics may likely be a combination of the internal politics of the business system, with the structure of external geopolitics among states.

nature of medieval Europe or China. Yet these economies clearly had capitalist characteristics. At least in the core sectors focused on in Chapter 3, they were dynamic economies organized around corporate entrepreneurs. Their technological innovativeness was of the sort that seems to be the result of ongoing economic expansion. Moreover, one of the conclusions of our general overview of technological innovation in Chapter 4 is that geographical movement, whether expansion into frontiers like those of northern Europe or south China, or the establishment of long-distance links that foster "diffusion," is equivalent to the process of expanding competition within a given economy; both foster innovation of techniques and products, and both open up new markets. From a larger perspective, the key to economic growth is the creation of new forms and areas of production, however this may be done. The growth of the market and its "demand" is a result of this process, not a precondition.

We should regard the nature of capitalism as a historical continuum. The banks were not the headquarters of capitalism in Buddhist China or medieval Christian Europe, although early financial institutions were gradually developed in the monasteries themselves. The Church did act as a storer of wealth and a source of loans, and eventually as an agency for investment and speculation. In Schumpeter's model, a key turning point is when banks not only loan out money but create new credit, by manipulating the time of repayment so that existing cash can be lent out many times over. For Schumpeter, this is the key to the existence of profit within the economic system. But this is precisely what ancient banks (such as the temples of ancient Greece) did not do; they took treasure in the form of hard specie, and lent it in concrete form, without interest and without creating any credit expansion in the system (Polanyi, 1977). It is not clear when and in what sense the medieval Buddhist and Christian monastic "banking" practices went beyond this. Nevertheless, by the time of the early Sung dynasty, monastic ordination certificates were part of a speculative market in financial paper, and there were no doubt other ways in which both Buddhist and Christian church finances acted to promote the circulation of credit, at least within their own religious economies (but also spilling over into secular society).

As Goldstone (1984) has shown for the Western Europe of 1500–1650, the process of growth in markets and occupational specialization is itself a major cause of monetary inflation, because of its effects on the velocity of circulation. The existence of inflation is a sign of the existence of capitalism, at least in some form. Such inflation goes along with growth, and with the expansion of monetary instruments. It is, of course, not alwa⋅s economically "healthy," and its ill effects, especially on government finances, can undermine institutional supports for further capitalist development. But that is only to say that capitalism is an unstable system, prone to shocks and crises. Sung China should be regarded as an instance of this rather than as a failure to achieve some ideal-typical level of capitalist takeoff.

If capitalism is a continuum, it may be measured institutionally according to how far this process has gone in creating superordinate markets for the instruments of market appropriation. We do not have to start with an ideal-type open market for the factors of production, nor with a financial "headquarters" creating credit and directing it to various areas of innovation. In one sense, the completely open market *never* comes into existence. The fundamental process of capitalist development is entrepreneurship (including in corporate form), and that always involves the search for areas of profit, areas in which competition does not exist. And ongoing enterprises, as both Weber and White emphasize, are always engaged in network-building and monitoring activities that focus on noncompetitive niches or otherwise appropriate market opportunities. At the same time, the very success of such enterprises creates markets: It creates them in the sense that new consumers are found and new networks of distribution are established; and it tends to create superordinate markets that bargain over the instruments of appropriation themselves. Financial networks emerge out of the success of lower-level units of production. Thus, finances become increasingly the "headquarters of capitalism," although financial institutions of any given degree of sophistication need not exist at earlier points in time. Schumpeter's banks that fuel economic expansion by multiplying credit are a higher-level growth. And if credit is expanded by manipulating the time periods of repayment, the development of still higher and more reflexive "loops" of financial speculation indicates that network complexity and hence the amount of credit that can be created can be escalated to still higher levels. There is no intrinsic point along this continuum at which "capitalism" begins. In fact, the nature of capitalism seems to be that it is always capable of adding such multiple levels onto it.

And here is a bottom line, if in fact one can say anything final about this dialectically self-transforming entity we are calling "capitalism." The entrepreneurial, profit-seeking organization of production always contains both "monopolistic" and market elements. Production itself creates markets and at the same time organizes itself socially to appropriate opportunities to deal upon them. If successful, this production not only spreads markets horizontally in space, but also tends to create superordinate markets, which become increasingly financial. On this higher level, the process can repeat itself. Appropriation of opportunities through network organization is much in evidence in financial markets, as well as through the special kind of power network that constitutes the state. But these financial markets are also subject to a competitive dynamic, which keeps reemerging "at the top" of the system, and which makes even the financiers and the state vulnerable to up-and-down processes they cannot control. It appears likely that new social loops can be added onto the top of this system, perhaps ad infinitum, without losing this basic characteristic.

To be sure, politics is capable of destroying economic development (as well as being destroyed by it). Weber's model of institutional preconditions shows us that the state has always been part of the economic process; and the fact that geopolitical patterns are crucial in at least some kinds of technological innovation shows that states can have an autonomous influence, equivalent to economic markets themselves. The nexus of causes thus leads us naturally into the topic of politics as an area to be explained in its own right.

Part II

Politics

6

Imperialism and legitimacy: Weber's theory of politics

Weber wrote a great deal about politics, but the general outline of his theory is surprisingly obscure. Apart from Weber's style of exposition, the reason appears to be that the causal dynamics of politics he indicates are not at all what one would expect. Weber's well-known political typologies are all conventionally internal to the state: the three forms of legitimacy, with their accompanying organizational forms of domination, plus the lineup of class, status, and party factions that contend for power. But the one place where Weber (1922/1968:901–40) offers a systematic introduction to politics, his chapter in *Economy and Society* entitled "Political Communities," has not been recognized as such. Instead of dealing with the internal affairs of a politically organized society, it devotes most of its attention to apparently subsidiary matters: imperialism and nationalism. But this chapter introduces the longest section of the book (Weber, 1922/1968:901–1372), which considers the state in all its historical forms; the fact that Weber found room here for a discussion of imperialism shows that he considered the topic to have a central importance for the whole of politics.

This sense of incongruity disappears once we get over the received notion that politics is essentially internal to a state. The thrust of Weber's thought is exactly the opposite: that politics works from the outside in, and that the external, military relations of states are crucial determinants of their internal politics. This is because of the centrality of legitimacy as a resource in the struggle for power. Legitimacy, as apprehended in the usual typological fashion, seems undertheorized. It is acknowledged to be important, but there seems to be no way to go beyond the static typology and set it in motion. How is legitimacy gained and lost, and who will get it under what conditions? Weber is suggesting that it is tied to the power position of the state in the international arena.

To the extent that this section of *Economy and Society* has been read

145

at all, it has most often been by commentators who have seen it as an expression of Weber's own nationalism. Weber has been accused of an overly admiring attitude toward the militarily powerful state, and of reflecting the German nationalism of his day. This approach to Weber's analysis is misleading and simplistic. The analytical value of Weber's theoretical approach is ignored in the haste to combat what is seen as its politically activist implications. In this ideological argument, the theoretical path forward is lost. Simply put: Weber is proposing a theory of the state from the "world system" perspective. The two main possibilities for such a theory are economic or military. Hence Weber begins with a discussion of the economic position, in the form of the Marxian view of imperialism.

By historical comparisons, Weber attempts to show that certain types of capitalist interests have been imperialistic, whereas other types of capitalism have not. Capitalism, although a contributing factor in imperialism, is not the only, or even the major, determinant. Weber then turns to a military theory of imperialism, which is linked both to a theory of internal political legitimacy and to the external context of the international prestige of states.

The theoretical viewpoint Weber was developing is a good deal more fundamental that those of Weber's critics who have accused him of merely expounding nationalist ideology. Weber does *not* assume a voracious drive for military expansion, everywhere and at all times. On the contrary, his concern is to show why and how military expansionism occurs, and when it does not. The driving force of militarism, he proposes, is in the realm of prestige: the lineup of state powers in the "world" arena (however that may be defined historically in particular locations), and its interconnection with the internal prestige lineup of contending factions, which is to say the basis of their varying legitimacy.

Following Weber's sequence of argument, we see that the discussion of imperialism is preceded by a discussion of the origins of legitimacy and of the state's power-prestige in the international arena. Imperialist capitalism is introduced as a possible alternative candidate for explaining the power dynamics of states. The verdict on this being largely negative, Weber turns to what he finds to be a more significant force, nationalism. But nationalism for Weber turns out to be not racial, ethnic, or language-based but something founded on specifically political sentiments tied to the international prestige of the states in its power relations with other states. The argument is incomplete, breaking off in the middle of a sentence. But it clearly leads us back to the beginning of the chapter: The legitimacy of state rulers and the state's tendency toward imperialist expansion are reciprocally related. A theory of imperialism is an intimate part of a theory of domestic legitimacy and domestic political domination, and vice versa.

A Weberian theory of politics, then, implies that internal politics is intimately connected with external *geo*politics. The ability of internal political factions to dominate a state depends considerably on the position of the state in the transnational situation or, as we might say today, on its place in the world system. A Weberian political sociology proceeds ultimately from the outside in, and the rhythms and struggles of internal politics are strongly affected by the external fate of the state in the world. I believe it is consistent with this interpretation that Weber's introduction to the state – the chapter "Political Communities" – begins with the questions of legitimacy and imperialism, and ends with a discussion of all the different internal factions that can play a part in the domestic struggle for power. The latter section has become famous taken out of this context under the title "Class, Status, and Party" (Weber, 1946:180–95). Yet, although this section has been rightly taken as the starting point for a theory of stratification, it was written not as a discussion of stratification per se but as a roll call of the various interest groups that can play a part in the political arena. The chapter encompasses the major parts of a theory of politics; it only remains to see them as a unity. Legitimacy and its origins: that is the question of how someone can dominate the state. Imperialism, power-prestige, and nationalism: these are the processes, international in character, that determine the dynamics of legitimacy. And class, status group, and party: these are the contenders for the throne. The national state is the stage on which the drama is played, but the international arena writes the plot.

A full-scale theory of politics along these lines has scarcely been sketched, let alone worked out. I will attempt to do no more than begin the project here. Among other things, it would have to delineate the internal dynamics of the economy that create classes, and the even more complex factors producing status groups. An inkling of how these internal actors on the political stage are formed was given in Chapter 5. Here, following Weber's own exposition, I propose to draw the general connections between internal and external politics and, following logically upon this, to try to fill in what a causal theory of the external politics of states would be like. This, in fact, is a theory of *geopolitics*. Hence, Chapters 7 and 8 will develop and illustrate the general principles of geopolitics I have proposed elsewhere. Chapters 9 and 10 will focus again on the internal arena, to pick up some of the features of the group struggle for legitimacy. We begin, though, where Weber does, in his debate with the Marxians over the nature of imperialism.

Politics

Economic interests, imperialist and nonimperialist

Weber begins his discussion with the question of whether economic trade may not be the cause of political expansion of state territories. He answers: not necessarily. The unification of Germany, for example, was carried out contrary to the natural trade lines rather than along them. The economically determined market for east German grains would be England, not west Germany, and the market for west German industrial goods would be France, whereas those from east Germany would go to Russia. On the contrary, trade often follows arbitrary lines of political unification rather than causes them, as in Austria, or in Russia, where north-south railway lines were established first for military purposes. Similarly, in ancient times, numerous empires were established irrespective of preexisting trade routes: the Persian Empire, the Roman Empire when it moved inland away from the coastal sealanes, the Chinese empires, the Mongols.[1]

On the other hand, Weber (1922/1968:914) points to both modern and ancient empires in which imperial expansion did "follow the tracks of previously existing capitalist interests." The continental expansion of the United States of America, like the expansion of Great Britain overseas and of Russia in Siberia, is of this type. Weber saw this as especially likely where the areas to be penetrated were politically weak (especially tribal areas). In ancient times as well, the Athenian and Carthaginian empires, as well as the Roman during its formative period when it was confined to the Mediterranean littoral, were influenced by interests in export trade.

One may well ask if it is legitimate to consider ancient and modern states together, given their very different economic systems and social structures. Often, modern capitalist imperialism is considered qualitatively different from anything found in premodern states. Yet Weber thinks the comparison instructive. This is partly because he believes there are noneconomic processes involved in imperialism (especially the dynamics of state prestige competition) that apply to all states, whether they have modern capitalism or not. But even in the realm of economic causes, Weber holds that the key to imperialist capitalism may be found in ancient Rome itself. "Rome's overseas expansion," he states, "as far as it was economically determined,

---

[1] Weber's statement is only partly correct. Chinese empires usually tried to control the Kansu–Sinkiang corridor to the west, because of its wealth as a trade route. The Mongols did so, too, although the major parts of their empire (China, Persia, Russia) did not comprise the trade routes per se, and the Mongols certainly were not capitalists.

148

shows features that have since recurred in basic outline again and again and which still recur today. These features occurred in Rome in pronounced fashion and in gigantic dimensions, for the first time in history. However fluid the transitions to other types may be, these 'Roman' features are peculiar to a specific type of capitalist relations, or rather, *they provide the conditions for the existence of this specific type,* which we wish to call *imperialist capitalism"* (Weber, 1946:166–7; italics added).

The economic interests favoring imperialism, however, are not generally those concerned with trade per se. Given that "the economic structure in general does co-determine the extent and manner of political expansion" (Weber, 1946:915), many of these economic interests may not be capitalist at all. Migrating peasant communities in the past have sought land and wiped out the previous settlers; conquering knights have taken the land with the settlers attached as a labor force for coerced production. Which alternative has occurred has depended on the economics of army supply itself; the massacres occurred when total populations were displaced, whereas serfdom resulted from armies of self-equipped knights living on a subsistence economy. Aside from these specifically predatory economic interests, however, others can be called capitalist. Plutocratic trading communities might also be interested in conquest, since the preferable investment for profits was land worked by indebted bondsmen, and warfare provided opportunities for such investment in land. This capitalist interest in the spoils of war might even come directly into conflict with a noncapitalist economic interest, such as in the struggles between the social classes in Rome in the period leading up to the political reforms of the Gracchi in the second century B.C., when the landless peasants of the expanding Roman population wanted land for themselves, whereas the wealthy investors wanted conquered lands to be leased at nominal rates.

The form of capitalist imperialism that came to dominate in Rome represents, for Weber, the type of such imperialism in world history. The Carthaginians pioneered its use on a large scale before Rome; it was later taken up "on the grand scale" by the Spaniards in South America, by the Dutch in Indonesia, and by the English, especially in the Caribbean and the American south. Colonial capitalists had tremendous opportunities for profit by enslaving the inhabitants or tying them to the soil as plantation laborers. In the absence of governmental apparatus suitable for collecting taxes, these might be farmed out to private tax-farmers, who thereby collected another form of capitalist profit. And the colonial government could enforce state

monopolies on trade in the interests of particular capitalist enterprises.

Such interests – colonial booty capitalists, tax-farmers, privileged
traders, together with suppliers of arms and credit to the state for
military expeditions – form a capitalist sector favoring imperialism.
Weber's thesis, however, is that these constitute only one sector of
capitalists and that their interests are not identical with those of capitalists concerned with normal manufacturing and trade, who may
find ample opportunities for profit without military expansion. The
relative strength of imperialist capitalism, compared to, shall we say,
pacifist capitalism, depends on *the degree to which the economy is dependent on the state for satisfying economic demands.*

Here, then, is Weber's major theoretical point regarding the power
of imperialist capitalism. Where business interests exist primarily to
sell goods to the state or loan capital to it, or rely on the state to
provide exploitable land, monopolized trade, or opportunities for tax
farming, then capitalists favor imperialism. Where the business economy is more private, less "collectivized," less dominated by politically connected monopolists, the capitalists favor pacifism. The latter
situation, Weber suggests, characterized Britain in the free-trade era
of the 1700s and early 1800s. The former, however, he saw (writing
about 1910) as coming again into prominence, because the balance of
potential profits had swung to government monopolies in foreign
railroad building and other construction, monopolist trade concessions, and governmental loans. "The universal revival of 'imperialist'
capitalism," Weber states, "which has always been the normal form
in which capitalist interests have influenced politics, and the revival
of political drives for expansion, are thus not accidental" (Weber,
1922/1968:919).

In Weber's view, if socialist states were to emerge in the future,
they would not escape from this dynamic.[2] For precisely because
such states have a highly collective economy, there is a strong tendency for economic interests to seek satisfaction by state action, or at
least not to oppose it. Socialist states would be just as liable as states
dominated by imperialist capitalists to use force to set favorable conditions of trade or otherwise squeeze tribute out of weaker states
elsewhere in the world. If Weber's theoretical proposition about the
conditions for economic imperialism is correct, socialist states should
be at the highly imperialist end of the continuum, along with other
states with highly politically oriented economies, and at the other end
from states with very privatized economies.

[2] Bergesen (1982) concurs from the point of view of world-system theory.

Imperialism and legitimacy

Nationalism

The extent to which particular social groups favor imperialism, however, is not solely determined by their opportunities for economic profit. Noncapitalist groups as well as capitalists may sometimes profit from successful imperialism. In ancient Athens, the profits for the Athenian citizens (the *demos*) were patently obvious, paid in the form of attendance fees at public ceremonies. In the modern world, the improvement in the standard of living of the working class in countries such as England, France, and Germany due to overseas imperialism is less visible, although Weber remarks that it would become apparent by its absence were the empires to disappear. In general, aside from capitalists directly involved in government business, the modern masses have little conscious conception of what is to be gained economically by a given foreign policy. In a remarkable passage, Weber assesses the war calculations of various groups:

In the case of a lost war, the "monarch" has to fear for his throne, republican power-holders and groups having vested interests in a "republican constitution" have to fear the victorious "general." The majority of the propertied bourgeoisie have to fear economic loss from the brakes being placed upon "business as usual." Under certain circumstances, should disorganization follow defeat, the ruling stratum of notables has to fear a violent shift in power in favor of the propertyless. The "masses" as such, at least in their subjective conception and in the extreme case, have nothing concrete to lose but their lives. The valuation and effect of this danger strongly fluctuates in their own minds. On the whole, it can easily be reduced to zero through emotional influence. [Weber, 1922/1968:921]

This emotional influence Weber describes as a sentiment of prestige of the state power, which may be called nationalism.

The feeling of nationalism, however, is not to be seen simply as a matter of primordial group identity. Nationalism is not identical with the solidarity of ethnic or language groups. Weber gives numerous examples of cases in which nationalist sentiments either pass beyond or subdivide ethnic or language lines. The French nation does not consist uniformly of French-speakers, nor is the nationalism of the United States confined to a particular ethnic group. Swiss nationalism cuts across three different language-speakers and ethnicities, and separates German-speaking Swiss from German-speakers in Germany. We could add examples from ancient societies: The common language of the Greeks did not give rise to a sense of political nationality, despite strong feelings of ethnic distinctiveness from the "barbarians" outside; whereas the nationalism of the Roman citizenry encompassed a steadily expanding ethnic coalition in Italy from the very beginning.

151

Nationalism, Weber insists, is rather a specifically political sentiment. It is "linked to memories of a common political destiny"
(Weber, 1922/1968:923). It is the history of having fought together as
part of a common state, against common enemies, for common political ideals, that constitutes the bond of national solidarity. Thus, the
German-speaking Alsatians are nevertheless highly nationalistic
French people, because their political identity comes from participation in the French Revolution and its ensuing wars against the reactionary powers of the rest of Europe. Every state, insofar as it has an
emotional appeal among its own populace, derives this not from a
preexisting ethnic unity in the population, but from the dramatic
struggles in which they have participated. It is because people have
fought on the same side either in internal conflicts for control of the
state, especially in a revolution, or in external wars against outside
enemies, that national sentiments exist. Participation in the state itself
is the sine qua non of nationalism.

One might question, however, whether nationalism is a relevant
political category for the large number of states that have little or no
democratic participation in politics. Weber does not address this issue, but implicitly it seems to follow that the sentiment of nationalism
has relevance to whatever groups are engaged in politics, be they
large masses or small military or aristocratic elites. In every state,
power depends on some degree of common sentiment. At a minimum, if a small armed elite coerces unwilling masses, nevertheless
sentiments of solidarity among that coercive minority are crucial in
binding it together as an effective fighting force. Beyond this minimum, the power of any state to command its populace is enhanced to
the degree that obedience can be enforced by prestige rather than by
the immediate application of force. And at the farthest extreme, we
have the entire nation-in-arms, where widespread and intense feelings of nationalism are decisive for political events.

In this sense, nationalism is a crucial political process in all states. It
is as significant in modern dictatorships as in democracies, perhaps
all the more so because modern authoritarian regimes have made the
most extensive efforts to mobilize public demonstrations of support
for the symbols of the regime. The mass rallies of the fascist states and
the omnipresent dramatization of leadership in communist states
both represent deliberate efforts to keep up a heightened level of
nationalist sentiment in support of the state's projects. By the same
token, nationalism in Weber's sense can be regarded as a crucial
factor in ancient states as well as in modern ones. Despite the fact that
most agrarian states limit political and military participation to a small
fraction of the population, the sentiments of nationalism are impor-

tant among that mobilized group. In the history of ancient Egypt, and of medieval China, we read of "nativist reactions," which throw out foreign regimes and reinstitute domestic ones that can claim inheritance of earlier state traditions.

"Nationalism" has always existed wherever there is a state; in the modern era, what has been called "nationalism" in a more conventional sense has usually been regarded as a feature that emerged in nineteenth-century Europe and has spread only in the twentieth century to the rest of the world, as urbanization, market economies and mass communications have mobilized the bulk of the populace for the first time. But this is only a special form of "nationalism": a type in which special claims are made for political autonomy based on ethnicity. Even in these cases, the common ethnicity is often quasi-mythical, creating imaginary territorial boundaries along the lines of political convenience. In Weber's sense, "nationalism" in this version has simply been an upsurge of efforts to divide particular states into other states along their lines of maximal internal weakness. Thus, the prime example of modern "national autonomy" movements are those that dismantled the Austro-Hungarian and Ottoman empires in the Balkans. Yet these were precisely the states that were crumbling under external geopolitical pressures; "ethnic" nationalism is merely the form in which the fragmentary states surviving the breakup were organized. The ethnic purity of many of these states has been a myth; Yugoslavia, for example, incorporates several ethnic groups, as a kind of miniature Austro-Hungarian Empire in itself. And at the same time that Austria-Hungary was breaking up, the Russian Empire was incorporating even more disparate ethnic groups in central Asia and the Caucasus, having earlier overridden the ethnic divisions of the Ukraine, White Russia, and the Baltic. In this case, "ethnic nationalism" was cast in a different form, one appropriate for a consolidating empire: pan-Slavism and its extensions, which attempted to claim a greater ethnic unity appropriate to an expanding state.

Moreover, in the ancient world nationalist sentiments have been important even for mass political participation. The politics of the Greek and Roman city-states were nationalistic in much the same way that those of modern states are; and even nondemocracies, such as the Mongol, Hunnic, Turkish, or German tribal armies, depended on sentiments mobilizing whole populations to act together in their wars or invasions. In each case, political unification was due to the prestige of the state within which people had a common participation and to the comparison between their own state's prestige and the prestige of foreign states.

Nationalism exists, in short, where a state is able to awe its own followers and hence to attract more followers. "The prestige of power," Weber says (1922/1968:911), "means in practice the glory of power over other communities." A successfully expanding state attracts supporters, flocking to the winning side. Political success is the generator of nationalism. It is also true that states attacked by outsiders can experience an upsurge of nationalist sentiment, although the extent of such nationalism is more conditional. The fervor of national defense exists to the degree that a people feels confident in its state's ability to successfully resist, or to come back from a defeat for future revenge. Too protracted or severe a defeat destroys nationalism, although an initial defeat can enhance it. We may assume, extrapolating Weber, that nationalism is attached to the viability of the state, but with a time lag due to memory. If a state has a previous history of success (and most states do, else they would no longer exist at that time), then its subjects will be most likely to be aroused into nationalist fervor when an attack comes, even from powerful outside forces. Even after a defeat, the memory of their old state's former prestige may still foster nationalist sentiments, especially given that a recent defeat would make the conquering state more hated for its oppression than admired for its power. If within this memory span the conquering state suffers reversals for other reasons, the stage is set for a nationalist revival and a war of liberation.

The defeat of Prussia by Napoleon in 1805 was followed by opportunities for revolt in 1813 when the Napoleonic army was beaten in Russia; the resulting upsurge of German nationalism was well within the memory span suggested here, and its success was especially likely because the French military occupation was not a very heavy one. The upsurge of "German" nationalism that followed and eventually led to German unification by 1870 was thus only superficially ethnic in character. In reality, it was a dynamic of the prestige of the Prussian state, which had expanded steadily throughout the 1700s and was able to continue in absorbing all of Germany in the 1800s. Prussia was especially able to identify its own prestige with that of German ethnicity because of the Napoleonic conquest of Germany; the "negative prestige" of the French state constituted the other pole of the drama that constituted the victory of German nationalism.

Nationalism, then, is the result of the success of a state in power politics. It is a feeling of awe toward the state, especially in regard to its proven ability to coerce domestic consent; and a feeling of subjective participation in the state's power in relation to other states. In this latter respect it is a vote of confidence in the ability of one's state to defend one against outside enemies, and, relatedly, in its ability to expand and conquer others. Like fans following a winning football

154

team, the loyalty of political subjects to their state depends on its victories. A victorious state experiences the greatest nationalism; an embattled one experiences nationalism to the extent that it can draw upon memories of past victories that can probably be repeated. A long string of defeats saps national loyalty, and eventually, after time periods we have not yet measured, national loyalty disappears. In its place comes a new nationalism, adhering to some new, victorious state, and cloaked in its particular symbolic formula, whether it be an ethnic or a more strictly political ideology.

Legitimacy

It should be apparent, then, that nationalism for Weber is the essence of political legitimacy. Legitimacy, as usually defined, is the willingness of followers to accept orders given to them as properly to be obeyed. Too often this is conceived of as a kind of psychological quantity impressed on individuals by socialization, and acting as an internal gyroscope bringing about political obedience. Yet Weber's discussion shows that legitimacy is nothing if not dynamic. It is not an internalized constant but an emotional feeling that arises from assessing the prestige of the state at any given moment. Weber's nationalism is simply legitimacy carried to fervid levels: In a condition of nationalist arousal, a populace does not merely passively accept the state's orders as legitimate but is actively enthusiastic to join in fighting the state's battles for it. But just as nationalism waxes and wanes with the degree of political conflict and the changing fortunes of states, legitimacy also fluctuates from high to low. In many cases it may be nonexistent.

Weber's discussion of the origins of legitimacy, which leads off his chapter on "Political Communities," makes clear the connection between legitimacy and national violence. Originally, Weber proposes, violence was not legitimate. He sketches a situation of loose tribal ties. Violent individuals form small marauding bands; men gather together in a closed "men's house" and subjugate the women and the weaker individuals. Such groups, he proposes, may cloak their power in the religious ceremonial and the fearsome masks of "supernatural" beings described in the ethnographic literature; but the religious legitimation is spurious, merely an effort to add symbolic terror to the real violence at their disposal. Inside the secret society, the attitude toward these spirits may remain cynical and skeptical. The warriors' domination over others is based ultimately on naked force, and not conceded as a legitimate right.

Nevertheless, a real sense of legitimacy does spring from this kind of

155

organization of violence. Legitimacy comes from a special type of emotion: the emotion that individuals feel when facing the threat of death in the company of others. The group that faces death together has a special bond. It is a "community of political destiny" of a sort matched by no other. Such groups acquire a solidarity deriving from a "community of memories" deeper than ethnic, linguistic, or other cultural ties. It is for this reason that nationalism is not linked to specific cultural backgrounds, but can bring together whoever happens to have been united by fighting together in a common organization.

So far we have seen only the source of a peculiar type of solidarity, confined within fighting groups. Legitimacy in the full sense arises from this, however, because the individual is expected to face death in the interest of the group as a whole. Accordingly, the individual concedes the right of the group to expect him (or her) to engage in self-sacrifice for the sake of the group, as well as to support the group in all aspects relating to the common safety. This gives rise to a particular type of violence that is accepted as legitimate by the members of the group on whom it may be turned: violent punishment directed by the group as punishment against any of its members who act treasonably or harm the group by disobedience or cowardice in warfare. For the first time, violence is now connected with a right that people (at least some of them) will concede applies to themselves as well as others.

At this level, it should be noted, violence is legitimate only as used within the fighting group, for purposes of disciplining its own members. The violence that the group uses against outsiders is not legitimate; it is merely successful coercion, or not. Thus, sentiments of legitimate authority exist only within particular disciplined groups; outside these groups, there is no claim of legitimacy. Weber extends this model to groups other than military ones, to other pockets of legitimacy that emerge in various premodern societies. Religious groups generate this sense of the obligation of the individual to the group, above all to the extent that in a hostile environment members are expected to undergo martyrdom for the faith. Kin groups with their obligation to take blood vengeance for injuries to any of their members; aristocracies with codes of honor requiring the settlement of affairs through dueling; the sworn secrecy of bandit societies: all of these generate specific sentiments of legitimate authority for insiders, even though outsiders are completely cut off from these inner realms.

The crucial development in the modern phenomenon of legitimacy occurs when the state manages to acquire a monopoly of violence on

156

a given territory. When this occurs, the collectivity involved in warfare becomes much more extended. When aristocracies no longer fight other small forces of opposing aristocracies in the midst of peasants indifferent to the outcomes, the sphere of legitimate authority is ready for a sizable extension. When an entire populace is attacked, it becomes realistic for states to claim that everyone is responsible for aiding in the group's defense. The sentiment that linked only the members of a fighting group together into an authority structure, conceding the legitimate rights of disciplinary coercion over its members, now becomes extended to the whole society. It is the military transition to mass warfare that makes every member of a modern state subject to the legitimate discipline of the state.

This is not to say that premodern rulers do not attempt to coerce their followers or to demand their unconditional obedience. What differs, rather, is the emotional mechanism. Where the masses had previously been coerced, so to speak, from "outside," now there is a psychological (more properly, in Durkheimian terms, ritual) mechanism that may sometimes produce a willingness of the masses to see each other coerced, and even to concede that they have duties the failure of which would rightly bring their own punishment. This does not happen all the time, and Weber was well aware (as surely we should be) that legitimacy is a fluctuating sentiment. But what is distinctive about modern politics is that such mass sentiments do regularly occur at times of major political events, and hence the fluctuation in legitimacy can be a crucial determinant of the fate of governments and of states.

The argument as stated gives too much of the impression of an evolutionary sequence from nonlegitimate violence, through the internal legitimacy of discipline in conflict groups, to the mass legitimacy of the modern state. In fact, we can easily give historical cases (many of them in the preceding pages) of mass political participation and hence mass sentiments of legitimacy in premodern states. The politics of Rome and the Greek city-states, and the mass posttribal nomad armies, provides examples; one might well add some of the Crusades and other cases. Conversely, the small-scale in-group legitimacy of fighting organizations does not disappear in the modern era, nor does illegitimate violence. What we have, rather, is a set of analytical constructs: three different conditions that give rise to varying sentiments conceding the legitimacy of violence used for group discipline. The major point is that whatever group is mobilized as a fighting group will undergo automatic processes that generate these emotions legitimating authority.

Legitimacy and imperialism

We may now attach the model of internal legitimacy to the Weberian theory of nationalism and imperialism. Legitimacy, for Weber, is not a constant quantity. It varies depending on the extent to which people feel their group is in a situation involving the potential threat of death. The group involved in a fight feels the pressure for group discipline, and concedes the legitimacy of its leadership, much more strongly than the same group in time of peace. The same applies on an extended scale to a whole society, if it is collectively organized for defense and attack. Legitimacy not only is intermittent over time; Weber (1922/1968:902) even remarks that in a prolonged state of peace, a society tends toward nonlegitimacy, in fact toward a condition of anarchy.

It is for this reason that so much of the peacetime discourse of politics nevertheless is aimed, overtly or covertly, at war. A state maintains its internal legitimacy to the extent that it can invoke its external power against threatening rival states. Its legitimacy depends not only on the actual emotions that take place during fighting but also on the sentiments that can be generated by waving the flag in peacetime. The state with high prestige vis-à-vis other states assures itself of a higher degree of legitimacy for its demands for internal obedience. Thus, Weber (1922/1968:904) can conclude that "it is on this prestige that the consensus of specific legitimacy of action is founded."

This analysis of legitimacy may sound strange in relation to Weber's better-known typology of charismatic, traditional, and rational-legal forms of legitimacy. Did Weber have two different and unrelated theories of legitimacy? I do not think so. The three types of legitimacy refer to the way that legitimacy is structured; the community-of-violence theory explains the source and strength of the feelings of legitimacy. Thus charismatic leaders become the personal focus of authority, whereas traditional leaders inherit their offices through kinship or religious practices, and rational-legal leaders are chosen and base their orders on enacted constitutions or laws. To what degree the populace accords legitimacy to such persons depends on the strength of emotions aroused by their political community of fate. The fate of the state's power-prestige determines the amount of legitimacy there will be; the typology merely indicates who will be the recipient of this legitimacy. For the dynamics of legitimacy, then, the power-prestige model is a more important predictor of the behavior of political *subjects* than the typology. In this view, previous discussion of legitimacy in terms of religious ceremonial or rational-

158

legal ideologies are too static. Such arguments place too much emphasis on the ability of religion or ideology to create legitimacy, whereas in fact these merely channel emotions onto particular recipients.[3]

One might nevertheless challenge this interpretation empirically on the grounds that it makes states' legitimacy depend unnecessarily on their belligerence. It would seem to make it impossible for a state to be legitimate in peacetime, thus proposing a highly pessimistic view of the world, as well as one that does not fit all the historical facts. Weber himself seems to give evidence against this theory, pointing out that political elites are not always nationalistic and imperialistic but are at times opposed to imperialism. The Spartan aristocracy for long periods was anti-expansionist; similarly, the Roman aristocracy after the Punic Wars, when the conquest of Italy had been completed, opposed further imperial expansion in favor of a "little Italy" policy. Similarly, the British aristocracy in the 1700s and 1800s favored a peaceful foreign policy, intervening merely to maintain the balance of power; their anti-imperialism continued up through political opposition to the wave of colonial expansion in the 1800s. Weber explains such anti-imperialistic sentiments on the grounds that these elites felt threatened domestically by political opponents who would benefit more from imperial expansion than themselves. The Spartans and Romans feared the democratization that had occurred in other city-states undergoing mass military mobilization, and felt their power challenged by imperialist demagogues appealing to the masses. The Roman aristocracy was right in their fears; the democratizing war party led by Marius and later by his relative, Julius Caesar, eventually

---

[3] This is consistent with a formal theory of rituals, which would apply to religious and political rituals as well. A ritual requires not only a particular formula, focus of attention, and an assembled group, but also a strong common emotion (Collins, 1975:153–5). Given the emotion, a ritual is an effective machine for creating sacred symbols and using them to designate social membership and authority. But the emotion comes from outside the ritual itself. The violence model explains where the most important emotional ingredient of legitimacy rituals comes from. In traditional societies we can systematically observe the connection between religious impressiveness and the hierarchy of political power (Swanson, 1962); and a similar connection seems to exist in modern secular regimes between the degree of political centralization and authoritarianism, and the extent of ideological ceremony and ideological sacredness. Such correlations, however, are static; and one may question whether the religion is so strongly believed in at all points in historical time. I would suggest, along the lines of Weber's analysis, that the impressiveness of the gods depends on the political success of the ruler, especially in military affairs. One might say: It is the gods (or other sacred objects) who are tested on the battlefield; some are promoted and exalted as a result, while others lose their holiness. Compare the argument of Girard (1977) that religious ceremonies always include an element of violence.

destroyed the oligarchy. A theoretical question remains, however: How can elites oppose imperialism if their sole base of legitimacy depends on belligerent sentiments and the prestige of military expansion?

I believe there are two answers to this question. These are barely touched by Weber, but they are not inconsistent with his analysis. One answer is that legitimacy is intermittent and not continuously necessary for domination. The second answer is that there are internal equivalents of war that create domestic legitimacy.

First, it should be recognized that political domination does not depend solely on legitimacy. Widespread emotions of legitimacy make it easier to rule; but the existence of armaments in the hands of a few can enforce domination a good deal of the time, especially in the absence of some strongly organized movement of revolt, which itself would require a strong counterlegitimacy. Moreover, from the point of view of a fine-grained microanalysis (Collins, 1981a) a great deal of social order is based on routine. Things stay the way they are because people are physically dispersed across the landscape in certain ways – the rich man in his castle, the poor man in his hut, and so forth – and the cognitive complexities of changing the physical organization of things tends to require more energy and more coordinative activities than simply leaving things as they are. This is not to say that the persons in power may not wish to generate strong sentiments of compliance in order to institute actions of their own; hence, some of the time they wish to arouse feelings of legitimacy. But this is intermittent. During any given 24-hour period, or any 365-day year, there are probably fairly few minutes during which many of the populace are called upon to experience the emotions endowing the state with legitimacy. Much of the time the state can survive by routine, or by a relatively low degree of "legitimacy arousal."

The second answer is that when legitimacy becomes important for politicians, it can be aroused domestically as well as on the international scene. It may be true historically, as Weber claims, that it is external violence that gives rise to the first and strongest feelings of legitimate obligation to the state. But the mechanism is a general one: Whenever a group finds itself in a community of fate regarding potential violence from some outside group, internal legitimacy for its authority structure is generated. Thus, internal conflicts can also generate legitimacy, provided they are potentially dangerous enough (and provided also that the group leaders can plausibly claim that they will win and crush their domestic enemies). Thus, class conflict may be a basis for internal legitimacy. The ruling class need not base its claims to domination entirely on some ideology proclaiming the justice of its rule; a challenge from some other class can be even more effective in stirring up the emotions buttressing or establishing its legitimacy. It then becomes the defender of order against the party of disorder, where "disorder" means explicitly violence in the streets, threats to persons and property.

Other domestic enemies may also be invoked. Religious heretics or supernaturally inspired threats (such as witches) may on occasion represent significant enough threats to generate legitimacy; other special minorities or deviants may also serve (Bergeson, 1977). Crime may also usefully serve this purpose. Perhaps the generalization may be made that in a society in which notions of class conflict are not part of the official ideology, and ethnic and religious persecution is taboo (as in the United States after 1960), crime is magnified as a violent threat in order to generate feelings of domestic legitimacy for the state.

It should be noted that, under certain circumstances, the two answers to the question of nonnationalist legitimacy can come together. Legitimacy may well be intermittent and largely superfluous to routine daily life. But this does not mean the state will fall apart from sheer lack of legitimacy. When the state does begin to crack, it is because organized groups spring up to claim legitimacy for themselves (expressly because they are combat groups). This in turn means that a situation of genuine domestic threat now exists, and hence politicians in power can point to an internal conflict of groups. Moreover, the more serious the rebellion, the more of the population it mobilizes into political participation. As the situation approaches a revolutionary crisis, everyone is forced to take an emotional stand by declaring his or her loyalty to one side or the other. This constitutes a Schelling-type "consensus-game," in which individuals try to join in the side they expect is most likely to win, lest they be endangered by being caught on the losing side (Schelling, 1962). Usually the side with the best "track record" of past coercive successes (the existing state) will gain most of these "swing votes," helping assure its victory. And from the point of view we are considering here, it gains something else: a renewed basis of legitimacy. In internal politics, as in external power-prestige games, the same dynamic applies: the state that successfully surmounts a situation of widespread violent threat gets a significant infusion of legitimacy. Ultimately this is the lifeblood (or should one say the heroin fix) of politics.

Geopolitics, external and internal

Returning now to the question with which we began: How are the dynamics of imperialism to be explained? We must confine ourselves here, as Weber does, to imperialism in the sense of foreign military intervention to establish an empire; covert forms of imperial domination, such as those promoted by unequal exchange in a formally free market (Emmanuel, 1972) are presumably the result of some other dynamic. Weber's argument is twofold: (1) Colonial booty capitalism plays a role in fostering imperialism; this is a strong influence to the degree that the economy revolves around provisions to and flowing from the state. Yet this economic interest in imperialism, even in these instances, is the less important factor. (2) The most important factor is the interests of political leaders in stirring up domestic legitimacy through success in the external military competition with other states. Internal legitimation is the good to be sought through engaging in the prestige game in the international arena; the prize for the rulers of the "Great Power" is paid in the coin of internal politics.

We have, however, just seen that there are alternative, homegrown ways of generating legitimacy without venturing abroad. How do we weigh these relative to foreign-military-based legitimacy? When will politicians attempt to play on one rather than the other? (And for that matter, why shouldn't they play on both at once?) The challenge is to take the elements Weber has provided and spin them into a full-blown predictive theory.

It is clear that such a theory must involve two different realms of explanation, the external arena of military relations among states, and the internal arena of domestic political factions. I propose that we know something of the determinants operating in both of these realms, and also that internal and external politics influence each other. The result of such a theory, then, should be to explain which states will be most (and least) imperialistic externally, and similarly, which factions will achieve the most legitimacy internally, and by which kind of appeal.

First the external arena. This may be defined as a network of states concerned about their military prestige vis-à-vis one another. The prestige emulation goes on constantly, during peacetime as well as during war. Thus the relations among states may be seen as a kind of status system analogous to that found among social groups within a society. Bendix (1967, 1978) has taken such concepts as the "reference group" from social psychology to apply to the process by which the leaders of an entire society take another as "reference society" to catch up with; hence, the process of "modernization" is an endless chain of emulation of successful "world powers" by aspiring ones. It follows that imperial expansion is carried out in order to claim or maintain one's status as a Great Power, rather than for economic motives per se.

162

Imperialism and legitimacy

This analysis helps make sense out of many phases of world history. Thus the scramble for colonies after 1880 was set off as the rising German state and the revived French one acted to emulate and challenge British domination of world power-prestige; the result was an "inflationary" phase of prestige competition. (Along this line of reasoning, it was the external prestige-dynamic that brought England unwillingly out of its anti-imperial mood – not because, as Weber stated, colonial booty capitalism became internally dominant; rather, the change in mood presumably occurred only as the result of the colonial race.) The possession of colonies was secondary and symbolic: Great Powers fought for such things, whether or not they were worth the cost in economic terms. It is consonant with this analysis that World War I was not fought between the states whose economic interests in the colonies were most clearly opposed (because this would have brought about a war between France and Russia on one side, against England as the principal enemy, probably in alliance with Germany); instead, England joined its colonial rivals against Germany, which was the state making the strongest bid to overtake England in international military prestige. Similarly, it can be argued that the post–World War II confrontation between the United States and the Soviet Union is fundamentally a prestige competition among the two Great Powers, and would exist whether or not economic interests were at stake. It is in keeping with this analysis that both U.S. and Soviet political elites have based their strongest claims for legitimacy on the foreign threat from the other.

It remains to make this theory more precise. After all, there are many states in the international arena. At any given time, which ones will be the most imperialistic, and against whom will their imperialism be directed? In Bendix's (1967) terms, who will be the "reference society," and who will be its primary emulator?

The answer, I would suggest, is that the militarily most powerful state becomes the "reference society" at any given time. (Thus, in Bendix's modernization sequence we see a series of attempts to catch up first with Spain, then with England, France – later with Germany, Soviet Russia, and the United States giving a choice of leading models.) This may serve as a provisional answer. To explain which states will be the prime emulators, the would-be challengers, we must go beyond this to consider the conditions that give a state a real chance of success. For if domestic legitimacy is to be gained by winning power in the international arena, it should also be kept in mind that legitimacy can also be lost as well as won. Rulers of states that fight unsuccessful wars jeopardize their own legitimacy at home, and would have been better off if they had not attempted the wars. Sometimes domestic politics leaves rulers little choice in this matter; but leaving this condition aside for the moment and considering only the external lineup of states, it is possible to say which states should be most likely to attempt external expansion – simply put, the states that have the greatest chance of military success. Here we may invoke geopolitical theory of the determinants of the expansion and contraction of states' borders (Collins, 1978; Chapter 7 of this volume). Without going into the details of this model, it can be noted that states that have a size and resource advantage over their neighbors, or that have a "marchland advantage" in the positional lineups among multifront confrontations, will be most tempted to expand at the expense of other states around them. It is these conditions that determine which states are relatively more and less imperialistic at any particular time in world history. In short, the dynamics of international prestige emulation, insofar as they can be predicted solely from the external relations among states, are based on the principles of geopolitics.

We turn now to the internal dynamics of imperialism. The most significant internal principle is that whichever political faction carries out a war will get the credit or blame for its success or failure. The party that carries out a successful war enhances its domestic legitimacy; that which leads a military defeat loses legitimacy. Within time limits that are still to be determined, this principle should help explain the ups and downs of domestic politics. At the extreme, this principle is congruent with a theory of revolution that emphasizes military defeat or exhaustion as its primary cause (Skocpol, 1979; Collins, 1978).[4] The argument made here implies that the revolutionary downfall of a state is due not simply to economic difficulties or disintegration of its military apparatus in defeat (which may not occur in every case of revolution) but also to its loss of legitimacy. Presumably this would depend on the regime's basing its claims strongly on prestige in the international arena.[5]

Short of revolution, one would expect that military success or defeat would affect the ascendancy and decline of domestic political factions. This analysis has yet to be tested empirically. The theoretical claim, though, is extensive. It implies that the fate of domestic parties depends largely on the fate of their state in the international arena. Since that international fate is predictable, in turn, from the geopoliti-

---

[4] The latter proposes that military overextension of states typically leads to rapid disintegration of territorial power.

[5] For example, the fall of the Shah's government in Iran in 1978 was to a considerable extent due to the fact that it was linked closely to U.S. military support. Defeat of a U.S.-supported regime in Vietnam caused a sharp drop in this source of power-prestige, and drastically curtailed the legitimacy of the Iranian government.

cal structure of the world system, the inference is that world geopolitics is a major determinant of the rise and fall of internal political factions in its constituent states.

The nature of this linkage is not yet specified. The geopolitical system does not tell us who will be the domestic actors in this drama; it only predicts the rise and fall of each, starting from the possession of domestic power by one or another state at a given time. Political theory as more conventionally pursued still holds a place in this kind of world-system theory; it shows the domestic social bases on which political factions are formed, and explains their domestic political resources and their lines of cleavage. Among these bases, several types of economic cleavage are prominent.[6] But this type of analysis is essentially static. It tells us who the political factions will be at a given time in a particular society. If we wish to predict their fortunes, their rise and fall into and out of power, we must turn to the world arena.[7]

Internal legitimacy and external power-prestige are connected. Weber's theory of imperialism was primarily an introduction to his theory of politics. Overall, Weber was more concerned with the political effects of imperialism than with its causes. But because he arrives at this conception by attempting to show that the causes of imperialism are primarily the internal struggle for legitimacy, we may extrapolate. Internal political factions rise and fall because they are tied to success or failure in foreign policy. This success or failure depends on the contingencies of the world system of geopolitical advantages and disadvantages. These dynamics of internal legitimacy-seeking create the impetus within any particular state for engaging in subsequent ventures in imperialism.

The theory may be extended on both fronts. We may examine the internal dynamics that produce classes and other factions, and the

[6] Among the best of such analyses are Wiley (1967) and Paige (1975). But see Sommers and Goldfrank (1979), for a critique of the latter as unable to predict the ascendancy of particular factions because it ignores the world context.

[7] Weber's point that certain political elites, such as the Spartan ruling class or the Roman or British aristocracy, were anti-imperialist because of fear of mass demagogic opposition at home suggests another refinement to this analysis. That is, not only do world geopolitical relations affect the internal fates of political factions, but also the contingencies of domestic political struggles affect whether or not a state tends to be imperialistic. Certain factions will throw the brakes to impede an imperial policy that might otherwise be favorable in the external arena. On the whole, though, I think this is a secondary factor. Rome and Britain eventually embarked on imperial expansion despite opposition by domestic elites; and Sparta's failure to do so may be attributed largely to the extent of opposition among its neighbors. On balance, I would judge that the dynamics of internal/external political relations are most heavily weighed by the external situation. The internal situation can slow down reaction to the external opportunities, but not by more than fifty years, if that.

economic conditions that constitute much of the internal environment of politics. Among these economic forces, though, will be precisely the demands made by the state to finance itself; and this is largely a matter of the military state's demands for the resources to take advantage of geopolitical opportunities in the external arena or merely to keep up with the degree of international competition in military technology. State fiscal crises, with their ramifying effects on domestic economies, are more often than not results of geopolitical overextension or other geopolitically determined pressures. The military resources of the state, of course, are also used to maintain internal "order," albeit often in the form of the authority of a privileged class over others. This privileged group may well take the form of parasitical inhabitants of the state itself. The growth of this group beyond certain bounds may become another cause of "fiscal crisis," such as the one that beset the top-heavy bureaucracy of Sung China (Chapter 3). In a sense, the state acts to extract resources from within a territory, in order to transfer them to a center that maintains coercive control. The state itself might be conceived as a form of "internal geopolitics," and its strains and dynamics can come from the contingencies of exerting military threat both internally and externally.

This leads us again to the external front, which is, of course, an object of interest in its own right. For if the causal dynamics of internal politics are related in so many ways to a state's external power position, an ultramacro viewpoint on the dynamics of the entire system of interacting states is what we must focus on theoretically. The following two chapters, therefore, treat some generalizations that have already been developed along these lines.

7

Modern technology and geopolitics

Most theories of geopolitics have been drawn from the histories of agrarian and early industrial states. In recent years, however, it has been argued that modern technologies have completely changed the principles of warfare and hence the geopolitical relations of states. The internal combustion engine, the airplane, the rocket – all have greatly increased the range and speed of movement and attack; and electronics makes global communications virtually instantaneous. Does it follow, then, that we are living in an era of entirely new geopolitical rules, in which all older principles of geopolitical explanation are outdated?

One prominent line of thought answers this strongly in the affirmative. Andreski (1968) states emphatically that the revolution in transportation and communication has already doomed the nation-state as an anachronism. The geopolitics of a plurality of states, such as has characterized the world up until now, no longer applies. The most powerful states now can make military strikes in a minimal time anywhere on the globe. Under these circumstances a world empire is not only possible but (barring total destruction) inevitable. Not only has the new military technology made it likely that such an empire can be won, but the rapid pace of modern transportation and communication make it feasible to administer a state of this size. Other analysts, too, have assumed that a unified world empire is not only possible but likely in the future; this has been argued by Wallerstein and his collaborators as a culmination of long-term trends in the capitalist world economy (Research Working Group, 1979).

This viewpoint implies that such geopolitical principles as formerly applied to the individual stages have been superseded. What takes their place is an economic dynamic which encompasses the entire world system, or alternatively, the strategies of nuclear war. The latter poses quite different possibilities than old-fashioned military

Originally published in *Journal of Political and Military Sociology*, 1981 (9):163–177.

expansion through conventional victory in warfare. In either case we appear to be in an entirely new geopolitical era.

On the other side it might be argued that nothing essential has changed that necessitates a revision of geopolitical principles for the contemporary period. This is the position that I will defend in this chapter. Classical geopolitical analysis has induced principles from the histories of the agrarian and early industrial states, ranging from the ancient Chinese, Middle Eastern, and Mediterranean empires, through the nineteenth century at the latest. A summary and extension of such theorizing is given in a previous publication (Collins, 1978). Although this material does not take account of the technological capacities of 20th century warfare, I will suggest that a closer look at modern warfare shows that the same sorts of principles continue to apply as in the past. Some major principles are:

(1) *Territorial resource advantage.* Other factors being equal, richer and more populous states win wars against smaller and poorer ones. Hence the former tend to expand over long periods of time, the smaller to contract.

(2) *Marchland advantage and corollaries.* The geographical location of states relative to each other, independently of their wealth and population, also affects their chances of victory in warfare and hence of long-term expansion or contraction. (A) States which are physically peripheral to others ("marchland states" in the terminology of McNeill, 1963) have an advantage over those which have potential enemies on more than one border. The marchland principle is especially important in that a series of other processes follow from it. These include (B) the tendency for interior states caught between several marchlands to fragment over long periods of time, and (C) the periodic simplification of geopolitics that occurs when rival marchland states have succeeded in fully assimilating the territories between them. The latter situation, I have suggested, constitutes (D) a crucial turning point, characterized by "showdown" wars of heightened military ferocity, and resulting either in local empires or renewed fragmentation.

(3) *Overextension and disintegration.* A related geographical consideration affects the possibility of states rapidly losing territory or disintegrating. Regimes undergo such crises because of military defeats and/or economic strains resulting from attempts to dominate territories which are too remote from their home base. Such geopolitical overextension, I have suggested, consists in fighting heavily on territories which are more than one ethnic/geographical heartland away from the political center. This principle may be of considerable impor-

tance for the sociology of revolution, in that military disintegration is a crucial precondition for revolution (Collins, 1975: 391; Skocpol, 1979). If this is so, geopolitical overextension is a key antecedent condition of revolution.

All of these principles appear to be called into question by 20th century technology. The *territorial resource advantage* (1) would be irrelevant once a single world empire was established. The *marchland principle* and its corollaries (2), and the *principle of military overextension* (3), are apparently challenged by modern technology even before a world-empire is established. For modern sea and air power have put all nations in direct contact with each other. Already the era of the sailing ship made England militarily contiguous to South Africa and India, and allowed Spain an empire stretching from Argentina to the Philippines. With modern air power, it would seem that even inland states are militarily accessible to any outsider that wishes to attack them. ICBMs can be launched virtually from anywhere to anywhere. Any country that has an airport can be invaded by plane, just as Soviet troops have landed in Afghanistan and Ethiopia, or Cuban troops in Angola. Air and sea power seem to mean that all the advantages of position are swept off the world chessboard. No country enjoys the advantage of having no enemies to the rear. Every country, no matter how distant, is potentially the enemy of every other. There are no more marchlands. It would then become impossible to say that marchland states will expand. Other geopolitical principles which follow from this one, such as the tendency of middle states to fragment or the occurence of turning points in military history, would no longer hold. Similarly, it could no longer be possible to characterize any military advance, no matter how distant, as overextension; hence military strains leading to the collapse of states would no longer hold.

In what follows, I will attempt to show that these criticisms are groundless. First, I will show that the size of states does not grow in the advanced industrial era nor do the effects of technology upon modern warfare lead us to expect that empires larger than the ones that have already existed are likely to be established. A unified world empire is highly unlikely even in the very long run, and there is every reason to expect that there will be multiple contending states into the indefinite future. Evidence bearing on this point is presented in Part I.

Next, I will take up the two forms of military power that seem to offer the greatest challenge to the geopolitical principles based on geographical location. These are sea and air power, which we will consider in Parts II and III. My conclusion will be that far from over-turning classical geopolitical rules based on land position, these two types of warfare are largely dependent upon the same principles which govern conventional land warfare.

I. The size of contemporary and traditional states

The speed of transportation has increased enormously in the past 150 years. In the Middle Ages, armies were limited to movement by foot (about 10 miles a day on the average, and up to 40 miles a day during emergencies), by horse, or by boat. Today cars and trucks can move, over suitable highways, 1000 miles in a day or even further. Modern ships can cover 500 miles a day, and jet aircraft can cover 12,000. If a state exists by being able to move troops to put down internal upris-ings or to repel external invaders, there is no doubt that a modern state can cover a large territory much more easily than a pre-industrial one could.

When the Ottoman Empire of the 1500s A.D. went on its annual campaigns in the Balkans, its effective range was about 900 miles: the distance its army could march from home base in three months and still be able to return home for the winter (McNeill, 1964). This was about the distance from Constantinople to Vienna, the point of far-thest Ottoman threat. A modern mechanized army could drive this distance, hypothetically, in a day or two. If transportation were all there was to it, there is no reason why a single empire could not extend all across the Eurasian continent from Vladivostok to Gibral-tar. One could easily imagine an empire of the entire globe in which every point would be accessible from any other within 24 hours by air and within a few weeks by sea.

But this has not happened yet, nor is it very likely. For the size of states is not only a matter of internal transportation but also of ex-ternal opposition and of relative expense. The most rapid and far-ranging military advances of modern times are small compared to the speed of unimpeded motor travel. Von Manstein's army in Russia in 1940 covered 40 miles a day for 5 consecutive days; this was consid-ered a very rapid advance, and it resulted in the army outrunning its supplies and being forced to stop and wait for them to catch up. Patton in 1944 advanced some 200 miles in 12 days, an average of 17 miles per day, in one of the most spectacular advances in military history (Van Creveld, 1977:159, 217). Despite motorization, it has been concluded that "the speed of strategic marches had not risen significantly" in modern warfare as compared to pre-motorized war-fare (Van Creveld, 1977:279).

Moreover, modern technology has become increasingly expensive. Even in classical times a distant campaign by foot soldiers was more expensive than a nearby one because every day of marching meant a day's worth of rations which had to be transported along with the army, as well as rations for the people and animals carrying the rations. Traditional armies attempted to circumvent this problem by foraging among the local population whenever possible (Van Creveld, 1977:5–108). This meant that an army would exhaust local sources of supplies and hence would have to keep moving if it were to be fed. When an army passed through barren territory or was tied down by a prolonged siege, the foraging method could not be used, and the length of supply lines became a crucial limit upon military expansion.

Today the logistics problem is much more severe. Traditional armies were usually small, on the order of 5,000 to 25,000 men in the 1400s A.D., or 60,000 to 100,000 in the 1600s and 1700s (Keegan, 1976:88; Van Creveld, 1977:34, 38). In the 20th century armies are much larger. Battlefield armies of World War I were on the order of 500,000 to 1,000,000 men; the German invasion of Russia in World War II was initiated with 3,500,000 soldiers (Keegan, 1976:271; Van Creveld, 1977:149). This has made foraging for supplies impossible, and modern armies have become absolutely dependent on their supply lines from home base.

The ramifications of this logistics problem are considerable. Trucks, tanks, and a supporting highway system eat up their equivalent of daily rations in the form of oil and spare parts. The most modern heavy tanks burn two gallons of gasoline per mile. The largest part of modern logistics has come to be the provision of ammunition. As late as the Franco-Prussian war of 1870, ammunition represented less than 1% of total supplies, with most of the rest being taken up with food and other subsistence. In World War II, these proportions were reversed, with total subsistence amounting to between 8% and 12% of supplies (Van Creveld, 1977:233). In the 1600s, artillery guns were supplied with 100 balls for an entire campaign; even two centuries later an infantryman might fire no more than 7 rounds during a war (Van Creveld, 1977:35, 81). By comparison, a single battle in World War I involved an artillery bombardment of 3 million rounds. This trend toward the massive expenditure of ammunition has continued; modern infantry are armed almost exclusively with automatic weapons firing at rates of up to 800 rounds per minute (Keegan, 1976:213, 307). A modern army can use up as much ammunition in a few weeks as previous armies fired off in years of fighting.

Thus although the baggage train of a modern army moves much

faster, hypothetically, than the Roman legions did, it has swollen to overwhelming size. Where an ancient army would have been made up largely of combat troops, in today's armies 90% of the troops are non-combatants. Behind the front is the great bulk of the army, manning a dense network of headquarters, supply dumps, medical facilities, motor pools, railheads, communications centers, and mechanical repair facilities (Keegan, 1977:293–4). Moving the front line is like nothing so much as an enormous traffic jam. Distant troop movements are more expensive than ever before. The cost of maintaining half a million U.S. troops in Vietnam, for instance, was $40 billion per year (Collins and Cordesman, 1978:14), an economic cost which had much to do with the difficulty of defending even a quasi-empire at that distance.

With these drawbacks to distant military operations, it ought to come as no surprise that *the maximal size of states has not changed in the last 2000 years.* Already at the time of the Roman Empire and the Chinese Han Dynasty, the largest states controlled several million square miles (Taagepera, 1979; Lenski, 1966). Today the scale remains about the same. The biggest states in the world today – Canada, China, the United States, Brazil, and Australia – are all approximately between 3 and 4 million square miles, while the rest of the world's nations are considerably smaller. There is one exception, the present-day U.S.S.R. at 8.6 million square miles. About 2/3 of this territory is the nearly-empty spaces of Siberia. And these lands were taken into the Russian empire in the 1500s and 1600s, long before the coming of the railroads or any of the appurtenances of industrialism (McEvedy, 1971:16, 48, 61). Russia was able to acquire Siberia purely because the geopolitical situation allowed it, especially because no other state was in a position to expand into it. Similarly, Canada is a huge state because it holds a large part of the barren sub-polar regions, in the absence of any military rivals for it.

The largest states of the pre-industrial past – Czarist Russia, the Mongol empire, the major Chinese dynasties, the Spanish empire – were also as large as those of today. They were a good deal larger than an average-sized modern state. France, whose boundaries have changed very little in the past 400 years (McEvedy, 1971:26, 80), is today the largest country in Europe at 210,000 square miles. And tiny Switzerland (16,000 square miles) has been independent almost continuously since the Middle Ages (McEvedy, 1971:26, 30) and shows every sign of continuing so for the foreseeable future.

In short, there is no historical trend toward bigger states in the modern world. There is no reason to expect that an empire subjugating the entire globe will ever come into existence. By the same token, there will be a good many medium and small-sized states in the centuries to come, as well as a few larger ones. The very technology of modern transportation and warfare which appears superficially to make a world empire possible actually carries such a heavy logistics load as to limit its own sphere of operations. The situation is analogous to the limits upon effective operation of a large-scale business organization under conditions of technical complexity and geographical dispersion. Such organizations had to shift to an autonomous divisional structure and away from a centralized one (Chandler, 1962). The military/political analogue of such decentralization is a plurality of states. Among this plurality, traditional geopolitical relations should continue to hold.

II. The vulnerability of sea power

We now turn to the question of whether land-based geopolitical principles hold when other forms of long-distance transportation are considered. Presumably all states which are accessible by water are militarily contiguous to each other, and hence any advantage or pattern associated with relative geographical location would be circumvented. Air power is an *a fortiori* instance of this mutual military accessibility. For this reason sea power is a particularly interesting test case, as it has existed already for several millennia, and its patterns may be seen in a good deal of historical evidence.

There have been relatively few overseas empires compared to the number of land-based conquest states throughout world history. This is especially true of the Orient. No significant maritime empires are found in the indigenous history of India, China, Korea, or Southeast Asia. Japan conquered Korea and Manchuria after 1885, and briefly held much of China, Southeast Asia, and Oceania in the 1930s–1940s. Many of the ancient Greek and Phoenician city-states founded colonies around the Mediterranean and Black Seas but were unable to keep control of them as overseas possessions. The only major sea-empire of ancient times was the Athenian, which controlled a tributary empire in the Aegean Sea during the mid 400s B.C. Rome used the Mediterranean sealanes for supplies, but its conquests were based primarily on land power. In the 800s–1000s A.D., Scandinavian sea raiders conquered England, Normandy, and Sicily, but except for a brief period of Danish overseas domination, these constituted population movements to new territories raher than multiterritorial empires. England held major parts of France during 1135–1200, and again 1350–1400, and made yet a third but ultimately unsuccessful attempt at conquest 1415–40. Venice held Crete and various Aegean posts from 1200 to 1700. Spain held Sicily 1400–1700, southern and Central Italy 1500–1700, much of North and South America 1550–1820, and the Philippines 1565–1900. Portugal held Brazil from the 1500s to 1820 and numerous trading posts along the coasts of Africa and South and East Asia in the 1500s and 1600s. The Netherlands seized a number of these coastal bases in the early 1600s and expanded to encompass all Indonesia from the late 1800s until 1940. France held Canada 1600–1760, portions of Africa from the 1870s to about 1960, and Indo-China from the 1880s to 1940. England held North American colonies 1620–1780, Canada 1760–1930, major portions of India from 1800–50 to 1945, Australia and New Zealand from 1800–40 to 1945, and large African territories from about 1880 to 1960. The United States held the Philippines 1900–40 and Puerto Rico and Hawaii from 1900 to the present. No Latin American, African, or Middle Eastern states have held significant overseas territories.

A number of generalizations can be made. (A) *Maritime empires are relatively hard to establish.* This is implied by the infrequency of sea conquests compared to the number of land-based conquests in world history. Moreover, unlike land conquests, successful maritime conquests have tended to move into a military vacuum. Rome's sea conquest of Britain was opposed only by small and disorganized tribes. The European empires in the Americas, Africa, the East Indies, and Oceania faced only tribal opposition, or at most the advanced horticultural states of Mexico and the Andes. India, when conquered by England, was on a higher level of civilization than the Aztecs, but it was militarily divided among a large number of contending states. The conquest of India was due primarily to the willingness of the Indian princes to bargain for alliances with the Europeans, as well as to the superiority of European troop discipline (Mason, 1976:39–60).

In almost every instance, sea power has been able to take land territory only when there was no more than minimal opposition. Virtually no sea-based power has ever conquered a civilized territory on the same level of economic and military organization as itself, whereas land-based conquests of this sort are frequent in world history. In the few cases where sea invasions have succeeded against opposition on a similar economic level, there has always been a conjuncture of conventional land-based enemies simultaneously pressing the defeated party. The Norman conquest of Sicily took advantage of a situation of feudal fragmentation, and the Norman landing in England in 1066 occurred at precisely the time that English forces were fighting (successfully) in the north against Norwegian invaders supporting a feudal rival. Japan's conquests took place at a time when China was fragmented by civil wars. Naval power thus is successful only on the same geopolitical rules as operate in conventional land warfare: the sea power can expand if it acts as one of several marchlands converging upon a land state. The conquered states (England, India, China) were caught in the disadvantageous position of being in the middle between opposing forces, and one or more of these multiple enemies has always been another land-based force.

(B) *Sea-based empires are especially vulnerable to disruption*. Most maritime empires have held foreign territories for relatively short periods in comparison to land conquests. The longest-held maritime possessions were the rather small conquests of Venice (500 years). Among major possessions, Portugal held Brazil 300 years while Spain held the Philippines 335 years, Sicily 300 years, Latin America 270 years, and Italy 200 years. England held Canada 170 years, the Atlantic colonies 150, and sizable portions of India 100–150 years. The Netherlands held major portions of Indonesia some 100 years. European possessions in Africa were mostly on the order of 50–80 years. Japan held Korea and Manchuria 50 years, and controlled China, Southeast Asia, and Oceania about 10 years. The ancient Athenian sea-empire lasted 60 years. The medieval Danish empire had major overseas power only 20 years. Even at the upper end of the spectrum, then, sea-empires do not match the length of the major land-empires of world history, of which there are numerous instances lasting 400–800 years (Collins, 1978).

The more long-lasting empires reigned over territories with a low level of indigenous social organization and isolated from significant military rivalries. Maritime conquest states which were close to the arena of major land powers have been extremely vulnerable. The Athenian sea-state was destroyed by war with neighboring land powers, Sparta and Macedonia. The dissolution of the modern European overseas empires has occurred, in virtually every instance, because of wars among the European homelands. France lost most of its overseas possessions to England while fighting Prussia in the Seven Years War (1756–63) and during the Revolutionary and Napoleonic wars (1789–1815). During the Napoleonic conquest of Spain, the Spanish colonists in Latin America refused to recognize French control. After 1815 the European powers tried to restore the Spanish empire, but the revolutionary armies were too strong and by 1823 all of Spanish America was independent. Portugal too lost Brazil in the aftermath of political upheaval following French and British military operations upon its home territory.

The U.S. owes its independence to the vulnerability of maritime empires to wars near their homelands. When the colonies seceded in 1776, they had little chance of military success because the resource advantage (principle #1) was overwhelmingly on the side of the British, with a population ratio of 12 million to 3 million. The British successfully occupied all major colonial cities, and the Americans lost virtually every battle for the first few years of the war. But the outbreak of European war made the British unable to keep an uninterrupted naval pipeline to their forces in America. A brief success by the French navy cut off British troops without supplies or reinforcements, forced their surrender in 1781, and assured American independence. It did not even take a very strong push to break the colonies loose. After the British pulled their forces out of America, they were able to beat the French rather badly at sea. But this illustrates what is fatal about maritime empires: the naval links need be broken only for a short time before the conquest slips away.

The same pattern is found in the wave of decolonization after World War II. The Japanese drove the French, British, and Dutch out of Southeast Asia, and when the Japanese were themselves defeated a few years later, the former owners could no longer get back in. With their forces pinned down with Germany and then the U.S.S.R., the European powers had no choice but to let their former colonies become independent. Essentially the same dynamics prevailed in India and Africa. The only colonial empire to hold out was the Portuguese, which had the advantage of staying neutral in World War II and could concentrate its troops on keeping Angola. Decolonization thus cannot be attributed simply to an upsurge of nationalism. For there is no evidence that ideological feelings *per se* result in transfers of power in the absence of military resources and vulnerabilities (Skocpol, 1979). Multi-ethnic conquest states like Russia, which expanded entirely on land frontiers, have not been decolonized. It is the special vulnerability of overseas empires that encourages both the 20th century national movements, and those at the turn of the 19th century in the Americas.

It is easy to see why sea power is so vulnerable to disruption. In order for naval power to operate offensively, it must succeed in putting land forces ashore to occupy territory. But sea-borne landings have never been very effective against serious resistance. The debacle of the Bay of Pigs in Cuba in 1961 is only one instance of this. Virtually the only landing operations that have been successful against a major power were those of the latter part of World War II. But the Japanese-held islands in the Pacific were vulnerable to American troops precisely because they were part of Japan's maritime empire; they were lost because they had to be supplied by sea. And the Allied landings in North Africa, Italy, and France were possible only because Germany was overextended and was collapsing under land attack on its eastern front.

(C) *Sea power is most effective defensively.* Naval forces add something to overall military strength, as in the American civil war or in World War II, provided they are combined with sufficiently strong land forces. But the real importance of sea power is defensive. The greatest weapon is the sea itself. It is much easier to destroy a fleet, and an army under convoy, than to destroy troops on land. That is why naval battles have always been much quicker and more decisive than land battles. The Greeks wrecked the Persian invasion fleet at Salamis in one day, just as the British cut short the entire German naval offensive of World War I in one day at Jutland in 1916, and the American navy crippled the Japanese at Midway on June 4, 1942. The crucial sea battles have been defensive ones: the Greeks at Salamis, the British beating back the invasion attempt of the Spanish Armada in 1588, and Lord Nelson breaking up Napoleon's invasion fleet in 1805 before it had a chance to clear the Mediterranean.

Precisely because it is so hard to mount an invasion across the water, islands have been the most impregnable of states. Japan, for example, has never been successfully invaded in its entire history. The Mongols tried it twice after conquering most of the rest of the world, but lost most of their forces each time. The U.S. obtained Japanese surrender after dropping atomic bombs on it, but hesitated to land otherwise for fear of expected enormous casualties to its own forces. At the other end of the world, England has been safe for almost a thousand years, since the Vikings attacked a weak and divided kingdom. The Byzantine Empire was able to survive in Constantinople for 100 years against strong Ottoman land forces because it was able to resupply through its control of the sea. And Holland held out against land invasion of Spanish forces in the 1570s by retreating for brief periods to their ships. Here naval power acted to preserve a state rather than to extend one.

I would conclude that sea power does not circumvent the marchland principle (#2) in geopolitics, and that sea power exemplifies rather than displaces other principles. Hypothetically, all countries that touch on the oceans are contiguous to each other, and hence none of them could be said to have a true marchland advantage. But it is very difficult for states to conquer others across the water; conversely, it is realtively easy to defend against seaborne attack. A state with maritime enemies is not usually much threatened unless it is overwhelmingly deficient in numbers and economic resources (principle #1), or if it is simultaneously threatened by land enemies on other fronts (principle #2). Moreover, it is not really accurate to regard waterways as making all coastal states equally vulnerable to each other's naval threats. Naval forces from nearby bases are much more likely to be successful than forces from distant ones. England thus served as a convenient jumping-off place for the 1944 landings in Normandy, and France was able to hold coastal Algeria longer (1830–1960) than more remote parts of its African empire. This suggests that a modified version of the marchland principle may be calculated for distances by water as well as by land. By the same token, the longer distance a naval power covers, the more vulnerable it is to disruption. States can risk collapse at home by overextension at sea as well as on land; here again a land-based geopolitical principle (#3) seems to hold for water as well.

The doctrine of Mahan (1918), then, is largely mistaken. The fate of naval empires themselves is largely determined by the balance of land forces affecting their homelands. Sea power is ancillary to land geopolitics.[1]

III. Air power and its geopolitical effects

Air power has become a major feature of 20th century warfare. Since all states are vulnerable to air attack from all other states, the existence of air power should presumably result in a total rewriting of the rules of geopolitics. All positional advantages and disadvantages would disappear. I will suggest, however, that this is not so, and that traditional land configurations continue to be central. The military use of air power takes a number of forms, which should be considered separately. We will deal in sequence with tactical air power, strategic air power (including nuclear), air power in relation to sea and land forces, and the use of air power in moving troops for land operations.

Tactical air power

The tactical use of air power in battle provides the strongest case for the uniqueness of modern warfare. Beginning in World War

---

[1] This points up one of the major weaknesses in the geopolitical approach of Modelski (1983), which measures world power by the size of navies. See also Zolberg (1983) for a critique of this overestimation of the role of sea power, which in fact appeared salient only during a few recent centuries of European history. In comparison to the full geopolitical theory presented in this chapter and in Chapter 8, the Modelski model deals only with a particular form of resource advantage, and omits all positional principles (marchlands and interior states, overextension). Hence it proposes a simplistic cyclic rise-and-fall of world hegemonies, in place of what is actually a much more complex pattern of world history.

Technology and geopolitics

II, control of the skies became an important element in land battles. The most striking victories of the war all occurred when one side had overwhelming air superiority. Early in the war the German *blitzkrieg* took Poland and most of the rest of Europe not only with tanks but with control of the air (Liddell Hart, 1970:28, 66–79, 135–6). German paratroopers and glider forces were instrumental in taking the Netherlands and Crete. Airplane firepower in the form of machine guns and bombs was particularly devastating against land forces on the march and against supply lines. It is partly for this reason that the Germans were able to make such rapid conquests at first, even though they frequently faced forces that outnumbered them locally. Similarly, the Japanese rapidly took Indo-China, Singapore, Malaya, and Burma in the opening months of 1942, sometimes against larger defensive forces, because Japan had the only substantial air force in the area and was able to exploit its advantage in maneuverability (Liddell Hart, 1970:212–237). Toward the end of the war, the situation was reversed. The Allies, especially the Americans, achieved complete air superiority. The D-day landings in Normandy in 1944 and the earlier landings in Sicily and Southern Italy were successful above all because the Germans were unable to counter them from the air (Liddell Hart, 1970:464, 547, 559). The final phase of the war, especially the rapid tank thrusts of Patton's army across the Rhone, were carried out with the Allies able to string out long supply lines in perfect immunity, while the Germans were limited to sporadic supply movements under the cover of darkness.

Nevertheless there were several clear limitations upon the effectiveness of air forces. They had little overall effect on the Russian front, where opposing air forces neutralized each other for most of the war. Air power proved insignificant in the island warfare of the Pacific. The U.S. generally had air superiority and was able to cover landing operations with it, but the long and difficult business of dislodging the Japanese from their defensive positions required a heavy expenditure of ground troops. The battle of Okinawa, for example, towards the end of the war, took 285,000 Americans to overcome 100,000 Japanese and resulted in 160,000 casualties on both sides (Liddell Hart, 1970:683–686). The Korean war showed the same limitation. Here U.S. air superiority was overwhelming. Chinese and North Korean aircraft were shot down at a 14 to 1 ratio. Nevertheless the war ended in a costly stalemate of massive ground forces.

Tactical air power, then, may sometimes make a difference in the conduct of battle. It is more effective in a highly fluid situation and when one or both sides are operating far from home base with greatly extended supply lines. As we have seen in the case of sea power, air power is militarily effective primarily when one side has overwhelming superiority in that arm. In other cases it is less effective, and conventional land forces are preeminent. In every case, however, the use of tactical air power is local, requiring bases within easy reach of the battlefield. These in turn usually depend upon control by land forces.

Strategic air power

A more geopolitically relevant use of air power is not its tactical use in battle but its use for strategic bombing. Here the aim is to knock out the main source of a state's geopolitical strength by destroying its industries and transport and terrorizing its population. The Germans tried to cripple British capacity to resist in World War II by bombing London and the industrial Midlands, first with conventional aircraft and later by V-1 and V-2 missiles. The Allies retaliated by massive bombing of German industrial cities, culminating in the destruction of Dresden in 1945. Other strategic bombing attacks included the fire-bombing of Tokyo and other Japanese cities towards the end of the war. In the Vietnam war the U.S. used both strategic bombing from long-range B-52s and short-range tactical strikes from helicopter gunships in an effort to cut supply lines and destroy enemy bases in the countryside.

The morality of attacking civilians in this kind of warfare has been severely criticized. From a strictly geopolitical standpoint, moreover, it has not usually been very effective. The U.S. air force expended more total firepower in Vietnam than did both sides together in World War II but without stopping the ultimate victory of the Communist ground forces. Probably the effect on the native population was the same as the effect of the German bombing of Britain, rousing hatred and stiffening the will to resist. Analyses of strategic bombing carried out after World War II concluded that the bombing attacks on German cities were more effective at killing civilians than in destroying German military installations and industry (Liddell Hart, 1970:589–612). The reason was that military and industrial installations were much better hidden and better defended, while civilians were left largely in the open. The same thing doubtless was true in Britain and Japan, and later in Vietnam.

The only unequalified success of strategic bombing was the A-bomb attacks which brought World War II to an end. Yet even this case does not add up to a major change in the principles of warfare. The nuclear attacks could only have been launched because U.S. forces had worn down the Japanese throughout the Pacific. Japanese air cover was gone, leaving the island open to U.S. raids, both conventional and nuclear. Three years of American advances across the Pacific had given them ample air bases within striking distance of Japan. It is doubtful that a U.S. nuclear attack would have forced Japan to surrender early in the war; a troop landing would still have been very difficult, and more likely Japan would simply have been forced to withdraw its offensive forces abroad and negotiate a peace settlement. The lesson, even in this extreme instance, is that air power can add something to conventional military factors, but only if those conventional factors are already strong.

The nuclear arms race of recent years and the extreme destructiveness of atomic weapons have convinced many observers that we are in an entirely new era of international politics. Because ICBMs can be launched from virtually anywhere on the globe, it appears that the world has shrunk to a single battlefield. Nevertheless, it does not follow that the growth or decline of states would occur in terms of principles other than those enunciated at the outset of this paper. For the relative nuclear striking power of states depends on their economic strength, which is the same factor determining conventional military power (principle #1).

If a nuclear war were to take place, there are two main outcomes possible: either one side would be devastated or both sides would be. In the first case, the state that would benefit from the destruction would be the one that could successfully move conventional ground forces onto the destroyed territory (when it became habitable again). This would undoubtedly be an *adjacent* state. If Iraq or Libya, for example, were to destroy Israel in a surprise nuclear attack, nevertheless it would not be Iraq or Libya that would pick up the territory; it would be one of Israel's immediate neighbors. Hence conventional positional advantages (principle #2) would still be borne out.

In the second case, both belligerent states would be destroyed. But this is not unprecedented. Such showdown wars to mutual destruction have occurred as far back as ancient China, as part of a conventional dynamic expansion of rival states (Collins, 1978). The outcome of mutual nuclear destruction today, as of self-destructive stalemates in the past, would be to remove these particular powers from international importance, and allow their territories to be picked up by new states on the periphery. The process is a corollary to principle 2(d) above.

Air vs. sea vs. land

The most important military use of air power is against ships. We have already noticed that sea battles have tended to be quick and decisive. The stronger fleet has usually put the weaker one on the bottom of the sea within a few hours, ending a naval threat once and for all. Modern air power has made navies even more vulnerable. Accordingly, the aircraft carrier has become the most important weapon in the fleet, and the old-fashioned battleship has become virtually extinct. In World War II the most important naval battles were fought by fleets that never came in sight of each other. At the battle of Midway in 1942 and at the Leyte Gulf in 1944, planes from the American carriers effectively destroyed the Japanese navy, although the fleets never got closer than 200 miles (Liddell Hart, 1970:349–53, 622–28). These battles were fought from aircraft carriers because the fleets were far out at sea. But ships are vulnerable whenever they are in range of land-based aircraft too. Hence air bases are a significant deterrent against naval attacks upon a coastal territory. Air power makes naval power even more difficult to apply than before, and makes any country protected by water even more impervious to invasion. The air power of the 20th century has negated what geopolitical effects sea power had in previous centuries.

Air power itself depends in the end upon land power. Although modern aircraft have a very long range, their effective military use depends upon there being bases which are close enough to their targets. Generally speaking, the more maneuverable the plane has to be in order to respond to battlefront conditions, the shorter the range of operation. Huge strategic bombers have a range of 12,000 miles. The target distance, of course, can be only half the total range if the plane expects to be able to return. The more air power is expected to play a role in actual fighting, the closer must be the bases to the battlefield. Maneuverable fighter-bombers suitable for ground support and for defense against enemy fighters have a range between 400 and 1500 miles, which means they must be based within 750 miles of the battlefield (Collins and Cordesman, 1978:140–1). These air bases could be on a carrier in nearby waters, unless the enemy has sufficient countervailing air power, in which case the bases must be on land held by one's own army. Local land power is necessary to make tactical air power possible.

We are getting down then, to relatively small spaces as geopolitics goes. It may be hypothetically true that air strikes make all nations vulnerable to every other nation, and hence that the pure marchland advantage no longer exists. But in the world of actual warfare, effective military strikes from the air require land bases within 1000 miles, which is well within the conventional scale of modern states. Effective air power is essentially local, and hence the geographical position of states, with or without enemies directly to the rear on land, continues to be important for their military fate.

Technology and geopolitics

Air troop landing

Paratroops might seem to be an exception. By combining air transportation with ground-holding forces, it might seem possible to pick up pieces of territory anywhere on the globe without having to move step by step across the land in between. But in fact, paratroop operations have been even more limited in range than air strikes. Troops dropped far behind enemy lines would soon be lost if there were no way to reinforce them. Hence paratroop operations are never carried out in hostile territory very far from a land force that is supposed to link up with it. In World War II the most remote paratroop operations were only 100 miles behind enemy lines, and most of the successful operations only leapfrogged 10 miles or so (Liddell Hart, 1970:67–69, 135–6, 544–5, 640–1).

Recently we have seen instances of troop air lifts into foreign territories. Soviet troops moved into Afghanistan in the winter of 1979 by first taking the airport at Kabul. Earlier, some 20,000 Cuban and Russian troops were moved to Ethiopia, 500 to South Yemen, and 15,000 to Angola. But in every instance there was already a foothold in the country. The Russians and Cubans were invited into Africa by their allies; hence there was no military problem in using local airports. The situation could hardly be the same if the territory were completely hostile. Even in Afghanistan, where the Russians have faced heavy opposition, the way for their invasion was prepared by a friendly head of government and by the fact that Russian advisers were already present at the airfield. The Russian airlift into Kabul speeded up Russian troop movement, but the land border between Afghanistan and the U.S.S.R. was primarily what made Afghanistan vulnerable.

Moreover, air transportation is the most expensive of all, and this is especially true for heavy military equipment. Airlifts are feasible only for short periods and under highly favorable conditions. Local allies are always needed where one lands, and any real opposition would make air-borne operations and supply extremely difficult to sustain. Given the expense alone, it is not surprising that no successful war (including the Vietnam war) has yet been carried out in which troops were moved mainly by air.

Overall, then, there is no evidence that airpower eliminates the importance of geographical contiguities by land. Tactical and strategic air power are effective only when combined with conventional ground forces, and the movement of such forces is strongly influenced by geographical configurations. Air power largely neutralizes sea power, hence making the sea transport of troops to hold overseas

183

territories even more difficult than in previous centuries. And the expense of moving troops by air is such that any heavy reliance upon it drastically escalates the costs of warfare, and enhances its chances of producing economic and political strain in the homeland, with all the political effects of overextension (principle #3). Air power, then, not only does not challenge conventional geopolitical patterns but appears to make them even stronger.

Conclusion

Modern technologies of long-distance warfare, along with modern transportation and communication, do not result in any major change in the underlying principles of geopolitics. Certainly it is highly unlikely that a global empire will ever be established. But is it not possible to reverse this expectation? Modern technology, instead of making a world empire possible, in fact seems to make it very difficult for any state to expand beyond its present boundaries. One might conjecture, then, that future geopolitics will differ from that of the past in that state boundaries will be much more stable than formerly. The defensive use of sea and air power, and above all the proliferation of nuclear arms, might seem to forestall *any* expansion at all.

This conclusion does not seem warranted. Empires cannot readily be established by modern sea or air power, but it remains possible to fight on land. There have been numerous conventional wars since the atomic era began in 1945, and these are likely to continue to change boundaries of control in the future in much the same way as in the past. The expansion of reunified Vietnam in Indo-China, for example, or of India against Pakistan and the Himalayan states, fits conventional principles quite well (Collins, 1978). The political future of Africa, to name just one area, seems certain to involve some geopolitical change, and this will doubtless follow conventional geopolitical principles.

Even outer space, which has opened up recently as a potential arena for military action, does not appear likely to violate the geopolitical principles defended in this chapter. Colonization of the moon or any other extraterrestrial satellite or planet would depend upon a type of air power and on air-borne supplies. For this reason, such outerspace empires would be very vulnerable to disruption and unusually expensive to maintain. States which tried to hold them against serious military opposition would almost certainly be unsuccessful and would also risk loss of their conventional territories via the dynamics of overextension.

In sum, the geopolitics of the future is by no means a total mystery.

Technology and geopolitics

The historical record provides a good basis for principles by means of which the future power of states may be projected. I will suggest in the next chapter that one such application can be made to long-term changes in the future power of the U.S.S.R.

8

The future decline of the Russian Empire

The power of states may be indexed by the expansion, contraction, or stability of state boundaries over long periods of time. This power depends on the ability of a government to concentrate more military forces at any point within these boundaries than any rival can bring to bear.

By this definition, the power of a state may overlap or fall short of its formal boundaries, although the long-term movement of boundaries is a good empirical approximation of this power. A state that can intervene militarily in other states beyond its formal boundaries may be referred to as possessing an "empire." In this sense, the Soviet Union has an empire, as indicated by the presence of its forces in Eastern Europe, Mongolia, and Afghanistan. We may speak of the Russian Empire in a broader sense as well, in that the long-term history of Russian expansion has brought a large number of non-Russian ethnic groups inside its borders by conquest. From a geopolitical viewpoint, there is complete continuity between Moscovite and Tsarist Russia and Soviet Russia.

Changes of state boundaries and of imperial controls almost always involve wars, including internal wars.[1] For this reason, long-term geopolitical changes are not smooth and continuous but occur in sudden jerks. Typically, geopolitical patterns take effect over a minimum of fifty years through several centuries, whereas wars typically last no longer than five years. There have been various approaches to predicting the outbreak of wars (Modelski, 1978; Doran and Parsons, 1980; Organski and Kuglen, 1980) although no clear-cut conclusions have yet been established. But if the timing of the initiation of wars remains uncertain, it is possible to show the long-term pattern of the outcomes of wars in terms of state expansion and contraction. The process may be stochastic rather than deterministic. The predicted decline of Russian power cannot be pinned down to a particular year.

---

[1] The sale or voluntary cession of territories also occurs occasionally in the historical record, but typically in a diplomatic context weighed by considerations of military alliance and vulnerability.

Future decline of the Russian Empire

It does appear, however, that the Russian Empire has already reached its limit after five hundred years of expansion and is entering a period of long-term decline. Particular combinations of events may even bring about precipitous losses of territorial power within the next thirty years, with the likelihood of extensive decline becoming very high for the twenty-first century.

The geopolitical theory presented here (Collins, 1978) contains a series of causal conditions, the results of which cumulate and interact. The fact that there is more than a single factor means that state power is not simply a cyclical rise and fall. In particular, economic and military resources interact with geographical position, in that the latter affects both the number of potential enemies faced by different states and the relative difficulty of using military force at frontiers of varying distances. Hence economic advantage alone is not enough to prevent a state's decline, in certain geopolitical configurations.

Each principle will first be presented separately, and then all will be applied to historical changes in Russian power.

Size and resource advantage

Other things being equal, larger and wealthier states will win wars against smaller and poorer states, and hence will expand while the latter contract. For much historical data, the relative strength of states is roughly indexed by sheer territorial size. But it is also the quality of the land that determines the size of the population on it, and hence the military resources that can be drawn from it. Where data are available, it is possible to measure the size and resource advantage by population and economic production (see Singer et al., 1972). Both are important, in that military power is a function of the size of the economy and of the population, not of the average economic level per individual. A very large country with a rather small GNP per capita will nevertheless be a significant military power. The size and resource advantage is cumulative over time, as territorially expanding states increase the base from which they can draw military resources, which in turn allows even greater territorial expansion.[2] Neighboring states at a size and resource disadvantage experience cumulative decline.

Positional advantage

States with militarily capable neighbors in fewer directions ("marchland states") have an advantage over states with powerful neighbors

[2] Boulding (1962:237–9) gives a formal representation of cumulative advantage in the particular case of two-person games.

Politics

in more directions ("interior states"). States that back up against a
natural barrier, in the form of high mountains, wide seas, or sparsely
inhabited territories, have a military advantage over those surrounded by accessible state borders on all sides. Over long time-
periods, interior states block each other's cumulative expansion,
whereas marchland states tend to expand because they are more
likely to fight enemies who are engaged in multifront conflicts. The
expansion possibilities of interior states are randomized with respect
to each other, whereas marchland states experience cumulative advantage. It follows that marchland advantage sets in motion cumulative size and resource advantage.

Fragmentation of interior states

Interior territories, facing enemies on several fronts, tend to fragment
into an increasing number of smaller states over long periods of time.
This occurs because the combination of alliances experienced by interior states is largely random, especially if balance-of-power principles
are followed,[3] and hence the power of such states fluctuates rather
than cumulates. Different overlapping slices of territory are conquered by such interior states at different times, leaving a residue of
numerous administrative jurisdictions. Territories that have been
fought over a good deal thus develop increasingly localistic political
infrastructure. The major powers on the periphery of such an interior
area often subsidize various factions within it, in order to keep them
out of alliance with their own major enemies. This increases fac-
tionalization within interior states and makes them more vulnerable
to outside intervention.

The positional advantage of marchland states and disadvantage of
interior states is found in much historical material. A high proportion
of the empire-building states of Chinese, Middle Eastern, and European history have been marchland states (Collins, 1978). The fragmentation of interior states has been observed in numerous historical
instances, including medieval Germany, Kievan Russia, the Balkans
after the decline of Ottoman power, and China during several of its
warring states periods. The rise of Moscovite Russia itself took advantage of this process as it afflicted the Mongol Empire in its successive
stages of fragmentation from the mid-1200s through the 1500s A.D.
(McEvedy, 1961, 1971; Chew, 1967; Spuler, 1972; Barraclough, 1979).
It can be questioned, however, whether positional advantages remain

[3] Thus the balance-of-power doctrine prominent in earlier geopolitical theory (Morgenthau, 1948) applies primarily to the position of interior states.

188

significant with the advent of modern sea and air power, which presumably make all states militarily contiguous. In the modern global world, have we now arrived at a balance in which all states are interior states?

But although some shift in scale has occurred, closer analysis (see Chapter 7) suggests that the change is only a matter of degree and that relative geographical contiguity of states to potential enemies continues to make a difference. Seaborne military power has been effective only to the extent that size and resource advantages have favored the overseas power, together with the extent to which land bases have been available near the point to be conquered. Air power, too, is affected by the closeness of bases to enemy territory; and air power alone is not sufficient for conquest in the absence of the ability to move large land forces. There continues to be a gradient of difficulty of military access among states, even in the industrial era. This is borne out by the continued evidence of positional patterns in World War II (which resulted in the defeat and fragmentation of Germany, an interior state). Some modern states thus continue to be favored by relatively greater inaccessibility to enemies from one or more directions, due to strong natural barriers (such as large mountain ranges or wide seas), whereas other states border on heavily inhabited territories on several sides. Such advantages or disadvantages of geographical position should continue to show up in the expansion and contraction of modern states over long time-periods.

Showdown wars and turning points

A consequence of the preceding is that if marchland states cumulatively advance in size and territorial resources, while interior states fragment, then eventually any interior territory will be totally absorbed by the marchland states surrounding it. This implies there will be periodic confrontations among the large marchland-based conquest states that had previously been separated by an internal buffer zone. From the historical record, there seems to be no way as yet of predicting whether a particular state will win this confrontation and establish a "world" empire. An alternative possibility is that the major states will fight to a mutually exhausting stalemate. In either case, certain empirical patterns do appear to be associated with such "showdown wars" (Collins, 1978).

One such pattern is that if a stalemate ensues from the confrontation of the giants, the long-term process of geopolitical simplification goes into reverse. If neither of the conquering marchland states is able to subjugate the other and establish a "world" empire, their mutual exhaustion tends to weaken their hold over their own client states. The geopolitical system begins to fragment again, with increasing division of the interior territory and the long-term growth of new marchland states on the periphery.

Overextension and disintegration

There is an additional reason, independent of the previous principles, why states may decline. Even "world" empires with no equivalent rivals have undergone weakening and long-term decay. A major reason is that military overextension beyond the resources of a territorial heartland results in disintegration of state power. This pattern is found in the decline of seven of eight major Chinese dynasties, and in numerous Western examples as recently as the decline of the Napoleonic French and the Nazi German empires after extension into Russia and North Africa (Collins, 1978). Such declines have begun quite abruptly, following long periods of military success, as the result of military defeats on extremely distant battlefields. The results of such overextension can include loss of territory, chronic fiscal weakness resulting in internal dissension and weakness to outside attack, and susceptibility of the regime to internal revolution (Skocpol, 1979; Collins, 1981b:63–9). There are two interpretations of this pattern:

1. The gradient of overextension is economic, involving the transportation costs of fighting at too great a physical distance from reliable supply bases. Economic overextension may be formally stated (Stinchcombe, 1968:218–30).[4] The vulnerability of any geographical point P_0 to a particular state, A, is given by:

$$V_{0A} = \Sigma_i \, (1 - cd_i) \, kIp_i \qquad \text{(Eq. 1)}$$

where k is a constant, I is average per capita income, p_i is the population of area i, d_i is the distance in kilometers from area i to point P_0, and c is the proportion of military resources used up in transporting it 1 kilometer.

When expanding armies from state A penetrate to a point P_0 that has a very low or even a negative value, total resources become rapidly depleted, and it becomes impossible for a state to muster military power to maintain order even at closer distances. This is especially so when $V_{0A} < V_{0B}$, that is, when the territory fought over

---

[4] A similar model, but one based on a different formalism, is found in Boulding (1962:227–76).

is within the "natural" range of some other state, *B*, and hence very large military resources are necessary to occupy it.

It is possible that the limits of overextension have expanded in the industrial era compared to the preceding era of agrarian states, from which the overextension rule was formulated. But although the cost of transportation generally has fallen and its range risen, the logistics costs of mechanized warfare have escalated as well. Ammunition in particular is expended in much greater quantities than any previous war materials; military forces are much larger, and hence create much greater supply problems as well as transportation bottlenecks (Keegan, 1976; Van Creveld, 1977). Hence overextension limits appear to be not greatly different than in agrarian states. This is consonant with the fact that the maximal size of states is little greater in industrial than in agrarian states (Chapter 7 in this volume; Taagepera, 1979). Economic overextension limits thus appear to be approximately on the same order as in previous centuries.

2. A second interpretation is that overextension is political, due to the strains of maintaining population acquiescence and troop morale across more than one ethnic border from the home ethnic base. Previous research (Collins, 1978) suggests the rule that military overextension consists in attempts to control ethnically distinct territories more distant than those immediately adjacent to one's own. This version of overextension remains significant today, since the strength of ethnic nationalism continues to be a powerful obstacle to unlimited military expansion.

Russian expansion and resource advantage

The historical expansion of Russia itself neatly illustrates the cumulative operation of the first two geopolitical principles (Chew, 1967). In the 1300s A.D., the territory of ethnic Russia (the deciduous- and mixed-forest plains from Lake Ladoga in the north to the Dnieper valley in the south) was divided among a large number of small states (Figures 8.1 and 8.2). The major military powers in the area were the Mongol Golden Horde, ruling the steppe from the Urals to the Caspian and Black Seas and extracting tribute from the Russians; and the Lithuanian Empire (succeeded by the Polish Empire) in the Baltic and the Ukraine. The impetus for Russian unification and expansion came from the principality of Moscow, a small state near the northeastern edge of Russian settlement. Its initial advantage consisted primarily of its marchland position, at the very edge of the relatively densely populated mixed-forest zone, with only the sparsely inhabited coniferous-forest area to its north and east. The other Russian states

VEGETATION ZONES

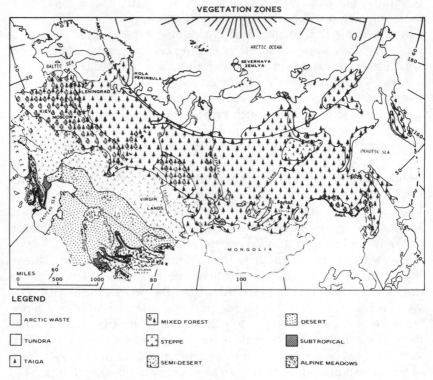

LEGEND

☐ ARCTIC WASTE   ▨ MIXED FOREST   ▦ DESERT

☐ TUNDRA   ▨ STEPPE   ▨ SUBTROPICAL

↑ TAIGA   ▨ SEMI-DESERT   ▨ ALPINE MEADOWS

Fig. 8.1 (from Chew, 1967)

to the south and west had the disadvantage of facing both each other
and the Lithuanian, Teutonic, and Polish forces. Moscow began to
expand at their expense, especially during the 1390s and in 1425–60,
when the Golden Horde was battling rival Mongol states, the Ilkans
in Persia and the Timurids in central Asia, and then splitting into
smaller states on the steppe. Fighting against fragmented rivals, by
1520 Moscow had absorbed virtually all of ethnic Russia.

Although the early expansion of Moscow was slow, the cumulative
population advantage over its immediate rivals became overwhelming after about 1480. To the west, Russia then came up against relatively sizable European states and made slow progress in further
territorial acquisitions. Russian expansion across Siberia began immediately, however, against minimal opposition from the sparse tribal
populations, reaching the Pacific by 1640. Infighting among the
Mongol khanates gave an opportunity for Russian conquest of the
southern steppes in the 1500s. Their subsequent colonization by Russian agriculturalists resulted in a further large boost in population,

192

Fig. 8.2 (from Chew, 1967)

which by the late 1700s made Russia a preeminent military power in
Europe (McEvedy and Jones, 1978). At that time Russia benefited
from the weakness of an interior state, Poland, which was attacked
on three sides and partitioned by Austria, Prussia, and Russia. With
the weakening of central-European states by French invasion in the
Napoleonic period, Russia made further gains on its western frontier,

Table 8.1. *Population, economic, and military resources of Russia and its allies and of Russia's enemies, 1975–7*

States	Population (in millions)	GNP (in billion $)	Active and reserve troops (in thousands)
Russia and allies			
Soviet Union	260	700	10,900
Other Warsaw Pact	108	304	3,075
Vietnam	50	8	2,185
Cuba	10	8	250
Other allies*a*	50	7	570
Total	478	1,027	16,980
Russian enemies			
United States	200	2,100	2,900
Other NATO	293	1,715	6,125
China	960	340	7,300–8,300
Japan	115	565	280
Pakistan	77	17	925
Yugoslavia	22	33	765
Total	1,687	4,770	18,320–19,320

*a*Mongolia, South Yemen, Ethiopia, Afghanistan.
Sources: U.N. Statistical Yearbook; U.S. Defense Intelligence Agency.

including the conquest of Finland. Russia's final territorial gains took place in the late 1800s at the expense of the disintegrating Ottoman Empire in the Caucasus, of the petty states of central Asia, and in the extreme Far East at the expense of China during its prolonged civil wars and colonial incursions (Clubb, 1971).

If Russian expansion was due to the combined effects of the size and resource advantage and the marchland advantage, however, *these two advantages have disappeared in the twentieth century.* The size and resource advantage now heavily favors Russia's enemies (Table 8.1). Their total population outnumbers that of the Soviets and their allies by 3.5 to 1, and their economic resources outweigh them 4.6 to 1. In troops the ratio is much closer, with an advantage of 1.1 to 1 favoring Russia's enemies in total troops including reserves. In troops on active duty, Russia's enemies total 9,320,000, Russia and its allies 5,500,000 – a ratio of 1.7 to 1.

The relative closeness of the troop figures is reflected in the current atmosphere of confrontation among equals. But in the long run of geopolitical time, it is the population and economic base from which troops may be raised that counts. For Russia and its allies are 3.5 times as heavily mobilized (3.84 percent of total population in active and reserve forces) as Russia's enemies (1.12 percent of population mobilized). Especially significant in the long run are two of Russia's enemies that have very small military mobilization ratios: China with 0.76–0.87 percent of population, and Japan with 0.24 percent. If the Soviet Union's enemies were to mobilize to the same level as the Soviet Union, their troop totals would come to 64 million: a staggering number that would represent virtually inexhaustible reserves.

Russian loss of marchland advantage

Russia has thus lost the size and resource advantage that favored its historical expansion. The marchland advantage has also disappeared. Through the very success of Russian expansion into Siberia, central Asia, and the Black Sea area, by the early twentieth century Russia had switched from a marchland state to an interior state. The lineup of size and resource disadvantages now facing Russia is the result of its having eliminated virtually all weak buffer states so that it faces powerful enemies in all directions. Russia now defends a frontier of 58,000 kilometers, stretching 8,000 kilometers east to Manchuria and another 5,000 to Alaska, and 3,500 kilometers from Norway in the north to the Caucasus in the south. Russia once expanded because of conflicts among the interior states Poland, Austria, Germany, and the Ottoman Empire, but now Russian imperial domination of Eastern Europe, and the corresponding tendency to military cooperation within Western Europe, brings Russia up against a unified enemy to the west. Similarly, the internal division and colonial invasion that allowed Russia to expand into the traditional territories of the Chinese Empire have given way to a strong Chinese state in the east.

The transition from a marchland to an interior position has taken place gradually over the past century. During that period, the overall expansion of Russian territory had already come to a halt. The European borders of Russia are approximately the same as in 1815. Finland has been lost, and the formal incorporation of much of Poland has been discarded. These losses are compensated by imperial control over the client states of Eastern Europe since 1945. Russian power in Eastern Europe has proved fluctuating and unstable since 1914, with much of Russian-controlled territory, including the Baltic states now formally incorporated in the Soviet Union, independent of Russia from 1914 to 1944. Russia's political difficulties in maintaining domination over Eastern Europe in recent decades suggest a continuation of the trend already established in the early twentieth century. On its eastern front, the greatest extent of Russian expansion was reached in the 1820s. Its border has drawn back since then, with the sale of its California outposts (1841) and of Alaska (1867) as a strategic retreat to avoid acquisitions by its British enemy (Chew, 1967:82–3). This contraction was balanced by an expansion in east Asia, beginning with the acquisition of the Amur-coastal region during the Chinese civil war and the Anglo-French incursions of the 1850s, and continuing when Russia took de facto control of northern Manchuria and the Liaotung Peninsula in the 1890s during the Sino-Japanese war. Defeat by Japan in Manchuria in 1904–5 marks the general limit of Russian expansion in east Asia; although minor advances were made after 1945, Russian imperial control of east Asia has retreated somewhat from its territories of 1900. In the Caucasus and central Asia, the advances achieved by 1890 have not been substantially extended, and some areas have fluctuated out of Russian control during wartime periods.

The size and resource advantage and the marchland advantage, which enabled Russia to expand steadily from the 1400s through the 1800s, have been neutralized and reversed in the twentieth century. Correspondingly, overall Russian expansion has ceased since around 1900.

Russia as an interior state

If Russia has shifted from a marchland to an interior position, it may be expected that in the long-term future Russia will fragment into successively smaller states. Such fragmentation would not begin until after an initial military defeat or political crisis but, once begun, would proceed at an accelerating rate. The very structure of the existing Russian state gives considerable potential for this fragmentation, because it was built up by conquest of disparate ethnic groups and of preexisting states. Fragmentation of the Russian Empire would become a cumulative process following upon the weakness of size and resource advantage and marchland advantage. These factors also produce negatively cumulative processes. An interior area tends to feed the cumulating strength of marchland states outside it, thus accentuating the military imbalance. In previous historical cases, the process of fragmentation has taken place over a period of two hundred to three hundred years (Collins, 1978). One might, therefore, project that the long-term fragmentation of the Russian Empire would last through the twenty-first and twenty-second centuries.

Future decline of the Russian Empire

The Cold War as a turning point

The long-term logic of geopolitical processes is for cumulative advantages to build in favor of marchland states at opposite ends of a civilized region. Eventually their cumulative growth, and the instability and fragmentation of the interior states, results in the disappearance of intervening buffer states and a military confrontation between the Great Powers. In the last several centuries this pattern may be seen in the expansion of two giant empires based at opposite ends of Europe, the Russian and the British. World War II and the immediately following Cold War period constituted a turning point. Power blocs had simplified down to two major forces, with all other states absorbed as clients of the two giants'. Among these a former segment of the British Empire, the United States, had inherited Britain's place as the marchland power farthest removed in the west from European vulnerabilities. The confrontation between Soviet and American blocs generated an atmosphere of impending nuclear showdown for world domination.

There are two possible outcomes of a geopolitical turning point. One possibility is victory of one side over the other, and the establishment of a world empire; the second is stalemate, resulting in the exhaustion of the two Great Powers and the renewed growth of independent powers outside the structure of enforced alliances. It appears now that the second alternative is being actualized. The apocalyptic atmosphere that characterized the foreign policies of the 1950s has given way to more modest claims that no longer envisage total displacement of one of the rival political systems. The reemergence of a polycentric world, with cracks in both the Eastern and Western alliances and the rise of many neutral powers, is in keeping with the predicted trend. If this hypothesis is correct, the power of the Soviet Union, as one of the major states that failed to achieve world domination at the showdown point, can be expected to go into long-term decline.

Russian overextension

There are two nonexclusive methods of calculating overextension, the ethnic and the economic. Present-day Russian power appears overextended according to both criteria. The ethnic as well as economic heartland of Russia is surrounded by a tier of ethnically alien territories within the formal boundaries of the Soviet Union, from Lithuania and other Baltic territories, through the Ukraine, to the Caucasus and central Asia. The Soviet Union not only has one of the world's highest rates of ethnolinguistic fractionalization, 0.67 on a scale of 0 to 1.0 (Taylor and Hudson, 1972),[5] but unlike other multiethnic societies such as the United States and (to a degree) Canada, the Soviet ethnic groups are highly localized geographically and hence maintain strong territorial identities. There is, however, ample historical precedent for the maintenance of political control over such ethnic groups *immediately adjacent* to the Russian heartland, *as long as no further geopolitical difficulties activate ethnic separatism* through weakness of the central government. But geopolitical strain is implied by Russian military domination of its Eastern European satellites, which are a second and, in some cases, a third tier removed. The Soviet Union's inability to control Yugoslavia and Albania (third- and fourth-tier states) is consonant with the "no intervening heartland" rule.

As a geopolitical time span, the four decades during which the Soviet Union has maintained domination over Eastern Europe are not a long period and do not indicate firm control. Russian intervention in Afghanistan, across the intervening Kazakh, Uzbek, Tadzhik, and Turkmen ethnic areas, also violates the hypothesized overextension limit. The Soviet Far East does not appear to be an instance of the ethnic version of overextension, as migrant Russians in Siberia far outnumber the indigenous inhabitants. But there are clear economic and logistic strains involved in defending this territory. It was on this frontier that a barely industrializing Japan defeated Russia in 1904–5, precipitating the first phase of the Russian Revolution. It is apparent that the vulnerability both of the Pacific Maritime Province and Amur valley, and of Outer Mongolia (currently occupied by Soviet troops), is higher to troops based in Chinese territory than to those in the Russian heartland. In the past, three Chinese dynasties occupied both of these territories (Figures 8.3–8.5), and troops of the Manchu dynasty decisively defeated Russian troops in the late 1600s in this area (Hermann, 1966; Clubb, 1971). Russian troops have won all recent battles there (in 1929, 1945, and 1969), but most of these encounters occurred when China was embroiled in civil war and foreign incursion on other fronts. Further economic and military recovery of China would increase the vulnerability of this area to China far above the level of vulnerability to Russia. In terms of Equation 1, assume c is the same for both; p is much higher for China, d_i much lower for the most populated areas of China than of the Soviet Union; GNP per capita need not reach equality with that of the Soviet Union for vulnerability to shift to the Chinese side.[6]

---

[5] Comparable scores are: Canada .75; United States .50; Sweden .08; Italy .04; West Germany .03; Japan .01.

[6] Setting average $d_{(Russia)}$ at 4,000 kilometers, average $d_{(China)}$ at 1,000 kilometers, the

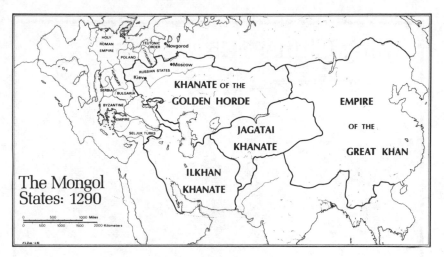

Fig. 8.3

Similarly in central Asia, Soviet Turkmenistan and possibly also Uzbekistan, Tadzhikistan, and Kirghizia appear in the long run to be geopolitically much more vulnerable to Iranian than to Russian control. During the past 2,600 years, Turkmenistan was united with Iran 73 percent of the time (1,900 years), and both were united with the other areas mentioned (traditional Transoxiana) 20 percent of the time (McEvedy, 1961, 1967, 1971; Barraclough, 1979). Russia has held these territories only 100–130 years, since 1850–80. Given the large population and potential economic resources of the Iranian plateau, Iran's future growth should pose yet another significant challenge to Russian territorial control. Current ethnic mobilization under the ideological aegis of Islamic militancy in this part of the world is in keeping with a pattern of increasing struggle for geopolitical control.

population of China at four times the population of Russia (p_R), and c at 10^{-4}, the vulnerability of east Asian Soviet territory to China exceeds its vulnerability to Russia when

$$(1 - 10^{-4} \cdot 10^3)_{KI(\text{China})^4 P_R} > (1 - 10^{-4} \cdot 4 \cdot 10^3)_{KI(\text{Russia})} P_R$$

Solving for $I_{(\text{China})}$:

$$I(\text{China}) > \frac{I_R}{6}$$

In other words, the vulnerability of east Asia switches toward China when Chinese GNP per capita reaches one-sixth of Russian GNP per capita. At current levels (Russian GNP per capita $2,600) the vulnerability would shift when Chinese GNP per capita rises from $355 to $420. If transportation cost c is set lower at 10^{-5}, Chinese GNP per capita would have to rise to approximately one-fourth of Russian or, at current levels, to $650.

199

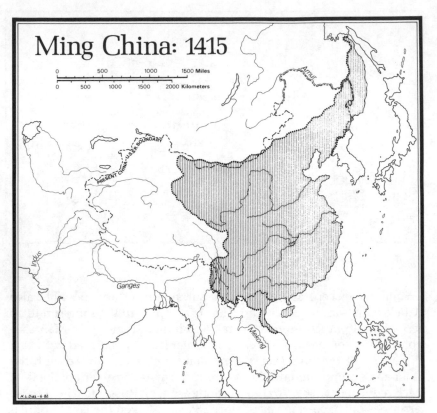

Fig. 8.4

The degree of overextension that already exists on several fronts has kept the Soviet military budget extremely high even in peacetime (variously estimated at 11 to 21 percent of GNP, when hidden expenditures are taken into account) (Collins and Cordesman, 1978). As a result, major strains exist within the Soviet economy. Besides these military forces on distant frontiers, a further expense is entailed by Soviet subsidies for Cuban troops in Africa and by foreign aid to bolster military allies. Any exacerbation of existing commitments, or extensions of Soviet military intervention to yet more distant territories, would constitute strains increasing at an accelerating rate. Similarly, the Russian naval buildup to a level challenging the United States constitutes an expensive overextension of military commitments. It is reminiscent of the effort of eighteenth-century France to maintain the largest army in Europe and simultaneously match Brit-

Fig. 8.5

ish power at sea. The financial strains of that policy brought on the French Revolution of 1789 (Collins, 1981b:63–8).

Interaction of geopolitical disadvantages

The various factors militating against the continuation of Russian power are interacting and cumulative. The activation of military crises in any area opens up vulnerabilities in other areas. If serious fighting were to break out in the Far East, or in central Asia, Russian power to deal with dissidence in Eastern Europe or the Caucasus would be diminished, thereby encouraging local efforts at autonomy. The current dissidence in Poland fits logically with a situation in which the Russians are hesitant to intervene militarily because of expensive

Politics

commitments in Afghanistan. Conversely, an Eastern European revolt would create vulnerabilities on southern and Asian fronts.

The Soviet Union has been able to meet each military crisis singly
during the past thirty years. But over long periods of time, the chance
rises toward certainty that several crises will arise simultaneously.
This would create a situation in which strains would prove militarily
intractable, resulting in the loss of control over at least one territory.
Moreover, losses beyond that point would probably become rapidly
cumulative. Since the Soviet Union has relied on loyal Warsaw Pact
forces to put down revolts (as in Hungary in 1956 and Czechoslovakia
in 1968), failure to control any particular Eastern European dissident
would tend to weaken control over the entire bloc. Any incident has
the potential for becoming a "tipping phenomenon" shifting the entire arrangement of tacit coordination, in Schelling's (1962:51–118)
terms. Simultaneous crises on several fronts, especially geographically far-flung ones, would encourage independence movements in
several places simultaneously, and the success that any one satellite
in pulling free sharply would increase the chance that a number of
adjacent states would also achieve independence. The necessity for
simultaneous crises to initiate the process makes it impossible to predict when such an incident might occur. But evidence on the mutual
escalation of rebellion and repression in other contexts typically
shows a pattern of logarithmic growth in rebellion (Hamblin et al.,
1977; Pitcher et al., 1978); if such a pattern may be extrapolated to the
series of Eastern European revolts and dissident movements, one can
expect an escalation of such dissidence within the next few decades.

Given the interlocking nature of the geopolitical weaknesses of
overextension and of a multifronted interior position, a serious crisis
of Soviet control would not be likely to involve Eastern Europe alone.
Activation of latent geopolitical weakness on the Far Eastern or central Asian territories would probably also be involved. A particularly
volatile area is likely to be the Middle East. Precisely because of its
natural resources and its internal instability, the Soviet Union will be
strongly tempted to intervene militarily in Iran, Iraq, or the Arabian
Peninsula in coming decades. Such an advance would constitute a
serious overextension, leapfrogging two or more ethnic heartlands
beyond the Russian home base. Given the high degree of class, religious, and national conflict in the Middle East, Russian client states
would be unlikely to be able to maintain themselves without active
intervention by Russian forces, such as those sent into Afghanistan in
1979. Internal weaknesses allowing Russian intervention would nevertheless call upon Russian resources to a degree that would be likely
to produce major political and economic strains for the Soviet Union.

Future decline of the Russian Empire

If an overextended imperial state becomes embroiled in ethnic and political conflicts within a distant client state, there is a strong tendency for these foreign instabilities to become gradually incorporated inside the imperial state's own boundaries. In the same way in which morale problems of U.S. troops intervening in the fragmented internal politics of Vietnam fed back into domestic American demoralization, Soviet overextensions create both economic strains and potential political problems at home. Thus it is highly likely that, once a first round of serious crises caused the loss of Eastern Europe or other distant territory, there would be set in motion cumulative processes of internal weakening, culminating in the eventual loss of the next tier of ethnically distinct conquest: the Baltic states, the Ukraine, the Caucasus, and the central-Asian Moslem territories. If such process matched prior rates of disintegration, it would extend well into the twenty-first century and perhaps beyond. A map for the year A.D. 2100 or 2200, by this projection, would show a number of separate states all across current Soviet territory.

It should be noted that the prime mechanism of change proposed is not ethnic revolt within the present-day Soviet Union. It is clear that Soviet mechanisms of internal surveillance and indoctrination operate effectively not only to curb dissidence but also to promote widespread popular agreement with official state ideology (Zaslavsky and Z, 1981).[7] Rather, the breakdown of the central power of the Russian state is a prerequisite for the emergence of strong ethnic separatist movements. Such a breakdown is projected to occur as the result of cumulative geopolitical weakness, resulting in an exhaustion of military resources that could be used for internal control. Simultaneous with such defeats would occur a loss of political confidence within the Russian states. This situation would then activate further ethnic separatism within the inner tier of Soviet-controlled territories.

Given the long-term nature of this process, extending into the next century or farther, it may be questioned whether ethnic identities can be expected to last long enough to have such an effect. But it appears now that ethnic identities, once thought to be fragile in the modern world, are remarkably resilient (Laumann, 1973; Greeley, 1974; Tudjman, 1981). Among the submerged ethnic groups in the Soviet Union, Ukrainian and Caucasian nationalisms continue strong despite two centuries of incorporation within the Russian state. Some ethnic groups, such as the Latvians, Estonians, and Lithuanians, were inde-

---

[7] This research consists of surveys carried out without official sanction in both private and public contexts by a Soviet sociologist, and includes data on privately expressed attitudes toward the Russian invasion of Czechoslovakia in 1968.

pendent as recently as 1940. Ethnic identity is often anchored by foreign ethnic populations, such as the overlap of Uyghur, Tadzhik, and Kirghiz in China and Russia; Uzbek in Russia and Afghanistan; Turkmens in Russia, Afghanistan, and Iran; and Azeri in Soviet Azerbaijan and Iran. Ethnic stratification, based on cultural discrimination in favor of Russian-speakers, continues to produce latent antagonism between Russian and other ethnic groups. Because Russian population growth has largely ended, while non-Russian, especially central Asian, populations continue to grow rapidly, population trends presage a steady decline in the proportion of Russians in the total population, from a current 52 percent to 40 percent or below in the twenty-first century (Clem, 1980). Soviet cultural policy, allowing considerable ethnic autonomy in language use and public communications for the mass of the populace, while reserving higher-ranking positions for Russian-speakers, thus manages both to preserve ethnic identities and to perpetuate a sense of ethnic discrimination and even latent class conflict (d'Encausse, 1979; Clem, 1980; McCagg and Silver, 1980).

The formal machinery for the dismemberment of the Soviet Union is already in place. The fifteen largest ethnically distinct areas are officially autonomous states, possessing local machinery of government (Figure 8.6). In current practice, this autonomy has little effect, as the armed forces, monetary system, and economic planning are controlled by organs of the central government and political control is organized by a single national Communist Party. The importance of the autonomous-ethnic-state structure, rather, is that it both maintains ethnic identities and provides an organizational framework that would allow genuinely separate states to emerge whenever the central government were seriously weakened.

Alternative perspectives

This projection of long-range Soviet decline is sufficiently unconventional to be profitably compared with more typical analyses.

Nuclear war

It is commonly assumed that the future of Soviet power revolves around the question of a nuclear war with the United States and around the technical factors determining the chances of one side or the other's winning such a war. But the significance of a nuclear war for altering long-term geopolitical patterns is not likely to override other geopolitical factors: (1) According to the previously presented projections, the Soviet Union is entering a long-term decline in

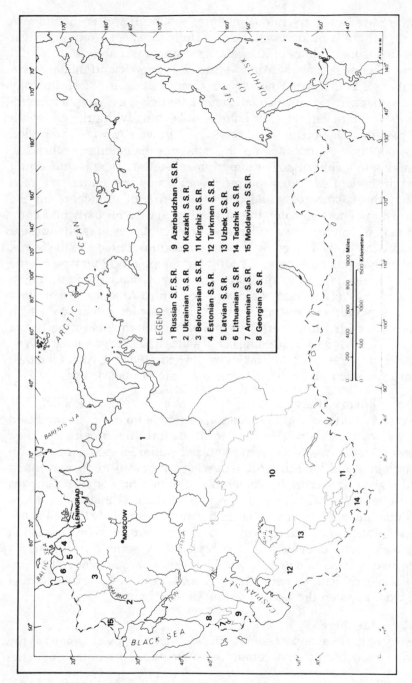

Fig. 8.6. The Soviet Union: present boundaries of union republics

LEGEND

1 Russian S.F.S.R.
2 Ukrainian S.S.R.
3 Belorussian S.S.R.
4 Estonian S.S.R.
5 Latvian S.S.R.
6 Lithuanian S.S.R.
7 Armenian S.S.R.
8 Georgian S.S.R.
9 Azerbaidzhan S.S.R.
10 Kazakh S.S.R.
11 Kirghiz S.S.R.
12 Turkmen S.S.R.
13 Uzbek S.S.R.
14 Tadzhik S.S.R.
15 Moldavian S.S.R.

Politics

power based on conventional military, political, and economic processes. There is no necessity for the United States to fight a nuclear war to ensure a failure of Russian expansion. (2) If a nuclear war did occur, the most likely outcome would be economic and military devastation of both Great Powers (U.S. Congress, Office of Technology Assessment, 1979). Such an outcome, although horrifying to contemplate, would nevertheless be entirely in keeping with prior geopolitical patterns. One possible outcome of a "showdown war" in a period of geopolitical simplification is the military exhaustion of both sides, resulting in a shift of power to peripheral states. There is little doubt that, if the United States and the Soviet Union were to cripple each other, the balance of world power would shift elsewhere on the globe.[8] (3) There remains the possibility that some particular combination of technical or accidental events would result in the nuclear destruction of the United States without serious damage to the Soviet Union. Nevertheless, from the long-term geopolitical viewpoint, the latter would have great difficulties in directly maintaining a permanent military occupation of a conquered North America. An attempt to do so would cause strain from an extremely long distance, which would be added to the array of military commitments of the Soviet Union vis-à-vis its surrounding client states and border enemies. One would still expect a decline in Soviet power in the long run of the next centuries, even given this extreme outcome of nuclear war.

Energy crisis

Would the world exhaustion of petroleum reserves, predicted for the years 2030–50 (Haefele, 1980), disturb this projection? Most likely it would not. Modern mechanized warfare depends heavily on petroleum, and long-distance (especially airborne) troop movement and logistics are crucially vulnerable to diminution of such supplies (see Chapter 7). The long-run prognosis, then, is that the strain of maintaining military operations in the future, especially long-distance and multifront operations, will become much greater. The exhaustion of world petroleum, unless it is replaced by some other militarily effective source of energy, would make a large-scale empire increasingly difficult to maintain in the next century. The exhaustion of oil would hasten the decline of the Russian Empire.

Ideology

Alternatively, it is often stressed that the Soviet Union, as the center of an international communist movement, promotes and bene-

[8] The Chinese government at one time explicitly stated this as a strategy (Clubb, 1971:423).

206

fits from ideological class conflict in all parts of the world. Such ideological connections give it special advantages against ordinary geopolitical constraints. But the historical evidence suggests that ideological movements, over long time-periods, tend to be subordinated to the patterns of geopolitics (Collins, 1978, and Chapter 9 in this volume). Modern political ideologies such as communism show a geopolitical structure like that of religions such as Christianity and Islam, within which heresies and splits emerged along lines of geopolitical antagonism. Current splits within the communist camp follow precisely those lines that would be expected on the basis of geopolitical considerations. Thus, despite the obvious ideological similarity between the Soviet Union and China, and the military advantages of alliance rather than enmity between them, the communist governments of the two countries maintained good relations for only ten years after the establishment of the People's Republic of China in 1950. China lays claim to the territory of Mongolia, the Amur region, and parts of central Asia on grounds of precedents established in the pre-Republic Ch'ing dynasty, and military clashes have occurred on the same territories in which imperial Chinese fought as long ago as 100 B.C. (Gronsset, 1953:58, 159–61; Clubb, 1971; Eberhard, 1977:182–3). Similarly, Soviet foreign policy has sought current geopolitical advantages rather than followed distinctively communist doctrine (Moore, 1965:350–408).

The preeminence of geopolitics over ideology does not mean that communism is irrelevant for the future of the Soviet Union. Russian alliances, victories, and defeats will continue to have their effects on communist doctrines and factions. Geopolitical theory does not predict that the decline of the Soviet Union would necessarily entail the overthrow of communist ideology in its territories. More in keeping with the precedent of religious ideologies would be the internal split of Russian communism into territorially localized heresies or factions. The projected disintegration of the Soviet Union would most likely occur under the leadership of dissident communist politicians. Given the current monopoly of communists over political organization in the Soviet Union, it would be difficult for political change to come about in any other way, at least initially. Geopolitically induced military and economic crises must give rise to debate within the Soviet Communist Party over possible courses of action, and rival recommendations would doubtless be couched in terms of varying interpretations of Marxism. With such ideological splits emerging with Soviet political organization, structural opportunities would motivate some Communist politicians to ally themselves with locally based ethnic populations. The breakdown of centralized Muscovite control over Soviet territories would result in ideological upheaval, but less probably in a complete disavowal of Marxism than in an efflorescence of heretical versions analogous to those that characterized the Protestant Reformation when the Papacy lost control of northern Europe.[9]

Conclusion

The foregoing analysis has of course policy implications for the Western powers. All major geopolitical processes appear to be working against the continuation of Soviet world power. Cumulative disadvantage should be expected to reach major proportions in the next century, and the coincidence of crises on several fronts simultaneously could occur at any time. One might well draw the conclusion that the major foreign-policy aim of the United States ought to be to avoid becoming involved in unnecessary showdown wars that would entangle it with the Soviet decline. Because their geopolitical situations differ, U.S. power is not in a zero-sum relation with that of Russia. Soviet decline does not depend on major U.S. intervention at Soviet borders, and the United States cannot be expected to gain territory or client states as the result of Russian decline. The long-term movement over the next several centuries, rather, should be in the direction of increasing pluralization of power in the world.

The major purpose of this analysis, however, has not been to suggest policy applications so much as to provide a concrete illustration of geopolitical principles. The underlying theory is not merely a conceptual viewpoint, but a means of explaining variations in the geopolitical power of states. We see, further, that a state's position of power-prestige in the international arena, in Weber's terms, is linked to the legitimacy of its internal rulers. Hence ideological movements

---

9 Could Russia be saved by a radical shift in alliances? It is true hypothetically that any possible pattern of alliances could occur among states. Any state could become isolated as an "interior" state surrounded by enemies elsewhere in the world; conversely, the same state could end its isolation and even turn the tables by making alliances with some of its neighbors and with states located on the far side of its enemies. In actuality, though, some patterns of alliance and rivalry are more "natural" than others. The historical relationship between China and Russia (discussed in this chapter under "Ideology") appears to be one such natural rivalry. Moreover, some states have less need to be concerned with patterns of alliance than others. Given the contingencies of politics, patterns of alliance are unstable and randomize over time. States with geopolitical advantages (fewer directions in which significant potential enemies must be faced, and hence less need to be concerned with alliance patterns) will be in a more favorable position than states with geopolitical disadvantages (more potential enemies and hence more need for balance-of-power alliances). The two types of states should differ in their long-term fates, according to the general principles suggested here. In the long run, alliances may put off but cannot avoid a decline in Russian territorial power.

within Russian Marxism can be expected to play an important part in the dynamics by which internal factions adjust to the new opportunities and liabilities of domestic power set in motion by the long-term geopolitical situation.

In general, ideology has a tendency to follow geopolitics. This lesson may be drawn from comparative history, of which the principal materials available are the histories of the world religions. Ideological struggle within religion has traditionally been the topic of heresy; but as we shall see, the secular political equivalent seems to move along similar contours.

Part III

Culture

9

Heresy, religious and secular

What is a heresy? It is an idea, a doctrine, or a symbolic action that provokes *righteous anger* and often violent repression. A heresy is not simply a position in intellectual discussion. The sides are already firmly chosen. Debate consists rather in showing deviation from canonical principles, and in name-calling. Pronouncing the name of a heresy in an angry tone is the last word in debating tactics: You are but an Albigensian! . . . a Manichee! . . . a Communist! . . . a Trotskyite!

The procedure is ritualistic in the Durkheimian sense. The conflict concerns group membership. The doctrine or gesture symbolizes the group and its standards of loyalty; it is a traditional formulation used on ritual occasions, and to depart from the accepted formula is to challenge the group structure: to split it, change its organization, or put forward a new leadership. Hence heresy debate is more than intellectual. The symbols are not necessarily matters of concern in themselves but are vehicles for organizational power and politics. Hence also the prevailing tone of righteous anger. Anger is the automatic response to a moral violation, the shattering of expected social solidarity. That this shades over into repressive violence is not surprising. For if morality extends only up to the boundary of the group, to break from the group puts one beyond the moral pale; those within can feel completely righteous in any degree of cruelty perpetrated against those who reject its community. Ironically, this is particularly so if the group is so constituted that dissidents are not simply destroyed but are strenuously to be brought back into membership's saving grace. Whether the group succeeds or not in this restraint is not so important, as Durkheim pointed out, as the sheer performance of the ritual. Punishment reinforces group solidarity and loyalty to the group's symbols among those who remain.

Durkheim's perspective provides us sociological entrée into the realm of heresy. But Durkheim was too insensitive to history and to the vagaries of politics to carry us very far. If God represents society, nevertheless the type of God represented has a great deal to do with the type of society in question, and with the organization of the church, the state, and the stratification of the populace as well. Weber can provide a necessary corrective here. But Weber had relatively little interest in heresy as such. He used the term occasionally, as loosely interchangeable with "heterodoxy." Thus he described Taoism and Buddhism as heterodox in Confucian China, Buddhism and Jainism as heterodoxies of Hindu culture, and even Samkhya (one of the "schools" of Hindu doctrine) as "more or less" heterodox to Hindu Vedanta (Weber, 1922/1963:192). The terminology is imprecise if we wish to isolate heresies as doctrines that provoke righteous anger and persecution.

Nevertheless, Weber's sociology of religion provides useful tools for understanding where and how heresy conflicts emerge. The dynamics of heresy connect with themes we have been pursuing throughout this book. For the essence of politics involves both violence and morality. On one side, its foundation is military and, I have argued, geographical. Violent threat always lurks in the background, and with it death – one certain doorway into the religious realm. On its other side, politics also concerns morality and ideals: ideology, if one likes, but ideology in a stronger, more morally compelling sense than is usually given to the term. The best example of such an all-encompassing ideology is religion.

Religion straddles the realm of culture and politics. Even where religions claim to be most apolitical, they cannot avoid having their own internal politics – the politics of the church organization itself; nor can they avoid connections, if unknowing ones, with the politics of the larger society. In many tribal and kinship-organized societies, the distinction is difficult to draw, and the Durkheimian cult is simultaneously religion, politics, and social structure. This is a lesson Durkheim must have learned from his teacher, Fustel de Coulanges, whose *Cité Antique* (1864) depicts the revolutions of ancient Greece and Roman city-states as a series of coalitions breaking through the restricted membership of prior family-based religious cults. The content of religious belief, including the degree of unity and transcendence of the spiritual, is correlated with the numbers of degrees of political hierarchy in the surrounding society (Swanson, 1962). Talcott Parsons (1967) stresses that the universalistic religions emerge in situations of cosmopolitan "world" ecumenes, which means either actual or potential empires. Clearly, political possibilities and actualities affect religious consciousness, just as political patronage or intolerance affects religious organization.

Theocracies apart, religion is often a motive force in modern politics. And it is akin to nationalism, crusades against "vice," and other forms of moralism that continually reappear in the political world. Such forces have an obvious staying power, however "irrational" they appear from the point of view of straightforward economic class interests. To analyze heresies poses the possibility of bringing all these types of phenomena back into a single overriding view of political process. Following Weber's lead, we shall look for a dynamic of struggle by organized groups and their leaders, in which the object is to benefit from emotional forces that confer legitimate identification with the essence of the community.

The universal church and the imperial state

Heresy can emerge only as an issue within a religion organized by universally oriented recruitment, rather than by heredity or membership in a preexisting community (such as the ritual cults of families, tribes, or kingdoms). A universal church is a special-purpose organization, and a new community created over and above traditionally existing ones. For this reason, each of the great "world religions" takes its origin from a prophet or other charismatic founder, whereas traditional and communal rites usually have more anonymous, unhistoricized origins.

According to Durkheimian theory, universalistic recruitment implies that the moral and spiritual ideal of the organization will also be universalistic. The moral code will be regarded as applying ultimately to everyone, and there is believed to be only one spiritual power or God. For these reasons, a universalistic church is a powerful political weapon. On both the organizational and doctrinal side, such a church is extremely useful for empire builders with ambitions of universal domination. This political connection is one of the sources of pressure that can lead to heresy conflicts. Conversely, when such states have acquired nonreligious, secular administration and legitimacy, this ingredient of heresy conflicts subsides.

Why is this universalistic-church structure crucial for heresy? Because if morality is more particularistic, and organizations are self-consciously local, then deviants from orthodoxy are simply outsiders. They can be treated callously, opportunistically, or in any other way, but they are not subject to demands for ritual conformity. The family cults of ancient Greece and Italy did not demand universal adherence, but, on the contrary, jealously guarded their ranks against outsiders. The theocracies of ancient Egypt and Mesopotamia were similarly particularistic, identifying the gods with the patronage of certain cities. Conquests by other cities and states usually resulted in the incorporation of the vanquished gods into subordinate positions

215

Culture

in a pantheon. The rival gods might be enemies, but they were not disbelieved for that reason. This phenomenon may be referred to as "preuniversalistic tolerance." It is found even among empire builders such as Rome, where the standard military procedure included a ceremony before the gates of a besieged city, calling upon its gods to desert their people and join the Roman pantheon (Fustel de Coulanges, 1864/1980:205–9).

Weber (1917–19/1952:139–46, 187–93) points out that this pluralistic structure was found even in early Judaism. The military sibs had their own exclusive cults, which only gradually gave way before the cult of the larger war coalition. Similarly, this Yahwe cult for some time coexisted with Canaanite cults of Baal, Moloch, and local syncretisms, which it only gradually displaced after the Yahwe partisans managed to identify themselves as the sole bearers of national legitimacy. This occurred in a manner that neatly illustrates Weber's general theory of politics. For it was the syncretisms that were "in office" when the Jewish state suffered its military downfall (actually deriving from the unfavorable geopolitical situation of Palestine between larger Mesopotamian and Egyptian empires). Thus the international situation delegitimated the Canaanite cults and gave impetus on the rebound to the "loyal opposition" of Yahwehists. The aggressive monotheism of Judaism, later inherited by Christianity, derives from this bitter political struggle against rival cults in Palestine. The exclusiveness and intolerance of these religions for long after made them stand out unfavorably in the eyes of the pluralistic "pagan" world.

As long as social groups and their politics were organized on the level of kinship structures, universalistic membership and hence heresy conflicts were not possible. This was the case, too, in state-organized societies, as long as the ruler claimed a familial charisma, which usually went along with the continued existence of household cults throughout the society. The Roman Empire, for all its potential for claiming universal domination and thus becoming a breeding ground for universal religion, nevertheless remained organized internally as an umbrella over a concatenation of autonomous households and municipalities with their own cult organization (MacMullen, 1974). Only when the growth of Roman bureaucracy (in the 200s and 300s A.D.) eroded and delegitimated this infrastructure could a universalistic church become politically popular.

A fortiori, smaller states with no realistic chance of establishing world empire had no choice but to regard the world as religiously pluralistic. An ecumene of military and commercial interchange, however, does foster the growth of cults that recruit membership

216

voluntarily, as autonomous, special-purpose organizations not rooted in family or city. The Greek oracles and their patron gods and goddesses were of this sort; so was the Bacchic cult, which cut across the usual lines of Greek society because it recruited women, who were politically disenfranchised at all levels and hence, in a sense, could be mobilized more easily. Roman conquest, which facilitated long-distance travel and cultural migration, structurally encouraged the growth of "denominational" cults. Some, such as the cults of Isis, Attis, Cybele, and others, were ancient civic cults of places long conquered, which had left their old community foundation to recruit universalistically. Others, like the popular cult of Mithra, had migrated across military frontiers from Persia. But although these were universalistic churches in a sense, they do not show the aggressive monotheism that sets the stage for persecution of heresies. One might call them semiuniversal, in that they emerged in an ecumenical world and broke free of old particularistic loyalties, but had not yet reached the level of social domination where they could claim to be the only true cult. Only Christianity and Judaism, with their distinctive political background, were so ambitious, and Christianity had to wait its time for Roman political conditions to ripen.[1]

The "semiuniversal" churches of antiquity often took the form of *mysteries:* which is to say, organizationally they were secret societies. The inner secret revealed might be that there is only one spiritual force permeating or standing behind everything. For the ancients, this was not merely a psychological message of personal identity with the godhead, because it also carried a social implication that the plurality of cults and gods in the surrounding society were but illusory manifestations of unity. Hidden in here was a potentially revolutionary message. If acted upon, it would have led to the overturning of the familistic and communal structure of ancient society. But the pluralism of the mystery cults was too strongly established for such a step. Hence the emphasis on remaining a *mystery*, that is, inner knowledge for an elite of initiates, that explicitly left the surrounding society and its cults intact. The mystery religions made no political claim, and hence had no struggles over heresy. They recognized illusions and lower levels of understanding, not morally reprehensible errors.

[1] The monotheistic claims of Judaism were always politically unrealistic insofar as they envisioned the restoration of the empire of David and Solomon. But the vision was politically attractive, once removed from its exclusive ethnic base. Hence the appeal of the Jewish model of monotheistic politics, not only in Christianity and later in Islam but also as evidenced by the religious prosperity of Judaism throughout the ancient diaspora, as in the wholesale conversion of the Kazars of the Russian steppe.

It is only when these organizational forms are transcended, and preuniversalistic tolerance gives way to a demand for subjugation to a spiritual monism, that heresies become possible. Heresy implies a particular kind of religious *and* political organization. It requires an overtly universalistic church, open not only to universal recruitment but to total community participation. And since the representation of the outer bounds of the community is always claimed by the military state, the successfully universalistic church tends to coincide with the state-supported church. This in turn gives a special impetus toward heresy conflicts, since the church is in a position to call upon the exercise of force to settle doctrinal orthodoxy, while conversely the state has an interest in maintaining a single source of legitimacy.

It is another peculiarity of heresies that they often involve intellectual matters, even though the core of the issue is not merely one of intellectual disagreement. The essence of a heresy dispute is the boundaries of religious membership, and hence the moral fervor and the violent punishments may be out of all proportion to the extent of intellectual disagreement. Heresy disputes often occur over minor and peripheral matters of doctrine (although they may occur over major issues as well), and sometimes over purely ritual procedures or other criteria of membership. But if it is of the essence of heresies that they are politicized, it also pertains to them that they are always in some degree intellectualized. The universal church must always be somewhat bureaucratized, that is, manned by literate specialists cut loose from family and community organization. Moreover, as a large-scale organization it makes provision for long-distance coordination and for training, which calls into being specialists in doctrine. The intellectual component becomes elaborated, and rivalries within the intellectual field take on potential for organizational and political maneuvering in the larger arena. Weber saw a continual tension between the different components of church organization, especially between the doctrinal specialists with their tendency to elaborate their own intellectual interests, and the "line authority" of bishops, abbots, and the like who have the ultimate responsibility for keeping the organization viable politically, economically, and morally.[2]

---

[2] This is another reason why one would not expect heresy conflicts to be possible within tribal societies. Nevertheless, I would not like to close the door completely on the possibility of finding political conflicts beneath tribal religious doctrine. It does not seem realistic to believe that intitutional practices having the motivational and legitimating power of religion should be passively and universally accepted in *any* type of society. We no longer believe that tribal societies are static and historyless, even though their politics usually must take the form of maneuvering in marriage politics, kinship coalitions, and the like. Given the mobilizing effects of religious cults, we should expect that they, too, have their maneuvers, their organizational

Heresy, religious and secular

For all these reasons, the *locus classicus* of heresy conflicts is the Christian Church, especially during the periods when it was politically Established. In searching out the principles of heresy, I shall draw primarily upon ancient Christianity in the following sections.[3] But it is also true that something like this dynamic is set up wherever the state upholds an official cult that has any intellectually elaborated doctrine. Islam as well as Chinese Confucianism fall into this category. We have, then, some comparative variants, in which pressures over heresy are a matter of degree.

Weber devoted considerable attention to the differences in organization and doctrine between Oriental and Occidental religions. In general, he held that only Christianity was organized in a sufficiently communal manner so that it could bring moral pressure for social transformation. His main concern was, of course, economic transformation, the development of capitalism, but the same factors apply to political transformation. On the one hand, Confucianism, Islam, and Judaism have no theological dogmas – apart from the cosmogenic and historical narratives in the latter two – but instead emphasize practical rules of conduct (Weber, 1922/1963:192). Theological disputes are not a feature of these religions, whereas Christianity is permeated with intellectuals and hence constantly in tension on this score.[4]

strains and conflicts. If so, these should be manifested in doctrinal controversies, hence in something *like* heresy disputes, if not in the same moral discourse as found within universalistic churches. The fashionable symbolic anthropology of today too easily reifies and sentimentalizes what is, after all, in many respects an ideology. Lévi-Strauss bears the responsibility for having set off a search for symbolic structures beyond the level of empirical interaction, but at the same time he had a streak of realism not found in many of his successors. Thus he views the elders of Australian tribes as politicians and intellectuals, deliberately organizing the totemic lineages (and hence their religious ideology) in response to some particular crisis of kinship politics (Lévi-Strauss, 1949/969:228, 314). Mary Douglas (1973:113–35) suggests some of the ways in which tribal politics affects its symbols, varying from egalitarian groups to ones in which the rivalry of powerful chiefs breaks down traditions and causes an alienated underclass to project their social fears in a religious guise. Similarly, Paige and Paige (1981) attempt to interpret reproductive rituals as tribal politics, although in an overly static way. More treatment of such ideological politics at the tribal level is distinctly called for.

3 This is another area Weber had intended to treat in his comparative studies of the world religions, left unfinished at his death.

4 "The Christian churches, as a consequence of the increasing intrusion of intellectualism and the growing opposition to it, produced an unexampled mass of official and binding rational dogmas, as well as a theological faith. In practice it is impossible to require both belief in dogma and the universal understanding of it. . . . A decisive influence was everywhere exerted on the character of religion by the relationships between the theological intellectuals, who were the virtuosi of religious knowledge, and the pious non-intellectuals, especially the virtuosi of religious asceticism and the virtuosi of religious contemplation, who equally regarded 'dead knowledge' as of negligible value in the quest for salvation" (Weber, 1922/1963:192–3).

Culture

The Oriental salvation religions, Hinduism, Buddhism, and Jainism, are in a different position. Weber (1922/1963:116–20, 227; 1916–17/1958:329–43) characterizes them as the creations of elitist intellectuals, oriented toward contemplative meditation rather than asceticism, and leaving no role for a lay congregation except to provide pious alms for the monks. Hence these religions can have neither contact nor conflict with politics, since all relations to the world are broken. Taoism, although not so extreme a religion of withdrawal, also shares this elitist and contemplative attitude. None of these religions is concerned with social reform, unlike the Occidental religions. Weber (1922/1963:50, 55) refers to Buddha and Lao-tzu as "prophets," but they are "exemplary prophets," enlightened humans who demonstrate the path to be followed, rather than "ethical prophets" (like Zoroaster, Jesus, Muhammad) who proclaim God and his will. It is the moralistic religions of participating congregations that are most influenced by and active in political circumstances. Even though a religion of love such as Christianity may originally be indifferent to worldly considerations, there is always a tension in the direction of social and hence political activism (Weber, 1922/1963:224). Once again we see why Christianity holds the greatest potential for heresy conflicts.

Weber was aware that the Oriental salvation religions also elaborated popular sides. Amidaist Buddhism offered salvation to the masses by calling on the name of Amida Buddha and various Bodhisattvas of mercy; Taoism developed a popular church with tutelary deities and a quasi-papal hierarchy; Hindu bhakti cults centered on devotion to merciful deities and spirit-infused gurus. But these Weber interprets as a retreat into popular wizardry and ritualism, lacking both world-transforming moral pressure and intellectual theology (Weber, 1922/1963:78, 102–3). Mahayana Buddhism Weber dismisses rather contemptuously as "a-literate . . . appealing especially to the feminine emotive aspect" (Weber 1916/1951:195). This is not quite an accurate characterization of Mahayana, which in fact was responsible for the high points of philosophical sophistication in both India and China. Nevertheless, Weber is not far off the mark when he emphasizes that intellectual doctrines in Buddhism, as in other Asian religions, were not the basis for factional schism of the same sort as in Christianity (Weber, 1922/1963:71–3). We shall pursue the point later in this chapter, in the discussion of mysticism.

The most politicized religious environment in the Orient, Weber felt, was Confucian China (apart from the unimportant case of Tibetan lamaist theocracy). Because there was an official state doctrine, it was the duty of the state, at least in principle, to persecute heresies (Weber 1916/1951:214–19). But this was confined to instances in which unauthorized congregations posed a political danger to the state, or promoted actual rebellions such as the T'ai P'ing syncretism of Taoism and Christianity, or various earlier secret societies of chiliastic popular Buddhism and Taoism. But Confucian officials were not imposing an intellectual orthodoxy. Confucianism itself Weber characterized as practical rather than intellectual, upholding the rituals of ancestor worship as a deliberate political policy for maintaining order, a kind of secular intellectual patronage of religion for cynical reasons. Although the Buddhist monasteries were plundered and partly suppressed in the 800s, they were nevertheless revived under a government regulation. "This tolerance by no means meant positive esteem," Weber remarks (1916/1951:217), "but rather the disdainful 'toleration' which is the natural attitude of every secular bureaucracy toward religion. It is an attitude moderated only by the need for taming the masses."

There is an element of polemic in Weber's discussion of toleration in China, as he pointedly denies the existence there of toleration in the modern liberal sense. But he sums up the entire Asian religious situation as one of tolerance (Weber 1916–17/1958a:329–30), in the sense that the various cults and sects all adapted to each other's presence. This was true even despite religious wars and militaristic monastic orders (the latter characteristic mainly of Tibet and Japan). In India in particular there was tremendous pluralism, which went along with a general political fragmentation. Only Confucianism was a political religion in the Western sense, but its peculiarly secular stance and its manipulative attitude toward religious practices kept it (for the most part) from engaging in heresy disputes. Weber's discussion thus provides some comparative proof for one basic condition for heresy: the need for it to be grounded in a universal, politically activist church.

Heresy and organizational power struggles

Heresies are produced by organizational power struggles within a universal church (cf. Kurtz, 1983). Such power struggles occur when there is a tension between the centralized and decentralized loci of resources. On the one hand there must exist sufficient organizational resources to make centralization a realistic ideal, but at the same time there is a dispersion among rival centers. The resources are those listed in Weber's theory of bureaucracy (1922/1968:956–65). These include literacy and readily available writing materials for records and communications, which make possible a ritual focus of loyalty around rules and sacred books rather than individual persons. Also important are the material conditions for long-distance movement: both the technology of transportation and a militarily or politically imposed peace covering sufficient territory and removing barriers to movement and communications. It is for these mundane reasons that universal churches tend to arise in political empires. A money economy further helps foster all these conditions.

In the early Christian Church (ca. A.D. 100–400), one can see the forming of a material organization from which arose the rivalries that led to heresy conflicts (Baynes, 1929; Jones, 1964; Chadwick, 1967; Brown, 1972). Christianity was based on the ceremonies of community worship. Thus it acquired as a material basis for this emotional production various forms of property: church buildings, graveyards, relics, books and other means of administration. The church collected money donations from its members, primarily for charity (which is to say, mutual aid among members and potential converts in times of sickness, burials, etc.), and to support missionaries and other Christian travelers. In the process of administering these resources, the Church began to lose its original form as a primitive democracy of all participants and to become centralized. Gradually, chief administrators emerged (bishops), and then paid priests. The pattern was adopted of having a single bishop per city, who gradually extended his power to veto the priests put forward by congregations and eventually to nominate them. By the second century of Christianity, the bishops of the major cities began to extend their power over the smaller cities in their areas. In time the number of principal bishops became reduced to a handful.

This extension of power occurred because bishops of the larger cities had more material resources than others. Accordingly, they held more money for charity, for the care of travelers, for sponsoring missionaries, for patronage within (and later without) the Church. They also held superior means of emotional production: larger and more impressive churches, finer vestments, nobler relics, and all the other paraphernalia of a compelling stage-setting for their rituals. Michels's Iron Law of Oligarchy stemming from the control of the means of administration applies equally well to organizations specializing in ritual production. There is, of course, also the centralizing implication of the universalistic ideology itself – the idea of one God – and one could bolster this by a charismatic succession of bishops from the Apostles and ultimately from Jesus. This ideology was gradually enhanced as the material administration became centralized. But this ideology could hardly have been decisive. Rome used it as the basis of its claim to primacy, but its claim became strong at a relatively late date and did not diminish the impressiveness of the rival claims of the bishops of Constantinople, Antioch, and Alexandria. (That the mere doctrine of universalistic monotheism does not necessarily entail the organizational centralization of the church is, of course, also illustrated by the Protestant Reformation.)

Heresies tended to develop around these rival organizational centers during the period of advancing centralization, and especially as the material resources of the Church escalated with the official adoption of Christianity by the Roman Emperors. But the adoption of Christianity was itself the result of its growing popularity and resources, especially in the urban upper classes of the Empire. The major persecutions of Christianity occurred at the time when it had become a serious political threat. The sympathy of the Emperor Alexander Severus to the church was followed by the hostility of his successor, Maximinus, in A.D. 235. Philip the Arab (244–9) was popularly rumored to be a believer. This, together with the Gothic invasions beginning in 248, which coincided with many mutinies, set the stage for the first systematic persecution when the Emperor Decius (249–51) ordered in 250 that everyone must possess a certificate of participation in the sacrifices to the gods (Chadwick, 1967:119–22). Christianity was becoming part of the "ins" and "outs" of imperial politics, and implicated in the legitimizing or delegitimizing effects of foreign policy as well as in the general "house-sweeping" of successive new administrations. Paganism was on the defensive, and Decius was referred to by his partisans as "Restorer of the Cults" (Brown, 1982:94).

The very instability of the succession contributed to the staying power of Christianity and ensured that persecutions were short and inconclusive enough to be morale-building rather than organization-destroying. Decius's edict was withdrawn in 260 by the Emperor Gallienus. In 274–5, Aurelian withdrew toleration as part of his attempt to impose monotheistic worship of the sun-god throughout the Empire; the effort failed but indicated that official policy was turning toward a state-established universal church as a replacement for the particularistic cults of the earlier pluralistic empire. Christianity's turn to play that role was clearly in the offing, as political observers must have been aware. Diocletian (284–305) temporarily turned reform efforts in a secular direction by imposing administrative bureaucratization, and by dividing the Empire into more manageable eastern and western units. But this division aggravated religious splits because Christianity had sympathetic support in the family of Constantius (father of Constantine), who ruled in the west. In the east, another pagan monotheism rose to the perceived threat (and opportunity), when Neoplatonist advisers gained influence at the end of

Diocletian's reign and launched a violent persecution of Christians in 304. This lasted through the ensuing civil war with Constantine until 311. The victory of Constantine's western forces and the reunification of the Empire resulted in the gradual adoption of Christianity as the state church by the time of Constantine's death in 337. The dismantling of the pagan cults and the monopolization of all means of religious-ritual production in the hands of the Christian Church was a slow process, and the continued vicissitudes of imperial succession and civil war gave the pagans at least one more chance in office in the reign of Julian (361–3). But Christianity was clearly the best organized of all the monotheistic candidates. Even Julian recognized the organizational realities by attempting to turn the traditional sacrifices into a universal church, although the attempt was doomed because he had backed a materially very weak candidate for an effort of this sort (Browning, 1976).

The main effect of the persecutions and civil wars on Christianity was to breach the organizational centralization of the Church and hence to produce heresies. The archetypal controversy was the Arian heresy, concerning the precise metaphysical relations between Father and Son within the Trinity. The content was esoteric, not to mention hairsplitting, but it aroused vehement passions on both sides. One can only conclude that the intellectual controversy came to be seized upon as a symbolic emblem of membership in the factions disputing control of the newly powerful Church. The theological issue goes back to the Monarchian controversy that had emerged in Rome and elsewhere around A.D. 200, which seemed to represent factions in church politics favoring or opposing the use of Platonic philosophy (rather than literal scripture) in debates with Gnostic intellectuals.

The doctrinal controversy was revived and sharpened in the years following the end of the Diocletian persecution (Chadwick, 1967:124, 129–51; Baynes, 1929). Arius, a popular preacher in Alexandria, apparently was locally elevated to bishop when the official bishop fled during the persecutions, then was reduced again to the rank of mere presbyter after an outside bishop was appointed. The treatment of Arius touched on partisan feelings; not only was there a schism of hard-liners (the Melitians, similar to the Donatists in Carthage), who held that Communion should be reserved for those who held firm under the persecution, but also a struggle over authority of appointment. Alexandria was one of the major independent sees of the Church, but its temporary weakness had invited the charitable intervention of the bishops of Syria and Asia Minor, as well as Rome. A full-fledged struggle over spheres of influence was occurring throughout the Church, heightened by the ongoing elevation of

Christianity to official status by the Emperor Constantine. The doctrinal dispute between Arius and his bishop spread rapidly as pro- and anti-Arian parties became the major vehicles of church politics.

Orthodoxy was imposed by the Creed adopted by the first ecumenical council of the Church, held at Nicaea in 325 under Constantine's personal supervision, although the civil wars and varying factional sympathies of his successors during the rest of the century brought numerous temporary shifts in the power of Arian and anti-Arian parties. The underlying issues were organizational. More important than its theological stands, the Nicene council voided previous practices of local autonomy and established veto power over appointments of all local bishops in the hands of the bishop of the provincial metropolis (Chadwick, 1967:131). Administrative division of the Roman Empire and resulting civil wars, as well as Julian's brief disestablishment of the Church, kept the situation unsettled for many decades. The growing tendency for the Church to split administratively between western and eastern branches became involved in new rounds of the Arian controversy, which only settled down after a new ecumenical council in 381 under the Emperor Theodosius enforced further centralization of appointments under Rome and Constantinople (Chadwick, 1967:150–1). After this time Arianism had a new political identity, since it had been spread by missionaries to the Goths outside the borders of the Empire. In the Visigothic kingdom, Arianism was rigidly upheld and the opposing Catholic ("Homoousian") doctrine was persecuted as heresy (Jones, 1959). As indicated in Chapter 8 of this volume, ideology follows geopolitics.

Orthodoxy as it eventually emerged was a theological compromise that avoided the extremes of Trinitarian controversies, although there was always the potential for reopening dispute by someone's insisting on theological clarification. In the nature of the case, it was always possible to provoke a battle by declaring that one's enemies held one or the other of the opposing heresies either by failing sufficiently to distinguish the members of the Trinity or by distinguishing them too much. This intellectual heritage remained a weapon that was trotted out when organizational politics made it convenient. Hence we find a replay in the Monophysite heresy, a slightly different metaphysical cut at the components of the Trinity, which emerged in Egypt and Syria during 430–530 as these provinces reacted to the breakup of the Roman Empire by attempting to reassert their independence from the church hierarchy (Chadwick, 1967:194–212).[5]

[5] Jones (1959) argues against a type of "sociological" explanation of heresies that holds they are expressions of nationalist movements in religious disguise. He points out

Culture

Geopolitical events and internal church conflicts

Conflicts among the external allies of a church, as well as other geopolitical crises, tend to produce heresy conflicts within it. This principle is a variant on the preceding theme of organizational politics. A church is a major political weapon, serving to manipulate loyalties and ideals and sometimes as an actual organization for material administration of the state. A universalistic church has frequently been either the vehicle for developing intensive political administration in a previously "uncivilized" area or an ally of such administrations. Christianity provided the literate administrators who turned the Germanic tribal kingdoms into organized states, just as Buddhism served politically to organize Tibet and central Asia. Confucianism, originally perhaps only marginally "religious," not only was instrumental in shaping the administration of the first bureaucratized Chinese dynasty, the Han, but became itself organized as more explicitly a religion in the process. We have seen that the adoption of Christianity as the official religion of the Roman Empire, although not itself a search for literate administrators, was part of a general effort in the late Empire to introduce rationally centralized administration and an accompanying universalistic mechanism for producing legitimacy.

A corollary is that if a state's organizational resources are split so as to produce its own factional struggles, its ties with a church tend to create a market for heretical variants of doctrine. Many of the Christian heresies were abetted by the Roman civil wars of the 300s A.D. The Arian heresy as well as others tended to prefigure the division of the Empire into east and west. The same applies to many medieval and Renaissance heresies in Europe. The Albigensians in Languedoc emerged from an unsettled geopolitical situation in which local borderlines were constantly redrawn among the kingdoms of France, Aragon, and England. Simultaneously the battle between Pope and German Emperor lined up secular allies and enemies of Roman Catholic orthodoxy. The Albigensian political base, however, was weak

that the Monophysite heresy in Egypt was not merely held by Coptic-speakers, but had its stronghold in Greek-speaking Alexandria, just as in Syria the Monophysite church did not include all Syriac-speaking areas and made inroads in Greek-speaking Asia Minor as well. The motivation of the heretics was religious rather than political, and in fact no political rebellions against the Roman Empire coincided with them. But Jones here is criticizing a narrowly reductionist thesis that does not recognize that politics occurs *within* the church organization in its own right. Jones himself refers to the doctrinal differences involved in the Monophysite dispute as "very minute," and comes close to the issue of organizational independence when he notes that Alexandria was unwilling to accept even a Monophysite patriarch when he was appointed at imperial command from outside.

226

and temporary, and the weakness of the English hold over this corner of France helped provoke the Crusade of French knights that plundered Albigensian strongholds in 1209–29 in the name of orthodoxy just as the English were being driven out (see McEvedy [1961:64–74] for historical maps of the geopolitical fluctuations). Similarly, the stirrings of the Hussites and other dissenters in central Europe foreshadowed the political restructurings of the Reformation.

Geopolitical factors do not enter into heresies merely as adjustments, so to speak, of religious lines to the realities of political borders. Even within a given state, the geopolitical situation affects the likelihood of religious controversy. The connection follows from Weber's general analysis of politics as the pursuit of internal legitimacy within a situation of international struggle for military prestige. If the church is a major source of legitimacy for the state, there is also a reciprocal relationship in which the "foreign policy" vicissitudes of the state react back upon the prestige of the church. In lay terms, if God is on our side, we conquer; hence when we are not conquering, there is some doubt whether our religious leaders are properly doing their job. We have already seen this principle at work in the religious crisis of the Roman Empire at the time of the Gothic invasions and the civil wars of the 200s. It is consonant with this principle that Constantine elevated Christianity to a state religion after attributing to it his victory in the civil war.

The major heresy dispute of the Byzantine Empire, Iconoclasm, was of this sort. The controversy broke out in 726, when the Emperor Leo III ordered the destruction of images representing Christ and the saints, and continued intermittently under different emperors for over a century. It has often been claimed that this movement was an imitation of Moslem precepts, but in fact both the worship of images and church prohibitions upon it go back to A.D. 100–200 (Chadwick, 1967:277–83), and there is little evidence of Moslem influence (Brown, 1982:251–7). What transpired instead was a genuine geopolitical crisis. The rise of Islam outside the borders of the warring Persian and Byzantine empires in the 600s was at first a somewhat remote threat, but by the end of the century all of the Byzantine provinces in North Africa and the Levant had been overrun. Closer to home, the borderline in Anatolia was slowly pushed back, and in 717–18 a seaborne attack was repulsed at Constantinople itself. Other cities of the Aegean heartland were at least briefly captured. Iconoclasm came in a wave of religious anxiety over the threatened end of both state and Church (Brown, 1982:284–301). It was an effort at religious purification from heretical practices that were being blamed for the geopolitical crisis.

The dynamic was not entirely external, however, but a combination of external events with an ongoing factional conflict within the Byzantine Church. Administrators of the central government and their allies, the regular clergy of the Church, had long been locked in a battle for influence with popular monastic holy men. The icons were associated with the cult of saints and their relics, and represented a decentralization of authority that the main-line administration had long deplored. The previous religious hegemony of the saints and holy men during a time of military decline thus worked against them as the foreign situation delegitimated their appeal. They were vulnerable to being represented as a heretical lapse responsible for the ill fortunes of the empire. The icon/saint axis was also weakened by the Arab raids that destroyed many of the autonomous cities and their pilgrimage sites. As refugees crowded into Constantinople, bringing with them their uprooted local icons, these once-sacred objects underwent what Brown (1982:289) refers to as a "giddy inflation." The very destruction of the raids encouraged recentralization. On this basis, as a more stable Byzantine state reemerged, the iconoclast controversy eventually quieted down and normality was restored.

In the history of Islam as well, geopolitical factors have been central in religious schisms (Lewis, 1967; Gibb, 1969). Initially Sunni and Shi'a were merely adherents of rival genealogical factions in the succession to Muhammad, but their support tended to divide along lines of ethnic conflict between the Arab elite and their forced converts to Islam. The later ramifications of the schism reflected political struggles among regional centers of the Islamic Empire. As the money economy of the empire and its means of military administration broke down, the empire came apart. The most remote province, Spain, seceded under the banner of loyalty to the orthodox Umayyad lineage when the core empire was taken over by the revolutionary Abassid Caliphate (which also claimed orthodoxy); then Morocco became independent as a heretical Shi'ite state. Further fragmentation produced a religio-political checkerboard. Heretical syncretisms of Zoroastrianism with Islam (as well as Shi'ite sympathies) served as vehicles for the reemergence of Persia as an independent political center, while the Fatimid Caliphate displaced Mesopotamian Sunni control with an Egypt-based Caliphate organized on its local doctrinal variant, Ismailism.

Islamic heresy differs from that of Christianity because politics is not external to the church. The religion itself is organized as a theocracy (the Caliphate, from *khalifah*, meaning a successor to Muhammad), and hence one does not find the same meshing of internal organizational struggles with external political ones (Levy, 1957;

Lewis, 1974). Officers of the state and other leading citizens looked after the material basis of religious activities, keeping up mosques, providing charity, and employing religious teachers and other functionaries. It is true that a general secularization of the court set in during the later Abassid period so that the Caliph gradually lost religious leadership to private specialists. The potential for theocratic revivals was exercised periodically in successive Islamic regimes but was followed by periodic relapses into political secularization.

Because of these organizational conditions, most Islamic heresies are not very intellectual in content. Weber characterizes Islam as scholastic and legalistic, with only a few heterodox sects influenced by Sufis being intellectualistic (Weber, 1922/1963:132). Unlike the abstruse theological disputes of the Christian heresies, in which rivalries among the intellectuals became embroiled in organizational and political struggle, Islamic heresies were couched more immediately in terms of political grievances and accusations of moral transgressions. The Sunni-Shi'a conflict concerned the proper line of transmission of hereditary charisma among the partisans of rival clans related to Muhammad. The more decentralized versions of heresy claimed to make an entirely new start after rejecting the moral degeneracy of the existing claimants; thus the figure of the Mahdi is a heretic leader who claims to bring a new prophecy and to create a new and pure Islamic state.

In general, the type of doctrine that is heretical is shaped by a church's organizational form. A highly political church produces explicitly political doctrines for schism; the relatively personalistic form of government characteristic of classical Islam produced heresies concerning the personal or family qualifications of leaders.

There is a general corollary. Heresies based on political conflicts have a peculiar pattern of resolution. When the possibility of a unified state is still strong, the heresy is fought over in a violent conflict. It becomes the occasion for execution, forced recantation, and crusade. But if separate states emerge and their military boundaries hold firm, their doctrinal differences become much less occasions for moral outrage and holy war and come to be accepted by canons of expediency. Thus the bitter separation of Latin and Greek Christianity was finally ratified after the political Empire became permanently divided. Similarly, there is a settling down of Catholic and Protestant relationships after the inconclusive wars and shifting alliances of the 1600s showed the impossibility of either side exterminating what it considered to be intolerable heresy. The result may be (as in seventeenth-century France) the peculiar pattern in which doctrines are considered heretical for purposes of internal power struggles but not in regard to the diplomacy of external relations. The pattern is repeated in the Communist–anti-Communist relations of twentieth-century politics.

The asymmetry of mystical and moralistic religions

Mystical religions are heretical to moralistic religions, but not vice versa. The difference derives from their principles of organization. Mysticism tends to be hierarchic, both externally and internally. Externally, its teachings are for an enlightened elite, not for the uncomprehending masses; mystical religions make no effort at mass conversion. Internally, a mystical religion is not a congregation but a school, a hierarchy of masters and pupils with varying levels of experience; each successive level of insight shows up the imperfections of lower levels. Doctrinally this is expressed as the successive freeing of oneself from attachments, including subtler ones such as attachment to nonattachment. Hierarchization here is, in principle, endless. This is illustrated by a dialogue between rival Buddhist masters of ninth-century China:

"Where are you going?"

"I'm going to a changeless place."

"If there's a changeless place, you won't be going there."

"Going is also changeless."

Organizationally, mystics are linked together vertically; fellow monks are connected only by having a common master. In contrast, moralistic religions emphasize community participation, in which the basic link is a horizontal one among the group of worshipers. It is true that moralistic religions (such as Christianity) also develop hierarchies that are at once administratively and ritualistically important. But group worship remains the core experience, and the hierarchy is legitimated only in that it ministers to the group. It is also true that the hierarchy can arrogate considerable power to itself; but if it is too extreme, it is regarded as a corruption. The Iron Law of Oligarchy operating within a congregationally based moralistic religion remains a constant source of tension and hence of controversy in its ranks (and the same may be said of analogous movements in secular politics, such as Communism and other forms of egalitarian radicalism).

According to Durkheimian theory, the group is the basis of all moralities. Thus, a moralistic religion is centered on membership as a whole, and its key ritual activity is one in which the group is assembled (for daily prayers in Islam, for church services in Christianity) and the god-emblems that symbolize the religion are evoked. Mysticism shows the negative side of the same variables. Its key ritual is the experience of the individual *alone*, in meditation, cut off from sensory contact with the world. Doctrinally, it goes farther and expresses its aim as liberation from all discursive thought (in Buddhism, "name-and-form"), which is to say, from all social symbols. If God represents the moralistic church, the highest spiritual state in mysticism, appropriately, is Nirvana, the Void.

There are, of course, Christian and Islamic mystics, just as at a more everyday level there is the practice of solitary prayer. But prayer is explicitly verbal, and the social aspect even of mysticism remains in the orthodox requirement that God has some personal aspect. If not strictly anthropomorphic, God nevertheless can speak, and hence command. Thus the great prophets like Moses, Jesus, and Muhammad can retire into solitude but nevertheless reemerge, with the word of God to be written down in sacred books. Even in Platonizing Christianity, God retains enough human qualities to be a *logos*, a word. The borderline into heresy is crossed when God becomes entirely an impersonal and agentless spiritual force, whether identified with the self or with the cosmos.

Weber stresses that the forms of self-discipline found in the moralistic Western religions are entirely different in their social consequences from those found in Oriental mysticism (Weber, 1922/1963:169–71). Any similarity in abnegation of the senses is superficial. The mystic controls the senses merely as a method of arriving at a pure state of contemplation. The Buddha shunned the torture of the flesh practiced by previous ascetic virtuosi, in favor of "the middle way" of quiet self-control; and both Hindu and Buddhist texts speak of the meditative experience as "bliss," frequently depicted in terms of sumptuous inner aesthetics. In contrast, the Western ascetic remains tied to the world, as an enduring entity to be rejected over and over again. The aim of that person's self-discipline is to prove his or her moral heroism by repeatedly fighting and conquering the temptations of the flesh. From the point of view of the Buddhist, the Christian ascetic is "attached" to his or her suffering. Conversely, from the Christian or Moslem viewpoint, the Oriental mystic is merely indulging in selfish withdrawal and delusion.

Weber regarded this as a fundamental difference between Oriental and Occidental salvation religions, because the asceticism-within-the-world ("inner-worldly asceticism") of the latter permeated all aspects of Christian life and, together with its moralism, shaped capitalism. It is apparent from Weber's tone (1922/1963:170–1, 176–7) that he shared the prejudices of the ascetic activist about the contemplative religions, which he speaks of rather insultingly. But more importantly for our purposes, Weber points out (1922/1963:178) that moralistic religions always regard the mystical path, when it crops up within their own orbit, as heretical. It does so on highly righteous grounds, since mysticism is not only egotistical and nonethical, but offends against God by identifying Him with oneself. The latter charge is not without grounds. For if God represents society and its morality, the mystic who successfully withdraws into completely inner contemplation must end up overthrowing conventional morality; the attempt to break all attachments leads to paradoxically amoral-sounding statements of the genre: "When you meet the Buddha on the road, kill the Buddha!"

The underlying problem is in the internal politics of a church. Mysticism is a serious organizational rival to moralistic organization. This is partly because any intellectualism within a church runs the risk of eliminating the anthropomorphic elements of doctrine and turning it into a mysticism. From a different direction, anti-intellectual ritualism and devotion tends to spill over beyond collective ceremonies into individual prayers, which often activate the mechanics of meditative experience. Thus there is the constant danger of mysticism emerging within moralistic religions, where it is usually treated as a heresy.

The first major heresy within Christianity, Gnosticism, arose because the growing proselytization of the educated classes fostered an intellectualism and syncretism with preexisting philosophical mysticisms in the Hellenic and Middle Eastern orbit (Jonas, 1963; Festugiere, 1967; Pagels, 1979). In some sense there may be a class conflict within Christianity involved in this, between its upper class and plebeian sectors. But the heresy dispute also indicates a struggle over the organizational form of the Church. The accusations made against Gnosticism show this structural rivalry. It was charged with being elitist, concerned only with individual salvation and not with morality, which are precisely the organizational forms at issue. Hence Christian monasticism was very early subjected to strict organizational controls. Individual contemplation was replaced by a communal life among the monks, which scheduled most of their time for verbal devotions symbolizing the empirical Church. Even in the High Middle Ages (ca. 1000–1300) when Greek philosophy dominated the philosophical education of European Christianity, guard was still kept against overly mystical themes. Thus these theological systems did not invoke the symbol-less mysticism of the Void but were rationalistic doctrines that placed spiritual reality in the hierarchy of Platonic forms or Aristotelian categories reaching from God and the angels down through the human soul and the lower material realms (Knowles, 1962). Where more individual-contemplative forms of mysticism reemerged, they were suppressed as heresy, as long as the

Church was capable of enforcing the repression. The growing popular mysticism of the 1300s and 1400s, such as German Pietism, were indicators of the dissolution of centralized control that, together with the impetus of political events in the surrounding states, foreshadowed the breakdown of the Reformation.

Does this dynamic hold within Islam as well as Christianity? There are several versions of mysticism within Islam (Arberry, 1950; Zaehner, 1960; Geertz, 1968).[6] The purest form was a hierarchy of illuminati, whose secret teachings included an esoteric, nonliteral interpretation of the Koran. These were the Ismailis, a Shi'a sect regarded as an extreme heresy by the orthodox theocracy. But true to the Islamic pattern, even among the Ismailis the emphasis was political. The religious doctrine became allied with a purely dynastic faction (the Fatimids) that maneuvered to gain control of the Egyptian state. Following the success of their sponsors, the Ismailis shifted back into another version of the particularistic lineage disputes that made up Islamic political controversy.

The Sufis, who emerged after the disintegration of the Islamic Empire in the 800s, were a mixture of mystical and moralistic organizational forms and doctrines. Although they derived their religious charisma individually through direct illumination and were relatively antagonistic to doctrine, their organizational pattern was less that of pure mystics than community spokesmen in local politics. The marabouts of North Africa described by Geertz (1968) are the voices of community morality demanding justice against higher political authorities. These Sufis were not generally treated as heretical. As Islamic political structure decentralized with the decline of the major empires, rulers began to be perceived as purely secular rather than theocratically legitimated. Because there was no formal religious hierarchy independent of the state, religious leadership devolved upon individually devout or charismatic lay people. This organizational diffuseness favored individualism and hence to a degree mysticism, which thereupon crept into Islam. Yet insofar as religious politics was still viable at the local level, the mysticism of the Sufis was tempered by a moralistic activism in their own communities.

---

[6] "Sufism, as an historical reality, consists of a series of different and even contradictory experiments, most of them occurring between the ninth and nineteenth centuries, in bringing orthodox Islam (itself no seamless unity) into effective relationship with the world, rendering it accessible to its adherents and its adherents accessible to it. In the Middle East, this seems mainly to have meant reconciling Arabian pantheism with Koranic legalism; in Indonesia, restating Indian illuminationism in Arabic phrases; in West Africa, defining sacrifice, possession, exorcism, and curing as Muslim rituals. In Morocco, it meant fusing the genealogical conception of sanctity with the miraculous – canonizing *les hommes fetiches*" (Geertz, 1968:48).

Wherever mysticism coexisted with more centrally organized Islam, however, it was treated as heretical. Thus intellectualistic mystics in the medieval Caliphates, pursuing a path of secular syncretism somewhat like the Christian Gnostics, ran the danger of being condemned as unorthodox. In modern times, when the Islamic states of the Middle East introduced centralized bureaucratic forms under European influence, the result was a shift back toward a more doctrinal and academic form of Islam. A typical case was the Wahabi reforms of the 1700s and 1800s. The result is the modern tendency to treat Sufi mystics as heretical or at least as selfish, doctrinally incorrect, and immoral (Geertz, 1968).

If mysticism is heretical to moralistic religions, however, the reverse is not the case. Buddhism and the mystical Hindu sects, although they exhibit occasional leanings toward moralism, do not have major heresy disputes and persecutions (Needham, 1956; Chan, 1963; Chattopadhyaya, 1969; Conze, 1969; De Bary, 1969). In Buddhism, some tendencies toward moralism emerged in the form of Mahayana, which emphasized the ideal of the Boddhisattva, the enlightened saint who forgoes entry into Nirvana in order to return to the world and aid others on the path. The Boddhisattva doctrine legitimated various world-oriented activities such as popular preaching, as well as fostering beliefs in deities (like the Chinese Kuan-yin, the goddess of mercy) who could be invoked for magical aid in time of distress. In China, popular versions of Mahayana, such as the worship of the future Buddha Amida, offered salvation for the masses through the ritual of calling on his name and renouncing one's sins. Amidaist mass movements were stirred up in medieval Japan by preachers who vividly depicted the delights of paradise and the tortures of hell in future incarnations and admonished the masses to follow Buddhist precepts of nonviolence and other moral injunctions. Some versions of Japanese popular Buddhism even underwent a kind of "protestant" reformation by sloughing off monastic celibacy and creating a married clergy preaching to lay congregations.

Following the usual pattern of moralistic/mystical relationships, Mahayana did accuse the original contemplative Buddhists (Theravadins – "the old ones") of selfishness. In contrast to their own self-designation as Mahayana, the "great vehicle," they scornfully referred to the Theravadins as Hinayana – the "lesser vehicle." But this stopped short of accusing the Theravadins of heresy. The canonical words of Buddha made it clear that Mahayana was the innovation, although the dating of texts was vague and Mahayana did have its own sutras that claimed to be original emanations. More importantly, the organizational anchor was still mystical. The basic structure of

Buddhism (except in the extreme Japanese innovations) remained an elite of world-renouncing monks. These could be venerated by the masses, who could perhaps achieve a form of salvation by being reborn in some future paradise, but this ranked below true Enlightenment, which was reserved for still further rebirths. Some Mahayana texts do speak of the evils of being "bound by the ropes of Hinayana" and admonish against the sin of heresy in splitting the congregation of monks. Nevertheless, there is no equivalent of excommunication in Buddhism, and there is no record of persecutions and forced recantations.

Moreover, even in Mahayana, the mystical element was still strong even if it was nearly lost at times. It appears that in the early period of Buddhist proselytization of China (ca. A.D. 300–500), especially among the barbarian northern dynasties but also in the Chinese south, contemplative meditation was little practiced, and Buddhism was regarded by outsiders as a form of magic. Buddhist practice consisted largely of the repetition of the sacred texts, together with aesthetically attractive ritual and monastic routine. But contemplative meditation was reintroduced. This was Ch'an (in Japan, Zen) Buddhism, deriving from the Hindu dhyana, concentration; literally, it was the meditation school of Buddhism. Meditation was also practiced in other sects, but Ch'an specialized in it and sharply abjured both intellectualism and ritualism. It re-created in Mahayana form the classical Buddhist hierarchy of mystical insights. Organizationally, as well, Ch'an monasteries were withdrawn from populated centers into remote areas and, far from appealing to the masses, set barriers to dissuade easy converts (Dumoulin, 1963).

The mystical side of Buddhism rarely regarded the moralistic variants as heretical. This was true even though there were many schisms as well as a history of vigorous doctrinal debate in both India and China. But these splits and philosophical disputes were not occasions for purges and efforts to impose dogmatic orthodoxy, even though the philosophical issues involved were profound and the moral pathways tortuous.[7] The development of Mahayana within traditional

[7] Weber (1922/1963:71–3) is mistaken in regarding the splits in Buddhism as merely disagreements over monastic regulations, and in contrasting an original intellectualism with a purely popularistic Mahayana. Again we see Weber's lack of information on the Asian Middle Ages. In fact, the centuries of developing split between Mahayana and Theravada in India (100 B.C.–A.D. 700) are a period of intense philosophical development in both camps, including the sophisticated logics and metaphysics of Nagarjuna, Vasubandhu, Asanga, Dignaga, Dharmakirti, among others, names as important in Oriental philosophy as Aristotle and Kant in the West. Similarly in China, Buddhism completely dominated philosophy from A.D. 400 to A.D. 1000, and produced numerous metaphysical systems of a much more sophisticated

Buddhism constituted an enormous set of deviations from original principles, including a shift from extreme atomistic phenomenalism and materialism to absolute idealism, as well as the rise of the Boddhisattva doctrine. By comparison, the Christian controversies over the Trinity are dwarfed.

Yet Mahayana and Theravada monks were found in the same monasteries in India; just as later, with the proliferation of sects within Chinese Buddhism, adherents of different doctrines could be found living together. How were these made compatible? The solution was hierarchical. Mahayana practitioners regarded themselves as a higher order of sophistication, a form of "advanced study" in mystical achievement. Thus the great Chinese T'ien T'ai sect (founded in south China ca. A.D. 580, and imported to Japan two hundred years later as Tendai) arranged all Buddhist doctrines in an order, with theism and demonology as the lowest level of relative and worldly truth, and more sophisticated doctrines and meditations ranked as progressive stages of spiritual development. Around 680, the Hua-yen doctrine reclassified all Buddhist schools in a similar hierarchy but added several other schools (including Ch'an) beyond the level of T'ien T'ai, with the top level reserved for Hua-yen itself.

One might argue that the relative peacefulness of Buddhist and Hindu sects in doctrinal matters had to do with their private status. India's usual political fragmentation kept religions from being identified with states and hence from enforcing their doctrines by means of a military arm. There are some exceptions, such as the one great empire nearly to unify the Indian subcontinent, Asoka's (reigned 273–232 B.C.) Maurya state, which adopted Buddhism as its official religion. What consequences followed for the enforcement of doctrinal orthodoxy are not known. But the Maurya hegemony was short-lived (the empire had disintegrated by 185 B.C.), and the long period of the Hindu revival and cultural colonization of the south, together with general political fragmentation, kept the Indian religions competing privately for adherents in a kind of generalized cultural market. If Hinduism eventually triumphed over Buddhism in India, it was because of a superior use of the hierarchizing strategy. The popular Hindu mystical sects regarded each other's gods as reincarnations of their own, lower manifestations to be worshiped by those not yet advanced to worship nearer the source. Buddha was incorporated as just another avatar.[8]

level than had previously been achieved by Chinese intellectuals (Needham, 1956; Stcherbatski, 1962; Chan, 1963; Das Gupta, 1963; Conze, 1967).

[8] This process is perhaps the best example of the principle of pure status hierarchy that

In China, however, Buddhism was introduced through state patronage and only gradually expanded by the Amidaist movements of the 500s and 600s A.D. (Wright, 1959; Ch'en, 1964; Eberhard, 1977). In the 700s and 800s, while Ch'an monasteries were moving to remote mountains, most Buddhist sects continued to be concentrated in the capital cities to be close to imperial patronage. Hence the fate of the latter tended to be closely tied to the rise or fall of particular dynasties, reigning monarchs, or governmental factions. Nevertheless, there was remarkably little effort to impose doctrinal orthodoxy, even with imperial patronage at stake. This was even the case in periods when the government appointed a kind of pope or head monk to oversee all Buddhist monks. There are occasional instances to the contrary. At the time of the rise of strongly pro-Buddhist Sui dynasty (reigned 589–618) the so-called Three Treatise school (advocates of the most venerated Mahayana philosopher, Nagarjuna) strongly attacked the theistic Buddhist cults as well as the Heaven cult of the Confucians and the Immortals cult of the Taoists. In the 580s, during the fighting that established the Sui dynasty, an extreme millennial "sect of the Three Stages" claimed to be the only true faith, and attacked all governments. It was opposed by all other Buddhist schools but was not finally suppressed by the emperor until more than a century later, in 713. In the northern capital immediately before the rise of the Sui, the T'ien T'ai originator Hui-ssu attacked the worldliness and corruption of the monks and was forced to flee because of threats on his life. And again in 753, Shen-hui, a dissident Ch'an monk who first launched the radical, paradoxical "Zen" style, was arrested and banished at the instigation of the orthodox Ch'an monks of the T'ang capital, whose authoritative lineage Shen-hui had attacked.

Except for the last, all these instances of intolerance and violence within Buddhism are clustered at a crucial political crisis: the rise of the Sui dynasty, when for the first time Buddhism achieved official patronage throughout China. Apparently the ambitious mood of Buddhist leaders at this moment was responsible for these efforts to impose a strict orthodoxy. But the rival Buddhist sects were too dispersed, and the Sui too short-lived to permit any such development.

Dumont (1970) finds exemplified in the Hindu caste system. It is a form of stratification based on the results of sheer cultural competition, apart from imposition based on economic class or political power (although these elements may have certain concrete influences as well). In my opinion, the caste system is a less pure case, since economic monopolization and political enforcement are hardly absent here. Insofar as the caste system does represent the operation of a pure hierarchization, I would suggest that this derived its force from the religious hierarchization, at least since the time of the classic Hindu revival (the post-Maurya period).

The internal Ch'an conflict referred to earlier was much more minor, although not only did it involve a dispute over which lineage should receive imperial patronage, but it also marks the point at which Ch'an policy switched over to abandoning the capital and founding self-sufficient (and antipolitical) monasteries in remote areas.

Japanese Buddhism was a good deal more violent. But its numerous sects, although rivals over Imperial favor, were nevertheless relatively tolerant of the wide doctrinal differences among themselves. The extreme form of popular Amidaist preaching did provoke the most intolerant form of Buddhism, Nichiren's Hokke (Lotus) sect, a "fundamentalist" revival of the 1200s. The Hokke sect condemned as heretical not only the popular Amidaist movements but also the ritualism of the elite sects (Sansom, 1958:220–6, 424–9; De Bary, 1969:345–7). But Nichiren's brand of Buddhism was itself unorthodoxly activist and came close to a Christian-like martyrdom cult. Monasteries formed their own armies, which exerted some power in the situation of a weakening court and growing feudal fragmentation. Armed monks from the Mount Hiei monastery above Kyoto terrorized the court at times, and rival monasteries (as well as Shinto shrines) fought over manorial boundaries and sometimes plundered each other's temples. But doctrinal disputes were not involved, merely material property claims. In the civil wars leading up to the Tokugawa unification of Japan, the Mount Hiei monastery and other strongholds were sacked by Nobunaga's armies in the 1570s (Sansom, 1961:283–90, 295–7, 343). Again, there was no question of suppressing heresy; the monastic armies were part of the feudal alliances of the time, and Nobunaga's massacres, though perhaps partly motivated by an effort to reestablish state monopoly over the use of force, were campaigns in a general military strategy.

To the extent that there was political suppression of Buddhism, it was from outside its ranks. In India, there were massacres of monks by Islamic invaders, acting on a typical enough scorn by a militantly moralistic religion for contemplative mystics. In China, Confucianism criticized Buddhism from the moralistic angle, charging that monks avoided their social obligations. But there were few actual persecutions of Buddhism mounted by Confucians, and even a certain amount of intellectual emulation, especially in the Sung and Ming dynasties, after Buddhism had lost all power to mount a threat to imperial patronage. The neo-Confucian philosophers may in fact be regarded (as was charged by their more traditional opponents) as Confucian versions of Buddhists: They had assimilated some of its metaphysics, and relabeled enlightenment as "Sagehood."

Most persecutions were instigated by Taoists, which is to say, by rivals on the mystical side. But by the 400s A.D., Taoism had changed from its original mysticism of private individuals, into a formal church with a pantheon and liturgy, preaching conventional morality and exorcizing spirits. In the foreign-dominated Toba state of north China in the 420s, the ruler established a Taoist "pope" in his capital. The same dynasty had also patronized Buddhism, and in 444–6 the struggle for influence between the two religions culminated in a brief persecution of Buddhism when Taoism was proclaimed the official faith. This type of struggle was repeated on several occasions. In 520 the Toba emperor banished the Taoists after they were proclaimed the losers in a court debate with the Buddhists. In 573 the ruler of one of the foreign northern states adopted Confucianism and confiscated the property of both Taoist and Buddhist churches. In 621, just after the pro-Buddhist Sui dynasty had been overthrown by the T'ang, the Taoists attempted to have Buddhism suppressed again, but effected only an order for government supervision of monasteries. In 712 a new emperor forced thirty thousand monks to return to secular life; but this followed a period (starting in 690) when several strongly pro-Buddhist empresses had reigned, and constituted an effort to return the state to secular control after a time of near theocracy.

These persecutions were not primarily doctrinal, but were explicit struggles for political control. Like the major persecutions of Christianity within the Roman Empire, they occurred when the relative power between different religions was swinging near the balance point. In the case of the Buddhist persecutions, there was also often a fiscal motive because the monasteries were repositories of considerable wealth and, in fact, were the nearest equivalents to banks. Hence the persecutions took the form not so much of violent repressions as of confiscation. As the finances of the T'ang and later dynasties worsened, another fiscal tactic was to require purchase of government ordination certifications for those wishing to become monks and, later, to sell higher monastic ranks. Such fiscal motives, rather than doctrinal passion, seem to have been behind most of the later persecutions, including the massive persecution of 845 that confiscated virtually all Buddhist property and defrocked 260,000 monks and nuns. Doctrinal rivalries could also be involved; the 845 event was instigated by Taoists who convinced the Emperor that Buddhism was responsible for a deteriorating military situation. The accession of a new Emperor the following year, however, called off the persecution and the Taoist "pope" was executed. As I have argued in Chapter 3, these political vicissitudes may have had fateful consequences for the possibilities of capitalist development in China.

Culture

Puritans versus compromisers within moralistic religions

Within moralistic religions, a recurrent theme in heresies is the conflict of puritans against compromisers. The Donatist and Pelagian heresies in the early Christian Church are of this type. The Donatists were a militant party that emerged after the Decian persecutions and forced recantations of the middle of the third century A.D. The Donatists were those who had weathered the storm and refused to recant; rallying around the symbols of their martyrs, they refused to take the trimmers back into the Church after the political winds had shifted. The moderate party, however, became the orthodoxy because their policy favored greater organizational expansion, taking in members on the basis of a less strict standard for admissions. The recalcitrant Donatists, in resisting this policy, doomed themselves to being a minority and became a heresy.[9] The Pelagian heresy (argued out during 411–28 by a British monk who had resided in Rome), had a more doctrinal focus, concerning the concept of free will (Chadwick, 1967:225–34). But its theme was essentially an attack by the purer, missionary church of Britain on the worldliness and corruption of the Roman bishopric. Again, the growing political weakness of Rome following the Visigothic raids of 401–16, the German invasions of Gaul from 407, and the departure of Roman legions from Britain in 411 provided the context in which doctrinal differences could be voiced. Doctrinal orthodoxy, though, went to the official Roman position voiced by Augustine, who reacted to Pelagius's doctrine by a sharp formulation of predestination. Once again, the puritans lost to the superior organizational resources of the compromisers, and their doctrines became heresies.

Does the principle of Orwellian relativism hold: that history is written by the winners, and a heresy is simply the doctrine of whoever has lost? This seems to be true of many heresies, especially the ones considered above as vehicles for organizational power struggles. But in this case there may be a natural selection of certain types of doctrines by organizational forces. The compromisers are those who react to what seems necessary to keep the organization prospering, and

[9] Jones (1959) criticizes interpretations that treat the Donatist heresy as a movement of Punic and Berber nationalism against Roman control, pointing out that the leaders of the movement came from the romanized classes and conducted their polemics entirely in Latin. Jones is no doubt correct that to refer to nationalism in this context is anachronistic. However, the persistence of a schismatic Donatist church for several centuries, located only in North Africa, can be better interpreted as an instance of the organizational politics of the Church as analyzed earlier in this chapter, in an area increasingly remote from the centers of control in the crumbling empire.

hence conserve and expand their membership and thier material resources. The puritans are utopians; when they do come to power (as
in various areas during the Reformation), they tend to lose power
rather quickly, or become compromisers themselves.

But they do not disappear. The pattern is a general one; puritans
and idealists are an element in virtually all heresies, Islamic as well as
Christian. If there are pressures toward compromise among the cosmopolitan administrators at the top of a church (following Michels's
principles), there seem to be corresponding pressures at the provincial levels, among the leaders of poorer and more heroically embattled communities, toward puritanism. When there is a weakness at
the center and corresponding devolution of initiative onto the periphery, the puritan attack may often be expected.

Equivalents in secular politics

The general Weberian model of politics, presented in Chapter 6,
holds that legitimacy is externally conferred, based on military prestige. Does this mean that the militarily successful state establishes its
own legitimacy and can forgo religious support? For short periods of
time this may be so. But if might makes right, this nevertheless holds
only in the external arena. The internal use of coercion creates an
atmosphere of illegitimacy and terroristic imposition unless, as with
the external use of force, it is authoritatively interpreted as protecting
the community. This can only be done with the proper ideological
apparatus.

We have seen that a universal church claims to represent the whole
community and thus pushes for expansion until it coincides with the
boundaries of the state, which makes a similar claim. The church
even tends to overlap state boundaries, and in its purer forms thus
gives impetus to political empire building. Conversely, there is a
trend for quasi-secular legitimating ideologies of states to become
increasingly religious over time. For example, Confucianism, once
adopted as official state doctrine, transformed itself into a theistic
church, raising Confucius himself (who had wished to keep spirits at
a distance) to an object of worship. The same pressure is evident in
the efforts of bureaucratizing states to acquire a universalistic religious legitimacy. Contending candidates in the Roman Empire included not only Christianity but Neoplatonism, Mithraist sun worship, and Julian's attempt to establish a universal and ethical church
of sacrifices. The usual glib interpretations of this countertrend
against secularism describe it as a "failure of nerve," but the gener-
ality of the process shows that it is structural.

241

Culture

The basic problem is that although the state gets its legitimacy from foreign military successes and loses it in military failure, legitimacy needs to be administered internally. It requires some organizational form of the means of emotional production. A universal church, not tying such resources to local communities or autonomous family cults, is a powerful support for a centralized state.

For these reasons, heresy conflicts tend to break out (among other reasons) when the state is badly shaken militarily. We see this in Iconoclasm at the time of the Arab raids on the Byzantium home provinces; Pelagianism coinciding with the Gothic and German breakthrough into the heart of the Roman Empire; Sufism and various heretical movements as the Islamic Empire crumbled; or Nichiren's atypically intolerant Buddhism in the anxiety over the imminent Mongol invasion of Japan.

The process casts some light on the phenomenon of nationalism. This is usually regarded as a feature of "modernization," based on mass communications, urbanization, and education, which for the first time mobilized most of the population into some consciousness of national identity. Before this we had what Eberhard (1965) referred to as "layer societies." Political awareness and participation were confined to a small cosmopolitan upper layer, while the bulk of peasants were localized below them, relatively indifferent to which masters were exploiting them at the moment. Nor was there much "national" loyalty even in the aristocratic-administrative layer; it was a common practice for ethnic outsiders (such as Marco Polo in Kublai Khan's China) to be used or even preferred as trusted administrators. Nevertheless, one sees religious conflicts in such societies that operate "nationalistically," not only in response to the kinds of geopolitical disasters just cited but also in internal conflicts among religions. For example, Confucians and Taoists reacted to Chinese Buddhism in intensely nationalist fashion (Ch'en, 1964). The former charged that foreign-style monks did not fit Chinese moral and social standards; the latter declared that the Buddha himself was only a follower of Lao-tzu, who had migrated to the West in his old age. These were unprecedentedly "modern" forms of chauvinism, given the usual permeable boundaries of the patrimonial bureaucratic state. The proper conclusion, I believe, is that Buddhism was instrumental in provoking and creating Chinese nationalism. (In a similar way, Islam's moralistic militancy can be credited with creating Indian nationalism, which otherwise tended to absorb dissident cultures through its usual hierarchizing pattern.)

Thus nationalism is a phenomenon not of modern mass mobilization per se but of the conflict of specialized religious intellectuals

242

contending for legitimacy at the state level. It is spread by religious proselytization rather than welling up from below under "modern" conditions. If nationalism has become more prominent in recent centuries, I would suggest that the reason is not so much economically based transformations of society, as the competitive development of mass religious organizations within the bounds of state regulation. It follows that the Reformation and Counter-Reformation are the foundations of nationalism in Europe.

We have still to consider secular politics. Economic and factional interest groups are usually regarded as the essence of politics. But this may be true only in a taxonomic sense; they are major actors, but the dynamic determining their victories and defeats is the legitimacy dynamic we have been considering. There is a commonly recognized pattern in modern politics: The party in office during a depression tends to be voted out, whereas those in office during a boom remain popular. This principle makes factional legitimacy depend on economic prosperity. This is one factor in a multiprocessual situation. Overlaying it is the geopolitically based legitimacy discussed above.

There are also noneconomic issues, sometimes referred to as "style issues" or analyzed as "status group politics": emotional issues of crime and "vice," scandal and corruption, loyalty and disloyalty, abortion, civil rights, and "moral politics" in general. Here we encounter the secular equivalent of religious politics and, indeed, of heresy disputes. By way of conclusion, we may reprise the above patterns of heresy in secular terms:

1. *Universalistic organization as a prerequisite for heresy conflicts.* In politics, this refers us to the great modern ideologies claiming universal validity: Jacobinism and its successor, Liberalism; socialism, and communism. Nonuniversalistic politics, on the other hand, are particularistic maneuvers on behalf of various local interests, individuals, families, and ethnic groups. The political ideology reflects its organizational base; the former are much more common in the churchlike political organizations of continental Europe, while the latter characterizes the fragmented and ad hoc personalistic party networks of the United States.

The politics of the right is more ambiguous. Its aim is to defend order, morally and socially. Rightist parties generally do not define themselves in terms of doing justice to social interest groups in the way that liberal/left parties do but may claim to be above "politics" (used as a pejorative term). Transcendent spiritual interests may be asserted to be primary, as by some European Catholic politicians; or (more in the American evangelical style) religion intervenes to impose the godly society. Whether explicitly or implicitly, conservative politics usually endorses a religious stance. By this standard, liberal and left parties are intrinsically heretical, simply by elevating secular politics above religion. The worst, of course, is atheistic communism, an explicit challenge, but godlessness and backsliding are suspected everywhere on the liberal side. There is, however, another version of the right, sometimes entwined with the religious version. This other "conservatism" is actually nineteenth-century "Liberalism," based on the principle of laissez-faire individualism. This version of the right is a genuinely universalistic political doctrine, for which all statist doctrines (and de facto statism) are heretical. In practice, the two forms of conservatism often overlap because of common enemies, although there is a tension between their basic ideologies; in the absence of external opposition, there is potential for breaking out into heresy disputes within their own ranks.

The liberal/left ideologies can also engage in heresy conflicts, especially when their adherents are in power or close to it. Liberalism (in the twentieth-century sense) is tolerant as a matter of one of its central principles; but it, too, can engage in heresy-hunting of its own on occasion, as in the persecutions of communism and attacks on the subsequent New Left, in the name of combating "extremism." *Any* universalistic ideology, in fact, insofar as it envisions itself as representing the ideals of the whole community, is capable of being intolerant to whoever violates its defining principles. Liberalism's tolerance has been supported mainly by a structural situation in which liberals themselves have been only one power group among others.

Despite the general absence of mass church-style party organizations in the United States, moralistic politics of a particular type has been extremely common. But these are not ideological disputes over issues of political doctrine, paralleling intellectually based heresy conflicts, but are instead particular scandals involving official misdeeds or failure to extirpate public "vices." This form of moralism may in fact be highly appropriate to the politics of personality-based, regional, ethnic, or other ad hoc political factions. Such particularistic politics by its nature lacks legitimacy, in that it has no principles upon which to make wider appeals. Lacking explicit political doctrines to amass moral support, American politicians tend to fall back on religiously based moralities in attacking conventionally defined vices and corruption. Probably this is one reason for the continuing prevalence of religion in the United States; it is supported by the form of political organization, rather than because it has a primordial grip on grass-roots culture.

2. *Imperfect centralization as a condition for heresy-producing organiza-*

tional power struggles and *3. similar pressures from geopolitical upheavals.* In politics, the clearest cases of ideological heresy disputes are found in the history of twentieth-century Marxism, produced by organizational struggles among the trade-union, parliamentary, and independent intellectual sections of Marxist parties in the West. In the Soviet Union of the 1920s and 1930s, the Stalin-Trotsky conflict was a heresy dispute tied to rival organizational bases within the state itself. For communist parties outside the Russian bloc, the question of how to link themselves internationally has been the major source of schism. The factionalism of such parties has often been explained by the alleged intellectualism and unrealism of "splinter groups" without serious political constituencies. But this explanation ignores the key organizational issue in these schisms: which branch of the universal "church" to treat as the orthodox center, in a situation of schism at the core itself. American and European Stalinists and Trotskyites reflected Russian politics, with further lines of strain because of the additional issue of how to maintain international organizational ties. The rise of further splits within and among the Communist states (such as the strains of Eastern Europe) has intensified these geopolitical pressures toward factionalism at the periphery of the movement.

Geopolitical strains, of course, affect all domestic parties everywhere on the spectrum, insofar as legitimacy declines with foreign-policy reverses. The actual outbreaks of political heresy hunts seem to be correlated with such crises. The upsurge of right-wing McCarthyism in the United States, for instance, must be understood in the context of the sudden challenge by Russia to U.S. military hegemony in the late 1940s (cf. Bergesen, 1977). The pattern, like that of the Pelagian heresy, may be quite widespread.

4. Mystics versus moralizers. It is hard to imagine what a political mystic would be, unless one thinks in organizational terms. Thus we find the heresy conflicts of Marxism involving the gnostic elitism of the pure intellectuals against the Stalinism of established party administrators. More generally, one might say that anarchists are the political equivalents of mystics, as illustrated organizationally by the waves of elite dropout movements from the early Saint-Simonians to the hippies. One's sympathies, perhaps, tend to go out to the gentle utopians and principled intellectuals in their uphill battle against the cynical realists. But an organizational analysis reveals a reason why the former, for all their idealism, tend to be delegitimated in the eyes of the public. They are intrinsically hierarchizing, expecting deference (and perhaps alms) from the unenlightened, whose ideal society they purport to exemplify. But, as Weber pointed out, exemplary prophets are always vulnerable to moralistic attack from the ascetic-activist side, and the latter hold the crucial weapon of invoking the moral symbols of the total community. "Mystical" idealists, however libertarian and nonviolent, commit the hidden sin of elitist arrogance from the point of view of the egalitarianism implicit in any moralistic criterion of membership.

Finally, *5. puritans versus compromisers* is a recurrent theme in modern politics. In the orbit of socialist parties and regimes, the conflict is chronic, in that the movement (or the state) is itself defined in terms of "puritan" ideals that are constantly undermined by Michelsian organizational resources. American-style particularistic politics starts with the center of gravity on the pragmatic side, whose lack of principled legitimacy constantly calls out "puritan" attacks.

From the point of view of any systematic political ideology, compromise with the organizational realities of politics always appears somewhat heretical. But in politics, as in religion, the puritans rarely are able to muster the sustained resources to acquire the title of orthodoxy, and too strong an insistence on their superior viewpoint tends to earn them the label of heresy. But all is not secure with the compromisers, since their own undignified maneuvers and their vulnerability to delegitimation from the swings of international prestige frequently leave an opening for new "puritan" attacks. Secular politics is as much delegitimation as legitimacy. In the next chapter, we shall go inside one such realm of the struggle over the delegitimation of modern society.

10

Alienation as ritual and ideology

The theory of alienation is often put forward as the Marxist contribution to micro-sociology. The Marxist tradition is, of course, largely macro, especially in its classical concerns with economy, the state, imperialism, revolution, and long-term social change. Where it touches base with the micro/phenomenological world of everyday life is at the concept of alienation. My argument, however, will be that this is not true. By the standards of current micro-sociology, the concept of alienation is not a micro one. It rests, rather, on a confusion of levels, a failure to understand the relationship between micro and macro levels of analysis. Behind the concept of alienation, I will suggest, is a long-standing tradition of intellectuals' elitism about working-class culture. It also has become involved in a distinctively modern romanticization of traditional societies, and with a fundamental misunderstanding of the nature of capitalism. The concept of alienation, I will conclude, is not necessary or desirable as the basis for a radical theory of conflict and domination, although it remains important as a phenomenon of political symbolism that can be central to the dynamics of political mobilization and political ritual.

The Hegelian background

The Marxist concept of alienation, as is well known, derives from Hegel's philosophy. Marx transformed Hegel's idealistic analysis into the materialism of economics, while retaining some of Hegel's specific formulations about consciousness *an sich* and *für sich*, consciousness in itself and for itself. An empirical side of this tradition has developed, including both Marxist analyses of work such as those of Braverman (1974) and Lefebvre (1971) and non-Marxist sociologies such as those of Seeman (1959) and Blauner (1964). Most recently, there has been a turn toward something more like the original Hegelianism, as modern Marxists have joined the vogue of anti-positivism and proclaimed a rapprochement with phenomenology and hence with micro-sociology. This has resulted in critical analyses

247

of everyday life in the modern world, some of which dovetail with earlier neo-Freudian critiques such as those of Fromm (1941) and Marcuse (1964).

The original Hegelian position, however, is well worth considering. In *The Phenomenology of Mind* (1807/1967:234–67), Hegel describes a basic human situation: the relation of Master and Bondsman. Although both are, in ultimate reality, pure Spirit and hence pure freedom, in their immediate social relationship both are chained to the other. The essence of the Bondsman is to exist for another, not for self. But the Master also lacks true independence, since his independent existence (consciousness *für sich*, for itself) is mediated by the Bondsman. Thus, unlike the later Marxist model, in which alienation is described as the fate of the propertyless laborer but not of the capitalist, Hegel sees alienation on both sides. Both parties experience an ironic twist. The Master, having attained lordship, nevertheless attains only a dependent consciousness. The situation of the Bondsman, too, "will pass into the opposite of what it immediately is" (1807/1967:237), and attain true independence. This dialectic, of course, has a revolutionary implication that Marx did not fail to pick up.

For Hegel, the route to liberation is through work. The Bondsman labors, and thereby externalizes himself in objects produced. This external thing confronts the Bondsman from outside and affirms his self-existence in his own right, *an und für sich*. This is the Bondsman's ultimate advantage over the Master; while the latter remains perpetually self-estranged, the former achieves spiritual realization, even under the condition of forced labor. This involves a rather romanticized conception of work, an idealization of the craftsman; this, too, was a tradition Marx did not fail to continue.

Hegel went on to sketch the human self's logical and historical development (two dimensions he did not sharply separate). Although the Master/Bondsman relation is something of a universal social archetype,[1] Hegel seems to situate it specifically in the slave-owning societies of classical antiquity. Its subsequent development can be represented by a succession of philosophical and religious systems. Stoicism attempts to overcome external unfreedom by declaring for the inner freedom of the individual, although this is a false freedom; skepticism goes farther and criticizes this as well as all other assertions. The result is consciousness in contradiction to itself, opening the way for what Hegel calls "the *Unhappy Consciousness*, the

[1] Jean-Paul Sartre (1943) took it as such.

Alienated Soul which is the consciousness of self as a divided nature, a doubled and merely contradictory being" (1807/1967:251).

The further history of this alienated self Hegel finds in Christianity. Expressing himself in rather guarded language (due no doubt to the political realities of his day), he describes the Christian conception of the soul as sinning and fallen from God, as the unhappy consciousness of the divided self. The very concept of the Trinity represents the split of absolute Being into its contradictory and fallen moments; the priesthood is a mediation, in the logical sense, among these elements. Despite his gnomic utterances (the meaning of which Hegel himself finally decided would have to clarified by footnote references to Christ, the Holy Ghost, and so on), Hegel's tone is clearly scornful of Christianity. Its asceticism, its rituals, its subordination of the self to God through prayer and humility, all are convulsions of the alienated self unable to realize the freedom of its true nature. Nevertheless, Christianity does mark a crucial transition; its emphasis on the God beyond opens the way to the realization of the idea of Reason, which in turn reveals the true nature of the Self. For Hegel ultimately is a kind of pantheist idealist; the world is absolute Spirit, and is identical with the self. Once the historical process is complete by which this can be realized, the long path of alienation is overcome, and the era of absolute Freedom is ushered in.

Hegel can be legitimately represented as doing a microanalysis of alienation, if only because of his Idealism. If, in fact, the whole world is an emanation of a single spiritual Self, everything is ultimately in microanalysis. Hegel can thus start his system with the immediate givens of consciousness, with the Cartesian situation of logical meditation that finds at first only an Ego, although, of course, Hegel develops his own distinctive dialectic of that situation. For Marx, however, the overturning of Idealism means that the micro underpinnings are no longer there. The external world of material things is real, in and of itself, and the human individual is part of it. It is true that the social world is not material nature per se, but nature transformed by human labor. It is a cumulating product of human selves (Marx and Engels, 1846/1947).

If, then, these products of human freedom turn around and constrain and oppress the humans who created them, we have an analogue to Hegel's idealist conception of alienation. In the one case, Spirit creates an external world but is oppressed by it and alienated from it because the self does not realize the world is its own creation; since there is ultimately only one Spirit, this alienation is simultaneously alienation from one's true self. In the other case, we have

249

human beings creating an external world of economic relations that take on the quality of oppressive and independent forces. Here, too, we have a claim that this is not merely oppression but alienation from the true self. Marx's eschatology, the final predicted overcoming of alienation, of oppression in all its forms with the ultimate attainment of Communism, follows only because Marx has retained the full force of Hegel's claims about the historical process of alienation and its overcoming. If the world is the product of the self, and is ultimately identical with the self, then a Hegelian realization is possible. (It could take the form of something like the Buddhist meditator's realization that the world is Nirvana.) But if the world is genuinely material and external, then it is no longer legitimate to expect that "alienation" can be absolutely overcome. It is not even legitimate to speak of alienation in the strict sense of self-alienation, for the world is not part of oneself and never was.

Alienation in Marx's system

Most Marxists are realistic enough not to concern themselves overmuch with the final overcoming of alienation; instead, they concentrate on the critique of existing societies. Here the concept of alienation is linked to the core of Marx's technical economic system by the concept of surplus value. Labor is the source of all value; capital can derive profit only by drawing more value for labor than it pays for it. But market forces should keep the price of labor down to the costs of reproducing it, while the necessity for propertyless workers to sell their time on the labor market allows capitalists to require them to work longer hours than the time necessary to cover the costs of reproduction. This extra labor time is the source of profit, and hence the key to capital itself. This is surplus value, and labor is alienated in precisely this sense. Moreover, the very downfall of the capitalist system is derived from the future history of the alienation of labor. Capitalists goaded by competition install laborsaving devices; but these cut into their source of profit, the surplus value made possible by the time-exploitation of labor. From this derives Marx's "law of the falling rate of profit," and ultimately the crisis of the capitalist system that will usher in socialism.

Alienation, then, has a precise economic sense within the Marxist system. It is also the connecting link between Marx's economics and his philosophy of history. The growth of alienation constitutes the establishment of the capitalist system; internal contradiction and crisis within this system usher in its antithesis, socialism. In socialism, alienation is overcome because the extraction of surplus value no longer takes place. Marx thus manages to reproduce the general form of Hegel's historical system, while translating it into an economics built on the premises of Smith and Ricardo.

Marxists are typically scornful of the empirical sociology of alienation (e.g., Seeman, 1959), because the latter changes its definition. For Seeman and his followers, alienation is a psychological concept, consisting of the features of powerlessness, meaninglessness, self-estrangement, and isolation. It no longer has a structural significance within world history, or the philosophical resonances that tie it to the emancipatory project of Marxism. Seeman and his followers are conservative in the sense that empirically they find only moderate amounts of alienation among the working class (though cf. Seeman, 1972). The Marxists can simply deny the relevance of this by asserting their structural economic definition: workers are alienated in a strict economic sense as long as capitalist profit still exists.

By stressing this, Marxists are making alienation exclusively a macro concept, and are conceding that it has no referent on the micro level. I think this concession is usually tacit rather than explicit (although Althusser [1969] is famous for rejecting any micro analysis at the level of mere human experience). Most Marxists who reject Seeman would nevertheless like to claim that alienation also exists on the micro level of everyday life. The beauty of Marx's system, for many, is that it is not merely economic; its economics interpenetrates its philosophy, its conception of history, and all of it together provides a cultural critique as well as promising a future fulfillment in the most complete humanistic sense.

The romanticization of past and present

A rendering of most of the typical themes is found, for example, in Giddens (1981). The impersonal control system of capitalism replaces the direct state coercion characteristic of agrarian societies with the indirect compulsion of the marketplace, driving propertyless workers to sell their labor time. The result is a mode of life that is alienated from top to bottom. In contrast to the embeddedness in nature characteristic of small-scale agrarian work, capitalism has removed meaning from work, enforced privatization, made surveillance anonymous, and commodified time itself. Giddens reinforces this with Heidegger's existentialism, in order to show that the change in the human experience of everyday time is a deprivation of human consciousness in a very deep sense. "In the world that capitalism has originated," Giddens declares (1981:251–2), "time is no longer understood as the medium of Being, and the gearing of daily life into comprehended tradition is replaced by the empty routines of every-day life."

Except for the Heideggerian flourish, this is a fairly standard position. It demonstrates rather clearly how much romanticism there is in this tradition about modern alienation. It establishes our alienated condition in contrast to an idyllic precapitalist world in which the economy does not rest on the extraction of surplus value and in which workers produce products for their own use. To be sure, the presence of a feudal or state-bureaucratc upper class is conceded; but they are depicted as appearing only occasionally to demand tribute. In daily life and work, there is the happy peasant, laboring in harmony with nature and seeing it transformed into useful products under his (or her?) own hands.

This is a sheerly imaginary social history. Agrarian societies, in fact, were the most stratified and unequal societies of all time. They had the most extreme concentration not only of wealth but of power as well (Lenski, 1966). At the daily level of the household, the manor, or the public place, people experienced the highest amount of humiliating deference of any societies that have ever existed. Ritual bowings and scrapings, and rank-displaying sumptuary regulations were at their height; mutilation and torture were common as means of punishment and political terrorization (Collins, 1981d). This daily grind of coercive deference existed everywhere, not merely in the proximity of the upper class; every household had its little hierarchy, reproducing the lordly oppressions of the top. Moreover, the every-day level of oppression had as its special victims women. Women are for the most part overlooked in this kind of Marxian analysis. Nevertheless, one can make out a good case that women were the predominant "industrial" or crafts workers in agrarian societies. For in a world in which the household is the unit of production, most of the manufactured goods are produced by women. Their spinning and weaving made the great bulk of the useable commodities that constituted the trade of that era. To see this as an idyllically unexploited situation for labor is to pay a very high price in realism for the sake of setting up a contrast with alienated modern society. In comparison, Hegel's history of alienation looks realistic. For Hegel, the height of alienation was the Christian Middle Ages; he was close enough to it so that he had no inclination to romanticize it.

The Marxian romanticization occurs at both ends of this historical scheme. Not only do they idealize the situation of labor and the tenor of everyday life in precapitalist society; they also depict the modern world in a negatively romanticized way. Braverman, Lefebvre, Giddens, Marcuse, and their followers see the modern world as dominated by commodities and the relentless ticking of clocks, subject to a commercialized mass culture and devoid of meaningful public ritual or satisfying personal experience. In other words, they assert that everyday microreality in capitalist society has a characteristically negative tone, which contrasts with the human warmth and ceremonial meaningfulness of traditional societies.

Cultural snobbery or revolution in ritual production?

This argument is rather widely accepted, far beyond Marxist circles. And small wonder; it has been a major theme of literary intellectuals since the early industrial revolution. There has been continual criticism of modern society in these terms ever since Wordsworth cried:

> I'd rather be
> A Pagan suckled in a creed outworn;
> So might I, standing on this pleasant lea,
> Have glimpses that would make me less forlorn;
> Have sight of Proteus rising from the sea;
> Or hear old Triton blow his wreathed horn.

The theme continues through T. S. Eliot's *Waste Land* and into the criticism of television today. It is, nevertheless, a peculiarly inappropriate theme for Marxists to adopt, because it rests largely on upper-class intellectuals' disdain for working-class culture. For the commercialized culture intellectuals ascribe to capitalist alienation consists of loud music, television, sensationalized drama, and the search for "action": in short, the main interests (along with sentimentalized religion) of working-class leisure.[2]

On the micro level, it is begging the question to assume that such culture is intrinsically meaningless and alienating. The Marxist critique seems to be animated by a deep-seated belief that true unalienated human nature prefers only to listen to Beethoven quartets and observe Kandinskys. I would say the burden of proof is on the other side: intellectuals ought to be held responsible for proving why

---

[2] Some Marxists, notably E. P. Thompson (1963), have made an effort to appreciate working-class culture. But notice that Thompson's historical studies of the early English working class concentrate on its respectable side: its religion, its efforts in local political thinking. Thompson prefers not to look at the gin mills, the Saturday night opium binges, the brawls that were the equivalent of latter-day soccer riots. In other words, what counts as working-class culture is what most nearly approximates upper-class culture; the rest, presumably, is a symptom of capitalist alienation. There is, however, a much simpler way to look at it. Life for the most part was hardly pleasant for these workers; instead of denigrating it, one ought to hope that their carousing gave them at least intermittent flashes of pleasure and control in their own lives.

people who watch television six hours a day do not find it meaningful in their own immediate experience. The fact that intellectuals themselves don't like to watch television is hardly an adequate criterion.

People in capitalist society are on the average probably no more alienated than people were in most other types of society. One might even make out a case that they spend *more* of their daily hours in meaningful activities than their forebears did. The reason is precisely the "commercialized" culture that now exists. For meaning does not emerge automatically; it requires a certain kind of social activity, the inputs of ceremonial labor and front-stage props that bring about ritual (Goffman, 1959; Collins, 1975:153–5, 364–80). It is these that produce the "sacred objects" and symbols that, as Durkheim argued, are the center of meaning. It is often asserted that modern life has robbed us of the rich tapestry of daily ceremonial that give meaning to premodern society. But I think that almost diametrically opposite is the case. What modern intellectuals usually fail to see is that the technology of ritual-production has gotten much more decentralized. People who carry around cassette recorders or radios blaring out popular music are literally wrapping themselves in a cocoon of self-chosen meaning almost every moment of the day; in a premodern society they were subject to the authoritarian scheduling of religious ceremonial, at which attendance was not free but enforced (see Laslett, 1971:55–83).

The modern technology of ritual production is in the hands of ordinary people to a much greater degree than ever before. Intellectuals miss this because the kinds of meaningful enactments with which ordinary people prefer to surround themselves are very different from the elitist forms of entertainment they themselves prefer, the so-called high arts. There is also a certain hankering after a past society dominated by public ceremonies, rather than the privatized experience of a television set or music player in one's home or car. What is overlooked here is the fact that rituals are not always so freely chosen and experienced. In agrarian societies, public rituals were for the most part compulsory. One could not evade the ceremonial debasement before the parades of the higher ranks or get away from witnessing the saying of the mass. These rituals were coercive, a weapon of domination. Hegel, whose late-eighteenth-century Germany was just fighting free of this kind of domination of the mind and the spirit, saw more clearly than subsequent intellectuals just how oppressive a society permeated by public rituals could be.

From this perspective, the trendy emphasis on the alienation of everyday life is more than a mistake; it is a blindness to a significant change in modern social structure. On the micro level, there has been a hidden revolution in the control of the means of ritual production. A great deal of the tenor of modern life hinges upon this; elitist culture critics have been unable to see what has happened, though, because they insist on seeing it through the eyeglasses of "alienation." It is entirely consistent with the hidden elitism of the intellectual tradition that communist regimes such as those in the Soviet Union and China officially sponsor the nineteenth-century *haut bourgeois* culture of opera, ballet, and the like while outlawing popular Western-style music. Nor does one have to be a Stalinist to be a principled culture snob. Witness, for example, Theodor Adorno's (1953/1977) absurdly bigoted description of jazz as the epitome of neurotic alienation. One can imagine what he must have thought of rock 'n' roll. Yet nothing demonstrates better the nature of the shift in the means of ritual production: Whereas opera and ballet are impossible without massive capitalist or state sponsorship, rock music has already been politically revolutionary because it is so portable. The propaganda of electric guitars was the indispensable organizing device of the radical counterculture of 1965–75, and its high ritual ceremonies were its rock festivals. If there is a democratization and a possibility of political rebellion in the modern world, it is due to a considerable extent to precisely this decentralization of the means of ritual production.

Surplus value versus the sociology of markets

The underlying problem with the Marxist tradition about alienation lies in its insistence on the concept of surplus value. The central point is that capitalism is uniquely based on the expropriation of labor from the means of production, leaving propertyless workers who are driven to subordinate themselves to the discipline of an employer in return for wages. Capitalism alone is an economy centered on the extraction of surplus value. Given this, alienation must follow, with all the possibilities of hitching onto it the romanticist and elitist critique of modern culture.

The scheme is founded on an antithesis between modern workers and a mythical economy of the past. The peasant serf had a direct access to the means of sustenance that a modern worker lacks, but also certain property debilities, such as the danger of being sold along with the land. The traffic in slaves in traditional societies is another instance of exploitation of humans by a system of property: in this case, humans as capital themselves. In kinship-based tribal societies, which are so often idealized by antimodernist critics, the entire political and economic superstructure is put together out of an interfamily alliance market of women. If women are valued and appropriated mainly as producers of children, who are subsequently alienated from them by the alliance market, that is certainly a very intimate form of domination by the products of one's own labor. The Marxists' failure to attend to the precapitalist sexual property system is a blind spot resulting from concentrating too exclusively on a favored image of surplus-value extraction in industrial capitalism.

Moreover, the theory of surplus value is at the heart of Marxian difficulties in explaining the actual operation of the capitalist economy. It is not literally true that capital is equivalent to surplus value extracted from workers. There are other ways to generate capital. Banks lend out several times more funds than they have; speculative markets as in real estate or stocks expand and contract by their own dynamics; and every time someone extends credit to a customer, he or she is freeing up some capital that can be put to use at least temporarily in investments. The financial system depends to a considerable extent on the endless roll-over of these kinds of time-bound transactions. Both Böhm-Bawerk and Schumpeter proposed models that made this time delay the key to capitalist profit, as was mentioned in Chapter 5.

Capital, in other words, is based primarily on a market, the market for credit. Such a conception is anathema to orthodox Marxism; after all, Marx (1857–8/1973) himself polemicized against the monetarists of his day. To base capitalism on the market instead of on the relationship to the means of production is a fundamental heresy; it is thus taken as a self-evident refutation of both Wallerstein and Weber. But Marx's archaic neo-Ricardian economic scheme never did work well in the real historical world, and there is no reason why, apart from its rhetorical glorification of factory workers, it should not be replaced by something more realistic. Marx's major contribution was to point to economic cycles and crises as a central phenomenon of capitalism. But Marx's own technical scheme has been incapable of handling this dynamic realistically. Conflicts and crises emerge from capitalism precisely because it is a set of markets, and above all because *capital is a credit market* with self-destructive tendencies. The concept of surplus value is not only unnecessary; it gets in the way of understanding the very essence of capitalist dynamics.

The primacy of capitalism as markets rather than as extraction of surplus value applies even to the case of the propertyless laborer. The Marxian argument poses the question, If people were not stripped of thier own productive property, why would anyone work for someone else? But in fact many small farmers have left their autonomous property, where they could have at worst eked out a subsistence quantity of food, to go to work in factories; and plenty of small business owners have sold out and gone to work for a corporation. The reason they left was as often as not economic compulsion, but *absolute* propertylessness was not required to make people go to work for wages. The farmer who could not stand the price competition with other farmers would find his standard of living dropping to the point where it was more remunerative to sell his labor instead. Thus, to get capitalism going originally, it was not necessary to expropriate the peasants; it was only necessary to amass some capital (including in the form of credit) and to set a market in motion, which eventually drove people into the labor force by itself. (This, for example, is roughly the means by which capitalism emerged in a nonfeudal society like the United States.) Marx failed to see this process because his Ricardian premises led him to deduce that wages under capitalism would always be as low as possible, and hence could never be an attraction in their own right.

This misses the location where the major struggle occurs under capitalism. Workers fight to make property out of their job positions themselves: to institute some degree of tenure, to win long-term wage provisions (e.g., salaries instead of wages), and cut down the amount of labor effort their bosses can get out of them. These tactics have been especially successful in the white-collar sector of the labor force. Hence, modern class dividing lines fall not where Marx classically had them (between owners of industrial capital and possessors of nothing but their own labor power) but between several classes fighting to win or maintain monopoly privileges over the labor market itself (Collins, 1979). Relative degrees of monopoly among organizations, similarly, enable bigger businesses to pay more in the form of "sinecure benefits" to their workers. It is no wonder, then, that big, rich organizations are often more attractive places to work than small individually owned businesses of the sort Marx and his followers have idealized. The actual experience of running a small business is often not so pleasant; the daily grind of operating a store, for instance, may well be a seven-days-a-week treadmill that many people actually on it find both oppressive and relatively unremunerative. For that very reason, it should not come as such a surprise that people who work in bureaucracies are typically more flexible and tolerant than people who work in entrepreneurial settings (Kohn, 1971). The big organization actually has more room to maneuver within it, precisely because it is a sinecure system; people may complain about it but nevertheless find it preferable to more oppressive traditional work settings.

In short, the essence of capitalism lies in the struggles that take place in markets. Its dynamics are indeed boom-and-bust cycles, but these cannot be explained in relation to a fictional construct of surplus value. Cycles are more profitably understood as processes that occur in the interdependent circulation of several social media: monetary credit, position-monopolizing credentials, and the cultural currencies passed around in the micro-level conversational markets of everyday life (Collins, 1981b). The Weberian emphasis on stratification via the market (Weber, 1922/1968:927–928) is precisely what is needed to understand capitalism.

It is one's position on the market, moreover, rather than one's relation to the means of production, that determines the political dynamics of capitalist societies. Weber (1922/1968:927–8) noted that class conflict may be mobilized in three different kinds of markets: the labor market (employers versus workers), the credit market (debtors versus lenders), and the commodity market (sellers versus consumers). The earliest class conflicts of the ancient Greek and medieval Italian city-states were uprisings of debtors; and in the modern United States, as Wiley (1967) points out, conflicts in the credit and commodity markets have often overshadowed labor-market class conflict. Even for Marx's own period, the early capitalism of 1800–40, the predominant mode of class conflict was not what is given in Marx's scheme. As Calhoun (1982:115) shows, workers revolted largely as communities of consumers; when they became organized as workers, the radical phase of class struggle settled down into the more limited demands of trade unions. For Marx, the small artisan who autonomously made a whole product was by definition unalienated. In fact, it was just this artisan who was most radically mobilized to fight against capitalism (Calhoun, 1982:123). The seeming contradiction disappears when we realize that the autonomous artisan is directly exposed to the vicissitudes of the market, because he (she) must dispose of his (her) goods directly. It is precisely the "alienated" factory worker who is shielded to some degree from market forces; hence the lessened radicalism of factory workers. Whereas a factory worker demands only a protected place within the capitalist system, the small artisan is an enemy of market capitalism precisely because he (she) is so immediately at its mercy.[3]

---

[3] This is, incidentally, the same process that transformed the consciousness and the political role of the modern intellectual. The eighteenth-century intellectual still worked for a patron; despite the lack of freedom this entailed, the intellectual had no ideology of alienation, because he (she) was not directly exposed to the market. The characteristic alienation of the intellectual from the world sets in when intellectuals become independent writers, making their living on the market for books and other publications. The writer, in short, becomes an artisan, producing a whole product to

Alienation as ritual and ideology

A micro-macro perspective

Let us recall clearly the difference between the micro and macro levels of analysis. Micro reality is the immediate empirical level; macro reality is an aggregate structure on the large scale, spread out in time and space. We live in micro reality. The macro world enters our lives mainly as an alienating experience. You have to deal with a bureaucrat, who can't do anything for you because of a rule made elsewhere. A bureaucratic functionary won't even talk to you about your problem, personally meaningful though it may be, because you need to consult someone elsewhere. *Elsewhere* – that is the hallmark of macro reality as it confronts us in everyday life. And if one's original emotion was annoyance or anger at the complaint one brought to this bureaucracy, one's encounter with the macro world often heats it up to boiling rage. Or if not rage, disgust, disgruntledness, exasperation – all variants on the experience of alienation. Kafka's alienated sensibility, which epitomizes the critique of the modern world, is merely a dramatic staging of this kind of experience.

Sociological studies of the micro world, however, show remarkably little evidence of alienation. For Garfinkel and his followers, who have looked at micro reality in minute, second-by-second detail, the prevailing tone seems to be predominantly neutral. Meanings, including such strong meanings as alienation, are largely attributed retrospectively, when something happens to disturb the natural, taken-for-granted flow of events (Scott and Lyman, 1969). For Goffman, too, the immediate social order is essentially accommodative; people go out of their way to maintain its normality. Even a conflict theory, I have concluded, operates on the micro level mainly with a reality of ritual order, not of overt conflicts. The main reality of everyday life is an enforced domination of power and property, not acts of rebellion against these (Collins, 1981a, 1981g). Conflict is mostly macro – in other words, an analytical conception of the larger movement of social patterns across longer periods of time and large numbers of persons.

We do not appear, then, to be essentially and personally alienated in society, as alienation theories usually imply. For this to be possible, the individual self would have to be intrinsically independent of the

his or her own specifications. But the very structure that gives this new freedom is the market, with its impersonal and pitiless decisions about literary careers. The alienated protest of modern intellectuals, we may conclude, is in fact entirely realistic at its basis – not in the condition of the larger world on which intellectuals reflect but in the actual economic conditions under which modern intellectuals try to survive and prosper.

social world; given this, the external world then can impose itself, alienating one from the products of one's labors, removing one's intrinsic powers and fulfillments. But surely this is an entirely un-sociological premise. As Goffman (1961:152) sarcastically remarks, it is "this touching tendency to keep a part of the world safe from sociology." Every social psychology shows the ways in which the individual is permeated through and through by social influences, down to the internalized conversation that makes up our conscious minds.

Moreover, the individual self, on analysis, turns out to be a *macro* concept, not a micro one. Though this may seem paradoxical, it is apparent that what we mean by a "self" is much broader across time than the brief moments captured by the ultraempiricism of an eth-nomethodologist's tape recorder. The actual moments of everyday life do not necessarily give a "self"; what they give are typically social encounters, out of which we might later *abstract* a self, as something that is not only part of each encounter but also cuts across many encounters. In short, the self is not only not primordially presocial and untrammeled; it is not even an immediate empirical entity. It is an abstract conception, a macro entity of some degree (even if a relatively small macro entity compared to big macro entities like orga-nizations or states). In the usual flow of ordinary life, the self is not alienated, because the self often does not exist. What exists instead is just the consciousness of the situation; the alienation, and the self, usually emerge only when something happens (not necessarily the same thing in both cases) that causes one to abstract out some larger meaning of events.

In the case of alienation, this usually happens because one encoun-ters the recalcitrance of the macro world. For the macro world, by its very nature, is a large-scale structure over and above the experience of the individual human. It is made up of nothing but other indi-viduals, but it has a structure of its own because of the way it is spread out in time and space, and in the numerical relationships among the individuals. There is nothing distinctive about the Marxist conception of capitalism as alienating individuals from the products of their own labors, or about individuals' being controlled by a struc-ture they themselves have created. For that is the way the macro world always is, in all of its forms. The Marxist conception of aliena-tion rests on the fallacy of confusing the micro with the macro level of analysis.

Large organizations and communities, moreover, are inevitably in-efficient and conflict-ridden. They are oppressive when some indi-viduals within them have enough resources to dominate others, and even in egalitarian circumstances they constantly manufacture controversy and disharmony. Large-scale economic coordination, however carried out, is laden with inefficiencies. Markets are inherently unstable; whatever equilibrium tendencies they may have are only analytical points around which the real world continually oscillates. Politically organized economies are no better; they simply transfer the inefficiencies of bureaucratization into the economic realm. This has always been true, and no doubt always will be. The vision of Heraclitus rules the world, not that of Hegel.

Nevertheless, the individual's encounters with the macro world are not always alienating. Many of the high points of life are there: the joy in the streets when one's side wins a war, the feeling of elation when one's political party is victorious at the polls. These positive macro experiences usually are crowd situations – which is to say, they are very big micro situations: a kind of continuous interpenetration of one's little micro world (a few square feet) and a larger one physically and emotionally connected to it, through the sheer presence of physical bodies. The rare elation that accompanies a revolutionary uprising is probably due to there being no apparent boundary between one's own micro situation and that prevailing anywhere else. One can anticipate that the crowd everywhere in the streets of St. Petersburg will share one's mood. For once, the boundary between micro and macro seems to have broken down.

Even so, such collective micro events have some of the same limitations as intimate micro experience. Although it is spread out in space, a crowd situation nevertheless is a meaningful unity only for a short period of time; like a purely personal event, the life of a crowd rarely exceeds three hours. Even the great and glorious revolutionary experiences (one thinks of the elation of Berkeley at the height of the Free Speech Movement in 1964) wind down into routinization as they go on for months; then even the movement itself becomes objectified as yet another macro object one must take into account.

The example seems to confirm my point: Macro experience is mostly alienating, at least when it has the large contours in time and space that are most characteristic of the macro. That we are not continually alienated by the macro world in which we live is largely because most of the time we don't think about it; we take the world locally, one micro encounter at a time.

Alienation as modern secular politics

Moments of political mobilization have a peculiarly two-sided quality. On the one hand, they constitute some of the biggest enjoyments in life: the magic moment when the micro-macro barrier seems to have broken down, and we have the feeling of at last being able to control the macro realm. But to bring about this mobilization, a feeling of alienation is often useful. If in ordinary everyday life we rarely feel alienated, the very experience of political mobilization may bring it about very strongly. I am reminded of the fact that the political protest movements of the 1960s were quite a high experience for those who participated in them. At the same time, the manifest content of the movements was a very strong sense of alienation from American society, from its political and racial policies, its sexual morals, deference standards, its whole construction of ordinary reality. It seems ironic that many persons who participated in those movements look back on them rather nostalgically; after all, one had been protesting against a quite unpleasant world, of napalm and genocide in Vietnam and racism in America. The paradox disappears when we see that the 1960s movements consisted of people who were consciously alienated but at the same time were experiencing the great solidarity and élan of collective participation.

Part of the continuing attractiveness of the concept of alienation, then, apart from its latent culture snobbery and its Marxist economic resonances, is just this sense in which it can function as a Sorelian myth. It does not simply mobilize a social movement; the sense of alienation is created in the very crowd experiences that constitute the movement. I am suggesting that people do not feel especially alienated before they experience the micro-macro–spanning occasions of a movement; they simply treat everyday life in its usual, neutral sense. It is those movement experiences themselves that create, or at least heighten, the sense of alienation. The collective experiences are a ritual in the Durkheimian sense; the idea of alienation then becomes the sacred object or symbol that represents the solidarity of the group. And like other great sacred symbols, it gives the individual energy, moral feelings, even joy. Thus the paradox that even an intense consciousness of alienation can be among the high points of one's life.

This leads to a conclusion about the status of alienation in sociological theory. The theory of alienation is fundamentally flawed. It cannot be used to analyze society, because it itself is an ideology arising from particular social circumstances. It is not necessary or desirable as part of our analytical apparatus for understanding capitalism, or political mobilization. But it does represent a phenomenon that is an important characteristic of modern intellectual life, and of modern politics as well. What we need is not a theory of alienation but a theory about alienation. I have suggested that such a theory can come from understanding the relationship between micro and macro levels in everyday life and seeing political ritual as a unique bridge between the levels.

Part IV

Sex

11

Weber's theory of the family

Max Weber is not usually thought of as a theorist of the family. Nevertheless, the topic is mentioned a good deal both in his comparative studies of the world religions and in his systematic treatments of capitalism. His main interest is in the family as an important obstacle to the development of rationalized capitalism. But he also deals with the topic in debating with Marxian theory, and in this connection he makes many penetrating observations on the subject of sex. From all of this together it is possible to extract a theory of the social determinants of family structure. It is a theory, I would contend, as yet unmatched in its historical breadth, as well as in its hardboiled realism and its emphasis on political – and even geopolitical – determining conditions.

Family obstacles to capitalism

"The great achievement of the ethical religions," Weber declares (1916/1951:237), "above all of the ethical and asceticist sects of Protestantism, was to shatter the fetters of the sib. These religions established the superior community of faith and a common ethical way of life in opposition to the community of blood, even to a large extent in opposition to the family." In his comparative studies of China and of India, he emphasizes that the family structure, especially the corporate kin group ("sib"), throttled capitalist development.

In China, for instance, where the sib was strongly organized on the basis of ancestor worship, it constituted local village government and controlled its economy (Weber, 1916/1951:86–100). Even cities were merely collections of mutually exclusive sibs around an imperial government center. Sib leaders administered roads and canals, provided local self-defense, operated courts and schools through their ancestral temple. The temple invested in land, which it leased, and operated as a pawnshop and moneylender. But these activities were carried out not as capitalist ventures for profit but as a type of welfare institution for the benefit of sib members. Finance and trade were kept limited below the level of "pure market capitalism, freely seeking trading opportunities" (Weber, 1916/1951:84). The main "investment" of the sib was in the education of its most scholarly sons, in order to pass the lengthy set of government examinations for official positions. A sib member in office was expected to make his fortune, through tax-farming, bribes, and other legal and illegal profits, and thereby enrich the prosperity of the entire sib.[1]

The Chinese sib, then, despite its corporate economic organization, promoted only what Weber called "internal booty capitalism" – capitalism oriented to political opportunities – rather than the rationalized capitalism concerned with the market. Moreover, there was a strong solidarity of sib members versus outsiders. Within the sib, the ethics of family brotherhood were supposed to prevail; loans and pawns were made without interest, in a spirit of welfare redistribution and emergency aid. Outsiders, on the other hand, were objects of distrust and manipulation, to be ruthlessly cheated or oppressed when possible. It is this that Weber refers to when he declares that a universalistic ethical religion had to break down the barrier between internal and external ethics in order for the full-scale market capitalism to develop. Similarly, he mentions that labor discipline was only enforceable within the sib; it could provide an economic unit of production in itself but constituted an obstacle to the free recruitment and mobility of labor that would be necessary for any large-scale factory production.

Weber makes a similar argument regarding India (Weber, 1916–17/1958a:49–54). He points out that unconditional credit and pawning of objects existed only within the sib; and he derives the caste system, with its strongly stabilizing effects on the traditional order, from (among other causes) an elaboration of the magical charisma of sibs. The breaking down of this corporate kin structure in the West, he felt, was a crucial turning point that led toward the possibility of rationalized capitalism. The same structure was found in early Judaism, for instance, as well as in the Greek and Italian world (Weber, 1917–19/1952:20), and his concluding words on India stressed that except for particular historical conditions in the Middle East, Occidental development "could easily have taken the course typical of Asia,

---

[1] Weber is referring to comparatively modern conditions in the Ming and Ch'ing dynasties (1368–1911), when the examination system was firmly in place. We have seen that Weber's treatment of China is skewed toward the conditions of the later dynasties and lacks sufficient information on the medieval period.

particularly of India" (Weber, 1916–17/1958a:343; similarly, Weber, 1923/1961:50–1).

It is scarcely too much to say, then, that for Weber the traditional family structure had to be overcome in order for rationalized capitalism to emerge. This gave him an interest in explaining both why particular family structures appeared in the first place and what the conditions are that break them down.

A combination of perspectives

Weber's approach to the family differs from most others, and not merely in his concerns for the family's economic consequences. Most of our treatments of the family come out of sharply specialized lines of scholarship. In addition to research on the contemporary (usually American) family, one can find anthropological studies of tribal societies and, in the last few years, efforts by historians of modern Europe to push the geneaology of the contemporary family back, usually to about the 1600s (e.g., Laslett, 1971, 1977; Stone, 1977/1979). What all three approaches leave out are the great historical civilizations, the agrarian state-societies from their origins up through medieval Europe and Asia. But this was of course Weber's specialty, so he fills a crucial gap in comparative family studies.

Weber moreover combined several different scholarly traditions. As a historical economist of the German school, he had been immersed in studies of the early stages of economic organization, which included the medieval organization of household production. Weber's own doctoral dissertation (1889) was on precisely this topic, with special emphasis on the family capitalism of the northern Italian cities of the Middle Ages. Thus he was primed to see the family as a changing economic institution, entwined with legal forms (see Weber, 1922/1968:359–60).

Weber was also much interested in the Marxist and feminist theories of the family. His own wife, Marianne Schnitger Weber, published in 1907 a major scholarly work *Ehefrau und Mutter in der Rechtsentwicklung* ("Wife and Mother in the Development of Law"), which Weber referred to as the most up-to-date treatment of the question of primal "matriarchy" (Weber, 1923/1961:271).[2] Given Weber's political and scholarly interests, and his wife's importance in the German

---

[2] This book was reviewed in the *Année Sociologigue* by Emile Durkheim (1910), who disliked its feminist position. In view of the question of why Durkheim and Weber, contemporaries and founders of modern sociology, ignored each other, it is interesting to note that Durkheim was familiar with the work of Weber's wife but not with that of Weber himself.

feminist movement[3] he could hardly avoid taking a position on the Marxist feminism set forth by Bebel (1883) and Engels (1884). It was via this route that Weber attended to anthropological researches on tribal family structures. Engels drew heavily on Lewis Henry Morgan's *Ancient Society* (1877), which in turn centered on Morgan's researches on North American Indian families. Weber comments that there are two kinds of empirical cases known, that of "primitive stages of civilized peoples" and that of "the so-called primitive tribes (*Naturvölker*)" (Weber, 1922/1968:370) – corresponding to the historical economic studies with which he was familiar, and the tribal societies on which the Marxists drew for their evolutionary schemes.

Weber thus had a dual interest in the family. His main purpose was always to show the conditions involved in the rise of modern capitalism, but in his systematic treatments he used the Marxian position as a foil against which to set up his own exposition (Weber, 1922/1968:356–65; 1923/1961:38–45). This meant that he always began by treating the topic of sex, and with considerable comparative scope, before settling back into his major concern with economic development. Moreover, Weber was quite polite toward the Marxian theory. Although he rejected its evolutionary stages and especially its claim of an ancient mother-right (matriarchy), he complemented the theory: "Although it is untenable in detail it forms, taken as a whole, a valuable contribution to the solution of the problem. Here again is the old truth exemplified that an ingenious error is more fruitful for science than stupid accuracy" (Weber, 1923/1961:40). Whereupon Weber embarked on many paragraphs discussing the history of prostitution.

In some ways this material appears tangential. But it enhances Weber's point that the family is a sexual institution as well as an economic one. In fact, we may take it as a definition that the family is the conjunction of these two spheres. Weber does not organize the sexual materials theoretically, beyond using them to refute Engels's arguments about the evolution of sexual domination. They intrude into his argument, almost like an excursus, probably evidencing the strength of Weber's intrinsic interest in the topic of sex. As well they might: Weber had a very troubled sexual life, and was both attracted

---

[3] Marianne Weber was an important figure in the German feminist movement, eventually becoming the first woman elected to public office in Germany after the extension of the suffrage. Max Weber read Bebel with her early in their marriage, and supported her feminist activities. Later, he defended her against public criticism when the convention of the Federation of German Women's Associations, which she had organized at Heidelberg in 1910, was criticized in the press as a movement of widows, Jewesses, sterile women, and those who did not want to perform the duties of mothers (Marianne Weber, 1925/1975:429–39). The result was a challenge to a duel, and a lawsuit that Max Weber eventually won.

and repelled by the radical Freudian movement that appeared in Germany at this time, including in his own circle of friends.[4] Weber's interest in Engels's theory was a way of focusing on sex, which doubtless comprised the element in Engels that Weber considered to be so promising for a theory of the family. Weber's treatment of the family is harsh, even brutal, in its realism. It remains for us to integrate this with the rest of Weber's comparative analyses on the family, in which he stressed that its sexual and economic aspects must always be seen in the context of political and military factors.

The geopolitics of the family

Weber's approach to the family does not begin in the usual starting place: with the nuclear family, matri- and patrilineages, and the like. Instead, these are matters to be derived later, from a more basic matrix. For Weber holds to a multileveled view of the family, a nesting of larger and smaller structures. Instead of starting with the nuclear family and working outward, it might be more accurate to say that Weber puts in view the largest political relations and works inward from there. His perspective on the family might best be labeled geopolitical.

Weber's two main structures are the *household* and the *kin group*.[5]

---

[4] Weber apparently had a virtually nonexistent sex life with Marianne, and only later achieved some fulfillment in an illicit affair with Else von Richthofen, his first female student, who later became part of the "sexual liberation" circle, including D. H. Lawrence (Green, 1974). His psychoneurotic breakdown, which incapacitated him for half a dozen years after 1897, must undoubtedly have involved these sexual tensions. The breakdown was precipitated after Weber took the side of his mother in a violent argument with his father, who died soon after. His mother, Helene Weber, was puritanical and moralistic, and influenced Max strongly; she apparently had some part in Max's marriage to Marianne, a cousin living with them in Berlin to whom Helene was quite close. Marianne Weber comes through in her biography of Max as very idealistic, after the flowery Victorian fashion. Early in their relationship Max seems to have treated her as a child; after his breakdown, Marianne welcomed the opportunity to mother him. The rise of the Freudian movement interested them both a great deal; from Marianne's viewpoint, at any rate, the two of them strongly agreed that sexual fidelity to marriage was an ethical obligation, although they were willing to consider sympathetically the position of contemporary young people, if only in the abstract. Max Weber rejected an article on Freudian theory for his *Archiv für Sozialwissenschaft*, replying to the author with a good deal of moral posturing; on other occasions, he denounced sexual "demagoguery" (Marianne Weber, 1926/1975:171–90, 229–33, 236, 371–90). In view of the affair that (earlier or later) took place between Max and Else von Richthofen – whom Marianne considered one of her close friends – it is obvious that there was a great deal beneath the surface that neither Marianne nor Max wished to make conscious. In short, the situation looks like a classic instance of Freudian repression. For a more extensive analysis of Weber's neurosis, see Collins, 1985, chapter 1.

[5] There is a good deal of inconsistency about how the latter term is translated. Weber

Neither is primal; rather, they conflict with and modify each other, with a considerable range of outcomes.

The basic form of the *household* is a group with common residence and consumption of the everyday means of subsistence within it, which Weber refers to as "household communism" (Weber, 1922/1968:359). But the household does not necessarily coincide with a family; it can include more than family members (servants, apprentices, slaves, retainers), as well as less (as in the case of tribal societies where husbands and wives take their meals separately in different households). The household, says Weber, does not exist in nomadic hunting societies, since it depends on settled cultivation of the soil. Even with the development of agriculture, "the household is often secondary with respect to a preceding state which accorded more power to the inclusive kinship and neighborhood group on the one hand, and more freedom to the individual vis-à-vis parents, children, grandchildren, and siblings on the other hand" (Weber, 1922/1968:358). Weber seems to have in mind, for instance, the situation of wandering hunters-and-gatherers, whose campsites fluctuate in membership on a day-to-day basis (Lee and DeVore, 1968); there is no authoritarian "head of the household," and political, religious, economic, and other powers and cooperation are grouped around larger kinship groups (or around local coalitions, the "neighbourhood group"). The household, then, is not at all a primitive stage from which larger structures developed, but rather itself the result of later developments.

The *kin group* (sib, clan) is just this larger network. It consists of all those who are related by blood in a certain way (e.g., through the male line, up to a certain degree), although as Weber points out, it can also be organized on the basis of fictitious kinship (Weber, 1917–19/1952:11, 1922/1968:366). It can be shattered and rebuilt when a charismatic leader brings together a new coalition, which thereupon becomes transmitted hereditarily, with its members tracing themselves back to this heroic "ancestor" (Weber, 1916–17/1958a:54). The kin group can act in a number of different ways. It can, for instance,

uses the German *Sippe,* which in English is rendered "sib." Gerth and Martindale (Weber, 1917–19/1952:475) argue that this is the best equivalent, in that the Irish term "clan" was rejected by Weber himself as ambiguous. But "clan" achieved a wide usage in the literature for referring to large kinship groups, and we find Gerth himself using the term in other translations (Weber, 1916–17/1958a), along with "sib." Frank Knight (Weber, 1923/1961) uses only "clan." Roth, finally, retranslates *Sippe* as "kin group" (Weber, 1922/1968). It is also equivalent to what contemporary anthropologists refer to as "corporate descent groups" or "lineage groups." In my opinion, there is little to be gained from trying to impose an arbitrary uniformity at this point, and I will use the terms interchangeably, with some effort to keep Roth's "kin group" as the principal usage.

be the main economic unit, as in the cooperative hunting expeditions characteristic of Paleolithic societies (an archeological example unknown to Weber himself; see Edwards et al., 1970:70–121). Weber stresses that the kin group is especially a military and protective unit, responsible for blood revenge for injuries to its members; it may be even more explicitly organized as a military secret society or "men's house" (Weber, 1923/1961:49; 1922/1968:365). Or it can be organized as a totemic clan, with magical and ritualistic rules separating insiders and outsiders, food prohibitions, taboos, and the like. Or again, it may be essentially a group of friends, conceiving of themselves as an artificial blood brotherhood.

Weber stresses that none of these is primordial. We have to visualize the *local geopolitics* of any tribal (or indeed, any other) society. Various political and economic opportunities, threats, and conflicts generate different sorts of coalitions among the people in an area. Sexual and blood relationships are a prime way of forging such coalitions, but because these are not flexible and rapid enough to keep up with events, sheer political expediency together with personal charisma can create ad hoc organizations. Later these tend to be regularized as kinship – partly fictional but also increasingly real as hereditary membership and sexual exchange cement the long-standing coalition.

A crucial point is that the larger coalition, the kin group, can have considerable power vis-à-vis the local group (the household, family, or shifting campsite group, whatever it may be). The kin group competes with these local groups in regard to sexual relations and group loyalty. It may be the kin group, organized as a military men's house, that appropriates women as sexual objects and assigns them to its members; it may be the kin group that arranges marriage exchanges, stakes its members to bride-prices, or exacts a kind of "intercourse tax" (my term, not Weber's) when a young member brings in a new woman in marriage.[6] Although Weber does not say so explicitly, one can extend this line of reasoning to conclude that the incest taboo within the nuclear family is enforced by the intrusion of the larger kin group and its political interests.[7] The kin group also maintains an

[6] For instance, among the Arunta of Australia, the elders of the kin group demanded the right to have group intercourse with any new wife before the husband could enjoy her (Spencer and Gillen, 1927:472–4). Explanations aimed at showing some symbolic significance in this are farfetched, in my opinion, in comparison to the obvious interest of this power group in securing their own sexual pleasure. After all, the household is nonexistent and the local "nuclear" kin group all but powerless; the larger kin group is the only organized power group, and there is nothing to stop it from exercising that power for erotic gratification.

[7] See my argument, based on Lévi-Strauss's theory that sexual exchange agreements are ways of bringing a negotiated settlement to intergroup conflicts, including raiding for women among demographically unbalanced groups (Collins, 1981e:115–21).

interest in family property, since it holds a residual interest in inheritance if immediate family heirs do not exist.

Furthermore, since the kin group has the all-important activity of blood revenge, it calls forth military loyalty (and hence legitimacy; see Chapter 6) that may be emotionally much more compelling than any authority within the local family or household. This is particularly true where different members of the same household belong to different kin groups, as for example, when father and children are assigned to different kin groups. Moreover, the kin group is often counted outward starting from each ego to a certain number of generations; hence, even in the absence of matrilineal complications each generation of a household will have a different, although overlapping, set of members of its kin group. (In China, the patrilineal sib was defined by the degree of kinship within which an individual was obligated to mourn relatives' deaths [Queen and Habenstein, 1967:93].) Different members of the same household may be required to participate on opposite sides in cases of blood revenge. Weber stresses the point that the kin group provides a countervailing force supporting the individual against the authority of the household patriarch: "the kin group guarantees the security and legal personality of the individual" (Weber, 1922/1968:366). This may be institutionalized in trials and laws organized by the kin group itself, including a veto over the sale of property, the right to participate in selling daughters in marriage, to receive part of the bride price, to provide legal guardians, and (as Weber stresses in the case of ancient Judaism) to interfere in domestic sexual practices (Weber, 1917–19/1952:401–3).

There is no fixed relationship, however, between the power of the local family/household group and the larger kin group. Neither is aboriginal, and hence neither constitutes a stage out of which the other grows. Weber repeatedly attacks evolutionary stage theories, both Marxist and those of earlier family and economic historians (Bachofen, Morgan, List, Hildebrand, Bücher).[8] Aboriginal "mother-right," or matriarchy, is a myth; the evidence from which it was

---

8 He even goes so far as to say, in his lectures on general economic history (Weber, 1923/1961:45), that there is no such thing as a primitive stage of hunting or pastoral peoples, existing apart from exchange with settled agricultural peoples. Weber was little interested in paleolithic archaeology, which to be sure was imbued with wild speculation and little advanced until after Weber's time. Obviously his claim about hunting peoples cannot be accepted, and he himself in another text seems to admit their primal existence (Weber, 1922/1968:358). His point does hold for pastoral peoples, however (McNeill, 1963), and in general Weber is correct in stressing the "horizontal" or "geopolitical" dimension of coexisting social forms, against the effort to derive one from another in stages. For an overview of the economic stage theories Weber was repudiating, see Hoselitz (1960).

inferred (instances of matrilocal residence and descent) really represents a very specific combination of factors bringing about a compromise between the powers of the kin group and the local household (Weber, 1922/1968:357). There is no original isolated nuclear family, gradually coming into contact with other units to form a larger exchange society (as in Bücher's theory); geopolitical linkages are there from the very beginning. The large extended-family households with their tendency to self-sufficiency and their household "communism," still found recently among the South Slavs or in the Swiss *Gemeinderschaften*, represent not a survival of a stage of "primitive communism" but a development of the strength of the household that could occur only when particular economic and political conditions weakened the power of the larger kin group (Weber, 1923/1961:51–2; 1922/1968:359–60).

On the other hand, the larger kin group is not primordial either. Weber would not have been sympathetic to Freud's primal "horde," nor did he admit Engels's and Morgan's stage of original undifferentiated promiscuity (Weber, 1922/1968:364). The power of the kin group, too, waxed and waned. The times when it did seem to approximate the sexual and other rights of the "horde" are actually determined by specific military and economic conditions, when the kin group was strongly organized into a military men's house – as in the duk-duk example from the Indonesian archipelago, which Weber frequently cites (Weber, 1922/1968:371; 1923/1961:46). Moreover, the kin group may actually be quite amorphous, acting only intermittently and without any formal association (Weber, 1922/1968:365). It may exist only in the claims that certain defined relatives have over vestigial inheritance rights, or merely negatively in prohibitions against marriage within its ranks. These various possible forms of kin group organization seem schematic and perhaps confusing in Weber's typological presentation in *Economy and Society*; but in his historical treatments (the *General Economic History*, the studies of the world religions), Weber devotes considerable attention to the conditions that can either reduce the power of the kin group to these vestigial rights or, conversely, build it up into a concretely organized and even dominant institution.

It remains only to point out that the household and other local groups on one side, and the larger kin group on the other, are not the only social actors in the arena. Beyond the kin group, there can emerge larger territorial groups: the village community, the tribe (which may be formally organized or exist merely as an ethnic-cultural homogeneity), and finally the organized state. All of these can interfere with, and cut across, the household and local family.

These are, in short, a larger geopolitical arena for the family; again, there is a tendency for causality to work from the outside in. The larger tribe is formed out of shifting coalitions among sibs, and eventually may acquire its own autonomous organization, and its own religious cult focus. The war coalition of the Jewish tribes under its war god, Yahwe, is an instance, to which Weber gives much attention, in which the larger organization make considerable inroads into the power of the kin group (sib) (Weber, 1917–19/1952:especially 174–87). And in general the power of the state is hostile to rival organization at the kin group level. Different levels of political organization might ally with one another: the state level helping to destroy the kin group level, thereby giving much greater authority to the household. The principles and variations of such dynamics make up the core of a Weberian theory of the family.

The family as sex and property

The family, then, is a complex of institutions, both local and spread out in space. But what is their specific nature, in short, the definition of "the family"?

For Weber, the family is not simply an agency for socializing children. Sheer biological parenthood, he points out, is a tenuous relationship unless based on the household as an economic unit (Weber, 1922/1968:357–8). Rather, the family is based on a specific kind of sexual relationship: one that takes place by the consent of the kin of both wife and husband, and out of which results the membership of children in the larger economic, political, and/or religious community belonged to by (at least one of) their parents. Weber defines marriage as a "stable sexual relationship" within the context of the larger community. Again, he does not build up from the small unit outward but from the outside in. It is the larger (kin) group that allows and enforces the sexual relationship; against their will, it is not legitimated, and may even be avenged by force. Equally important, the larger group determines the rules according to which children born of particular kinds of sexual unions will have property rights as well as political membership.

Two comments are worth making. First, although Weber's conception bears some resemblance to the Malinowskian functionalist position, that the family is based on a universal need for children to be legitimate members of society, the argument is not a functionalist one. Weber does not say that it is a universal normative rule that all children should be legitimate; in fact, he points to considerable variation in the kinds of sexual union that occur historically and resulting

276

in various rights or lack of rights involving the children, including concubinage and slavery. He shows, rather, a principle of privilege or stratification: only certain kinds of regulated sexual relations bring with them property rights, as well as power and status, and these relations (legitimate marriages) dominate other sexual relationships, which also may exist on a regular basis.

Second, we might wonder about a possible circularity in the argument. If marriage and legitimate offspring are only constituted by the larger kin group, how in turn could the kin group have become constituted *as kin* without prior marriages? I think that the clue to the puzzle is in Weber's point that the kin group may actually begin as the ad hoc following of a charismatic leader and only later glosses this over with fictitious bonds of kinship. In short, sexual unions are at first *not* legitimated; it is only after a larger coalition is charismatically formed that it comes to regulate sexual unions (probably through exchange politics). This in turn makes possible the transition to an ideology of fictional (and later real) kinship in the larger group.

Weber's conception of the family is very close to a conflict theory (Collins, 1975:225–85). The family is essentially a set of sexual and economic relationships regulated by political power (such as the military enforcement of the larger group). Politically regulated rights translate into "property." The rights over sexual access are what Kingsley Davis (1949) and others (Collins, 1975) have called "sexual property," whereas the economic goods and services involved in and resulting from sexual *property* (as opposed to merely casual, unregulated sexual intercourse) constitute family economic property. It is only when sex becomes property that inheritance also appears.

When these sexual property rights are organized so that the resulting children are members of a common economic institution – the household – we have the family in its familiar form (Weber, 1922/1968:358). The family, in this "modern" sense, may be summed up as: sexual property (and its offspring) as the unit for economic property. But as we have seen, the household is hardly primitive or universal; we should treat the "family," then, as the entire complex of variations in which sexual and economic property are conjoined. This includes all the different ways that the larger kin group interacts (and conflicts) with smaller sexual groupings and living arrangements.

Political and economic determinants of family organization

Weber states that the organization of male and female work influences family structure (Weber, 1923/1961:45–9). Women's work is wild-plant gathering and, later, horticulture, weaving, pottery, and

277

care of small domesticated animals; men's work is hunting, heavy plow agriculture, care of large animals such as cattle, plus wood- and metalworking. When horticulture dominates the economy, family organization is frequently centered on the woman's house, where she has control over the work process. Conversely, economies based predominantly on hunting, pastoralism, or plow agriculture have family structures organized around men, upon whom the women are economically dependent.

Thus far Weber is in keeping with the familiar anthropological picture. Where Weber differs is in his emphasis on the military factor as always significant. The female-centered household, even in the cases where it is matrilineal as well as matrilocal, is not matriarchy; in fact he describes it as a "traditional bondage and a corresponding patriarchal position within the house" (Weber, 1923/1961:46). The men are always organized in some version of the larger kin group (clan, sib), frequently with a separate men's house. This is a sort of club where men live, make weapons and other metal tools, and organize their military and hunting expeditions. Above all, it is a type of terrorist institution, surrounding itself with fear-inspiring artifacts such as masks and hideous emblems. It maintains strict secrecy against outsiders, especially women, who are forbidden to enter under violent penalties such as gang rape (Murphy, 1959). Weber stresses that its procedures "were specifically invented to intimidate and rob women" (Weber, 1922/1968:371).[9]

The rationale for the secrecy of the men's house is the magic practiced there. In more contemporary terms, one could say that magic is the ideology of this terrorist group, and that the fearful apparatus represents their monopolization of the means of impression management or emotional production. Initiation rites for adolescent boys are part of this same use of ritual for terroristic domination, this time for age stratification within the group; such rites include circumcision,

---

[9] Later he continues, "The members of the fraternity . . . live on war booty and on the contributions they levy on non-members, especially on the women by whom the agricultural work is done. . . . Depending on the social regulations in question, the warriors steal or purchase girls in common, or demand as their right the prostitution of all the girls of the territory dominated. . . . In order to secure their economic position, which is based on the continuous plundering of outsiders, especially women, the consociated warriors resort under certain circumstances to the use of religiously colored means of intimidation. The spirit manifestations which they stage with masked processions very often are nothing but plundering campaigns which require for their undisrupted execution that, on the first sound of the tom-tom, the women and all outsiders flee, on pain of instant death, from the villages into the woods and thus allow the 'spirits' conveniently and without danger of being unmasked to take from the houses whatever may please them. The well-known procession of the Duk-Duks in Indonesia is an example in point" (Weber, 1922/1968:906–7).

which is frequently practiced in tribal military groups as a form of discipline.[10]

The men's house, which is primarily a military barrack, was found not only in tribal societies but also among the Spartans – another society in which men lived under strict discipline and women were relatively independent because the men lived away. Weber gives great emphasis to this form of organization in his theory of the development of the state (see Chapter 6). Males typically live in a tribal men's house from adolescence through mid-adulthood, after which they are finally "discharged from service," so to speak (my phrase, not Weber's), and go to live with their wives. Thus the men's house is frequently connected with matrilineal kinship, and with the avunculate – the authority of a woman's oldest brother over her children.[11]

Weber stresses that the military organization brings sexual domina-

---

[10] Paige and Paige (1981:122–66) propose a political theory of circumcision ritual, as a ceremony that assembles the tribal coalition, and shows the father's good faith in them by his willingness to place in their hands his son's penis. This represented considerable risk, given the rudimentary sanitary and medical practices of these tribes, to the reproductive organ upon which rested the patriarch's hopes of grandchildren to add to the strength of his faction. Such rituals, Paige and Paige argue, are especially important in pastoral societies, in which the environment imposed no constraints on splits in the lineage coalition. The theory is plausible in general (although not in all of its details). It reinforces Weber's point that circumcision relates to the military group. It was originally carried out in adulthood, and the demilitarized lower classes were exempted from it (Weber, 1917–19/1952:91–5). But Weber shows that its significance need not be related to its kinship implications; circumcision is only one part of the discipline exacted within military groups (which may of course be ad hoc, nonkin coalitions), including ritual fasting and sexual abstinence prior to battle. These are connected to the ritualistic revving up of emotions for the battle itself, including war dances, cannibalism, or human sacrifice (for which Hebrew circumcision was apparently a later substitute). In Egypt (where military circumcision was also practiced) the foreskin of the enemy was taken as a trophy, like the Indian scalp.

[11] Murphy's (1957, 1959) theory of sex antagonism, based on the Mundurucu of Brazil, argues that the men's house arises where patrilineality is combined with local exogamy, so that the men stay together while their female siblings go to other villages. But the Mundurucu happen to be unusual in that they combine patrilineality with matrilocal residence (together with exogamy at the village level, whereas most matrilocal societies have local endogamy). It may well be that the geopolitical situation is the missing element in the explanation; the Brazilian jungle is notably warfare-prone, with the level of technical organization ruling out permanent conquests and confining war to chronic headhunting expeditions. Murphy's logic exemplifies the tendency to reify residence and lineage rules as an ultimate cultural explanation, instead of seeing these as political arrangements that are themselves to be explained. Murphy's analysis of the sexual antagonism of the men's house situation, however, is congruent with Weber's. Murphy emphasizes the extreme hostility of men toward women, their beliefs that women are polluting, and their use of sex to dominate them, arguing that these are methods of controlling female-based work groups while not living with them. Similarly, Weber refers to the terroristic methods of the men's house as "an attempt by the men who have left the household to strengthen their threatened authority" (Weber, 1922/1968:371).

279

tion. Wives may be obtained by group capture (which Weber, perhaps dubiously, believes can result in polyandry), or group members may buy them. He accepts the occasional possibility of group marriage (Weber, 1923/1961:48–9) but denies that it is a normal stage as in the Morgan-Engels theories. More importantly, Weber stresses that a woman is always under the authority of males, either the men of her own house community or those who bought her. "Woman is regarded as labor power, and is bought as an object of value, as a work animal" (Weber, 1923/1961:48). Marriage by purchase (the brideprice) requires some differentiation of wealth. This in turn tends to break up the solidarity of a men's military group. Wealthy men can buy many wives, resulting in polygamy; whereas poor men (usually a group of brothers) may have to pool their resources to buy one to share among themselves (polyandry). More commonly, a poor man may acquire a wife by going to live in her house, temporarily or permanently, paying for her by his services. Unlike contemporary anthropology, with its tendency to explain kinship practices by abstract cultural rules, Weber stresses the force of economic and political realities. Above all, he never loses sight of the possible existence of stratificaticn; both patrilocal and matrilocal institutions may exist in the same place and indeed within the same household, depending on whether the men in question are rich or poor (Weber, 1922/1968: 368).

In sum, both economic and military factors determine family organization. There is no evolutionary sequence, but rather a set of shifting possibilities determined by the particular configuration of factors holding at that time. Although Weber does not use the example, one could illustrate his approach by pointing out that paleolithic societies may have shifted back and forth between more sedentary, quite possibly female-centered families, during periods when gathering predominated, and male-centered organization, when there was exclusive dependence on hunting – as in the glacial epochs when Cro-Magnon peoples followed the reindeer herds (Maringer and Bandi, 1953).

But these economic factors must always be overlaid with military conditions. The larger kin group/clan is always crucial for fighting (as well as for the collective hunting necessary to kill the larger game animals). This kin group can be organized in different ways; the residential men's house/barrack is a form it takes when economic organization centers around the women's houses. It can take other forms as well, including those in which there are male-centered families, or in which there is virtually no stable household at all (as in the Australian desert) but only continually shifting campsite groups. Weber describes the totemic group as another variant on the patterns

of military organization of the kin group. It is a peace union, organized around magical beliefs and using emblems of a totemic animal
or being to symbolize the brotherhood of members who must not kill
one another. (Similarly, it is exogamous, because the group wishes to
avoid sexual jealousy within its ranks.) Unlike the case of the men's
house, the men live with their wives but come together for totemic
festivals and for political discussions and military expeditions.[12]

Whether particular kinds of military coalitions form – as men's
houses, totemic groups or merely ad hoc gatherings – depends, I
suggest, on geopolitical conditions. The sheer density of settlement
and degree of competition among adjacent tribes would be affected
by scarcity or abundance of natural resources, and by the presence or
absence of natural barriers to movement. These would affect the incidence of warfare and consequently the importance and relative institutionalization of military coalitions. A full-fledged theory of this
sort remains to be created. But following the logic of Weber's theory
of the state, the external military situation sets the stage for internal
political maneuvering; and in a tribal society, this internal organization takes the form of family and kinship structure.

Weber does point out the ways in which the family organization
depends on existing weapons technology. The men's house and
other forms of collective military operations, mobilizing the entire
adult male population, depend on relatively cheap weapons (as well
as on an economy that uses either women for subsistence work or
else a male group intermittently practicing hunting and readily trans-
formable into a military group). With the invention of heavy weapons, especially the chariot, and horse-mounted combat, war comes to
be monopolized by an elite. This tends to dissolve the clan (especially
the men's house) in favor of individuals withdrawing to their own
families and property. The clan/men's house may also disintegrate
owing to demilitarization – either because of ecological dispersion
and low competition or because outside conquest forcibly creates a

---

12 Weber erroneously states that totemic organization is connected with matrilineality
   (Weber, 1923/1961:47), whereas in fact Australian and other examples show that it
   can exist in a number of different forms. Weber was concerned here mainly to
   combat evolutionary theories that see totemism as an aboriginal stage. Weber's
   source is Frazer (1910); apparently he was also acquainted with Spencer and Gillen's
   (1899) work on central Australia, the source that both Durkheim (in *The Elementary
   Forms of the Religious Life*) and Freud (in *Totem and Taboo*) used for their theories
   regarding primitive social organization. Weber's treatment of this material, in general, is the most realistic and currently defensible of the three, as far as historical and
   social-structural dynamics are concerned. (To be sure, Durkheim made brilliant use
   of the totemic materials to show the social-psychological dynamics of ritual, morality, and symbolism.) The geopolitical analysis of Australian kinship, following
   Weber's insights, remains to be written.

hierarchic society with an aristocracy ruling over disarmed peasants. In both cases, men return permanently to their families. The result is a tendency to patriarchy, "paternal dominance with paternal inheritance." Among the conquerors of land, as well, property is automatically assigned in the male line, and women are excluded from inheritance.

Sexual rights are determined as part of this same complex. Marriage is an institution of sexual appropriation. It is restricted by incest prohibitions, which Weber points out are the obverse of exogamy. Both are due to the avoidance of jealousy among the *males* of the household (and of the clan, where the kin group is strongly organized, especially in a common men's house [Weber, 1922/1968:364–5]). Exogamous practices are furthered by exchange agreements among allied groups; here Weber anticipates Lévi-Strauss.[13] The extent of incest prohibitions, and hence of exogamy, is determined by the political organization of these groups (and, it follows, not by any primal psychological mechanism). Endogamy is likewise a phenomenon of political organization. Where clans become stratified by differences in wealth and power, endogamy appears, setting status bounds on alliances. Similar considerations lead to hypergamy. The levirate, Weber points out, is not a survival of a stage of group marriage, but part of a situation in which the clan takes it upon itself to provide a husband for widows of its members, so that its property will not fall into alien hands and its full military ranks will be preserved.

Sex is not merely regulated by the kinship system, however. In general, men have full sexual freedom beyond marriage, until the restrictions imposed (rather late, Weber remarks) by the monotheistic religions. Weber seems to vacillate on the subject of female sexual freedom. At one point (Weber, 1923/1961:42) he mentions "originally equal sexual freedom for women" and refers to the Arabs at the time of Muhammad (not a very primordial example, to be sure), when temporary marriage in exchange for support, and trial marriage, existed alongside regular marriage. But in general Weber regards marriage as a set of variations in degree on prostitution: "Between professional prostitution and the various forms of marriage may intervene all possible intermediate arrangements of permanent or occasional sexual relations" (Weber, 1923/1961:40). Weber, in fact, begins his discussion of the family with a comparative analysis of prostitution

---

13 Weber (1922/1968:364–5) refers to the male appropriation of particular women within the household as the first breach in its primitive communism. Here Weber seems to be lapsing into the archaic Morgan-Engels stage of primitive communism, which he explicitly rejects elsewhere (Weber, 1923/1961:51).

Weber's theory of the family

("in which connection, it goes without saying, no ethical evaluation is involved" [Weber, 1923/1961:40]), which he regards as the great positive contribution of the socialist theories of the family. His aim is partly to criticize Engels by showing that prostitution is much older than the monogamous form of marriage, both of which Engels claimed were introduced with private property. But Weber also wishes to show that sexual relations and their appropriation are central to comparative variations in family politics.

In tribal socieites women may be sexually exploited for gain, hired out by the clan in exchange for provisions. Relatedly, there is sexual hospitality, the giving of wives and daughters to cement relations with honored guests. Also in this category are arrangements in which males receive sex in return for living in the house of a woman's kin and performing services for the male household head. Weber comments, somewhat polemically, "this 'prostitution' of female household members accounts for many cases that are subsumed under the imprecise collective name of *matriarchy*" (Weber, 1922/1968:368). What seems like the sexual freedom of women, by modern bourgeois standards, is actually a form of sexual exploitation by her relatives.

On the other hand, the existence of something closer to independent prostitution, which is arranged by women themselves and from which they receive the economic rewards, is a version of the emancipation of women. In a class-stratified society, "girls of upper class families were especially reluctant to submit to the harsh domestic confinement of the patriarchal marriage, but clung to their sexual liberty, remaining in their parental homes and entering into contracts with men to whatever extent they pleased" (Weber, 1923/1961:42). Weber's main example is Ptolemaic Egypt, when there was "sexual freedom of contract with enforceable exchange by the woman of sex gratification for sustenance, rights in estates, or other considerations" (Weber, 1923/1961:40). Such arrangements might just as well be called marriages with liberalized legal rights for women, and explicit recognition and regulation of the sexual element (see Chapter 12 for further discussion of his case). Contrary to Engels, it is not merely bourgeois marriage that is a form of prostitution; Weber implies that all forms of marriage have their varying elements of prostitution, and some of the most explicit prostitution may actually be a liberalization of the status of women.

Weber is particularly interested in temple prostitution. Its origins, he suggests, are in the magical practices of ensuring the fertility of the fields by ritual copulation. This is, of course, the theme of Frazer, whom Weber explicitly cites. When independent religious organizations arose in technologically more advanced societies, they took over

283

this fertility magic.[14] Orgiastic ceremonies were especially important in the agricultural societies of India and the ancient Middle East, such as the Canaanite kingdom abominated by their Hebrew neighbors. The hierodules, or ritual prostitutes, were female temple slaves; in addition to performing in ceremonial orgies, they also prostituted themselves to the public for pay. In Babylon and in Jerusalem (during the period when the Yahwe cult had not yet monopolized religion), they catered especially to traveling merchants (Weber, 1923/1961:41; 1917–19/1952:189–91). Even after the decline of fertility magic, temples continued to maintain prostitutes as part of their material interests. As an offshoot, prostitutes became independent in India, Greece, and elsewhere (one might also cite China and Japan), amalgamating with entertainers and sometimes becoming highly cultured consorts of the upper classes. Here again Weber describes prostitution as a way women improved upon a restricted social position.

Political and religious attacks on prostitution occurred when rival cults became powerful. The pastoral peoples of Palestine who organized an intertribal coalition under the emblem of Yahwe were bitter enemies of the Canaanites and their fertility cults. The puritanical injunctions of Judaism arose from this conflict; for instance, the strong condemnation of male nudity (one of the most heinous offenses) and of masturbation were due to the presence of these elements in the ceremonies of Moloch (Weber, 1917–19/1952:187–93, 202). Because cults of this sort were present in the urban areas of Palestine itself, and were encouraged under some of the despotic kings (Weber, 1917–19/1952:189, 212), the attack on sexual practices had something of the character of class war within Judaism. The political onslaught of the rural clans, the main upholders of the Yahwe war federation, involved delegitimating the urban rulers by branding their sexual practices as immoral and foreign – a tactic often found in prerevolutionary situations (such as before both the Puritan revolution and the 1688 revolution in England and the 1789 French Revolution [Stone, 1977/1979:335]). In general, Weber comments, the prophets were always attuned to foreign policy (Weber, 1917–

---

14 Weber's cryptic remarks need to be developed from a consistent geopolitical and conflict perspective. Frazer is notorious for ignoring historical sequences and citing comparatively modern practices as primitive "survivals." His most explicit material shows that in certain tribal societies (examples from America, Africa, and southeast Asia), men copulated with their wives, or the chief with his wife, at certain crucial points in the agricultural season (Gaster, 1959:124–8). But these do not involve autonomously organized religious cults, with their own priesthood. Fertility cults in the later context must surely have had an additional, or entirely different, political and social significance, which as yet remains to be investigated from the point of view of the politics of sexuality.

19/1952:109, 267–9) and thus to the legitimation of the state by its power position in the international arena.

Once in control, a priestly faction based on a tradition of ethical prophecy has an additional reason to continue its hostility to orgiasticism. From the priests' viewpoint, eroticism is a primal urge to be overcome on the way to religious fulfillment; thus it was condemned by all the religions of salvation, by Brahmanism as well as by Zarathustra and the Jewish and Christian prophets and priests (Weber, 1923/1961:41). The upper-class state, too, promulgated a status honor based on self-disciplined impressiveness, and feared the possible outbreaks of revolutionary violence stirred up by the emotional excitement of orgiastic festivals. Still later, prostitution (as well as concubinage) was decisively condemned only with the rise of ascetic Protestantism in Europe. There are many variations here. The main point that emerges from Weber's discussion is that the restriction of sex to the regulated bonds of the family occurs only when the state and church are organized at a level that transcends all kinship organization, and thus takes over public morality as part of its own claim for political legitimation.

The kin group and its transformations

We have already seen the major variations on the structure of the kin group. Everywhere, Weber emphasizes, it is a military organization, whether existing loosely and intermittently as a group of men who can call upon one another for blood revenge, or as the peace union of a totemic group, or in the tightly regimented form of the men's house/barrack. In *Ancient Judaism*, Weber (1917–19/1952:139–48) examines the politics of the kin group (sib) at considerable length, as its coalitions were transcended by an even larger coalition of tribes, whose cult eventually became autonomously powerful and destroyed the sibs themselves.

Weber stresses that the shape of world history was determined by the differing fates of this military kin group. In the Occident it disappeared, even though it had been instrumental in the founding of not only the Jewish, Moslem, and other Middle Eastern states but also the Greek and Italian city-states.[15] In the Orient, the kin group was maintained and even strengthened (Weber, 1923/1961:50). The result of

---

[15] Originally these were coalitions of kin groups (*gens, phratry, curia*). Weber did not live to write his planned volume on the religious organization of Mediterranean antiquity. He does treat the political transformation of the Greek and Roman family, up through the "crisis of the clan state," in his *Agrarian Sociology of Ancient Civilizations* (Weber, 1909/1976:148–52, 172–5, 273–85).

this, as we have already seen, was crucial for the development of capitalism in the West but not the East.

The causes of this important shift in family organization were essentially political, including religious politics. Weber argues that the rise of chariot and horseback warfare and other heavy weapons brought about the end of the men's house, since warriors were now a specialized elite group, residing on their own property. But as we can see from China, this did not necessarily spell the end of the kin group (clan) in general. The rise of the bureaucratic state is one factor that broke down the clan; Weber remarks that the state feared the clan as a source of rival political factions, and hence relentlessly destroyed it, as in the New Kingdom of Egypt (Weber, 1923/1961:51). At the same time, Weber has to admit that even though the Chinese state was bureaucratized quite early, it was never able to break the power of the clan. It appears that state bureaucracy may also adjust to the clan, by using it as a convenient unit of local administration, when it is organized into villages jointly responsible for fiscal and other duties.

Weber's other candidate for the clan-destroying force is religious prophecy (Weber, 1923/1961:50). Charismatic religious leaders seek to build up their following without the restrictions of kin groups and their localized cults. This was especially the case with Christianity, to which Weber gives pride of place in destroying this major obstacle to the development of capitalism. But he also notes that Judaism gradually put the clan into the background, though it coexisted with the Yahwe cult down through the period of the exile. After that, it lost its purpose because of the demilitarization of Jewish society. Once again, it appears that one can point to a variety of routes to the same destination. As mentioned, the Greek and Italian clans, although originally strong, were eventually transcended by the new civic structure that became the focus of military and political organization. Even here, for a long time the clans lingered on as units within which the army was mustered. But these became mere vestiges after a series of political revolutions that widened political membership, connected with the change in military technique to the large-scale phalanx. In northern Europe, again, the clan was the unit for Celtic and Germanic military organization. Here it was broken, partly because of opposition by the Christian Church, and especially by the organization of the feudal status system. This grouped men not by the democracy of clan descent, but by estates differentiated according to knightly or nonknightly style of life. For this reason, Weber (1917–19/1952:5) included the medieval order of estates as one of the half-dozen crucial historical developments of the West.

Weber's theory of the family

The rise and fall of the household

We arrive, finally, at the household organization of the family. This comes late in the analysis, because as we have already seen, the household is not primordial, and does not dominate the scene as long as the larger kin group is important. Weber rejects earlier schemes of economic history, in which household production is regarded as the first stage. When the household does become the center of the economy, it is generally in advanced agrarian societies, in which military and political developments have destroyed the importance of the clan. (There are exceptions: In India, the caste takes the clan's place; in China, the clan continues to exist at the village level, alongside the household.)

This form is what Weber calls the patriarchal household: a despotism of the male head, in whose home all family members reside and from whom all inheritance takes place. The patriarch has the power to assign both his sons and daughters in marriage; traditional exchange rules (cross-cousin marriage and the like) and other forms of kin group influence over marriage have now shrunk to mere vestiges or disappeared entirely. The kin group ceases to be economically important. The patriarchal household concentrates virtually all property rights, and may operate in the various forms of a farm or manor, an urban capitalist business (such as craft, trade, or banking), or an *oikos*. The last, a term introduced by the earlier economic historian Rodbertus, is a large aristocratic estate that engages in production of a variety of both agricultural and industrial products. But it is not a stage on the way to industrial capitalism, Weber points out, because its aim is not production for the market but an effort to supply all the needs of the lord out of his own lands and by the labor of his own servants – in short, a marketless form of industry (Weber, 1922/1968:381–3).

In any of these forms, the patriarchal household may be very large. Its membership may include a number of wives and concubines with their children, as well as servants, slaves, and military retainers. There may also be the practice of sending children of the noble classes to be educated in the households of higher lords while serving as pages or ladies-in-waiting; closely related to this is the practice of taking hostages to ensure military compliance.

The existence of this large-scale household has been challenged by a recent wave of historical scholarship (Laslett, 1971, 1977). But this argument rests on a conceptual misunderstanding. It has been shown that most households in late medieval Western Europe were not large; due to demographic and other reasons, several generations did

287

not usually live together, and extended kinship ties were not important. It has been claimed that the nuclear family has been the primary form of organization, perhaps perennially (Goody, 1976). This does not touch on the Weberian conception, for two reasons. The first is that the two pictures refer to different ends of the social scale. Laslett and his followers have concentrated on the lower orders, where households have always been small, whereas Weber's patriarchal household is at the center of the political and economic order, in the higher classes. And in fact there is little real argument on this score. Laslett's (1971:1) own materials show vivid examples of how a prosperous urban bakery, for example, consisted of master, wife, children, apprentices, and servants, to a total of some fourteen persons. In England in particular there was a widespread custom of young people of both sexes leaving home to serve in larger households until they could afford to marry and form a (usually small) rural household of their own (Laslett, 1977).

The second error is to confuse the kinship system with the household. Weber of course separates them clearly and points out that the rise of the household to economic dominance accompanies the decline of the extended kinship group. To be sure, under certain conditions the multigenerational family does act as a cooperative economic unit. Laslett and his followers describe this as an Eastern European form, and Weber similarly cites the *zadruga* of the South Slavs, and the Swiss *Gemeinderschaften* as examples of joint family property. Weber, too, carefully points out that this is far from a universal stage (although he is more concerned to combat the idea that it is a vestige of primitive communism) and is merely one variant that agrarian household organization may take after the disintegration of the clan confederation.

The crucial point is that the patriarchal household may be large, but it is not intrinsically a form of extended kinship. The joint and stem families are sometimes found, but mainly in politically unimportant rural areas, and below the level of the aristocracy or the bourgeois patriciate. The main characteristic of the large patriarchal household, in fact, is that it brings together many persons who are *not* kin. It is the servants, slaves, apprentices, military retainers, pages, and hostages that make it an important form of organization (along with the concubines and secondary wives, who are kin but certainly would not be called "extended family"). The patriarchal household is at least halfway along the road to the breakdown of the kinship-based society; although it is centered on a family – that of the despotic household head – it brings in large numbers of nonfamily members to act as part of the military, political, and/or economic unit.[16] When such a household becomes politically powerful, it can act as a unit of government or administration, in which case Weber calls it *patrimonial domination*.

One can see now where the confusion has arisen. Modern sociologists, familiar only with contemporary societies, have usually operated with gross distinctions. On the one hand there has been the nuclear family (and small nuclear household) visible in industrial societies; on the other, there are still-surviving tribal societies, for the most part with complex kinship systems (usually extra-household, although that point has not been so much noticed), and a memory of rural societies in which the family seems to have been much larger and more important than it has since come to be. Hence the mythical sequence of extended families in bucolic agricultural times, shifting under the pressure of industrialization to the stripped-down nuclear form. Laslett and his followers, starting from recent historical times and working backward, examine the extended family and conclude that it was a myth.

Until recently, many comparative sociologists have had little idea of what the historical agrarian societies were like, preferring to substitute a horizontal comparison across alleged stages in which tribal societies serve as a facsimile for all earlier "extended" forms. They might have saved themselves the trouble by consulting Weber. He shows us that the dominant households of the societies immediately preceding our own were large but that the kinship was not extended; in fact, the households were large precisely because the more remote links of kinship were now forgotten or at least supplemented by relationships that were not based on kinship.

The patriarchal or patrimonial household is thus already a relatively "modern" form. Nevertheless, although it opened the way for the development of the rationalized market economy and for bureaucratic administration by "breaking the bonds of the clan," it remained in its own way an obstacle to more impersonal developments. It did retain one crucial element of kinship organization: not that it relied primarily on family labor or connections (since it was able to transcend these by incorporating nonkin into the household) but that its core was still a family. A nuclear family, to be sure, but nevertheless a

---

[16] Cf. the argument of Miller (1981:41) and of Patterson (1982) that slavery was crucial for breaking the limitations of kinship in creating larger economic and political organization. It was especially important in matrilineal societies in giving men control over their own property (Patterson, 1982:232). Since in these societies slaves tended to be women, this provided a form of patrilineal sexual property.

kin group in which authority coincided with marital status as head of household and was perhaps further channeled by primogeniture or other inheritance rules. This was not necessarily an obstacle to capitalist industry, because the family enterprise was the rule throughout the early industrial revolution and even later. But it limited the impersonal operation of government, the necessary regulative framework for a market economy. As long as government was patrimonial (whether in the decentralized feudal or the centralized patrimonial-bureaucratic version), private and public property were confounded, and impersonal administration of laws and public finances was impossible.

A crucial development in the rise of capitalism had to be yet a further transformation of the family structure, in which the patrimonial household was broken down or at least separated from government administration. Here again the change worked from the outside in. Political and especially military factors – above all the development of professional standing armies supplied by a continuous and centralized administration – brought about the strengthening of the power of the state. The state then acted directly to break down the great patrimonial households by attacking the private armies of retainers who lived at the tables of the feudal lords (cf. Stone, 1967).[17] Of course, the Crown itself began as one patrimonial household among others, but the military revolution soon made it necessary to create a bureaucracy – literally, bureaus – that was not part of its own household and yet no longer merely delegated authority to subsidiary lords' households (which had been the essence of feudalism).

It is in the political sphere, then, that the crucial separation of work from the household first took place. One might say there was a two-stage decline of the organizational significance of the family. First, kinship itself was severely limited with the rise of the large household; then the patrimonial household was reduced as separate workplaces appeared. The development had to happen first in the sphere of the state: partly because a more impersonal form of the state was a necessary precondition for the rise of the market economy, and partly because the state itself exerted its force to shape family structure in the rest of society. As usual in Weber's approach, politics continues to be the major determinant of the family.

Once industrial capitalism was under way, to be sure, it further

---

[17] It is no wonder, then, that Laslett (1971:1–11) finds even aristocratic households in England in the late 1600s and the 1700s to be relatively small, rarely exceeding thirty persons. For it was the preceding Elizabethan state that had successfully campaigned to reduce or eliminate the military followings of the lords.

disintegrated the patrimonial household. But even this did not necessarily follow. Weber points out (1922/1968:377–80) that large capitalistic enterprises could be maintained in the form of households, especially where their prime asset was land or other property that was most effective economically (and brought the greatest prestige) if kept undivided. Such households might even become bigger, and kin ties remain strong, precisely where the family was most prosperous. Weber refers to his own dissertation (Weber, 1889) to point out that the laws of joint liability developed in this type of household enterprise were the basis for the later extrafamilial business corporation.

Nevertheless, political developments pushed in the other direction, away from the household enterprise. With the monopolization of violence by the state and the disarming of the household, the need for armed retainers disappeared, and the individual no longer had to look to the household and kinship group for protection. The fiscal interest of the state in a more intensive exploitation of the individual taxpayer resulted in legal changes, particularly in the area of inheritance. The separation of household and business accounts for legal purposes, Weber remarks, was the crucial difference between modern Western commercial law and that of classical antiquity; characteristically, the difference first manifested itself in the Middle Ages (Weber, 1922/1968:379).

This brings us to a final aspect of family structure: inheritance. The topic, of course, has been with us implicitly all along, since lineage structure is to a large extent a matter of inheritance. We have already noted that matrilineal and patrilineal structures in stateless societies are determined by the form of production – whether subsistence is largely male or female work – overlaid by the form of military organization (with matrilineality reinforced by a men's house form of barracks, patrilineality by self-equipped military aristocracy) (Weber, 1922/1968:370–2). With the decline of the clan, brought about by the hostility of the centralized state, the patriarchal household becomes predominant, and with it the unlimited power of the patriarch to dispose of property. But as Weber points out (1922/1968:372), the property law of the great empires moves toward steadily weakening patriarchal power. One reason is a political motive, as rulers attempt to reduce the concentration of power in the hands of potential rivals.

Connected with this is another important set of forces, in this case involving women. The unlimited patriarchal household is likely to be polygamous (which of course is restricted to the upper classes, who alone can afford it). The maximal power of the patriarch is when he has numerous wives and can choose who among his offspring will inherit. In this situation there is little distinction among wives, concubines, and slaves. Particularly in horticultural societies in which women are economically productive, the possession of many women is itself merely a form of wealth; in these societies, women are most likely to be acquired by paying a brideprice.[18]

In agrarian societies, however, women are no longer primary producers but (especially in upper-class families) more nearly mere luxuries, and the brideprice disappears. It tends to be replaced by the institution of the dowry, sometimes described as giving wealth as an incentive to another family to take the cost of maintaining a woman off one's hands. Along with this shift goes a clear differentiation among women, between primary and secondary wives and concubines; in some cases there is a shift to monogamy.

It has not been generally recognized how much of a puzzle this poses. Brideprice and dowry are formal opposites, to be sure, but the economic motivation in one is not merely the obverse of the other. When women are economically valuable, it makes sense for powerful men to pay for them. On the other hand, when women are no longer valuable, it does not follow that men would pay to give them away. After all, in extremely male-dominated societies, there is no reason why men should wish to incur any expense at all in connection with maintaining women; more logically, they could simply kill them off (through infanticide, which in fact is widely practiced in many such societies) until they are scarce enough so that others will pay for them merely for sexual purposes. One cannot invoke "natural" love among parents and children as an inhibition; the notion is anachronistic, and patriarchal agrarian societies have notably harsh and authoritarian emotional relationships within the family (Stone, 1977/1979:81–8).

The dowry, rather, shows something different. On the average, it cannot bring any economic gain; if families tend to have the same number of daughters as sons, what they give out in dowries should be received back (de facto if not de jure) when their sons marry. But in fact the dowry is vested as property in the married daughter, and even if sons get control of the dowries through their power as husbands, it is an intergenerational transfer and a diminution of the father's resources. (See Goody and Tambiah, 1973.) The significance of dowry, rather, appears to be in the realm of status. One can see that by comparing it with the brideprice. If a brideprice were offered today, it would be considered scandalous and demeaning to the woman, a form of prostitution. Dowry, the opposite situation, ap-

[18] This is sometimes euphemistically referred to a "bridewealth," a term that obscures the nature of the transaction.

pears to indicate the high status of women. Its vestige today exists in the custom in which the bride's father pays for the wedding ceremony; the more lavish the wedding, the more prestige attaches to the father. This is particularly notable in traditional rural sectors, where the number of guests entertained at a wedding is the primary way of displaying status. The dowry system thus appears as a kind of potlatch, a pure status competition among the weathier classes, emulated by those below to the extent they can afford it.

Weber adds another dimension. For the shift to the dowry system and the concomitant rise in the status of (upper-class) women goes along with notable changes in inheritance. We can see this in the differentiation of sexual partners into primary and secondary wives, concubines, and so forth. These status distinctions are primarily concerned with property. The primary wife is the one whose offspring are guaranteed inheritance, and so on through various gradations. The distinction becomes strongly made between legitimate and illegitimate children (Weber, 1922/1968:372): Contrary to Malinowski-type theories, this is not an historical constant but varies according to the relative strength of the patriarch vis-à-vis the families of his wives. The differentiation of the surrounding society into strata brings about a status interest in class endogamy, "according to which upper-class clans married their daughters only to equals and demanded that they receive a status superior to that of female slaves" (Weber, 1923/1961:52). The dowry is connected with a situation in which the woman's relatives stipulate in the marriage agreement that she should become head wife and that only her children should succeed as heirs. Weber stresses, in opposition to Engels, that the interest in legitimate heirs does not come from the father, who could have secured this in numerous ways, but from outside, from the woman's family. It is out of this claim that pressure was first set up in the direction of monogamy (Weber, 1923/1961:53).

Polygamy could be afforded only by the wealthy (at least in societies in which male work predominated), and monogamy long existed in the middle and lower classes, but out of economic necessity rather than preference. It became raised to an enforceable ideal first among the Hellenes and especially the Romans (Weber, 1922/1968:373–5). Weber sees it as evolving from the status system of the dowry, pointing out that the Egyptians distinguished legally between higher-status marriages, with dowry, and lower-status marriages, without (Weber, 1923/1961:53). Only the former had full legal protection of inheritance arrangements. Weber comments that Christianity later raised monogamy to a norm for ascetic reasons. I would suggest that we cannot simply take this for granted, however, as none of the other monotheistic or ascetic religions did so. Instead, we seem to have Christianity adopting and extending a Roman custom. It might be most accurate to say that monogamy developed out of the tendency to set one wife above other sexual partners in the status system of class-stratified and hence class-endogamous societies, the same societies that developed the dowry "potlatch."[19] This status system gave rise to an elaborated law of inheritance, which brought marriages within the provenance of the state and its fiscal interests; thus political as well as status pressures converged on enforcing monogamy.[20]

Women's position was thus sharply raised during the centuries of the agrarian state societies, from being a form of chattel, a "work animal" or a kind of domestic prostitute, to an individual of high status (provided her class status was high), even with certain independent economic rights. These developments did not all move in the same direction at the same time. In Ancient Rome, the woman arrived at the right of divorce and hence the right to dispose of her own property, but at the same time she had no power over her children, nor did she have protection as a widow (Weber, 1922/1968:373). In medieval England, the situation was almost the reverse; widows were maintained by a rent on family property but had no economic and legal independence of their husbands. Later, women's independent property rights (and hence liabilities) were recognized because of the capitalist need to protect creditors. Weber's somewhat cryptic remarks on the subject provide little more than a starting place for further investigation. Some efforts in this direction are the subject of the following chapter.

Appendix: The question of Iroquois matriarchy

Weber strongly argued that tribal societies, including matrilineal/matrilocal forms, are male-dominated and that the emancipation of

[19] It is consonant with this interpretation that the emphasis on the dowry was most extreme in classical India, where the caste system made the sharpest status distinctions. Even in this situation, only the higher castes can afford to give dowries (Goody and Tambiah, 1973:69).

[20] Goody (1983) investigates the question of the rise of the Western European family, which he sees primarily in terms of prohibitions on marriage with relatives (both close and distant), on widow remarriage, and on concubinage and other multiple marriages. All of these can be interpreted as prohibitions on classical strategies for ensuring heirs and continuity of family property. Goody argues that the Christian church forced these changes in order to receive inheritances for itself. He places the origins of the Western family in the 300s and 400s A.D., although it took more than half a millennium for the full rigor of church policy to take effect. This analysis places the emphasis on a different time period than what is implied in Weber, although it is stressing different aspects of a multisided situation. In general, Goody's emphasis on the economic politics of the Church seems in keeping with Weber's theoretical themes.

women begins only with the politics of the patrimonial, agrarian societies. The Iroquois are often cited as a counterexample to this type of generalization, the strongest instance known of female power in any tribal society. The Iroquois lived in longhouses, inhabited by a number of families related through the female line, and under a female ceremonial head. The Confederation of Iroquois tribes was headed by a council of men, but its members were nominated and replaceable by the senior woman of each longhouse. Tribal lands were regarded as the property of women. Brown (1970) and Blumberg (1984b) attribute Iroquois female dominance to the female basis of economic production (corn horticulture), Sanday (1981) to religious myths exalting women's productive place in the cosmos.

An alternative explanation is geopolitical. The Iroquois Confederation came into existence in the years between A.D. 1475 and 1570, as a result of the efforts of two (male) tribal diplomats to end the internecine wars among related tribes (Fenton, 1951; Ritchie, 1965; Goldenweiser, 1967). There had been prior confederations among the longhouse peoples, but these had always been unstable. The innovation of the new Confederation – which remained a major military force for more than two hundred years, even against the colonial powers – was precisely its use of female nominators of council members. The elevated political position of women arose with the Confederacy, not before; previously women had no more influence than was common in numerous other tribes centered on female horticultural production.

The political genius of the Iroquois Confederation seems to have been that it curbed the ambition of individual war chiefs. The requirement of unanimous decision by a council was one method of limiting individual power; the nomination of leaders, and veto powers on them, by women was another. Female political participation – which was nevertheless kept to the background – was a mechanism chosen by the males to prevent ambitious individuals from destroying the Confederation as in the past. The vesting of property and lineage membership in female lines was adopted as a political extension of the matri-centered local economy. Contrary to Sanday's (1981) claim that female fertility-nurturant mythologies produce female power, Iroquois culture in many respects was extremely macho. The Iroquois were unusually disciplined fighters (Otterbein, 1967), feared by their neighbors for their cannibalism and the practice of torture, which they regarded as an ordeal of honor. All these attributes are strongly reminiscent of the all-male warrior groups Weber described as typical tribal power centers. If in the case of the Iroquois Confederation, the politics did raise to a degree the political status of women, this should be regarded as the result of two geopolitical processes: (1) the tendency to make women the "home base" in a highly militarized situation that often took men away to distant wars (Ember and Ember, 1971) and (2) power struggle among males, resulting in a stalemate, in which situation women could be introduced as additional political actors. The latter process plays an important role in Chapter 12, in explaining historical rises in the status of women.

12

Courtly politics and the status of women

One of the most famous puzzles in the comparative study of the family is the case of the Nayar of south India. They practiced a form of plural mating that has led observers to question whether the Nayar had the family as conventionally defined at all. The importance of the Nayar case is not confined to questions of the universality or fundamental characteristics of the family. The Nayar family is one of a set of similar structures, and its analysis illuminates an important theme in family structure generally: its connection with politics. I shall attempt to show comparatively that the peculiarities of the Nayar family were due to its political circumstances. Moreover, a number of key developments in the history of the family have been brought about by political processes in the surrounding society. Such processes may even shed some light on the origins of the family structure that we associate with modern Western society, and of the position of women within it.

Comparative research on the family has relied heavily on anthropological materials about tribal societies. The Nayar are an anomaly in this context because they were not a tribe at all. They were part of an agrarian state society, literate and hence "historical," rather than one of the so-called historyless peoples. The Nayar were the warrior caste in the small Hindu kingdoms of the Malabar coast (Kerala). Marriages with the higher Brahman caste were crucial in establishing the Nayar family system; the Nayar life-style was supported by castes of peasant serfs and untouchable laborers below them. The Nayar family system has largely died out in modern times, surviving most recently in rural villages, where it has been fair game for anthropological fieldwork. But it originally had its heart in political capitals, the cities of Cochin and Calicut, which had populations of 25,000–60,000 during the medieval period (Chandler and Fox, 1974: 243, 246).

At first glance, the Nayar look even more out of place among agrarian state societies; most of these (India, China, Islam, ancient Greece and Rome) were rigidly patrilineal/patrilocal. Nevertheless there is at least one similar case. In Heian Japan (ca.A.D. 800–1200), residence was often matrilocal, descent was counted in both paternal and maternal lines, and possession of daughters was more important to a family's fortune than possession of sons; court men and women both had multiple sexual partners, and jealousy was disparaged. Heian society is a less extreme version of the family structure found among the Nayar but is similar enough to give us comparative leverage to find what features seem to be causally important and potentially generalizable.

This type of comparison has perhaps been overlooked because the Nayar have been treated as part of the anthropological literature along with other nonliterate and stateless societies. Despite their historical background, the Nayar resemble a tribal society because matrilineality, matrilocality, and corporate kin groups are characteristics usually found only in such societies. Many comparativists deliberately exclude agrarian state societies from their analyses, precisely because these "complex" societies are believed to introduce spurious relationships because of diffusion, outside influences, or imposed dominance structures. In my opinion, this is a false dichotomy. Tribal societies are not immune to external influences, and may even be constituted by them (Strathern, 1973). In actuality the anthropological literature is rarely consistent on what it calls a separate "society." Nor is "diffusion" a purely accidental contaminating agent that requires us to throw out certain data as tainted; it is the very nature of history itself. To exclude such cases is to base comparative family theory almost entirely on the small tribal societies that made up a tiny proportion of the total historical population of the world, and to ignore the family experience of 80 percent of the people who have ever lived.[1]

The result of excluding the historical agrarian family is that when sociologists look comparatively at their own society's family structure, their eye leaps directly from the complex "extended" family structure of tribal societies to the nuclear family of industrial society. It was this contrast that motivated Linton's (1936) classic distinction between "ascription" and "achievement," which most observers take as the main difference between industrial and preindustrial societies. In recent years, however, the blank space between illiterate tribes and the twentieth-century West has begun to be filled in by the emergence of a historical sociology of the family (e.g., Ariès, 1962; Ladurie,

---

[1] Members of tribal societies make up less than 2 percent of the approximately 43 billion persons who have lived in the last 10,000 years. Calculated from McEvedy and Jones, 1978:15, 342.

1976; Laslett, 1980). What it finds contradicts the view that industrialism is responsible for the rise of the nuclear family with all its
"modern" traits. Historical research finds the modern family almost
as far back as it has looked. Romantic love, emphasis on personal
happiness in choice of mates, economic power of women, and relative freedom of divorce have been found in the early 1800s and even
the 1700s in the North American colonies and early United States
(Lantz et al. 1968; Lantz, 1976). The nuclear family household, late
marriage for women, small age gap between the spouses and com-
panionate form of marriage were characteristic of England and northwestern Europe as far back as the 1600s and 1500s (Laslett, 1977).
Where, then, does the modern family begin? And if not because of
industrialism, why?

I submit that the Nayar-Heian comparison can contribute to an-
swering this question. In brief, the Nayar represent a type of "court
nobility" situation of marriage politics, as does more obviously the
Heian aristocracy. Agrarian state societies practice such politics because major political positions are hereditary. But such societies
should not be regarded as instances of "ascription" in the sense of
being static. In fact, people in such societies actively and consciously
schemed to get ahead. This could be done by advancing one's family
connections; the family patriarch, if successful, could reap the benefits of this *in his own lifetime.* The Nayar and Heian marriage politics
differ from those found in most agrarian states, but they reveal a
crucial mechanism affecting the sexual status of women. A similar
mechanism, I will conclude, may be responsible for the beginning of
the modern Western family structure in the courtly society of medieval Europe.

The Nayar puzzle

The Nayar were organized in exogamous matrilineages (Gough, 1959;
Mencher, 1965; Fuller, 1976). Each of these consisted of a number of
matrilocal households call *taravads*. The women lived together with
their children and brothers. Property was held in common under the
authority of the eldest male, the *karanavan*, and could not be divided.
The *taravad* was a large fortified household surrounded by walls or
moat, and usually containing twenty or more adults.

The Nayar combined two different kinds of marriages. The first,
was *tali*-tying ceremony, was held before a girl reached puberty, and
consisted of a ritual in which she was married and then in effect
divorced four days later. The *tali* marriage partner was always from a
particular other matrilineage, called *enangar*. Thus lineages were per-

petually linked through the hereditary relationship of giving *tali* partners to another; representatives of the *enangar* lineage were always invited to the Nayar household for important family ceremonies such as births and deaths.

After this childhood marriage-and-divorce, the Nayar woman was free to take a number of visiting husbands, called *sambandham*. The number of such husbands could be as many as a dozen, but more usually there were three or four regular *sambandham* husbands, plus temporary liaisons with Nayar soldiers passing through the area. There was no jealousy among the visiting husbands, who could have a number of *sambandham* wives in different lineages. There was a type of incest prohibition, in that sexual intercourse was not allowed among members of the same lineage, nor could two members of the same household share the same woman or man. Husbands visited their wives at night, often arranging schedules to avoid overlaps. The visiting husband placed his weapons outside the wife's bedroom door; another husband who saw them there might sleep outside on the veranda. When a woman became pregnant, one of her husbands usually acknowledged the child. This involved very little besides some small gifts; it had no effect on inheritance or lineage membership, since these remained strictly in the female line.

The Nayar caste did not comprise the only members of Malabar society. The foregoing description applies especially to the commoners, nonnoble subcastes of the Nayar. These rural lineages held land on feudal tenure from the headman's lineage, who in turn had received it from district chiefs, and they in turn from a royal lineage. The Nayar were professional soldiers and owed military service to their feudal superiors. They were frequently away from home, at least during the nonmonsoon season, training in the local gymnasium, fighting in incessant wars, or taking part in military ceremonies at the capitals. Below the Nayar were the castes of serfs and artisans who worked their property for them; above them were some small military castes of nobles, chiefs, and kings, and the wealthy landowning priestly caste of Namboodiri Brahmans. The Nayar themselves made up approximately 15 percent of the population.

The Nayar nobles and the higher non-Nayar castes also practiced Nayar-style marriage, with a particular emphasis upon hypergamy (female up-marriage) and a strict prohibition of hypogamy (female down-marriage). This was particularly strong among the Namboodiri Brahmans, who were divided into ten subcastes ranked by prestige. Unlike Brahmans elsewhere in India, the Namboodiri practiced strict primogeniture (Mencher, 1965:175). Only the eldest son was allowed to marry a Brahman woman and produce an heir to the family property. The younger sons visited Nayar women in *sambandham* relationships; elder sons might also have such relationships in addition to their Brahman wives. From the Brahman viewpoint, these were considered concubinage, although the Nayar considered them to be legitimate marriages. Because lineage passed in a strictly paternal line for the Brahmans, and in the maternal line for the Nayar, there was no loss of status for Brahmans in fathering Nayar children, whom they willingly acknowledged with the traditional birth gifts. But since the Brahman man was of a higher ritual rank than his *sambandham* wife, he could not eat in her house, nor could he touch her or his children during the daytime while he was in a state of ritual purity. The higher Nayar subcastes, when married to lower-ranking Nayar women, imitated the Brahmans in this pollution avoidance, confining their visits strictly to nighttime hours.

The entire Malabar society was permeated by rigid pollution rules that were considered by observers to be the most extreme in all of India. Caste rules regulated food, dress, style of houses, and all other aspects of life. Low-caste persons could use only certain paths, and their huts were in out-of-the-way places where they could not be seen. Only in Kerala did lower castes pollute not merely by touch but by approaching within a certain number of feet of a Brahman or a Nayar. Nayar warriors could kill a Pulaya on sight if they met a member of this low caste on the highway: an example that reminds us that the caste system was not merely upheld by beliefs. Because of this extreme caste-consciousness, Nayar women's sexual activities had to be strictly confined to identifiable caste members of equal or higher rank. Hence a woman who did not have the *tali* ceremony performed by puberty, linking her to an appropriate *enangar* lineage, lost caste. A Nayar woman who had a child that was not acknowledged by an appropriate man was assumed to have had intercourse with someone of lower caste (who might even be someone of a lower Nayar subcaste); the woman was punished by the entire *enangar* in a neighborhood assembly, was dismissed from caste and household, and could be sold as a slave.

Historical background

The Nayar family system has been described by anthropologists relying on informants in remote rural villages in the twentieth century, and appears to have been intact there until the late 1800s. According to European and Arab travelers, it appears to have flourished from the 1300s to the 1700s. It began to decline after Kerala passed into British control during 1792–1850.[2] Under pressure from

[2] Sir Richard Burton visited Zamorin's palace at Calicut in 1850 and reported: "We

the British (and also Moslem rulers on the northern edges of Kerala), who considered the Nayar marriage system decidely immoral, the *sambandham* marriage began to decline. Along with it, Nayar women lost many of their privileges and shifted toward the patriarchal domination characteristic of the rest of India.

Many observers, including the Nayar themselves, have noted the connection between the marriage system and the military situation of Kerala (Mencher, 1965:176). Before the advent of British-imposed peace, the Malabar coast was made up of many small states, in incessant warfare among themselves. Hence the men spent much of their time traveling to war while the women remained at home. This of course cannot be the whole explanation, since other parts of India also had incessant warfare without the Nayar type of family system. Geopolitical factors nevertheless are an important background. Kerala, the western coast of south India, is a narrow strip of very fertile land cut off from the rest of the continent by the Ghats, a rugged mountain range 8,000 feet high. Kerala is almost on the equator, and the climate is tropical with heavy rainfall. Lacking roads, wheeled vehicles, or pack animals, transportation through the jungle was extremely difficult. Although warfare was rife among local rulers, no extended kingdoms were ever created, no doubt due to the difficulties of logistics and communications. Compared to the rest of India, south India had an unusual degree of autonomy at the district and village level (Thapar, 1966:173). The Kerala kingdoms never expanded to conquer outside territories; alone in all of India, they were never incorporated into any northern or Deccan (central) conquest state (Davies, 1949).[3]

Kerala, then, was a situation of unusual political decentralization. At the same time, it was by no means a thinly populated tribal area, but an agrarian civilization. Cultivation of rice, coconuts, mangoes, plantains, and cotton supported the highest-density population in India. Moreover, Kerala's favorable location in relation to the trade winds of the Indian Ocean made its ports the principal entrepôts of Western trade, which was largely in the hands of Arabs. Medieval

---

were gratified to catch a sight of Nair female beauty. The ladies are very young and pretty – their long jetty tresses, small soft features, clear dark olive-colored skin, and delicate limbs – their *toilette*, in all save the ornamental part of rings and necklaces, was decidedly scanty." Quoted in Fuller, 1976:15.

[3] Although the history is obscure, it is possible that Kerala was nominally part of a south Indian empire based on Madras (the opposite, eastern coast) during A.D. 1000–1200 in the period immediately preceding the rise of the system under consideration here (Davies, 1949; Thapar, 1966:195–6, 334). Further evidence of its medieval isolation is the fact that Kerala developed its own language, Malayalam, from A.D. 1200 to about A.D. 1500.

Courtly politics and the status of women

Kerala had a higher volume of trade and more urban development than northern India (Thapar, 1966:328). Arabs, Jews, Christians, and others created a multi-ethnic environment. Kerala had an unusually high degree of literacy for a traditional society. Apparently virtually all Nayar men and most of the women could read and write Malayalam (Gough, 1968:146). Every Nayar child went through a ceremony of "first writing" at about age five (Mencher, 1965:186), indicating that writing had become a ritualized emblem of cultural status.

This situation, I would suggest, produced an interrelated complex of elements: chivalrous practice of warfare, extreme rank consciousness, and status competitiveness expressed in marriage politics. Foreign observers of medieval Kerala noted all three of these elements (Fuller, 1976:8–10). The Nayar were described as extremely proud and arrogant but also as courteous, warlike, and courtly. They always went armed and were involved in frequent altercations. Warfare was incessant, but because it never resulted in annexation of territory, it was carried out with elaborate rules of honor that made it a gentlemanly game.

Fighting took place only in daylight; in the morning, the opposed forces bathed together and chatted and joked, exchanging betel, until the battle was heralded by drums. The armies then formed up: a vanguard of swordsmen, a middle rank of archers and men armed with clubs, with lancers bringing up the rear. There was no cavalry. The armies advanced slowly, intermittently retreating. When ranks finally broke, a general bloody melee developed, inevitably resulting in many deaths and woundings. When sunset approached, the drums sounded the battle's end; it ceased at once. The antagonists again mingled together as they had done in the morning. [Fuller, 1976:8]

This chivalrous style of fighting is characteristic of geopolitical situations in which power is fragmented and large-scale conquests are not possible (Collins, 1981c:94–5).

Moreover, the extreme elaborateness of the caste system, with its many subcastes, sumptuary regulations, and minute gradations of prestige, also fits this situation. High degrees of status competition are characteristic of societies with decentralized power and a wealthy leisure class, and especially in multi-ethnic situations (Collins, 1977). Thus the very wide penetration of literacy among the Nayar fits the more general atmosphere of competition over cultural status.

The Nayar, then, were a courtly aristocracy in a wealthy but decentralized situation. Status competition took place primarily through marriage politics. But this competition was not a matter of prestige alone; it also provided the basis for alliances among families, which

303

were crucial to the political fortunes of families in this situation of constant warfare among shifting coalitions.

Among the higher Nayar, there was much rivalry among lineages (Gough, 1959:84). Political fortunes could rise and fall with a family's prestige. Important families placed great stress on marrying their daughters and sisters to men of higher subcastes, virtually never to equals. The royal lineages staked their prestige on having Namboodiri Brahmans (and especially high-ranking ones) father their kings. Both *sambandham* marriages and the *tali*-tying rites among *enangar* lineages were hypergamous, if a family could accomplish it. To fail to do so was to lose status, and hence political allies. Lower-ranking Nayar families, to be sure, were unable to keep up, and were forced to accept *sambandham* and *enangar* relationships with equals. The *tali*-tying ceremony was expensive, involving a four-day feast with entertainment for many guests and distribution of food to low-caste agricultural workers outside the gate (Mencher, 1965:171). Hence it constituted a potlatch-like display of wealth that only the higher ranking could easily afford. Wealthy Nayar might allow poorer families to present their daughters collectively at their own ceremony; this of course created both enhanced honor for the higher family, and obligations of loyalty on the lower that could be called on in military feuds.

The entire Nayar feudal system was thus tied together by marriage politics. Hypergamous unions and the *enangar* relationships "linked office-bearing lineages to each other and to their retainers in a complicated manner. And Nayar men phrased their loyalty to higher-ranking leaders, rulers and Brahmins in terms of a debt owed to benevolent paternal figures whose forebears had collectively fathered them and whose blood they were proud to share" (Gough, 1959:88). The system was highly dynamic, and an ambitious family could raise its status by cutting off prior equal-status *sambandham* marriages and permitting only hypergamous ones.

For this reason, although Nayar women had an unusual degree of sexual freedom as conventionally defined, they were nevertheless under strict control. *Sambandham* relationships were usually arranged by the woman's uncle; if the *karanavan* did not approve of a woman's husband, he could require her to dismiss him (Mencher, 1965:183–4). Women after puberty were restricted, rarely leaving the women's section of the house. Because these were fortified households, husbands could not reach their wives without the consent of her armed male relatives. Women in Nayar society were a crucial possession in the game of marriage politics, upon which the family's entire status (and its military connections) rested. It was more important for a man to have sisters, and for them to have daughters, than it was for he himself to have sons (Mencher, 1965:183).

How did the Nayar family system originate? Some observers have connected it with the survival of ancient matrilineal systems in south India, evidenced by the queens who ruled the Pandya states in the southeast (Thapar, 1966:103–5, 202). On the other hand, it has also been claimed that indigenous castes of Kerala had a patrilineal kinship system until matrilineal polyandry was forced upon them by the Namboodiri Brahmans from the 1100s onward (E. K. Pillai, cited in Fuller, 1976:121). It is not likely, however, that a family system was imposed by force. More probably it was the result of a process of marriage politics spread by emulation in the decentralized situation of status competition. The early kings and chiefs of Kerala encouraged the immigration of Brahmans by giving them tax-exempt land, while employing Brahmans to perform Vedic rituals supporting the kings' claims for status (Thapar, 1966:184). The Brahmans thus played a part in the initial phase of consolidation of small states of Kerala, under the stimulus of the new trading wealth; economic prosperity of the Malabar trading coast began at this time.

The existing tribal society was already organized into intermarrying lineages, the later *enangars*. As Dumont (1961) has pointed out, the *tali* ceremonies tie together lineages in much the same manner as cross-cousin marriage rules elsewhere in south India. And in fact the *tali* (a leaf-shaped emblem tied around the woman's neck) is the common symbol for marriage throughout south India. The Nayar marriage system seems to show two marriage systems superimposed one upon the other. The original *enangar* tribal alliance system, with its egalitarian tendencies, was relegated to the background once tribal society gave way to the highly stratified feudal society of the Middle Ages. It was reduced to a pro forma marking of the vestigial *enangar* alliance, together with a quick divorce, which allowed the woman freedom to contract further marriages (Unni, 1958:72).

The way in which the later *sambandham* came about, I would suggest, is by a process similar to that which we shall see in Heian Japan. The indigenous kings found it possible to raise their status by making their daughters concubines of the Namboodiri Brahmans. By stressing matrilocality and matrilineality, the Nayar retained control of the women and their children. This strategy fitted well enough with the status claims of the Brahmans, who would have refused regular patrilineal marriages with lower castes. A Nayar women could not have entered a Brahman's house. The system spread from the courts to the rest of the Nayar nobility and then into the lower nonnoble subcastes of Nayar. The process was not simply a trickle-down of cultural diffusion: It was an explicitly hypergamous system that emphasized vertical exchanges. As Tambiah (1973) has shown for the caste system generally, under a system of hypergamy status is not lost by men marrying down, whereas it can be gained by a woman's family as long as she marries up. The hypergamy of Indian kinship generally, introduced into Kerala by the Brahmans, combined with the extreme status competition of decentralized feudalism to favor the spread of the Nayar system of courtly marriage politics.

Marriage politics in Heian Japan

Heian Japan shows us in historical detail how a female-centered family system can develop as the result of deliberate political strategy, beginning at the top of society and spreading downward. From the late 700s A.D. onward, the Japanese Emperors came under the control of a series of regents of the Fujiwara clan (Sansom, 1958:139–42, 155–7; Morris, 1964:63–6). The prevailing practice was for adult emperors to abdicate in favor of a child, who was duly married to a daughter of the Fujiwara family. When he was old enough to have a son, he abdicated in turn. The head of the Fujiwara family thus usually had his own grandson on the throne, and during the emperor's minority exercised power as regent or sometimes in an even more behind-the-scenes capacity through the agency of figureheads holding official titles. Even adult emperors could be controlled by family influences through marriage politics.

The key to this system was the presence of attractive and intelligent daughters who could be married to the emperor, if not as official wife, then as favorite concubine. Although the official family structure was patrilineal and patrilocal, matrilineal and matrilocal elements were introduced into it as much as possible (Morris, 1964:59–60, 218–19; Frédéric, 1972:27, 46). Matrilocal residence was emphasized by the practice of having the Emperor live with his wife's family during his minority, and also during the frequent periods when the Imperial palace was destroyed by fire. (Such fires were often likely deliberate, as they were a common tactic in political infighting [Sansom, 1958: 169].) Furthermore, the woman returned to her parental home during menstruation and while giving birth, and usually stayed there while her child grew up. This bolstered the power of the patriarch over his Imperial relatives, by having them live in his own home.

This structure also emphasized the maternal line. Despite an apparent ancient period of matrilineality, Japan in historical times had a patrilineal family system, and male primogeniture was the inheritance rule (Frédéric, 1972:34). In these respects, medieval Japan was

306

similar to virtually all agrarian state societies. Nevertheless, the female line was stressed precisely because it was by this means that the Fujiwara regency was able to take effect. As a result, women acquired the rights to hold and inherit property in their own names (Morris, 1964:92, 217). This in turn made women even more valuable in marriage, and matri-centered marriage politics spread from the Imperial family itself to the surrounding aristocracy, and even into the provincial clans (Frédéric, 1972:47). In emulation of the Fujiwaras, matri-residences became the high-status form, and matrilineal descent was given a prominent place in the political connections of the aristocracy.

We see, then, a way in which royal marriage politics introduces matrilocality and matrilineality into a patrilocal and patrilineal family system. Heian Japan also developed two other features similar to the Nayar situation: elaborate status-ranking, and prevailing sexual affairs amounting to polyandry. Again this can be traced to the Imperial family itself. Polygamy was common among the Japanese aristocracy, as in other agrarian state societies. But given the matrilineal and matrilocal cast to Fujiwara marriage politics, this meant that concubines became equally important as an avenue to family power as legitimate wives. Fujiwara control did not come automatically, as other clans also attempted to practice marriage politics. The Fujiwara themselves tended to split into rival branches, each of which tried to produce heirs to the royal line (Sansom, 1958:160–3). To maximize family leverage, the claims of grandsons through Imperial concubines could be pressed. This gave an even greater prominence to the sexual element in politics as different claimants to control strove to have attractive daughters to whom a young adult Emperor would become especially attached.

This type of sexual politics extended into the entire structure of court positions. The Heian court aristocracy (both men and women) was divided into some thirty ranks and subranks, minutely graded by sumptuary regulations, forms of etiquette, and other privileges (Morris, 1964:78–83; Sansom, 1958:170). These rankings were not purely cultural; they carried with them access to powers of office, as well as graded stipends of riceland, the basis of the Heian economy. Acquiring such positions was the subject of incessant maneuvering among the courtiers, and for this purpose personal and family prestige were essential. Thus the aristocracy as a whole came to emphasize Fujiwara-style marriage politics. Daughters were more important than sons for a family that wished to rise or even to maintain its position in the court hierarchy, and a man's ranking might depend even more on his mother's rank than on his father's (Morris, 1964:219; Frédéric,

1972:33). This reversed the usual male-dominated status structure of agrarian state societies; Heian Japan was even more extreme than the Nayar in this respect.

This situation produced a version of polyandry. Unlike other agrarian states, in which aristocrats' women were typically guarded as exclusive sexual property in fortified harems, the matri-focal structure of Heian Japan tended to give women their own residences. Plural wives or concubines of the Emperor or other high officials usually had their own palace wings or detached residences, or lived with their own families, with the husband visiting each in turn (Morris, 1964: 232–5). Women with money could own their own houses and estates. Among the middle ranks of the aristocracy (or even higher), prestige could be acquired not only by marrying their daughters to high officials but also by having them serve as concubines or as courtiers (ladies-in-waiting) of high-ranking women. Especially among these unmarried (or divorced) women, there was a great deal of sexual freedom. Much time was spent in affairs, sending love poems with appropriate classical allusions, and preparing and commenting on the elaborate clothing worn by both men and women. There was great emphasis on one's status in the aesthetic rankings of court life, and having numerous and well-conducted sexual affairs was a major basis of prestige (Morris, 1964:237–9, 248). The man who did not have mistresses was regarded as provincial and even his wife would thereby be lowered in public esteem (Morris, 1964:250). Jealousy existed privately, to be sure, but its public expression was the most scorned of emotions; jealousy was even regarded as a spiritual evil and was an official ground for divorce (Morris, 1964:260, 298).

Multiple affairs on the part of women were less highly esteemed than those on the part of men, but were nevertheless tolerated and even to some extent admired.[4] Married women, as opposed to un-

[4] Sei Shonagon's diary gives a vivid example:

"It is dawn and a woman is lying in bed after her lover has taken his leave. She is covered up to her head with a light mauve robe that has a lining of dark violet; the colour of both the outside and the lining is fresh and glossy. The woman, who appears to be asleep, wears an unlined orange robe and a dark crimson skirt of stiff silk whose cords hang loosely by her side, as if they have been left untied. Her thick tresses tumble over each other in cascades, and one can imagine how long her hair must be when it falls freely down her back.

"Near by another woman's lover is making his way home in the misty dawn. He is wearing loose violet trousers, an orange hunting costume, so lightly coloured that one can hardly tell whether it has been dyed or not, a white robe of stiff silk, and a scarlet robe of glossy, beaten silk. His clothes, which are damp from the mist, hang loosely about him. From the dishevelment of his side locks one can tell how negligently he must have tucked his hair into his black lacquered head-dress when he got up. He wants to return and write his next-morning letter before the dew on the

married courtiers, were expected to be sexually faithful to their husbands (but not vice versa), but in court circles, at least, adultery was not taken as a serious offense. Given the prevalence of affairs, which usually took place in semidarkness behind the elaborate ceremonial screens of the women's quarters, it was not always clear who was mating with whom. The legitimacy of offspring was thus often questionable, even in the Imperial line itself (Frédéric, 1972:58–9; Morris, 1964:238–9). Such issues, however, were not given much public weight. Because of the de facto importance of the female line in Heian marriage politics, illegitimacy was never an important concern.

The degree to which this system depended on political considerations can be seen by comparison of the higher with the lower ranks of Japanese society. Among the farmers and the lower warrior families of the provinces, the family was strongly patrilineal, usually monogamous, and patrilocal.[5] Male sexual property rights were strongly emphasized and adultery was severely punished (Frédéric, 1972:42, 54–58, 66). Moreover, as the dominance of the Heian court eventually

morning glories has had time to vanish; but the path seems endless, and to divert himself he hums 'The sprouts in the flax fields.'

"As he walks along, he passes a house with an open lattice. He is on his way to report for official duty, but cannot help stopping to lift up the blind and peep into the room. It amuses him to think that a man has probably been spending the night here and has only recently got up to leave, just as happened to himself. Perhaps that man too had felt the charm of the dew. . . .

"The woman senses that someone is watching her and, looking up from under her bedclothes, sees a gentleman leaning against the wall by the threshold, a smile on his face. She can tell at once that he is the sort of man with whom she need feel no reserve. All the same, she does not want to enter into any familiar relations with him, and she is annoyed that he should have seen her asleep. . . .

"Now the gentleman leans further forward and, using his own fan, tries to get hold of the fan by the woman's pillow. Fearing his closeness, she moves back further back into her curtain enclosure, her heart pounding. The gentleman picks up the magnolia fan and, while examining it, says in a slightly bitter tone, 'How standoffish you are!'

"But now it is growing light; there is a sound of people's voices, and it looks as if the sun will soon be up. Only a short while ago this same man was hurrying home to write his next-morning letter before the mists had time to clear. Alas, how easily his intentions have been forgotten!

"While all this is afoot, the woman's original lover has been busy with his own next-morning letter, and now, quite unexpectedly, the messenger arrives at her house. The letter is attached to a spray of bush-clover, still damp with dew, and the paper gives off a delicious aroma of incense. Because of the new visitor, however, the woman's servants cannot deliver it to her.

"Finally it becomes unseemly for the gentleman to stay any longer. As he goes, he is amused to think that a similar scene may be taking place in the house he left earlier that morning." (*The Pillow Book of Sei Shonagon*, 1971:60–62. Original ca. A.D. 1000).

5 There were apparent matrilocal and matrilineal elements in the practice of families adopting a son-in-law if they lacked a son (Frédéric, 1972:46, 64); but this may be better interpreted as a means of continuing the paternal line. Expansion of the practice of adoption may be one basis of the nonkin group-loyalty system characteristic of modern Japan (Nakane, 1970).

gave way to the power of the feudal nobility and then to the Tokugawa military dictatorship, even the aristocracy shifted back toward a more typically agrarian patriarchal family system. The economic and inheritance rights of women disappeared, and women were forced into the highly subordinated position characteristic of Japanese society in more recent centuries (Dunn, 1972:44–6, 69–71, 173–4; Frédéric, 1972:63).

Historical development of the Heian system

The Heian family system represents a shift toward a matrilineal/local structure within a society that was patrilineal/patrilocal. It was true that there are indications of a matrilineal system in the remote background. Chinese visitors to Japan around A.D. 100 refer to a number of tribes under the jurisdiction of a queen, which has been interpreted as a matrilineal ruling house (Sansom, 1958:16–17). The official Shinto cult as it emerged by the 600 A.D. worshiped a sun goddess who is described as the ancestress of all the other gods, as well as of the Imperial house (Sansom, 1958:20–22). This may be related to matrilineal family systems of the Polynesian type. It is believed that Malayo-Polynesian mariners migrated to southern Japan in the last millennium B.C. (Eberhard, 1977:5–7), at the same time as their dispersion into Oceania. These were not the only peoples to colonize Japan, however, as Bronze Age Tungusic groups also migrated to Japan from Korea by 200 B.C. (Sansom, 1958:13). These various tribes eventually formed a federation, through a process of warfare and (if tribal precedents from elsewhere can be extrapolated [Lévi-Strauss, 1969]) kinship alliances. Matrilineal and patrilineal systems apparently clashed, as indicated by the myth that the sun goddess battled with her male relatives (Sansom, 1958:30–32; Nihongi, 1972:1–41). In the myth, the sun goddess prevailed; in actuality, a strictly male line of her descendants held the throne throughout historical times.

In the 400s and 500s A.D., military struggles were still going on among the rival clans. The clan chiefs of the more ancient lineages were priests of their own family cults. As the centralized Japanese state emerged, the Imperial House acquired absolute religious authority, but the earliest historical records show that it was already politically impotent, a figurehead controlled by nonroyal clans. It has been suggested (Sansom, 1958:55) that the unbroken reign of the Imperial family is primarily a result of its having reigned instead of ruled; it provided the ceremonial continuity of the Japanese state, whereas transitions of power always occurred unofficially and usually behind the scenes among the warring clans.[6]

[6] Japanese early clan structure is much like that of archaic Greece (Fustel de Cou-

Courtly politics and the status of women

As early as the 500s A.D., we find the system of royal marriage politics. A daughter of the Soga clan married to the Emperor initiated a series of Soga regents and child emperors. The one reigning queen in Japanese history since mythical times was a Soga woman (reigned 593–628), but it was during her nominal reign that her nephew Prince Shotoku served as regent and carried out the major reforms that introduced Buddhism into Japan and created a Chinese-style imperial bureaucracy (Sansom, 1958:50, 91). Thereafter the system of courtly marriage politics gradually spread to encompass the entire upper administrative class, reaching its height under the Fujiwara but continuing after their downfall in the 1100s.

At that time, a peculiar twist on the system of behind-the-scenes rule occurred: the reign of "cloistered Emperors" (Sansom, 1958:201–2). It was usual for a retired emperor to join a Buddhist monastery. He would likely be still a young man, while the reigning Emperor was a child. During the 1100s, emperors took advantage of gaps in the production of Fujiwara daughters to ally themselves with other countervailing clans, and to assert their own controls over government. Thus the retired Emperor would exercise control through his own son, the nominal Emperor. This constituted a reassertion of patrilineal control inside a system that was de facto matrilineal, if nominally patrilineal. But because several retired Emperors might be alive at the same time, rival behind-the-scenes rulers sometimes existed, and they too usually became pawns to clan leaders. Eventually military clans in eastern Japan established the Shogunate, a military headquarters that exercized real administrative control over the country. Even here, the system of marriage politics tended to insinuate itself. The Hojo clan controlled the Kamakura Shogunate for a time as regents by marrying their daughters to the nominal high official (Sansom, 1958:416–21). Still later the Ashikaga Shogunate established at Heian-kyo (Kyoto) itself produced multiple layers of behind-the-scenes rule. As the Japanese state lost centralized control to warring feudal lords after 1300, however, the importance of marriage politics diminished. With the recentralization of Japan under the Tokugawa Shoguns (1600–1850), the last vestige of Heian-style matri-families

langes, 1864/1980), where ancient families were organized as religious cults, and early kings were merely religious figureheads. A major difference is that the Greek tribes became organized into city-states; and in the cities kings often acquired despotic political powers with the support of the urban lower classes in their battles against the aristocracy. In Japan, the clans remained rural and became increasingly feudal; Heian-kyo, the capital, remained for a long time the only city of consequence, and one in which the lower classes had no military or political significance. Without counterbalancing class to support it, the Emperor remained at the mercy of the aristocracy.

was extinguished, replaced by a typically agrarian state system of patriarchal control.

Conclusions: courtly politics and the status of women in world history

The Nayar and the Heian systems are not identical, of course. But they have enough features in common for us to understand some of the tendencies toward matri-families within agrarian state societies. Both Heian Japan and medieval Malabar were far in the direction of a courtly system of political maneuvering, rather than strictly military determination of power. That is not to say that either of them was a peaceful society. The Nayar were in fact very highly militarized. But the geographical barriers that made Kerala impervious to outside conquest also meant that the localized form of state power was continuous and decentralized. Families could change their ranking by astute alliance-making, but only in terms of an autonomous prestige system that could not be arbitrarily imposed by a conquering king.

Similarly, Japan was geographically isolated from foreign attack (with the brief exception of the abortive Mongol invasions of 1274 and 1281). Japanese politics was often violent enough. Assassinations and armed uprisings took place even in the comparatively centralized Heian period. There were numerous unexplained deaths in the Imperial family, and the ever present danger of exile for courtiers accused of religious heresy or violation of the many superstitions and taboos (Sansom, 1958:151; Morris, 1964:136–52). But the sporadic and individualistic pattern of such conflicts illustrates the weakness of force as a systematic influence in Japanese politics; in its place arose a system of prestige competition in terms of autonomous standards. It is for this reason that both the Nayar and the Heian courtiers stand out from most agrarian state societies;[7] both had extremely developed systems of ranks with sumptuary regulations, taboos, and the like. In Malabar this was set within the terms of the Indian caste system, but elaborated in a much more extreme form than elsewhere in India. In Japan, it took the form of purely social and aesthetic snobbery. In actual practice, both came to much the same thing: a continuous competition among minutely described ranks manifested in styles of dress, ritualized manners, and sexual attractiveness.

Is there a wider significance of the Nayar and Heian cases? They

---

[7] Heian Japan is notable as one of the greatest periods of female cultural creativity in all of world history. At the height of the Fujiwara regime, female courtiers produced such works as Lady Murasaki's *Tale of Genji* and Sei Shonagon's *Pillowbook*, along with many others.

312

suggest the general principle that the status of women improves in periods of courtly status politics. Maneuvering over lines of succession emphasized matrilineal descent and inheritance, which in turn can become the basis for independent property rights held by women themselves. Prestige based on sexual alliances brings about greater sexual freedom for women, which is enhanced by matrilocal residence. This in turn can lead to a cult of female desirability and to aesthetic idealization of women.

The implication is that a political element must be added to any general theory of the status of women. Blumberg's theory (1978, 1984b), based on cross-cultural evidence, argues that the status of women depends largely on their contribution to, and control over, economic subsistence and on the relative labor supply of men and women. Neither Nayar or Heian aristocratic women contributed economically by their work. But Blumberg's theory implies that factors determining property rights are essential if working women are to reap social benefits from their economic contributions; the line of theory suggested here may be complementary to the economic theory in showing some of the autonomous dynamics of kinship politics that can bring about female property rights.

The historical pattern of the family is not a simple lineal evolution through a set series of stages. We have seen how matrilineal/local forms may be created (or re-created) within patrilineal/local systems. Similarly, when the conditions favoring courtly matri-politics disappear, the status of women may again shift to a situation of patriarchal domination. We see this pattern with the rise of military dictatorship in post-Heian Japan, and in Kerala after British domination.

Periods of courtly politics also occurred in Europe and may have played an important role in the rise of the modern Western family. This family system, with its bilateral kinship, love-based monogamous marriages, and relative autonomy of women, stands in sharp contrast to the strictly patriarchal family system of most agrarian state societies, including those of ancient Greece, Rome and much of early medieval Europe.[8] But we know that it existed in the West long

---

[8] Women in early medieval Germany and in the Frankish kingdoms had few economic rights and could not inherit land. Women were effectively property of husbands or fathers; high-ranking men (including Charlemagne) might be polygamous or own concubines (Bullough, 1973:154–7; Goody, 1976:18). In southern France and in Italy, the old Roman exclusive paternal rights remained strong. In Normandy, and presumably in the ancestral Viking lands of Scandinavia, women were excluded from inheritance (Ladurie, 1976). In Anglo-Saxon England, however, women could play a legal part in land transactions; these rights were diminished after the Norman conquest (Goody, 1976:15, 24, 30). In the lands of the Capetian monarchy around Paris, inheritance rights for women developed from the 1300s and 1400s (Ladurie, 1976).

before the rise of industrialism. I would suggest that it arose within agrarian states, precisely because of a period of intense, decentralized courtly status competition. The cult of courtly love, which began at noble courts in northern Spain and southern France during the 1100s and 1200s (Bullough, 1973:181–3) may be due to dynamics similar to the Heian and Nayar situations.

The development of the Western family from the High Middle Ages onward is not a linear pattern but intermittent periods of gains and declines in female status. The crucial development of medieval courtly politics, I suggest, was that it emphasized female lines of inheritance and descent. The original purpose was for dynastic politics, by which kingdoms, but also the properties of dukes and other higher noblemen, could be acquired through strategic intermarriages, even by the woman-giving line. This led to the institutionalization of property rights vested in women themselves. These legal rights survived even after the decline of specifically courtly situations. Furthermore, although such legal rights were initially established for the benefit of the aristocracy, they could also be applied to women of the middle classes. The fact that women could be heirs in their own right, whether of landed estates or of middle-class businesses, meant that they acquired a special value in the individually based marriage markets that emerged with commercial and urbanized societies. It is this special economic value of women that is behind the distinctively Western style of courtly politeness to women, and it also contributed to the love-match ideal that went along with the rise of the individual marriage market (Collins, 1971).

In conclusion let us consider a somewhat paradoxical point. The institutionalization of female property rights and the rise in the status of women begin with the aristocracy and depend on periods of highly rank-conscious, snobbish status competition. For this reason, periods of democratic politics have often tended to be harshly antifeminist. The most extreme period of the subjugation of women in ancient Greece, for example, was during the time of Athenian democracy; the rights of women were much more extensive in conservative Sparta (Pomeroy, 1975:59–73, 80). The reason was perhaps that the male democracy of Athens found the wealth and lavish display of aristocratic women an especially easy target for their attacks on aristocracy. Conversely, it was after the downfall of Greek democracy, in the strictly hereditary kingdoms of the Hellenistic period, that women acquired rights to hold independent property (Pomeroy, 1975:121–7, 130–1). Here we can trace the role of marriage politics as Hellenistic kings attempted to set their own grandchildren on the thrones of neighboring kingdoms by marrying away their daughters (Pomeroy, 1975: 121–3).[9]

This suggests a major problem in the spread of women's rights generally. The cutting edge of women's rights has usually been in the upper classes. For such rights to become general they must spread downward to the middle and lower classes. The mechanisms of status emulation and legal universalism can help produce such a downward spread. At the same time, democratization tends to mobilize attacks on the privileges and innovations of upper-class women. This pattern has been seen recently in the sexual conservatism and anti-feminism that have been rallying points for the mass movements of the revolutionary Khomeini regime in Iran. The conditions for the spread of women's rights appear to require a complex balance of political and social equality and inequality.

Appendix: Moral politics in ancient Rome

The shifting rights of women during the history of ancient Rome (Friedlander, 1908–13; Carcopino, 1940; Pomeroy, 1975) show another aspect of this political process: that the liberalization of women's rights can accompany a "liberal" movement in male politics, and that conservative reactions can take place simultaneously in both spheres. In this case, we are dealing with far more "democratic" and "mass" politics than in the courtly politics considered earlier. And the Roman instance shows a more deliberate effort to change the family. At least on the conservative side, this took the form of a "politics of morality" not unlike the tone of family traditionalists in the United States in the late twentieth century.

We can distinguish at least three periods of controversy over the Roman family. The most recent was during the reign of Domitian (A.D. 81–96), when Juvenal wrote his scathing satires on the looseness of Roman women, stressing the prevalence of adultery and licentiousness among the rich, and Tacitus compared Roman wives unfavorably to German ones. This image of moral decay has colored our historical image of Roman society, although as we shall see, it is more reasonably attributed to the "moral politics" of the time.

Earlier, during the reigns (27 B.C.–A.D. 37) of the first Emperor, Augustus, and his successor, Tiberius, there was a determined effort

---

[9] It is in this period that the romantic love-story appears in Greek literature, paralleling the ideological glorification of women in medieval European courtly love poems (Hadas, 1950:189–90, 201–10, 223, 291–8).

to reestablish what was regarded as the traditional family. Laws were promulgated requiring all men to marry by age twenty-five and all women by age twenty; penalties were set for failure to remarry after widowhood or divorce; incentives in the form of improved legal status were given to women (both slaves and free women) who bore more than three children. Augustus Caesar himself tried to restore the old-fashioned virtue of women staying at home spinning wool, by setting the ladies of the imperial household to work and even wearing their homespun clothes (somewhat comparable to U.S. President Jimmy Carter's turning out lights in the White House to save electricity during an oil crisis). Traditional religious cults of the female virtues (chastity, loyalty, fertility) were reestablished, and nonfamilistic foreign cults, such as the worship of Isis, were suppressed. Moreover, because the principal historians and poetic chroniclers of the earlier period – Livy and Virgil – were part of Augustus's propaganda machine, their contrasting picture of the ideal Roman family of early, "nondegenerate" times has covered up the reality of what the ancient family had actually been like.

The earliest period of "moral politics" took place between the beginning of the great showdown war with Carthage (216–202 B.C.) and the war that broke the Macedonian power and gave Rome effective control of Greece (171–168 B.C.). This period of forty-five years has the appearance of a major struggle between the sexes inside Rome, at the same time that the Roman army went from fighting for its life to clear hegemony of the Mediterranean world. Rome's defeat by Hannibal in 216, the worst it ever suffered, actually left Roman women in a temporarily strengthened position. With the loss of so many males, women were emboldened to enter the political arena and entreat the Senate to ransom prisoners (which it refused to do). The slaughter also left many women as heiresses to family property. The Senate reacted by passing the Oppian Laws (215 B.C.), which prohibited public display of wealth by women and confiscated much of their property for the war fund. In 195 B.C., after the war had been won, women demonstrated successfully for the repeal of the Oppian Laws, despite the opposition of the famous reactionary misogynist Cato the Elder. But the war of the sexes was not over. Nine years later, thousands of women (and men as well) were executed for participating in the Bacchic rites imported from Greece. These rites were reportedly orgiastic, but that may have been exaggerated by the propaganda of moral politics. In any case, it was an attack on women who dared to join an organization outside the family and its traditional rites. Two years later, in 184 B.C., Cato, who had been elected Censor, confiscated jewels and other displays of luxury on the part of women. And in 169 B.C., during the victorious war with the Macedonians, the Voconian Law was passed, severely restricting the right of women to inherit.

All these were political efforts to control the shape of the family. One might question, though, whether they were effective. Despite the Oppian and Voconian legislation, women continued to acquire wealth and to display it lavishly; indeed, after the conquest of Greece, upper-class Roman families had become opulent, owning huge estates and many slaves. Hence one might conclude that these political efforts – as well as the reactionary romanticism of Augustus and the later criticisms at the time of Domitian – illustrate more than anything the impotence of the state to affect the drift of the family caused by deeper forces. But this, I argue, is a simplistic view of politics. One can say that politics is like a game of billiards: One rarely gets what one is directly aiming at; the outcomes usually happen on the rebound, and more than likely involve ricochets of several forces, combining to produce an unforeseen vector of their own.

Let me illustrate first by examining certain aspects of the Roman family where the effects of politics are fairly clear. Roman law gave severe control over family members, and especially women, to the *pater*, the male head of the family, or to some other male guardian. This included the power to kill a wife or daughter for certain offenses, including not only adultery but also drinking wine. He also had sole power of divorce, not only over his own wife but over the wives of his children. This seems to be a case where the family is completely autonomous of the state. But not so. For one thing, the state itself established and upheld this law. In the case of the women condemned for participation in the Bacchic rites in 186 B.C., it was the state that pronounced the condemnation and then handed them over to their families for execution. (The severe prohibition against the drinking of wine by women, incidentally, may perhaps derive from either this incident or a similar cast of moral politics.) Moreover, the state at various times set express limits on what the *pater familias* could do. Although under early law a wife was the absolute property of such a man, and hence could be sold into slavery, later laws decreed that a man who actually sold his wife would be executed and his property confiscated. This sounds like a legal contradiction, but it merely indicates political conflict. A different political faction was now intent on breaking the power of the *pater familias,* and we get some inkling of who they were by the provision that the confiscated property went half to the woman, half to the temple of Ceres, whose guardians happened to be the leading politicians of the plebeian faction. Similarly, later political interventions acted to restrict the uni-

317

lateral power to divorce or punish family members: in the interest sometimes of the wife's family, sometimes of the larger group of kinsmen *(gens)*.

Another example shows the indirect effect of state policies on the family. The law stated that the *pater* should decide whether newborn infants should be raised or exposed to die, but it also stipulated that all males should be raised but only the firstborn female. In the late Republic, the political policy of maintaining the poorer classes on a dole of bread applied only to males, because females were not voters and their support was not solicited. These policies seem to have produced a decidedly skewed sex ratio, which in turn reinforced a family structure in which all females were married. We might also notice the effect of slavery, a politically determined institution, on the family. This affected the structure of upper-class, slave-owning families, where strict regulations allowed some sexual access of males to slaves and set an equally strict prohibition regarding upper-class females. The structural contradiction between the property and status system and the ubiquity of slaves (again, the majority of whom were male) is certainly behind much of the denunciations of women in the moral politics of the Juvenalian type. The types of family structures possible among the slaves themselves were even more sharply determined by the laws regulating slavery.

The family structure of a society is never static, and it is inaccurate to speak of "the Roman family" as if there were only a single such entity. Political change alone is enough to determine that the family will have a history. In the case of the Roman family, these changes were intimately connected with the shifting forms of politics. The classic account of this remains that of Emile Durkheim's teacher Fustel de Coulanges (1864/1980). Initially, the family was organized politically around a domestic cult dominated by the *pater* as priest. Like other ancient cities, Rome was formed as a civic cult, a coalition of the heads of the family cults. The result was an oligarchy of family heads exclusively possessing political and legal rights. Subsequent Roman political history took the form of a series of revolutionary movements, as the clients (junior family members and collateral branches) and then the plebeians (alien migrants who lacked family cults) pressed for admittance into the ruling institutions of the state. In Rome, the most conservative of the ancient cities, the earlier revolution of the clients was relatively successful, but the plebeians acquired only limited concessions.

What looks at first glance like a war between the sexes in Roman politics is actually entwined in this factional history. The struggle during and after the Second Punic War (between the Oppian and

Voconian legislation, and including the purges of the Bacchic rites) did not simply pit women against men, but pitted women with the support of a male political faction against the defenders of the old-line family structure, which was in turn an agency of oligarchy among males as well. Women evaded restrictive legislation and gradually acquired property, not because politics was weak against other forces but because those other forces were themselves political, the rise of a democratic faction.

When the ritual-based family cult was in force, marriage took the form of *manus*, a ceremony in which the bride was transferred from the religion of her father to that of her husband's family. The political structure built on this cult, as we have seen, was gradually widened and broken down by successive revolutions, although the conservative faction in Rome clung to it longer than in the more democratic cities of Greece. After the Punic wars, though, the family cult no longer corresponded to any political reality and was kept alive merely as a kind of ideological self-identification for a faction that actually operated in an entirely different political arena. The new political realities did foster a different type of marriage. In place of *manus*, marriage now came to be arranged by a kind of legal fiction, as if it were a tentative agreement between the families, in which the woman (and her inheritance rights) actually remained in the hands of her father. At the same time, divorce became much easier and could be initiated from either side.

What was the point of this? Amid the factional politics and civil wars of the late Republic, intermarriage was a principal form of alliance. The household, now swollen by enormous wealth and the patronage of the leading politicians, remained the organizational basis of politics. Hence, party alliances were necessarily interhousehold alliances. Pompey, Sulla, Caesar, Antony, Octavian – all were multiply married, since divorces were necessary in order to break up alliances and keep up the rapid flow of political maneuver. This is one reason why the woman's family kept up active ties with her rather than handing her over exclusively to her husband's family, as in the older form. A married woman could even be ordered by her father to divorce her husband when political alliances shifted.

Amid these clashing billiard balls of politics, an unintended result was that upper-class Roman women's status and power rose. The political maneuver gave increasing property rights to the female line, which might vest in a woman herself under certain circumstances (such as male deaths). Some women, such as Antony's first wife, Fulvia, took advantage of the shifting alliances to play politics on their own behalf and became personages of some influence. (They were fiercely hated by their political opponents, who were the source of much misogynist propaganda.) Women also acquired fame because of their prominence in these family alliances; early in his career, Julius Caesar first made a notable impact by the innovation of delivering a public funeral oration for his female relative, through whom he was related to the popular general and politician Marius. Later, women of the imperial family were deified, along with their husbands and fathers—again, as part of the political package.

The propagandistic and legal reaction of the early Empire in favor of an idealized traditional family must be seen in the context of the politics that preceded. Augustus and Tiberius were attempting to bring to an end the factional politics of the period of the civil wars. They and their propagandists attempted to discourage divorce because divorce had been a major part of the mechanism of factional alliance. In attacking the fluid family structure, they were attacking the main instrument of upper-class politics. The moral politics of Augustus was part of the effort to consolidate the power of imperial rule. Ostensibly, the policy was aimed at overcoming the moral degeneracy of the age, combating the bachelorhood that had become quite common, and promoting fertility and hence manpower for the Roman army. But army manpower can hardly have been the issue in the laws to compel marriage, since in fact this was not a time of military crisis; conversely, such legal expedients had not been resorted to earlier when military demands were much more severe. We are instead in the realm of moral politics, with its symbolic issues designed to stir up emotional legitimacy for a policy whose real object is to undermine the structures that mobilized its enemies.

Later in the Empire, the legal structure of the family shifted again. The law of inheritance changed so that a woman was again a member more of her husband's family than of her father's. Attacks on women's dissoluteness and freedom continued, especially in the reign of Domitian. The reasons for this are not readily apparent, but we can see the atmosphere of moral politics of the time from the fact that the Emperor instituted trials of some of the Vestal Virgins for unchastity. These women were daughters of high-ranking families, who officiated at the civic cult of Rome. The cult's origins went back to the early interfamily coalition that founded the city, and it had long since lost its political religious significance. Thus the ritually prescribed chastity of the Vestals was for the most part a dead letter, despite the severe penalties (scourging, being buried alive) for violations. Domitian or the political cliques surrounding him, however, found some moral legitimacy to be gained by claiming to revive the old rules and carrying out dramatic punishments. That this was an aspect of the factional politics of the time can be inferred from the fact that earlier such prosecutions (114–13 B.C. in the period of the "social wars," 73 B.C. in that of the Cataline conspiracy) were selectively directed against alleged lovers of the Vestals who were active in the leading political conflicts of the time. Again in the period A.D. 190–220, there was an upsurge of anti-abortion legislation under the banner of the restoration of the traditional family. What caused this particular upsurge of moral politics can only be guessed at.

References

Adcock, F. E. 1957. *The Greek and Macedonian art of war*. Berkeley: University of California Press.

Adorno, Theodor. 1953/1977. "Zeitlose mode. Zum jazz." In *Gesammelte Schriften*, volume 10. Frankfurt: Suhrkamp.

Aldrich, Howard. 1979. *Organizations and environments*. Englewood Cliffs, N.J.: Prentice-Hall.

Althusser, Louis. 1969. *For Marx*. New York: Random House (Vintage Books).

Andreski, Stanislav. 1968. *Military organization and society*. Boston: Routledge & Kegan Paul.

Arberry, A. J. 1950. *Sufism*. London: Allen & Unwin.

Ariès, Phillippe. 1961. *Centuries of childhood*. New York: Random House.

Barraclough, Geoffrey (ed.). 1979. *The Times atlas of world history*. Maplewood, N.J.: Hammond.

Bartholomew, John. 1954. *Physical world atlas*. New York: American Map Company.

Baynes, N. H. 1929. *Constantine and the Christian Church*. New York: Oxford University Press.

Bebel, August. 1892. *Die Frau und der Socialismus*. Stuttgart: J. H. W. Dietz.

Bellah, Robert N. 1957. *Tokugawa religion*. New York: Free Press.

Bellwood, P. S. 1981. The peopling of the Pacific. *Scientific American*: 174–85.

Bendix, Reinhard. 1960. *Max Weber: An intellectual portrait*. New York: Doubleday.

　　1967. Tradition and modernity reconsidered. *Comparative Studies in Society and History* 9: 292–346.

　　1978. *Kings or people: Power and the mandate to rule*. Berkeley: University of California Press.

　　and Roth, Guenther. 1971. *Scholarship and partisanship: Essays on Max Weber*. Berkeley: University of California Press.

Bergesen, Albert James. 1977. Political witch hunts: The sacred and the subversive in cross-national perspective. *American Sociological Review*: 222–32.

　　1982. Rethinking the role of socialist states in the capitalist world economy. In Christopher K. Chase-Dunn (ed.), *Socialist states in the capitalist world-economy*. Beverly Hills, Calif.: Sage.

　　1984. The critique of world-systems theory: Class relations or division of labor? *Sociological Theory 1984*. San Francisco: Jossey-Bass.

323

References

Beveridge, Andrew. Unpublished manuscript. New York, Columbia University Department of Sociology.

Blauner, Robert. 1964. *Alienation and freedom*. Chicago: University of Chicago Press.

Bloch, Marc. 1961. *Feudal society*. Chicago: University of Chicago Press.

Blumberg, Rae Lesser. 1978. *Stratification: Socioeconomic and sexual inequality*. Dubuque, Iowa: William C. Brown.

——— 1984a. Personal communication.

——— 1984b. A general theory of gender stratification. In *Sociological Theory 1984*. San Francisco: Jossey-Bass.

Böhm-Bawerk, Eugen von. 1896/1949. *Karl Marx and the close of his system*. New York: Augustus Kelley.

Borkenau, Franz. 1981. *End and beginning: On the generations of cultures and the origins of the West*. New York: Columbia University Press.

Bortkiewicz, Ladislas von. 1907. Wertrechnung und Preisrechnung im Marxschen System. *Archiv für Sozialwissenschaft und Sozialpolitik 24*.

Boulding, Kenneth. 1962. *Conflict and defense*. New York: Harper & Row.

Bourdieu, Pierre, and Passeron, Jean-Claude. 1970/1977. *Reproduction: In education, society, and culture*. Beverly Hills, Calif.: Sage.

Bousquet, Nicole. 1979. Esquisse d'une Théorie de l'altérnance de périodes de concurrence et d'hégémonie au centre de l'économie-monde capitaliste. *Review* 2 (Spring): 501–17.

Braudel, Fernand. 1967/1973. *Capitalism and material life, 1400–1800*. New York: Harper & Row.

Braverman, Harry. 1974. *Labor and monopoly capital*. New York: Monthly Review Press.

Brown, Judith K. 1970. Economic organization and the position of women among the Iroquois. *Ethnohistory* 17: 131–67.

Brown, Peter. 1972. *Religion and society in the age of Saint Augustine*. London: Faber & Faber.

——— 1982. *Society and the holy in late antiquity*. Berkeley: University of California Press.

Browning, Robert. 1976. *The Emperor Julian*. Berkeley: University of California Press.

Bullough, Vern L. 1973. *The subordinate sex: A history of attitudes towards women*. Urbana: University of Illinois Press.

Burger, Thomas. 1976. *Max Weber's theory of concept formation*. Durham, N.C.: Duke University Press.

Burt, Ronald S. 1982. *Toward a structural theory of action*. New York: Academic Press.

——— 1983. *Corporate profits and cooperation: Networks of market constraints and directorate ties in the American economy*. New York: Academic Press.

Calhoun, Craig. 1982. *The question of class struggle*. Chicago: University of Chicago Press.

Carcopino, Jerome. 1940. *Daily life in ancient Rome*. New Haven, Conn.: Yale University Press.

Chadwick, Henry. 1967. *The early Church*. New York: Penguin Books.

Chan, Wing-tsit. 1963. *A sourcebook in Chinese philosophy*. Princeton, N.J.: Princeton University Press.

324

References

Chandler, Alfred D. 1962. *Strategy and structure*. Cambridge, Mass.: MIT Press.

Chandler, Tertius, and Fox, Gerald. 1974. *Three thousand years of urban growth*. New York: Academic Press.

Chattopadhyaya, Debiprasad. 1969. *Indian philosophy*. Delhi: People's Publishing House.

Ch'en, Kenneth. 1964. *Buddhism in China*. Princeton, N.J.: Princeton University Press.

Chew, Allan F. 1967. *An atlas of Russian history*, New Haven, Conn.: Yale University Press.

Clark, Terry Nichols. 1973. *Prophets and patrons: The French university and the emergence of the social sciences*. Cambridge, Mass.: Harvard University Press.

Clem, Ralph S. 1980. The ethnic dimension. In Jerry G. Pankhurst and Michael Paul Sacks, (eds.) *Contemporary Soviet society*. New York: Praeger.

Clubb, O. Edmund. 1971. *China and Russia*. New York: Columbia University Press.

Cohen, Jere. 1980. Rational capitalism in Renaissance Italy. *American Journal of Sociology* 85:1340–55.

Hazelrigg, Lawrence E., and Pope, Whitney. 1975. De-Parsonizing Weber: A critique of Parsons' interpretation of Weber's sociology. *American Sociological Review* 40: 229–41.

Cohen, Mark. 1977. *The food crisis in prehistory: Overpopulation and the origins of agriculture*. New Haven, Conn.: Yale University Press.

Collins, John M., and Cordesman, Anthony H. 1978. *Imbalance of Power: An analysis of shifting U.S.-Soviet military strengths*. London: Presidio Press.

Collins, Randall. 1971. A conflict theory of sexual stratification. *Social Problems* 19: 2–21.

1975. *Conflict sociology*. New York: Academic Press.

1977. Some comparative principles of educational stratification. *Harvard Educational Review* 47: 1–27.

1978. Some principles of long-term social change: The territorial power of states. In Louis Kriesberg (ed.), *Research in social movements, conflicts, and change*, volume 1. Greenwich, Conn.: JAI Press.

1979. *The credential society: An historical sociology of education and stratification*. New York: Academic Press.

1981a. "On the Micro-foundations of Macro-sociology," *American Journal of Sociology* 86 (March), 984–1014.

1981b. *Sociology since midcentury: Essays in theory cumulation*. New York: Academic Press.

1981c. Long-term social change and the territorial power of states. In *Sociology since midcentury: Essays in theory cumulation*. New York: Academic Press.

1981d. Three faces of cruelty: Toward a comparative sociology of violence. In *Sociology since midcentury: Essays in theory cumulation*. New York: Academic Press.

1981e. Lévi-Strauss' structural history. In *Sociology since midcentury: Essays in theory cumulation*. New York: Academic Press, pp. 109–32.

References

1981f. Crises and declines in credential systems. In *Sociology since midcentury: Essays in theory cumulation*. New York: Academic Press.

1981g. Micro-translation as a theory-building strategy. In K. Knorr-Cetina and A. V. Cicourel (eds.), *Advances in social theory and methodology: Toward an integration of micro- and macro-sociologies*. Boston: Routledge & Kegan Paul.

1985. *Max Weber: A skeleton key*. Beverly Hills, Calif.: Sage.

Conze, Edward. 1969. *Buddhist thought in India*. Ann Arbor: University of Michigan Press.

Das Gupta, S. N. 1963. *History of Indian philosophy*. Cambridge University Press.

Davies, C. Collin. 1949. *An historical atlas of the Indian Peninsula*. New York: Oxford University Press.

Davis, John P. 1904/1961. *Corporations*. New York: Capricorn.

Davis, Kingsley. 1949. Jealousy and sexual property. In *Human Society*. New York: Macmillan, pp. 175–94.

De Bary, William Theodore (ed.). 1969. *The Buddhist tradition in India, China and Japan*. New York: Random House.

d'Encausse, H. C. 1979. *Decline of an empire: the Soviet Socialist Republics in revolt*. New York: Harper & Row.

Doran, Charles F., and Parsons, Wes. 1980. War and the cycle of relative power. *American Political Science Review* 74: 947–65.

Douglas, Mary. 1973. *Natural symbols*. New York: Penguin Books.

Dumont, Louis. 1961. Les mariages Nayar comme faits Indiens. *L'Homme* 1: 11–36.

1970. *Homo Hierarchicus. The caste system and its implications*. Chicago: University of Chicago Press.

Dumoulin, Heinrich. 1963. *A history of Zen Buddhism*. Boston: Beacon Press.

Dunn, Charles J. 1972. *Everyday life in traditional Japan*. Tokyo: Tuttle.

Durkheim, Emile. 1892/1960. *Montesquieu and Rousseau*. Ann Arbor: University of Michigan Press.

1910. Review of Marianne Weber, *Ehefrau und Mutter in der Rechtsentwicklung*. *L'Année Sociologique* 11: 363–9. Reprinted in Emile Durkheim, *Journal Sociologique*. Paris: Presses Universitaires de France, 1969, pp. 644–9.

Eberhard, Wolfram. 1965. *Conquerors and rulers: Social forces in medieval China*. Leiden: E. J. Brill.

1977. *A history of China*. 4th ed. Berkeley: University of California Press.

Edge, David O., and Mulkay, Michael J. 1976. *Astronomy transformed*. New York: Wiley.

Edwards, I. E. S., Gadd, C. J., and Hammond, N. G. L. 1970. *The Cambridge ancient history*. 3rd ed. Volume 1, part 1. Cambridge University Press.

1971. *The Cambridge ancient history*. 3rd ed. Volume 1, part 2. Cambridge University Press.

and Sollberger, E. 1973. *The Cambridge ancient history*. 3rd ed. Volume 2, part 1. Cambridge University Press.

1975. *The Cambridge ancient history*. 3rd ed. Volume 2, part 2. Cambridge University Press.

ade, Mircea. 1962. *The forge and the crucible*. London: Rider.

References

Elvin, Mark. 1973. *The pattern of the Chinese past*. London: Methuen.

Ember, Melvin, and Ember, Carol. 1971. The conditions favoring matrilocal vs. patrilocal residence. *American Anthropologist* 73: 571–94.

Emmanuel, Arghiri. 1972. *Unequal exchange*. New York: Monthly Review Press.

Engels, Friedrich. 1884/1972. *The origin of the family, private property and the state*. New York: International Publishers.

Farrington, Benjamin. 1953. *Greek science*. New York: Penguin Books.

Fenton, William N. 1951. Locality as a basic factor in the development of Iroqouis social structure. In *Symposium on Local Diversity in Iroquois Culture*. Washington D.C.: Smithsonian Institution.

Festugiere, A. J. 1967. *Hermetisme et Mystique Painne*. Paris: Aubier-Montaigne.

Fieldhouse, D. K. 1966. *The colonial empires*. London: Weidenfeld & Nicolson.

Finley, M. I. 1973. *The ancient economy*. Berkeley: University of California Press.

Flannery, Kent. 1973. The origins of agriculture. *Annual Review of Anthropology* 2: 270–310.

Foley, Vernard, and Soedel, Werner. 1981. Ancient oared warships. *Scientific American* 244 (April): 148–63.

Forbes, R. J. 1950. *Metallurgy in antiquity*. Leiden: E. J. Brill.

Franke, W. 1960. *The reform and abolition of the traditional Chinese examination system*. Cambridge, Mass.: Harvard University Press.

Frazer, James G. 1910. *Totemism and exogamy*. London: Macmillan.

Frédéric, Louis. 1972. *Daily life in Japan at the time of the Samurai, 1185–1603*. London: Allen & Unwin.

Friedlander, Ludwig. 1908–13. *Roman life and manners under the early empire*. New York: Dutton.

Fromm, Erich. 1941. *Escape from freedom*. New York: Farrar and Rinehart.

Fuller, C. J. 1976. *The Nayars today*. Cambridge University Press.

Fustel de Coulanges, Numa Denis. 1864/1980. *The ancient city*. Baltimore: Johns Hopkins University Press.

Galt, Howard S. 1951. *A history of Chinese educational institutions*. London: Probsthain.

Gartman, David. 1979. Origins of the assembly line and capitalist control of work at Ford. In Andrew Zimbalist (ed.), *Case studies on the labor process*. New York: Monthly Review Press.

Gaster, Theodor H. 1959. *The New Golden Bough*. New York: S. G. Phillips. Revision of James G. Frazer, *The Golden Bough*, London, 1890.

Geertz, Clifford. 1960. *The religion of Java*. New York: Free Press.

1968. *Islam observed*. New Haven, Conn.: Yale University Press.

Gerhard, Dietrich. 1981. *Old Europe. A study of continuity, 1000–1800*. New York: Academic Press.

Gernet, Jacques. 1956. *Les Aspects économiques du Bouddhisme dans la société chinoise du Vᵉ au Xᵉ siècle*. Saigon.

Gerth, Hans. 1982. *Politics, character and culture: Perspectives from Hans Gerth*. Edited by Joseph Bensman, Arthur J. Vidich, and Habuko Gerth. Westport, Conn.: Greenwood Press.

and Mills, C. Wright (eds.). 1946. *From Max Weber: Essays in sociology*. New York: Oxford University Press.

References

Gibb, H. A. R. 1969. *Mohammedanism: A historical survey*. New York: Oxford University Press.

Giddens, Anthony. 1981. *A contemporary critique of historical materialism*. Berkeley: University of California Press.

Gimpel, Jean. 1976. *The medieval machine*. New York: Penguin Books.

Girard, Réné. 1977. *Violence and the sacred*. Baltimore: Johns Hopkins University Press.

Goffman, Erving. 1959. *The presentation of self in everyday life*. New York: Doubleday (Anchor Books).

   1961. *Encounters*. Indianapolis: Bobbs-Merrill.

Goldenweiser, Alexander A. 1967. Iroquois social organization. In Roger C. Owen, James F. Deetz, and Anthony D. Fisher (eds.), *The North American Indians, a sourcebook*. New York: Macmillan.

Goldstone, Jack A. 1983. Personal communication.

   1984. Urbanization and inflation: Lessons from the English price revolution of the sixteenth and seventeenth centuries. *American Journal of Sociology* 89:1120–60.

Goody, Jack. 1976. Inheritance, property, and women: Some comparative considerations. In Jack Goody, Joan Thirsk, and E. P. Thompson (eds.), *Family and inheritance: Rural society in Western Europe 1200–1800*. Cambridge University Press, pp. 10–36.

   1983. *The development of the family and marriage in Europe*. Cambridge University Press.

   and Tambiah, S. J. 1973. *Bridewealth and dowry*. Cambridge University Press.

Gough, E. Kathleen. 1959. The Nayars and the definition of marriage. *Journal of the Royal Anthropological Institute* 89: 23–34.

   1968. Literacy in Kerala. In Jack Goody (ed.), *Literacy in traditional societies*. Cambridge University Press.

Greeley, Andrew M. 1974. *Ethnicity in the United States*. New York: Wiley.

Green, Martin. 1974. *The Von Richthofen sisters*. New York: Basic Books.

Grousset, René. 1953. *The rise and splendour of the Chinese Empire*. Berkeley: University of California Press.

Habermas, Jurgen. 1979. *Communication and the evolution of society*. Boston: Beacon Press.

Hadas, Moses. 1950. *A history of Greek literature*. New Hork: Columbia University Press.

Haefele, Wolf. 1980. A global and long-range picture of energy developments. *Science* 209: 174–82.

Hamblin, Robert L., Hout, Michael, Miller, Jerry L. L., and Pitcher, Brian L. 1977. Arms races: A test of two models. *American Sociological Review* 42: 338–54.

Hannan, Michael, and Freeman, John. 1977. The population ecology of organizations. *American Journal of Sociology* 82: 929–40.

Hartwell, Robert. 1966. Markets, technology, and the structure of enterprise in the development of the eleventh-century Chinese iron and steel industry. *Journal of Economic History* 26: 29–58.

   1967. A cycle of economic change in imperial China: Coal and iron in

References

northeast China, 750–1350. *Journal of Economic and Social History of the Orient* 10: 103–59.

Hegel, G. W. F. 1807/1967. *The phenomenology of mind*. New York: Harper & Row.

Hermann, A. 1966. *An historical atlas of China*. Chicago: Aldine.

Hirsch, Paul M. 1983. The study of industries. University of Chicago Graduate School of Business.

Hirst, Paul Q. 1976. *Evolution and social categories*. London: Allen & Unwin.

Hobsbawm, E. J. 1964. Introduction. In Karl Marx, *Precapitalist economic formations*. New York: International Publishers.

Hoselitz, Bert F. 1960. Theories of stages of economic growth. In Bert F. Hoselitz (ed.), *Theories of economic growth*. New York: Free Press, pp. 193–238.

Hughes, Thomas Parke. 1969. Technological momentum in history: Hydrogenation in Germany 1898–1933. *Past and Present* 44: 106–32.

Jeremy, David. 1981. *Transatlantic industrial revolution: The diffusion of textile technologies between Britain and America, 1790–1830s*. Oxford: Blackwell.

Jonas, Hans. 1963. *The Gnostic religion*. Boston: Beacon Press.

Jones, A. H. M. 1959. Were ancient heresies national or social movements in disguise? *The Journal of Theological Studies*. New series, 10, part 2: 280–97.

   1964. *The later Roman Empire 284–602. A social, economic and administrative survey*. New York: Oxford University Press.

Jones, Eric L. 1981. *The European miracle: Environments, economies, and geopolitics in the history of Europe and Asia*. Cambridge University Press.

Kalberg, Stephen. 1979. The search for thematic orientations in a fragmented oeuvre: The discussion of Max Weber in recent German sociological literature. *Sociology* 13: 127-39.

   1980. Max Weber's types of rationality. *American Journal of Sociology* 85: 1145–79.

Kanter, Rosabeth M. 1977. *Men and women of the corporation*. New York: Basic Books.

Keegan, John. 1976. *The face of battle. A study of Agincourt, Waterloo, and the Somme*. New York: Random House.

Knowles, David. 1962. *The evolution of medieval thought*. New York: Random House (Vintage Books).

Kohn, Melvin L. 1971. Bureaucratic man: A portrait and an interpretation. *American Sociological Review* 36: 461–74.

Kurtz, Lester. 1983. The politics of heresy. *American Journal of Sociology* 88: 1085–1115.

Ladurie, Emmanuel LeRoy. 1976. Family structure and inheritance customs in sixteenth century France. In Jack Goody, Joan Thirsk, and E. P. Thompson (eds.), *Family and inheritance: Rural society in Western Europe 1200–1800*. Cambridge University Press.

Landes, David S. 1969. *The unbound Prometheus. Technological change and industrial development in Western Europe from 1750 to the present*. Cambridge University Press.

References

Lane, Frederic C. 1973. *Venice. A maritime republic.* Baltimore: Johns Hopkins University Press.

Lantz, Herman. 1976. Marital incompatibility and social change in early America. *Sage Research Papers in the Social Sciences.* volume 4, Series No. 90–026. Beverly Hills, Calif.: Sage.

  Britton, Margaret, Schmitt, Raymond, and Snyder, Eloise C. 1968. Pre-industrial patterns in the colonial family in America. *American Sociological Review* 33: 413–26.

Laslett, Barbara. 1980. Beyond methodology: The place of theory in quantitative historical research. *American Sociological Review* 45: 214–28.

Laslett, Peter. 1971. *The world we have lost. England before the industrial age.* 2nd ed. New York: Scribner.

  1977. Characteristics of the Western family considered over time. In Peter Laslett, *Family life and illicit love in earlier generations.* Cambridge University Press, pp. 12–47.

Laumann, Edward O. 1973. *The bonds of pluralism.* New York: Wiley.

Lee, Richard B., and DeVore, Irven. 1968. *Man the hunter.* Chicago: Aldine.

Lefebvre, Henri. 1971. *Everyday life in the modern world.* London: Allen Lane.

Lenski, Gerhard E. 1966. *Power and privilege. A theory of stratification.* New York: McGraw-Hill.

Leontieff, Wassily. 1982. Academic economics. *Science* 217: 104–7.

Lévi-Strauss, Claude. 1949/1969. *The elementary structures of kinship.* Boston: Beacon Press.

Levy, R. 1957. *The social structure of Islam.* Cambridge University Press.

Lewis, Bernard. 1967. *The Arabs in history.* New York: Harper & Row.

  (ed.) 1974. *Islam from the Prophet Muhammad to the capture of Constantinople.* New York: Harper & Row.

Liddell Hart, B. H. 1970. *History of the Second World War.* New York: Putnam.

Linton, Ralph. 1936. *The study of man.* New York: Appleton-Century.

Lukes, Steven. 1973. *Emile Durkheim: His life and works.* London: Allen Lane.

McCagg, W. O., and B. D. Silver. 1980. *Soviet Asian ethnic frontiers.* Elmsford, N.Y.: Pergamon Press.

McClelland, David C. 1961. *The achieving society.* New York: Van Nostrand.

McEvedy, Colin. 1961. *The Penguin atlas of medieval history.* New York: Penguin Books.

  1967. *The Penguin atlas of ancient history.* New York: Penguin Books.

  1972. *The Penguin atlas of modern history.* New York: Penguin Books.

  and Jones, Richard. 1978. *Atlas of world population history.* New York: Penguin Books.

Macfarlane, Alan. 1978. *The origins of English individualism.* Oxford: Blackwell.

MacMullen, Ramsay. 1974. *Roman social relations, 50 B.C. to A.D. 284.* New Haven, Conn.: Yale University Press.

McNeill, William H. 1963. *The rise of the West. A history of the human community.* Chicago: University of Chicago Press.

  1964. *Europe's steppe frontier.* Chicago: University of Chicago Press.

  1982. *The pursuit of power: Technology, armed force, and society since A.D. 1000.* Chicago: University of Chicago Press.

Mahan, Alfred Thayer. 1918. *The influence of sea power upon history.* Boston: Ginn.

330

References

Mannheim, Karl. 1935/1940. *Man and society in an age of reconstruction.* New York: Harcourt Brace.

Marcuse, Herbert. 1964. *One-dimensional Man.* Boston: Beacon Press.

Maringer, Johannes, and Bandi, Hans-Georg. 1953. *Art in the Ice Age.* New York: Praeger.

Marx, Karl. 1856/1959. *Preface to a contribution to the critique of political economy.* In L. Feuer (ed.), *Marx and Engels: Basic writings on politics and philosophy.* New York: Doubleday.

1857–8/1973. *Grundrisse.* New York: Random House.

1867, 1885, 1894/1967. *Capital.* New York: International Publishers.

and Engels, Friedrich. 1846/1947. *The German ideology.* New York: International Publishers.

Mason, Philip. 1976. *A matter of honor: An account of the Indian Army, its officers and men.* New York: Penguin Books.

Mayer, Martin. 1976. *The bankers.* New York: Random House.

Mencher, Joan. 1965. The Nayars of South Malabar. In Meyer Nimkoff (ed.), *Comparative family systems.* New York: Houghton Mifflin.

Miller, Joseph C. 1981. Lineages, ideology and the history of slavery in western central Africa. In Paul E. Lovejoy (ed.), *The ideology of slavery in Africa.* Beverly Hills, Calif.: Sage, pp. 41–71.

Mills, C. Wright. 1956. *The power elite.* New York: Oxford University Press.

Mitzman, Arthur. 1970. *The iron cage.* New York: Knopf.

Modelski, G. 1978. The long cycle of global politics and the nation state. *Comparative Studies in Society and History* 20: 214–35.

1983. Long cycles of world leadership. In William R. Thompson (ed.), *Contending approaches to world system analysis.* Beverly Hills, Calif.: Sage.

Mommsen, Wolfgang. 1959. *Max Weber und die deutsche Politik, 1890–1920.* Tübingen: Mohr.

Moore, Barrington, Jr. 1965. *Soviet politics.* New York: Harper & Row.

1966. *Social origins of dictatorship and democracy.* Boston: Beacon Press.

Morgenthau, Hans J. 1948. *Politics among nations.* New York: Knopf.

Morris, Ivan. 1964. *The world of the shining prince. Court life in ancient Japan.* New York: Oxford University Press.

Murasaki Shikibu. 1970. (original ca. A.D. 1008). *The Tale of Genji.* Tokyo: Tuttle.

Murdock, George Peter. 1967. Ethnographic atlas: A summary. *Ethology* 6: 109–236.

Murphy, Robert F. 1957. Intergroup hostility and social cohesion. *American Anthropologist* 59: 1018–35.

1959. Social structure and sex antagonism. *Southwestern Journal of Anthropology* 15: 89–98.

Nakane, Chie. 1970. *Japanese society.* Berkeley: University of California Press.

Needham, Joseph. 1956. *Science and civilisation in China.* Volume 2: *History of scientific thought.* Cambridge University Press.

1964. *The development of iron and steel technology in China.* Cambridge: Heffer.

1965. *Science and civilization in China.* Volume 4, part 2: *Mechanical engineering.* Cambridge University Press.

1971. *Science and civilization in China.* Volume 4, part 3: *Civil Engineering and nautics.* Cambridge University Press.

References

Nelson, Benjamin. 1949. *The idea of usury*. Princeton, N.J.: Princeton University Press.

Nihongi: Chronicles of Japan from the earliest times to A.D. 697. 1972. Tokyo: Tuttle.

O'Connor, James. 1973. *The fiscal crisis of the state*. New York: St. Martin's Press.

Organski, A. F. K., and Kugler, Jack. 1980. *The war ledger*. Chicago: University of Chicago Press.

Otterbein, Keith F. 1967. An analysis of Iroquois military tactics. In Paul Bohannon (ed.), *Law and warfare*. New York: Natural History Press.

Pagels, Elaine H. 1979. *The Gnostic gospels*. New York: Random House.

Paige, Jeffrey M. 1975. *Agrarian revolution*. New York: Free Press.

Paige, Karen Ericksen, and Paige, Jeffrey M. 1981. *The politics of reproductive ritual*. Berkeley: University of California Press.

Parsons, Talcott. 1937. *The structure of social action*. New York: McGraw-Hill.

1947. Introduction. In Max Weber, *The theory of social and economic organization*. Translated by A. M. Henderson and Talcott Parsons. New York: Oxford University Press.

1951. *The social system*. New York: Free Press.

1963. Introduction. In Max Weber, *The sociology of religion*. Boston: Beacon Press.

1967. *Societies: Comparative and evolutionary perspectives*. Englewood Cliffs, N.J.: Prentice-Hall.

1971. *The system of modern societies*. Englewood Cliffs, N.J.: Prentice-Hall.

and Shils, Edward. 1951. *Toward a general theory of action*. Cambridge, Mass.: Harvard University Press.

Patinkin, Don. 1983. Multiple discoveries and the central message. *American Journal of Sociology* 89: 306–23.

Patterson, Orlando. 1982. *Slavery and social death: A comparative study*. Cambridge, Mass.: Harvard University Press.

Perrin, Noel. 1979. *Giving up the gun: Japan's reversion to the sword, 1543–1879*. New York: Random House.

Pfeffer, Jeffrey, and Salancik, Gerald. 1978. *The external control of organizations: A resource dependence perspective*. New York: Harper & Row.

Pitcher, Brian L., Hamblin, Robert L., and Miller, Jerry L. L. The diffusion of collective violence. *American Sociological Review* 43: 23–35.

Polanyi, Karl. 1944. *The great transformation*. New York: Rinehart.

1977. *The livelihood of man*. Edited by Harry W. Pearson. New York: Academic Press.

Pomeroy, Sarah B. 1975. *Goddesses, whores, wives, and slaves: Women in classical antiquity*. New York: Schocken.

Price, Derek J. de Solla. 1969. The structure of publication in science and technology. In W. H. Gruber and D. R. Marquis (eds.), *Factors in the transfer of technology*. Cambridge, Mass.: MIT Press.

Queen, Stuart A., and Habenstein, Robert W. 1967. *The family in various cultures*. Philadelphia: Lippincott.

Renfrew, Colin. 1976. *Before civilization: The radiocarbon revolution and prehistoric Europe*. New York: Penguin Books.

Research Working Group on Cyclical Rhythms and Secular Trends. 1979.

References

Cyclical rhythms and secular trends of the capitalist world-economy: Some premises, hypotheses, and questions. *Review* 2 (Spring): 483–500.

Ritchie, William A. 1965. *The archaeology of New York State*. New York: Natural History Press.

Sahal, Devendra. 1981. *Patterns of technological innovation*. Reading, Mass.: Addison-Wesley.

Samuelsson, Kurt. 1961. *Religion and economic action*. New York: Basic Books.

Sanday, Peggy Reeves. 1981. *Female power and male dominance: On the origins of sexual inequality*. Cambridge University Press.

Sansom, George. 1958. *A history of Japan to 1334*. Stanford, Calif.: Stanford University Press.

1961. *A history of Japan 1334–1615*. Stanford, Calif.: Stanford University Press.

Sartre, Jean-Paul. 1943. *L'Etre et le néant*. Paris: Gallimard.

Scammell, G. V. 1981. *The world encompassed. The first European maritime empires, c. 800–1650*. Berkeley: University of California Press.

Schelling, Thomas C. 1962. *The strategy of conflict*. Cambridge, Mass.: Harvard University Press.

Schluchter, Wolfgang. 1981. *The rise of Western rationalism*. Berkeley: University of California Press.

Schumpeter, Joseph A. 1911/1961. *The theory of economic development*. New York: Oxford University Press.

1914. *Epochen der Dogmen- und Methodengeschichte*. In *Grundriss der Sozialoekonomik*, 1. Abteilung, *Wirtschaft und Wirtschaftswissenschaft*. Tübingen: Mohr (Paul Siebeck), pp. 19–124.

1918. *Das Sozialprodukt and die Rechenpfennige*. *Archiv für Sozialwissenschaft* 44.

1939. *Business Cycles: A theoretical, historical, and statistical analysis of the capitalist process*. New York: McGraw-Hill.

1942. *Capitalism, socialism, and democracy*. New York: Harper.

1954. *History of economic analysis*. New York: Oxford University Press.

Scott, Marvin B., and Lyman, Stanford M. 1969. Accounts. *American Sociological Review* 33: 46–62.

Seeman, Melvin. 1959. On the meaning of alienation. *American Sociological Review* 24: 783–91.

1972. Alienation in pre-crisis France. *American Sociological Review* 37: 385–402.

Sei Shonagon. 1971. (original ca. 1000 A.D.). *The pillow book of Sei Shonagon*. New York: Penguin Books.

Seidman, Steven. 1980. *Enlightenment and reaction: Aspects of the Enlightenment origins of Marxism and sociology*. Unpublished dissertation, University of Virginia.

Semenov, S. A. 1964. *Prehistoric technology*. New York: Cory, Adams and MacKay.

Singer, J. D., Bremer, S., and Stuckey, J. 1972. Capability distribution, uncertainty, and major power war. In B. Russett (ed.), *Peace, war, and numbers*. Beverly Hills, Calif.: Sage.

Skocpol, Theda. 1979. *States and social revolutions*. Cambridge University Press.

References

Snodgrass, Anthony. 1980. *Archaic Greece*. Berkeley: University of California Press.

Sommers, Margaret R., and Goldfrank, Walter L. 1979. The limits of agronomic determinism. *Comparative Studies in Society and History* 21: 443–58.

Southern, R. W. 1953. *The making of the Middle Ages*. New Haven, Conn.: Yale University Press.

1970. *Western society and the Church in the Middle Ages*. New York: Penguin Books.

Spencer, Baldwin, and Gillen, F. J. 1899. *The native tribes of central Australia*. London: Macmillan.

1927. *The Arunta*. London: Macmillan.

Spuler, Bertold. 1972. *History of the Mongols*. Berkeley: University of California Press.

Stcherbatski, Theodore. 1962. *Buddhist logic*. New York: Dover.

Stinchcombe, Arthur L. 1968. *Constructing social theories*. New York: Harcourt Brace Jovanovich.

Stone, Lawrence. 1967. *The crisis of the aristocracy, 1558–1641*. New York: Oxford University Press.

1977/1979. *The family, sex and marriage in England, 1500–1800*. London: Weidenfeld & Nicolson.

Strathern, Andrew. 1973. Kinship, descent, and locality: Some new Guinea examples. In Jack Goody (ed.), *The character of kinship*. Cambridge University Press.

Struver, Stuart. 1971. *Prehistoric agriculture*. Garden City, N.Y.: Natural History Press.

Swanson, Guy E. 1962. *The birth of the gods*. Ann Arbor: University of Michigan Press.

Sweezy, Paul M. 1942. *The theory of capitalist development*. New York: Oxford University Press.

Taagepera, Rein. 1979. Size and duration of empires: Growth-decline curves, 600 B.C. to 600 A.D. *Social Science History* 3: 115–38.

Tambiah, S. J. 1973. From Varna to caste through mixed unions. In Jack Goody (ed.), *The character of kinship*. Cambridge University Press.

Tawney, R. H. 1938. *Religion and the rise of capitalism*. New York: Penguin Books.

Taylor, C. L., and M. Hudson. 1972. *World handbook of political and social indicators*. New Haven, Conn.: Yale University Press.

Tenbruck, F. H. 1975. Das Werk Max Webers. *Kölner Zeitschrift für Soziologie und Sozialpsychologie* 27: 663–702.

Thapar, Romila. 1966. *A history of India*. New York: Penguin Books.

Thompson, E. P. 1963. *The making of the English working class*. London: Gollancz.

Thompson, William R. 1983. Cycles, capabilities, and war: An ecumenical view. In William R. Thompson (ed.), *Contending approaches to world system analysis*. Beverly Hills, Calif.: Sage.

Tudjman, F. 1981. *Nationalism in contemporary Europe*. New York: Columbia University Press.

Udelson, Joseph H. 1982. *The great television race: A history of the American television industry 1925–1941*. University: University of Alabama Press.

References

United States Congress, Office of Technology Assessment. 1979. *The effects of nuclear war*. Washington, D.C.: U.S. Government Printing Office.

Unni, K. Raman. 1958. Polyandry in Malabar. *Journal of the M.S. University of Baroda* 5: 71–2.

Van Creveld, Martin. 1977. *Supplying war: Logistics from Wallenstein to Patton*. Cambridge University Press.

Wallerstein, Immanuel. 1974. *The modern world system: Capitalist agriculture and the origins of the European world-economy in the sixteenth century*. New York: Academic Press.

Weber, Marianne. 1907. *Ehefrau und Mutter in der Rechtsentwicklung*. Tübingen: Mohr.

1925/1975. *Max Weber: A biography*. New York: Wiley. Translation of *Max Weber: Ein Lebensbild*.

Weber, Max. 1889. *Zur Geschichte der Handelsgesellschaften im Mittelalter*. Stuttgart.

1903–6/1975. *Roscher and Knies: The logical problems of historical economics*. New York: Free Press. Originally published in *Schmoller's Jahrbuch*.

1904–5/1930. *The Protestant ethic and the spirit of capitalism*. Translated by Talcott Parsons. New York: Scribner.

1904, 1906, 1917–19/1949. *The methodology of the social sciences*. Translated by Edward A. Shils and Henry A. Finch. New York: Free Press.

1909/1976. *The Agrarian sociology of ancient civilizations*. London: New Left Books.

1916/1951. *The religion of China*. Translated by Hans H. Gerth. New York: Free Press. Originally published in *Archiv für Sozialwissenschaft und Sozialforschung*.

1916–17/1958a. *The religion of India*. Translated by Hans H. Gerth and Don Martindale. New York: Free Press. Originally published in *Archiv für Sozialwissenschaft und Sozialforschung*.

1917–19/1952. *Ancient Judaism*. Translated by Hans H. Gerth and Don Martindale. New York: Free Press. Originally published in *Archiv für Sozialwissenschaft und Sozialforschung*.

1922/1947. *The theory of social and economic organization*. Translated by A. M. Henderson and Talcott Parsons. New York: Oxford University Press.

1922/1954. *Max Weber on law in economy and society*. Translated by Edward A. Shils and Max Rheinstein. Cambridge, Mass.: Harvard University Press.

1922/1958b. *The city*. Translated by Don Martindale and Gertrud Neuworth. Glencoe, Ill.: Free Press.

1922/1963. *The sociology of religion*. Translated by Ephraim Fischoff. Boston: Beacon Press.

1922/1968. *Economy and society*. Edited by Guenter Roth and Klaus Wittich. New York: Bedminster Press.

1923/1961. *General economic history*. Translated by Frank H. Knight. New York: Collier-Macmillan. Original from 1919–20 lectures.

1946. *From Max Weber: Essays in Sociology*. Translated and edited by Hans H. Gerth and C. Wright Mills. New York: Oxford University Press.

Wertime, Theodore A. and Muhly, James D. (eds.). 1980. *The coming of the Age of Iron*. New Haven, Conn.: Yale University Press.

References

White, Harrison C. 1981. Where do markets come from? *American Journal of Sociology* 87: 517–47.

Whyte, Lynn, Jr. 1962. *Medieval technology and social change.* New York: Oxford University Press.

Wiley, Norbert F. 1967. America's unique class politics: The interplay of the labor, credit, and commodity markets. *American Sociological Review* 32: 529–40.

——— 1983. On the congruence of Weber and Keynes. In Randall Collins (ed.), *Sociological theory 1983.* San Francisco: Jossey-Bass.

Williamson, Oliver E. 1975. *Markets and hierarchies: A study of the economics of internal organization.* New York: Free Press.

Wright, Arthur F. 1959. *Buddhism in Chinese history.* Stanford, Calif.: Stanford University Press.

Zaehner, R. E. 1960. *Hindu and Muslim mysticism.* New York: Schocken Books.

Zaslavsky, Victor, and Z. 1981. Adult political socialization in the USSR: A study of attitudes of Soviet workers to the invasion of Czechoslovakia. *Sociology* 15: 407–23.

Zolberg, Aristide R. 1983. "World" and "System": A misalliance. In William R. Thompson (ed.), *Contending approaches to world system analysis.* Beverly Hills: Sage.

Index

Abassid Caliphate, 228, 229
absolutism (absolutist state), 30, 34, 88
"Adam Smith paradox," 14
adjudication, 24, 31
administration, 49, 222–3
administrators, 30, 33, 43, 51
adoption, 309n5
Adorno, Theodor, 1, 255
adultery, 309, 315
Afghanistan, 169, 183, 186, 198, 202, 204
Africa, 81n3, 82, 174, 175, 176
agrarian economies, 26, 27, 71
agrarian societies, 40, 49, 97, 254, 287,
    292; family structure in, 289, 312, 313,
    314; innovation in, 102–4; romanticiza-
    tion of, 251–2
agrarian state societies, 168, 269, 294;
    courtly politics of, 15–16; family struc-
    ture in, 297, 299; inheritance rules in,
    307; nationalism in, 152–3; overexten-
    sion, 191; status structure, 308; tech-
    nological innovation, 107
agricultural revolution, 95, 104, 110
agriculture, 25, 86, 101, 107; China, 61,
    62, 63; commercialization of, 40n19,
    79n1; discovery of, 81–2; effect on
    family structure, 272, 278; Middle
    Ages, 47, 96; rationalization of, 33,
    111; technological innovation in, 102,
    103, 118
air power, 169–70, 173, 189; geopolitical
    effects of, 178–84
Alaska, 195, 196
Albania, 198
Albigensians, 226–7
Alexander Severus, Emperor, 223
Alexander the Great, 94
Alexandria, 108, 223, 224, 226n5
Algeria, 178
alienation, 14–15; macro/micro experi-
    ence of, 259–60, 262, 263; as modern
    secular politics, 261–3; as ritual and
    ideology, 247–63

alliances, 14, 32, 91, 188, 208n9, 303–4,
    310; family, in Rome, 319–20; sexual,
    313
alphabet(s), 104, 108n17
Amida Buddha, 220, 234
Amidaism, 67, 220, 234, 237, 238
Amitabha (deity), 66
ammunition, 17, 191
Amur valley, 198, 207
anarchists, anarchy, 158, 245
Anatolia, 82, 93, 103n12, 227
ancestor worship, 221, 267
ancient states, nationalism in, 151, 152,
    153
Andes (the), 99, 174
Andreski, Stanislav, 167
Angola, 169, 176, 183
animals, animal power, 99, 100, 103–4,
    110
anthropology, symbolic, 219n2
antifeminism, 315
Antioch, 223
appropriation, 23, 40, 123, 131–2;
    feudal, 45; form of, 43; instruments
    of, 141; of opportunities, 131, 133,
    139, 141, 142; patrimonial, of proper-
    ty, 109, 110; of women, 273, 278n9,
    282
Arabian Peninsula, 202
Arabs, 47
Aragon, 226
Argentina, 169
Arian heresy, 224–5, 226
aristocracy(ies), 40, 54, 128, 159–60,
    165n7, 282; Heian Japan, 307, 308; le-
    gitimacy and, 156, 157, 159; and mar-
    riage politics, 307, 310; military, 85,
    87; Spartan, 159; and status of wom-
    en, 314–15
Arius (preacher, bishop), 224–5
Armenia, 103n12, 108
armies, 35n13, 91, 92, 157, 290; move-
    ment of, 170–2

Index

Index

Calhoun, Craig, 258
Calicut (city), 297
Caliphates, 234
Calvinism, 21, 33–4, 46
Canaanite cults, 216
Canaanite kingdom, 284
Canada, 172, 174, 175, 198
cannon, 85–6, 90–1, 92, 95
Canon law, 50–1, 213
Capetian monarchy, 313n8
capital: basis of, 256–7; conversational,
137; entrepreneurial organization of,
27, 46, 54, 118; mobile, 42, 43, 54–5;
social organization of, 136; surplus
value key to, 250
capital accounting, 22, 23, 25, 54
capitalism, 7, 9–10, 36n14, 79n1, 121,
136, 141, 247; and alienation, 251–3,
254, 255; basis of, in Middle Ages, 45–
76; components of, 21–6, 46, 54; crisis
of, 250; defined, 14, 21–2, 109, 135,
139; dynamic processes in, 12, 117,
121, 125n3, 135, 258; essence of, in
markets, 256–8; family, 269, 270, 290–
1; family as obstacle to, 267–9; future
of, 44; genesis of, 75, 96; as historical
continuum, 140–2; and imperialism,
146, 148–50; institutional characteristics and social prerequisites of, 8–
10, 25, 26–34, 35, 39–44, 46, 47, 48,
49, 54, 57, 70, 142; international character of, 41–4; nature of, 139–42;
obstacles to, 29, 34, 35, 45, 286; pacifist, 150; and religion, 7–8, 75, 231,
268; religious, 7–8, 45, 48–75, 239; rise
of, 34–7, 46; sociology of, 117–42; and
state, 138; struggle in, 257–8; traditional, 136; Weber's theory of, 1, 19–
44; world-transforming force in West,
20, 26–34, 286
capitalist takeoff, 24, 25, 26, 33n11, 35,
76, 141; preconditions for, 40–1
Cardan, Jerome, 114
Caribbean, 149
cart(s), 47, 102
cartelization, 130
Carter, Jimmy, 316
Carthage, 316
Carthaginian empire, 148, 149
Cartwright, Edmund, 112
Cartwright power loom, 78
caste system, 24, 29, 32, 35, 237n8, 268,
287, 294n19, 297; Nayar, 300–1, 303,
304, 312
Catal Huyuk (town), 104n14
Cataline conspiracy, 321
catapults, 85, 88

cathedrals, 55
Catholic Church, 34, 46; organization of,
as basis of capitalism, 8n3, 45, 48–52,
71, 74; see also Christianity; church
Cato the Elder, 316
Caucasus, 153, 195, 196, 197, 203
Caursines (people), 29n8
cavalry, 87
celibacy, 49, 67–8, 234
Celts, 286
centralization, 31, 106, 159n3, 228, 242,
290, 291; China, 60–1; imperfect, as
condition for power struggle, 221–5,
244–5
Ceres, temple of, 317
challenge-and-response model, 45, 79n1
Ch'an (Zen) Buddhism, 67, 235, 237, 238
chariot, 93n6, 103, 286
charisma, 1, 2, 216, 229; in kin group
formation, 268, 272, 273; of leaders
(founders), 6, 158, 215, 272, 277, 286;
office, 36; routinization of, 6, 8
charity, 29
Charlemagne, 313n8
chemicals, 80, 81
Cheng Ho, 82
children, 256, 276–7, 287, 291–2, 293,
294, 309, 318; Nayar, 300, 301
China, 27, 34, 35, 38, 84, 92n5, 131, 173,
214; agrarian state society, 297; barbarian conquests, 63; Buddhism, 235, 236,
237–8; capitalism, 10, 118, 140; communism, 207; Confucian, 220–1; construction, 109; dynasties, 190, 198;
family structure, 267–8; fragmentation,
188; Great Wall, 105; Japan's conquest
of, 174, 175; kin groups, 274, 286, 287;
labor-intensive methods, 110–11; Mahayana, 234; military technology, 85,
86, 87, 89–90, 93n6, 95; Ming, 200f;
mobilization ratio, 195; money economy, 110; nationalism, 153, 242; prostitution, 284; relationship with Russia,
207, 208n9; religions, 46; religious capitalism in, 58–73; size of state, 172;
superficial bureaucratization, 31; technological innovation, 80, 83, 96, 101;
Weber on, 58–9
Chinese empires, 148, 168, 195
Ch'ing (Manchu) dynasty, 10, 59, 63,
66n4, 198, 207, 268n1
Christianity, 29n8, 32, 207, 216, 217, 249;
as basis of capitalism, 20, 33–4, 35, 46,
71, 76; doctrinal orthodoxy, 240–1;
and end of kin groups, 286; family
structure, 293–4; geopolitical events
and conflicts in, 226–30; group in,

339

Index

Index

Index

Index

household, 277, 287–94, 319; as family
structure, 271–6; matrilocal, Nayar, 299
"household communism," 272, 275,
282n13, 288
household production, 77, 269, 287
Hua-yen, 236
Hui-ssu, 237
Hungary, 202
Huns, 61, 153
Hussites, 227
Huygens, Christian, 114
hypergamy, 282, 300, 304, 306
hypogamy, 300

ICBMs, 169, 181
Ice Age, 98, 99
Iconoclasm, 227–8, 242
ideal types, 4, 6, 24, 120, 121
Idealism, 4n1, 249
ideas, 3–4, 5, 20; diffusion of, 84–5;
new, 100–1, 115; in politics, 214; religious, 20; scientific, 115
ideology, 12, 94n7, 159, 241; alienation
as, 247–63; in decline of Soviet Union,
206–9; and geopolitics, 207–9, 225;
and heresy conflicts, 243–4, 245; political, 214, 246; state, of China, 10; universalistic, 222–3, 243, 244, 245
Ilkans, 192
Immortals cult, 237
imperialism, 13, 145–66; dynamics of,
161–6; legitimacy and, 158–61
incest prohibitions, 273, 282, 300
India, 15, 20n2, 29, 32, 38, 173, 184;
agrarian state society, 104, 297; Buddhism, 235, 236; caste system, 287,
294n19; family structure, 267, 268; fertility rituals, 284; held by England, 92,
169, 174, 175, 176; military technology, 91, 92, 95; nationalism, 242;
obstacles to capitalism, 35, 42; political
fragmentation, 236; religious pluralism, 46, 221; technological innovation, 94n7; temple shape, 105
individualism, 9, 76, 244
Indo-China, 174, 179, 184
Indonesia, 149, 174, 175
Indus, 84
industrial society(ies), 24–5, 168; continuation of capitalism in, 37; family
structure in, 298–9; and industrialism,
9, 72, 299, 314
industrialization, 25, 30, 79, 83, 91, 97,
110, 253, 289, 290; China, 62, 63, 72
industry and science, 26n5, 112
inequality(ies): in agrarian societies, 252;
economic, 117, 119, 123, 136

infanticide, 292
inflation, 41, 62, 139, 140–1
information, market, 132–3; monopolization of, 130
inheritance, 274, 275, 277, 282, 287, 290,
291–2, 293–4, 312, 314; Japan, 306–7;
women, 316–17, 320–1
initiation rites, 278–9
Innocent IV, Pope, 52
innovation, 83, 98, 101, 104; capitalist,
111–15; and growth of new monopolies, 130; locus of, 93–5; and profit,
125; requires credit, 135; sector-specific, 94; over time, 78, 80–1, 82, 83, 85,
86, 88, 90, 94, 95–7, 98, 100, 107, 109–
10; see also technological innovation
institutional forms (capitalism), 43, 76
instrumentation, 114–15
intellectualism in religion, 219, 220, 232,
242–3
intellectuals: alienation of, 258n3; elitism
about working-class culture, 247, 253–
5, 262; and Marxism, 121–2; Platonic,
224
interest, 135; see also usury
interest groups, 2, 147
interior states, 168, 188; fragmentation
of, 188–9, 197; Russia as, 195, 196
"internal booty capitalism," 268
invention(s), 25, 78, 80–5, 112; ideas in,
115; locus of, 93; possibility of future,
116
inventors, 83–4, 112–13
Iran, 86, 91, 164n5, 199, 202, 204, 315
Iraq, 202
Ireland, 58
iron, 47, 80, 103
Iron Age, 82
Iron Authority (China), 64
Iron Law of Oligarchy, 222, 230
iron production, 54, 62
ironworking, 64, 82, 93
Iroquois matriarchy, 294–6
irrigation, 30, 32, 102, 105, 107
Isis, cult of, 217, 316
Islam, 46, 207, 217n1, 230, 241, 242;
agrarian state society, 297; history of,
38, 227; mysticism in, 233–4; schisms
in, 228–9; state support for, 219
Islamic Empire, 228, 233, 242
Islamic madrasahs, 8
islands, 177
Ismailis(ism), 228, 233
isolation, 251; geopolitical, 95
Italian city-states, 258, 285
Italy, 58, 174, 175, 176, 179, 198n5,
313n8; arms race, 94–5; clans (sibs),

345

Index

Italy (*cont.*)
268, 286; conquest of, 159; paper industry, 82; revolution in, 41

Jacobinism, 243
Jainism, 214, 220
Japan, 15, 67, 70, 72, 92n5, 242; air power, 179; Buddhism, 234, 236, 238; defeat of Russia, 196, 198; history of, 38; impregnability of, 177; military technology, 87–8; mobilization ratio, 195; monastic orders, 221; overseas empire, 173, 174, 175, 176; prostitution, 284
jealousy, 282, 308
Jericho, 104n14
Jerusalem, 284
Jesus, 220, 222, 231
Jevons, William Stanley, 117
Jewish tribes, 276
Jews, 29n8, 285; *see also* Judaism
joint liability, law of, 291
Jones, A. H. M., 225n5, 240n9
Judaism, 44n23, 46, 216, 219, 274; and end of kin groups, 286; ethical prophecy in, 32; puritanism in, 284; sib structure in, 268; as universal religion, 217
Julian, emperor, 224, 225, 241
Julius Caesar, 159–60, 319, 320
Jurchen regime, 89
Jurchen Tartars, 63
Jutland, 177
Juvenal, 315

Kabul, 183
Kafka, Franz, 259
Kalberg, Stephen, 22n3
Kamakura Shogunate, 311
Kathedersozialisten, 121
Kautsky, Karl J., 38
Kazakh area, 198
Kazars (people), 217n1
Kerala, *see* Malabar (Kerala)
Keynes, John Maynard, 11
Kiangsi, 62
kin groups (sibs), 9, 216, 267–8, 277, 285, 318; confused with household, 288–9; and family structure, 271–6, 277, 287, 289–90, 291; legitimacy in, 156; marriage and, 277; among Nayar, 298; organization of, 280–1; transformation of, 285–6
kinship, 15, 98, 306, 310
kinship-organized societies, 214; sexual property system, 255–6
Kirghiz (people), 204

Kirghizia, 199
Knies, Karl, 4n1
Knight, Frank, 272n5
knights, armored, 85, 86, 93n6
Knights Hospitalers of St. John, 52–3
Koran, 233
Korea, 70, 88, 173, 175, 310
Korean war, 179
Kuan-yin (goddess), 234
Kublai Khan, 242

labor, 9, 34, 127, 252, 268; alienation of, 250–1; China, 64n2, 67; exploitation of, 123–4; free, 23, 24, 27, 29, 39, 46, 54, 55, 62–3, 71; massed force of, 105, 106, 107; supply/demand, 131; *see also* working class
labor discipline: in factory, 77, 78–9; in sib, 268
labor force, 26, 128, 257
labor market(s), 14, 126, 127, 131; in Catholic Church, 55; class conflict in, 258
labor theory of value, 123, 250
laissez-faire, 24, 122
land, 26, 128; *see also* property system(s)
land power, 182
land warfare, 170, 174, 175, 180, 184
Landes, David S., 79, 112
Lane, Frederic, 47
Lao-tzu, 59, 220, 242
Laslett, Peter, 289, 299, 290n17
Latin America, 138n8, 175
Latvians, 203–4
law, legal system, 9, 24, 30, 34, 36, 41, 131n5; based on citizenship, 33; calculable, 24, 27, 30, 36n14, 39, 47, 50; church law in development of, 51–2, 71; precapitalist, 26; property, 71; rationalized, 48; in rise of capitalism, 27–9, 43, 51–2
Lawrence, D. H., 271n4
lawyers, 51
leaders, political, 160, 162
Lebanon, 108
Lefebvre, Henri, 247, 252–3
left (the), 244
legitimacy, 2, 145–66; defined, 155; domestic, 160–6; dynamics of, 147, 155, 158–9; emotional, 320; externally conferred, 241–3; and imperialism, 158–61; internal, 227; kin group, 274; military force and, 15; origins of, 155–7; religious, 12, 215, 216, 241, 243; state, 208–9, 215, 241–3, 245, 285; status and, 6; three forms of, 145, 158
legitimation, 6, 44

346

Index

Index

matrilineages, (matrilineality), 271, 274, 278, 279, 281n12, 289n16, 291, 294–5, 298; in agrarian state societies, 312; in India, 305; among Nayar, 299–300; and status of women, 306–7, 309, 310, 311, 313, 314

Maurya state (India), 236

Mauss, Marcel, 12

Maximinus, Emperor, 223

Maxwell, James Clerk, 114

Mayans, 105

meaning, 254, 259

means of production: monopolization of, 130; relationship to, 126, 129–30; *see also* factors of production

measurement, 115

mechanics, 114

mechanization, 23, 25, 111n19

meditation, 66, 220, 230–1, 235, 249

Mediterranean antiquity, 9, 27n6, 31, 38, 47, 104

Mediterranean empires, 168

Mediterranean Sea, 173

Melanesia, 99

Melitians, 224

Mencius, 59

mendicant orders, 52, 55

Menger, Carl, 4n1, 117, 120

"men's houses," 273, 275, 278–9, 280, 281, 282, 285, 286, 291

mercenaries, 95

merchants, 108–9

Mesolithic period, 93, 100

Mesopotamia, 81, 98, 101, 103, 106, 107n16; theocracy, 215, 216; urban revolution, 102

metallurgy, 80, 81n2, 85, 89, 96, 113

metalworking, 47, 102

meteorites, 103n12

Methodenstreit, 4n1, 120–1

Mexico, 81, 91, 98, 99, 101, 174; pyramids, 105

Michels, Robert, 241; Iron Law of Oligarchy, 222

micro-sociology, 247

microscope, 114

middle class, 314

Middle East, 32, 91, 93, 99, 102n4, 104, 202, 234, 268, 284

Middle Eastern empires, 168

Midway, 177, 182

migration(s), 80, 100, 101n11, 103n11, 217

military (the), 11, 30, 31–2, 87, 146, 279n10; legitimacy in, 156, 157, 161; *see also* army supply

military crises, 201, 202, 207

military factors: in family organization, 271, 278, 280–1, 290, 302, 312; in kin group organization, 273, 274, 285–6; in politics, 214

military force, power, 2, 12, 15, 107, 187

military intervention, foreign, 162, 186

military organization, 43, 286; and sexual domination, 279–80

military relations, determinant of internal politics, 145, 146, 153–4, 159–60, 162–4, 281

military technology, 85–92, 93–5, 96, 118, 167; in China, 65, 69–70

Miller, Joseph C., 289n16

Mills, C. Wright, 1, 2

Ming dynasty, 10, 59, 63, 66n4, 67n4, 71, 95, 200, 238, 268n1

mining, 47–8, 78

missionaries, 51, 110, 222, 225; Buddhist, 65, 67

Mississippi valley, 105

Mithra, cult of, 217, 241

mobilization ratios, 195

Modelski, G., 178n1

modernity, modernization, 19, 45, 62, 79, 162, 242

Mogul Empire, 27

Moloch (god), 216, 284

Mommsen, Wolfgang, 1

Monarchian controversy, 224

monasteries, 10, 33, 46, 49, 51, 96, 140; Buddhist, 58–73, 238; as economic entrepreneurs, 50, 52–4, 55, 69–70, 71, 74, 109, 118; as repositories of wealth, 239

monastic orders, 50, 52–5, 56, 58; militaristic, 221, 238

monastic religion, organizational structure of, 72

monastic revolution, 9

monastic titles, sale of, 72–3, 131, 140, 239

monasticism, 35, 36, 57–8, 75, 76

money, 36n15, 108, 122–3, 130; borrowed/lent, 79n1, 109; organizational politics of, 134–9; social organization of, 11–12, 119, 130, 137–139; veil theory, 123, 135, 136

money economy(ies), 222, 228; China, 61, 62, 67, 68, 110

money market, 69, 139; *see also* credit

Mongol Empire, 172, 188, 192

Mongol Golden Horde, 191, 192

Mongolia, 186, 207

Mongols, 61, 63, 67n4, 90, 110, 148, 153, 177, 242; military organization, 88–9

monism, 218

348

Index

monks, 33, 52–4, 56; Buddhist, 66, 67–8, 238; military, 53, 57, 238
monogamy, 292, 294–5
Monophysite heresy, 225
monopoly, monopolization, 11, 32, 118–19, 130, 141–2; class, 24; of innovation, 125; as key economic process, 125–33; labor markets, 14; of means of emotional production, 278–9; of means of religious-ritual production, 224; occupational, 128–9, 130; of opportunities, 6, 11–12; among organizations, 257; state, 149, 150; term, 131; trade, 136; ubiquitous and transitory, 129; of war, 281–2, 286, 291
monopoly price, 125
monotheism, 216, 217, 223–4, 282; universalistic, 222–3
Montesquieu, Baron de la Brède et de, 4n1
monuments, 102, 104, 106
Moore, Barrington, 40n19
moral code, universalistic, 215
moral politics in ancient Rome, 315–21
moralism, 215, 244
moralistic religions: asymmetry with mystical, 230–9; puritans vs. compromisers in, 240–1, 246
morality, 213, 214, 215, 232, 285
moralizers, political, 245–6
Morgan, Lewis Henry, 274, 275, 280, 282n12; *Ancient Society*, 270
Morocco, 228
Moscow (state), 191–2
Moses, 231
Moslems, 90, 91, 95, 285
mounds, 105, 106
Mughals (India), 91
Muhammad, 220, 228, 229, 231
Mulkay, Michael, 115
Mundurucu (people), 279n11
Murasaki, Lady: *Tale of Genji*, 312n7
Murdock, George P., 5
Murphy, Robert F., 279n11
muskets, 87, 90, 91, 92; *see also* weapons
mysteries, 217
mystical religions, 230–9
mysticism, 220
mystics, political, 245–6

Nagarjuna (philosopher), 235n7, 237
Namboodiri Brahmans, 300–1, 304, 305, 306
Napoleon I, 154, 175, 177
nation-state(s), 134n6, 167
national autonomy movements, 153
nationalism, 145, 146, 147, 151–5, 158, 214; and decolonization, 176; ethnicity

and, 153, 154, 191; heresy and, 242–3; and legitimacy, 155, 156; and military expansion, 191
natural resources, 81, 93, 281
naval technology, 85, 94, 95, 96
naval warfare, 65, 87, 90, 94
Nayar (people), 297–8, 299–306; family structure, 312–13, 314
Needham, Joseph, 64
Nelson, Lord Horatio, 177
neo-Kantianism, 4n1
neoclassical economics, 4n1, 11, 24, 25, 38, 117
neolithic period, 98–100, 101n11, 104n14
Neoplatonism(ists), 223–4, 241
Netherlands, 41n20, 174, 175, 179
networks, 132, 133; financial system, 136, 137, 138, 139, 141, 142; geopolitical, 85; kinship, 98
New Zealand, 174
Newcomen, Thomas, 82
Nicaea, 225
Nichiren (Buddhist monk), 238, 242
Nirvana, 231
Nobunaga, 87–8, 238
nomadic hunting societies, 272
Normandy, 173, 178, 179, 313n8
Normans, 174
North America, 99, 174; Indians, 270, 294–6
Norway, 56, 195
nuclear family, 271, 273, 275, 288, 289–90, 298, 299
nuclear war, 167–8, 181, 197, 204–6
nuclear weapons, 184
number systems, 102

Occident, 285; religious organization and doctrine of, 219–21
occupations, 26, 140; fixed, 126, 130–1
Oceania, 100, 173, 174, 175, 310
Octavian, 319
Oersted, Hans Christian, 82
Ohio valley, 105
oikos, 287
Okinawa, 179
oligopoly, 131, 132
Olmecs (people), 105
Oppian Laws (Rome), 316–19
opportunities: appropriation of, 131, 133, 139, 141, 142; monopolization of, 119, 128
oppression, 250, 252; in large organizations, 260–1
organization(s), 6, 257; conflict in, 245, 260–1; fixed positions in, 130–1; interplay of religious and political forms

349

Index

Index

Index

Index

sexual hospitality, 283
sexual politics, 307–8; *see also* marriage politics
sexual property system, 256, 277, 289n16
sexual relationships, 15, 273, 283
sexual rights, 282
Shang dynasty, 104n14
Shen-hui, 237
Shi'a, 228, 229, 233
Shinto cult, 310
ships, 83, 90, 94; sailing, 102, 169
Shogunate, 311
Shotoku, Prince, 311
Siberia, 148, 172, 192, 195, 198
sibs, *see* kin groups (sibs)
Sicily, 173, 174, 175, 179
siege warfare, 86, 90, 94
silk industry, 65
sinecure sector, 131, 257
Singapore, 179
Sino-Japanese war, 196
slave economy, 107–8
slaves, slavery, 26, 255, 277, 289n16; ancient Rome. 317, 318; female, 292, 293; temple, 284
Smith, Adam, 27, 123–4, 251
Social Democrats (Germany), 121
socialism, 25, 35, 38n17, 44, 60, 130, 250; alienation overcome in, 250–1; capitalistic, 57, 76; claim of universal validity, 243; state, 110
socialist parties, states, 150, 246, 261
Socialist Party (Germany), 121
Soga clan (Japan), 311
Solutrian period, 99
Sombart, Werner, 26, 38, 42n22, 120
Sommers, Margaret R., 165n6
soul, 249
South Africa, 169
South America, 149, 174
South Yemen, 183
Southeast Asia, 173, 174, 175
Soviet Union, 163, 176, 183, 245; future decline of, 185–209; hidden elitism in, 255; imperialism, 169; mobilization ratio, 195; size of state, 172
space, 184
Spain, 82, 91, 94n7, 163, 228; imperialism, 149, 169; infantry, 87, 90; overseas empire, 174, 175
Spanish Armada, 177
Sparta, 159, 165n7, 175, 279, 314
specialization, 4, 27, 35, 77, 78, 79n1, 101, 218
speculation, 73, 131, 136, 140, 141, 256
Spencer, Baldwin, 281n12

Sphinx, 105
spindle, 78
stagecoach, 110
Stalin-Trotsky conflict, 245
Standestaat, 50
state (the), 2–3, 8, 39n18, 106–7; in China, 10, 68, 69, 72–3; and economy, 118, 142, 150; effect of religious organization on rise of, 74, 75; and family, 275–6, 290–1, 294, 317–18; fragmentation of, 168, 169, 188–9, 190, 196, 197, 203–4; men's house organization in development of, 279; monopoly on violence, 156–7, 291; overextension and disintegration of, 168–9, 178, 184, 190–1, 197–201, 202, 203, 207–8; power position of, in international arena, 145, 146, 147, 148, 153–4, 158, 208–9 (*see also* state prestige); and religion, 13, 218, 219, 223, 226, 229–30, 237, 239, 241, 243; in rise of capitalism, 42–4, 138, 143; size of, 164, 168–9, 170–3, 177, 187, 188, 189, 191, 194; theory of, 146; threat to legitimacy of, 161; universal church and, 215–21, 243–4
state boundaries, 241; expansion and contraction of, 164, 168, 184, 186–7, 188; Russia, 191–6
state prestige, 147, 149, 153–4, 158–9, 161, 162–4, 208–9, 227, 246; and legitimacy, 155; and nationalism, 151; religion and, 241–3
statism, 244
status, 2, 6, 7, 13, 29, 88, 111, 277, 292–3; hierarchy, 236n8; in/and legitimacy, 145, 147; of women, 3, 295–6, 297, 299, 319
status-competition, 74–5, 293; and family structure, 312–13; international arena of, 12–13; in marriage politics, 303–4, 305–8, 212, 314–16
status groups, 8, 14, 128–9, 147, 243; finance system, 137–9
status networks, 12
status systems, 9, 286; of business, 113; among states, 3, 162–4; of women in household, 292, 293, 294
steam engine, 78, 81, 82, 111, 112, 114
steam power, 81
steamship, 90
stock market, 23, 136
stoicism, 248
Stonehenge, 106
stonemasons, 55
strategic air power, 180–1, 183

Index

Index

Transoxiana, 199
transportation, 24, 26, 27n6, 30, 47, 102, 110; and modern warfare, 184, 190, 191; revolution in, 167; sea, 47, 62 (*see also* ships); speed of, and movement of armies, 170–3; technology of, 222
travel, 217, 222
tribal societies, 5, 29, 104, 289; anthropological studies of, 269, 270; birthrate, 101; Easter Island, 106; family structure, 272, 294–5, 297, 298; fertility rites, 284n14; heresy conflicts, 218n2; religion, 214; technology, 97–102; women in, 283
tribe(s), 270, 275–6, 281; Australian, 219n2; coalitions of, 285
Trinitarian controversies, 224, 225, 236
Trinity (the) (concept), 249
Tugan-Baranowski, Mikhail, 38
Tungusic groups, 310
Turkmenistan, 198, 199
Turkmens (people), 204
Turks, 61, 153
two-person games, 187n2

Ukraine, 153, 197, 203
Umayyad lineage, 228
U.S.S.R., *see* Soviet Union
unions, 127, 258
United States, 148, 151, 198, 258; civil war, 177; class conflict in, 258; overseas empire, 174; politics, 243, 244, 246; size of state, 172; and Soviet Union, 163, 197, 204, 206, 208; war for independence, 41n2, 175–6
universalism, 34, 315
universities, 51, 73, 75
urban revolution, 102, 104, 106–7
urbanization, 60, 61, 79n1, 153, 242
usury, 35n12, 40; laws regarding, 29, 55, 56, 57–8
utopians, 245
Uyghur, 204
Uzbek (people), 204
Uzbekistan, 198, 199

valuation, 124
value-freedom issue, 2, 120
values, 7; ultimate, 23n4
Vasubandhu (philosopher), 235n7
Vedanta, 214
Venice, 9, 48, 56–7, 173–5
Verein für Sozialpolitik, 120, 121
Verstehen, 120
Vestal Virgins, 320–1
Vietnam, 165n5, 172, 184

Vietnam war, 180, 183
Vikings, 47, 82, 177
village community, 275–6
Vinaya (code), 71
Vinci, Leonardo da, 78, 80, 114
violence: legitimacy of national, 155–7, 158, 160, 161; monopolization of, by state, 156–7, 291; in politics, 214; as ritual display, 13n4
Virgil, 316
Visigothic kingdom, 225, 240
Voconian Law (Rome), 317, 319
Volksgeist, 4n1

wages, 41
Wahabi reforms (Islam), 234
Wallerstein, Immanuel, 2, 21, 27, 39, 45, 46, 79n1, 85, 96, 126, 167, 256; preconditions of capitalism, 41, 42–3
Walras, Leon, 117, 122
Wang An-shih, 62
war(s), warfare, 13, 24, 26, 87, 102n11, 136, 139n8, 151, 158, 186, 221; as business, 95; chariot, 93n6, 103; chivalrous, 303; horseback, 93, 281, 286; incidence of, 281; internal equivalents of, 160–1; Malabar, 302; mass, 157; Rome, 316, 321; showdown, 168, 181, 189–90, 206; technology and, 167–8, 169, 170–2, 173–84, 191, 206; *see also* civil war(s)
Warring States period (China), 59–60, 61, 64, 87, 105
Warsaw Pact, 202
water mill, 48, 64n2, 69–70, 104
water power, 48, 62–3, 82
Watt, James, 80, 112, 113
wealth: in China, 62, 68–9; concentration of, 40; differentiation of, 280; distribution of, 27, 252; women as, 292
weapons, 30, 31, 43, 85–91; and family organization, 281–2, 286
Weber, Helene, 271n4
Weber, Marianne Schnitger, 269–70; *Ehefrau und Mutter in der Rechtsentwicklung*, 269
Weber, Max: *Agrarian Sociology of Ancient Civilizations*, 285n15; *Ancient Judaism*, 285; doctoral dissertation, 269, 291; *Economy and Society*, 20, 21, 22, 23n4, 29–30, 31n10, 145–6, 275; *General Economic History*, 11, 19, 20–1, 30, 31n10, 37, 39, 40, 44, 46, 275; importance of, 1–7; "Protestant Ethic and the Spirit of Capitalism, The," 1; *Protestant Ethic and the Spirit of Capitalism, The*, 19–20,

Index

Weber, Max (*cont.*)
21, 22n3, 46, 119–20; *Religion of China, The,* 20n2, 59; *Religion of India, The,* 20n2, 59; "Science as a Vocation," 1–2; sexual life of, 270–1; "Social Psychology of the World Religions, The," 22n3; sociology of capitalism and, 117–42; *Wirtschaft und Gesellschaft,* 1, 2, 120
"Weber thesis," 19, 20, 21
Weberian revolution, 71, 76
West Germany, 198n5
Western Europe, 195
wheelbarrow, 64n2
wheels, 100
White, Harrison, 64, 132–3, 137, 139, 141
White, Lynn, 47
White Russia, 153
Wiley, Norbert, 11, 165n6, 258
windmills, 48, 104
women, 15–16, 217, 280, 299; aesthetic idealization of, 313, 315n9; in ancient Rome, 315–21; cultural creativity of, 312n7; as labor power, 280, 281, 294; in patriarchal household, 291–4; position of, 294–5, 297, 299, 310; as property, 256, 308, 317; sexual freedom for, 282–3; symbolic exchanges of, 12; as victims of oppression, 252; work of, 277–8, 291
women's house(s), 278, 280
women's rights, spread of, 315
wood, 98
woodworking, 100
wool-export trade, 54, 56

Wordsworth, William, 253
work ethic, 46
workers and sociology of markets, 255–8
working class: alienation of, 251; romanticization of, 252; standard of living of, 151
working-class culture, elitism about, 247, 253–5
working class revolution, 37
world, external, 249, 259, 259–60
world empire, 167, 169, 172–3, 184, 189–90, 197, 216
world market, 85
world religions, 34–5, 46; comparative study of, 1, 10, 20, 46
world system (theory), 2, 21, 43, 57, 126, 146, 150n2; diffusion and, 85; geopolitical structure of, 165; state's place in, 147; technology in, 167
World War I, 163, 170, 177
World War II, 92n5, 170, 176–7, 180, 182, 183, 189; air power in, 178–9
worship, community, 222, 230
writing, 30, 221, 303
writing-systems, 84, 102, 107, 109n17
wrought iron, 81
Wu, empress of China, 73

Yahwe, 276; cult of, 44n23, 216, 284, 286
Yugoslavia, 153, 198

Zarathustra, 285
Zolberg, Aristide R., 178n1
Zoroaster, 220
Zoroastrianism, 228

356